THE
Foolproof Foodservice Selection System

The Complete Manual for Creating a Quality Staff

Bill Marvin
The Restaurant Doctor™

John Wiley & Sons, Inc.

New York • Chichester • Brisbane • Toronto • Singapore

The Restaurant Doctor is a registered trademark of William R. Marvin

This publication is designed to provide accurate and authoritative information in regard to the subject matter covered. It is sold with the understanding that the publisher is not engaged in rendering legal, accounting, or other professional service. If legal advice or other expert assistance is required, the services of a competent professional person should be sought. FROM A DECLARATION OF PRINCIPLES JOINTLY ADOPTED BY A COMMITTEE OF THE AMERICAN BAR ASSOCIATION AND A COMMITTEE OF PUBLISHERS.

Library of Congress Cataloging-in-Publication Data

Marvin, Bill.
   The foolproof foodservice selection system : the complete manual
for creating a quality staff / Bill Marvin.
     p.   cm.
  Includes bibliographical references and index.
  ISBN 0-471-57431-7
   1. Food service—Personnel management—Handbooks, manuals, etc.
TX911.3.P4M38   1992
647.95′068′3—dc20   92-29649
                                                 CIP

Printed in the United States of America

10 9 8 7 6 5 4 3 2 1

C O N T E N T S

Preface   v

Acknowledgments   ix

EXECUTIVE INSIGHTS

  1. The Foolproof Foodservice Selection System   3

  2. The Best Employer in Town   7

  3. Productive Positions   9

  4. Recruiting Requisites   13

SYSTEM SUMMARY

  5. The Advice to Applicants Letter   21

  6. The Application   23

  7. The Tracking Sheet   25

  8. The Screening Interview   28

  9. The Sanitation Screening Test   31

10. The Professional Screening Test   33

11. The Lifting Test   35

12. The Demonstration Tests   37

13. The Interviews   39

14. The Professional Test   41

15. The Situation Tests   43

16. Background Research   45

17. Making the Offer   48

CLOSING COMMENTS

18. Selection Is Just the Start   55

SUGGESTED READINGS   **58**

APPENDICES

    A. **Position Descriptions**   **A-1**

    B. **Selection Documents**   **B-1**

    C. **Screening Tests**   **C-1**

    D. **Interview Guides**   **D-1**

    E. **Coaching Staff Tests**   **E-1**

    F. **Beverage Staff Tests**   **F-1**

    G. **Production Staff Tests**   **G-1**

    H. **Service Staff Tests**   **H-1**

    I. **Legal Summaries**   **I-1**

P R E F A C E

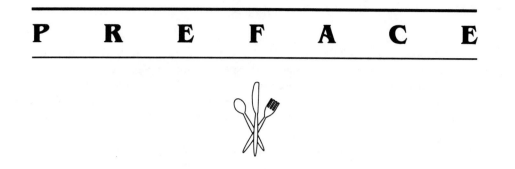

You wouldn't serve a sandwich on moldy bread, would you? No. Would you be famous for your chili if you made it with spoiled beef? Of course not. These questions sound silly because it is obvious that even the greatest culinary skill cannot produce quality food from substandard ingredients.

In a similar vein, who would deny that foodservice is a people business? This means that people are an ingredient in your recipe for success. The quality of your staff determines the level of your guest service and produces your sales volume. It also determines your principal operating costs. Even so, many operators still try to produce a quality dining experience with substandard staff. This practice will not work with people any more than it will work with food. Operators do not intentionally assemble an ineffective staff, but few will deny that they could do a better job when it comes to hiring.

"My guests are the most important assets I have," says W. C. Wells, partner in Taylor Vaughn's Old-Fashioned Dinner House in Portland, Oregon. "I won't risk their patronage by placing them in the hands of just anyone. Hiring warm bodies is an injustice to me and my staff and a disservice to my guests." Wells, who has been a restaurateur in the Northwest for over twenty years, is proud of the difficulty in qualifying as a member of his staff: "The real value is to our guests who really receive the benefit of our commitment to select only people who show a service attitude. With most of our staff oriented toward delighting our guests, we create stability and consistent high standards in our company. We think this helps *good* workers become *excellent* workers."

Staff selection is perhaps the most important aspect of guest service. In the real world of foodservice operations, however, it seems managers never have enough time to spend in the hiring process—because they must spend too much time cleaning up the messes made by the marginal workers who are there because there wasn't enough time to spend in the hiring process! Does this sound familiar?

You know that warm bodies make for lukewarm business, so how can you break the cycle? If you were a human resources expert, that would be one thing, but who has the time to study personnel theory when there are meals to get out and deadlines to meet? Just staying on top of labor laws and regulations can be a full-time career! If you want to pursue the subject, there are many excellent books on interviewing and hiring. I always had two problems with such books, however, no matter how well crafted: They were not specific to the needs of the foodservice industry, and they all required that the information they provided be further interpreted and adapted before it could be used. As an operator, I wanted a more effective way to select quality staff, but I never had time to develop one.

Finding a workable approach to picking the right people the first time became a project. I took the best ideas from the most practical sources I could find and combined them with secrets I learned during my foodservice management and consulting career. From all this I developed a structured format that makes sense within the operating reality of most foodservice operations. As the format evolved, what at first started as a basic text on hiring turned into a full-fledged staffing program—**The Foolproof Foodservice Selection System**.

If you have been in this business for any length of time, you must know that nothing is beyond the ability of someone to screw it up! Given this, how can a system be foolproof? Perhaps **The Foolproof Foodservice Selection System** is not *exactly* foolproof because it cannot guarantee that you will never hire a dud. After all, the System doesn't decide who gets the offer—*you do!* I *can* guarantee, however, that by following the System you will measurably improve the quality of your foodservice staff selections, and that is not a bad start.

The Foolproof Foodservice Selection System is an organized plan for creating a quality foodservice staff. Without a plan, you are merely making things up, and when you make things up, you run the risk of making mistakes, either by hiring the wrong person or by violating employment laws. Working this way takes more time, is less effective, and produces more stress. Worse than that, you don't get the best people, and that is the greatest loss of all—for you, your staff, and especially for your guests.

Without a plan, you are not selecting, you are only hiring, and there is a significant difference. Hiring is simply filling an employment vacancy, whereas selecting is the conscientious choosing of a person to join your staff. Selection implies that you know what you are looking for and make an informed choice from candidates who meet your preestablished criteria.

The Foolproof Foodservice Selection System offers operators a way to identify the right people the first time. If you use it, it will work. This manual contains everything you will need to put the System to work for you this afternoon. It is all in here—the forms, the tests (and the answers), and the basic information needed to fit the pieces together. All it takes to customize the System is putting your operation's name at the top of the forms and making copies!

The Foolproof Foodservice Selection System gives foodservice managers a powerful tool for improving their ability to recognize the right people the first time around. Here are the results you can expect by following the System:

You will stack the odds in your favor.
Your chances of making a personnel mistake will drop significantly. The selection errors that arise when you make a superficial judgment are reduced by a program that allows you to verify and document all personal impressions from several points of view.

You will make a clear statement to applicants.
By following the System you will deliver a clear message to applicants that you are serious about your business. There will be no question that you will accept only the very best people on your team. High standards attract professional people who will be proud that they can measure up.

You will stand out from your competition.
Most foodservice operations do an uninspired job of staff selection, relying on generic forms from the stationery store and haphazard interviewing. In contrast, the organized, professional face you will present to job seekers by following the System will immediately place you in a clearly different category.

You will help create a positive working climate.
Climate is a measure of the mental health and attitude in an organization. The majority rules. If you staff your operation with quality workers, you ensure that the prevailing climate will foster professional excellence and exemplary guest service.

You will improve your level of guest service.
The way *you* treat your staff is the way *they* will treat your guests. The System will improve your treatment of applicants, which will ultimately work to the benefit of your patrons.

You will have a better idea of what you are getting.
When you select new people using the System, you will have an accurate idea of what skills they bring to the job. You will also know how much additional training they require to meet the professional standards of your operation.

You will keep your options open as long as possible.
You will have more time to observe and evaluate a candidate's performance before making a final employment commitment and assuming the financial risks that come with it.

You can decline or release marginal candidates without backlash.
In our suit-happy society, it seems people are always looking for someone to blame if life does not work out the way they planned. Following the System will give you a defensible way to do what you need to do to control your staff and your business.

You will reduce stress and free up time to manage.
A high-quality staff means fewer problems for you to solve. The less time you need to solve problems, the more time you have to be a leader.

You can safely delegate the responsibility for staff selection.
The System clearly outlines the procedures and desired results during each step of the selection process. This makes it easier for others to assume some of the responsibility for staff selection while allowing management to retain overall control. If you can involve your present staff in the selection process, you will free your personal time and improve the level of job satisfaction in the operation.

You will reduce turnover and related expense.

The seeds of turnover are sown by "warm-body hiring," and you must break the cycle. While not all turnover is unhealthy, 300 percent a year is hazardous to your professional health. Following the System will help you identify people who are likely to stick around, primarily because the selection process is not quick. Only those with perseverance and a desire to become part of your team will complete it. High retention decreases costs and increases the quality of guest service. The result is higher profits and improved satisfaction at all levels.

You will improve your reputation with minorities.

The System provides all appropriate documents in both Spanish and English. By allowing Spanish-speaking applicants to take tests in their own language, you will earn a reputation as a conscientious employer who is sensitive to the needs of minorities.

You will stay out of trouble with the law.

Following the System will document the fact that you treat all applicants with fairness and equality. The System has been reviewed by knowledgeable human resources professionals to ensure that it complies with existing labor laws, including the Americans with Disabilities Act (ADA). Individual states may have specific requirements that could require modifying some System elements. Appendix I includes summaries of relevant federal laws (and states with exceptions to them). *I suggest you consult your legal counsel to be sure you conform to all applicable rules in your area.*

Best of all, if you grasp the spirit behind **The Foolproof Foodservice Selection System**, you will create a stronger magnet in the employment market. More qualified workers will be drawn to your doors, decreasing your turnover, increasing your profitability, and raising your level of guest satisfaction and repeat business.

THE SYSTEM ON DISK

The Foolproof Foodservice Selection System is ready for use as presented. However, you may wish to modify portions of the System to more closely fit your needs. To facilitate this process, certain sections of **The Foolproof Foodservice Selection System** are available on computer disk in most popular word processing formats. For further information and prices, please contact the author at PROTOTYPE RESTAURANTS, 332 West Bijou Street, Suite 107, Colorado Springs, CO 80905. The toll free number is (800) 767-1055.

A c k n o w l e d g m e n t s

Creating this manual was far from a solo effort. It involved finding the common threads in the many ideas and insights I have been privileged to absorb in my professional career and synthesizing these gems into something cohesive. My sources, then, are effectively everyone I have ever worked for or with, everything I have ever heard about our industry, and every triumph and tragedy I have ever experienced in 33 plus years in foodservice. What you have here is a true group effort! However, since the publisher thought it might be confusing to put everyone's name on the cover, I need to acknowledge a few other members of the team.

First and always, I thank my wife, Margene, for believing in my ideas and enduring the creative process with such love and good humor. To say that I couldn't have done it without her would be an understatement. Also, the book could never have happened without the support and encouragement of Claire Thompson of John Wiley & Sons and Mike Bartlett of *Restaurants & Institutions*. These wonderful people have a real love for our industry and a strong commitment to help all of us do a better job. Their goal is to create a series of working books for working professionals, and I hope this book reflects favorably on that intent.

Personally and professionally, I am grateful to Robert Kausen, president of Life Education, Inc., in Coffee Creek, California. Robert helped me understand what makes people tick and made common sense fashionable again. Michael Hurst and Donald I. Smith, whose perspectives always color my thinking, deserve recognition for their ongoing contributions to expanding excellence, spirit, and fun in our profession.

The ideas in this manual came from many talented professionals. I am indebted to Linda Beethe of Benefit & Personnel Resources in Colorado Springs for her counsel and perceptive review of the human resources materials. I never would have dared to tiptoe through the mine field of labor laws and their interpretations without a guide of her caliber.

I particularly appreciate the contributions of Marv Hunt, one of the few operating managers who really understood what I was trying to accomplish. Marv is a kindred soul who played devil's advocate and helped clarify my thinking in many areas. The System would be much less comprehensive without his professional insights.

Fred Burky shared the screening interview with me six years ago, saved my professional neck at the World Cycling Championships, and gave me a glimpse of the possibilities for a better way to select staff. George and Mary Atwell are great chefs and good friends whose guidance and input on all things culinary is a valued resource. Chef Stephanie Cardwell was a sympathetic ear and contributed so much to the selection process for the production staff. And when it comes to beverage operations, I couldn't have had a better advisor than Nick Dunn, partner in The Shore Bird Restaurant, Princeton-by-the-Sea, California.

Every time I got stuck, some talented operator always appeared to help me sort things out. A few who come immediately to mind are Mike Nemeth of Nemeth's El Tejon in Colorado Springs, Colorado, Bill Blistain of Phillips Waterside in Norfolk, Virginia, and Hap Gray of The Watermark Restaurant in Cleveland, Ohio.

Good ideas aren't worth much if they don't work in the real world, so I appreciate W. C. Wells, manager/partner of Taylor Vaughn's Old-Fashioned Dinner House in Portland, Oregon, for having the belief and courage to field-test the original rough materials on something as important as starting a new restaurant. His comments and suggestions helped me understand and refine many notions that eventually found their way into the System.

I am grateful to Pauleta Terven of Memorial Hospital in Colorado Springs, Randy Thurman of Azteca Mexican Restaurants in Seattle, Larry Stakes of Phillips Waterside Restaurant in Norfolk, Virginia, Cameron Janati of the Overlake Golf & Country Club in Medina, Washington, Patty Evans of the Westin Galleria Hotel in Dallas, and Shirley Waterfield of the Gideon-Putnam Hotel in Saratoga Springs, New York, for putting the final draft to the test and proving the worth of the System in a variety of operating formats. Muchas gracias as well to Claudia Pineda of Azteca Mexican Restaurants for making time in the middle of a hectic schedule to create the Spanish translations.

Finally, thanks to the many others who have attended my seminars around the country whose questions, comments, and insights have helped make this work more coherent. And to every unnamed person whose ideas and passions are directly or indirectly reflected in the pages that follow, my sincere thanks for your professional expertise and best wishes for your continued success.

Bill Marvin
The Restaurant Doctor™
Colorado Springs, Colorado
October 1992

Executive
Insights

The Foolproof Foodservice Selection System

System Overview

Here is a summary of the elements of **The Foolproof Foodservice Selection System**, all of which are explained in greater detail in following chapters. An asterisk following an element indicates that a Spanish-language version is included.

ACTIVITY	PURPOSE/FACTORS MEASURED OR VERIFIED
INITIAL CONTACT	
Advice to Applicants Letter*	General company information, self-screening
Application for Employment*	Background, personal, and professional information
SCREENING	
Screening Interview	Extroversion, pride, responsibility, energy
Sanitation Screening Test*	Basic sanitation knowledge
Professional Screening Test*	Basic professional knowledge
APPLICATION REVIEW	General qualifications review
FIRST DEMONSTRATIONS	
Lifting Test	Physical qualifications
Demonstration Test 1	Basic professional skill
FIRST INTERVIEW	Personal patterns and motives
SECOND INTERVIEW	Willingness, approach, coachability, professional curiosity, status
PROFESSIONAL TEST*	Professional knowledge

SITUATION TEST*	Professional perspective and priorities
SECOND DEMONSTRATION	Professional skill
THIRD INTERVIEW	Willingness, approach, coachability, professional curiosity, status
BACKGROUND RESEARCH	
Supervisor Reference Check	Verification of application information; work habits and patterns
Co-Worker Reference Check	Work habits and patterns
Law Enforcement Report	Application information verification
Medical Exam	Application information verification
OFFER OF EMPLOYMENT	Formal job offer

At the heart of **The Foolproof Foodservice Selection System** is a series of tests and interviews. These elements will give you better insights into the skills, attitudes, and priorities of prospective staff members.

The Tests

Some companies have elevated the role of pre-employment testing to an art form. Armed with a battery of personality profiles, honesty tests, and psychological probes into every imaginable corner of the psyche, they attempt to find the best candidates for a job opening. Structured tests are clearly preferable to a simple "chemistry test" (the "I like you" judgment) that defines the hiring process in many operations, but they can be expensive and they do not eliminate the need for several complete interviews and a thorough background check. For most foodservice operations, structured industrial tests are overkill.

In contrast, there is nothing deep, psychological, or expensive about the tests in **The Foolproof Foodservice Selection System**. The System uses four general test types, explained in the following paragraphs.

Screening Tests   The Screening Tests identify candidates most likely to be successful. They quickly separate applicants with good potential from those who are unlikely to be as productive. The Sanitation and Professional Screening Tests are simple quizzes for identifying those applicants who obviously have no familiarity with the technical basics of the position.

Professional Tests   The Professional Tests for management, production, service, and beverage staffs identify a candidate's level of professional awareness. They are lengthy (150-question) examinations of technical and professional knowledge. In particular the Professional Tests provide an excellent outline for future staff training.

Demonstration Tests   The Demonstration Tests identify proficiency in specific job-related skills and measure the practical aspects of job performance. The Lifting Test verifies the candidate's ability to meet principal physical requirements of the job.

Situation Tests   The Situation Tests are plausible foodservice scenarios that place applicants in sticky situations and ask them how they would handle them. They show how the candidates think, give insight into their professional perspective, and help gauge their priorities under stress.

It is inappropriate (and illegal) to use pre-employment testing as a means to discriminate against anyone. The Equal Employment Opportunity Commission (EEOC) regulations include lengthy definitions of "protected classes" of workers and other legalisms, but the simple fact is that people are people, and you must treat them all equally—period. If challenged, you must be able to justify the purposes of the tests and show how the testing relates to the selection process. I outline the purpose behind each test in case the question ever arises.

An Important Note About Tests

On the basis of my experience, the tests in **The Foolproof Foodservice Selection System** are valid and accurate. To be safe, however, I suggest you keep track of your own test results so you can be sure you are getting the quality of people you want. You can also verify that you are not categorically eliminating members of any protected group. All other things being equal (which they seldom are), candidates with the highest test scores are more likely than lower-scoring candidates to be successful on the job. Nevertheless, it is important to keep in mind that the actual test *score* is less important than what the answers reveal about an applicant's professional knowledge, skills, and personal approach.

Measuring an applicant's knowledge is only one purpose of a test. It can also help you decide *where* in the organization otherwise qualified candidates should start, not just *if* they should start. For that reason, I do not recommend that you use the written tests as the *sole* selection criterion. Serious staff selection is not that simple.

Serious staff selection is multifaceted. Demonstration tests give candidates a chance to prove their job skills, and checking references helps you find out if applicants are truly who they represent themselves to be. Several interviews, particularly if conducted by different people, give a clearer idea of motives and patterns in a candidate's history. You will also achieve consensus regarding how the applicant is likely to fit into your operation. Lifting tests will demonstrate physical ability to do the work required, and situation tests will show you how an applicant thinks. Finally, observation of the candidate's bearing, appearance, and punctuality will give insight into his or her likely conduct on the job. All of these tests are appropriate steps in conscientious staff selection.

The Interviews

Interviewing is not a natural skill, as anyone who has done it can attest. The best book I know on the subject is *Swan's How to Pick the Right People Program*. In it, William S. Swan points out the most common interviewing errors. Some of his conclusions are based on self-evaluation by interviewers, and some come from observing interviews in progress. The most telling source of errors, however, was reports by job applicants on what interviewers do that reduces the effectiveness of the interviewing process. Dr. Swan's observations are outlined in the following paragraphs.

Talking Too Much Most interviewers talk half the time or more during an interview, but it is the candidate who should be talking 80 or 90 percent of the time. After all, how much can you learn about an applicant if you do all the talking?

Telegraphing Desired Responses When you give applicants too much information in the early part of the interview, you often tip them off to the type of answers you want to hear. No wonder so many people seem like such a natural fit!

Jumping to Conclusions We often make judgments about people quickly, usually reaching a decision during the first six to eight minutes. Once the judgment is formed, it is difficult to change

Not Using an Organized Approach Interviews conducted off the top of your head typically come down to variations of "tell me about yourself." You then ask a few questions, get some minor information, and the interview is over. The problem with this haphazard approach is that it does not give you a basis for comparing candidates. When several interviewers talk to a candidate without any common plan, it is often impossible to reconcile their observations. Interviewing is more stressful without a structured approach because every time you interview a candidate you have to decide on the spot what to do and how to do it. This explains why so many people hate interviewing.

The interviews in **The Foolproof Foodservice Selection System** were designed with Swan's observations (and a few pet peeves) in mind. Chapter 13 details the mechanics of the interview process under the System. Here are a few of the design parameters.

No Distracting Note Taking   I always found note taking during an interview to be distracting. When I was conducting the interview, I found it difficult to listen and write simultaneously. And when I was the one being interviewed, I got nervous when the interviewer started writing after I said something—I was never sure if what I had said was right or wrong! The interviews in **The Foolproof Foodservice Selection System** require only that the interviewer check a box showing the degree to which the candidate's answer matches the desired response.

Reasonable Time Frame   The first interview will take 30 to 45 minutes to complete. The second and third interviews for hourly staff will take 20 to 30 minutes each, and the second and third interviews for supervisory staff will take 30 to 45 minutes each. Compare this to your last "endless interview."

Distinct Structure and Goals   The interviews are organized. Interviewers know exactly what qualities they are measuring, what questions they will be asking, what answers they are looking for, and how long the interview will take. They score each interview to give a clearer basis for comparison between candidates.

Clear Guidelines for Inexperienced Interviewers   The structure of the interviews allows more members of the staff to become involved in the selection process. This relieves management of the time demands of doing it all alone, spreads out the responsibility for staff selection, and contributes to the participatory atmosphere of your operation.

Simple to Administer   The interviews are ready to go. The interviewer does not have to decide what to say or worry about how much time to spend. It is obvious how the interviews are supposed to start and equally obvious when they are over.

At first glance, the System seems to impose a tremendous amount of detail—definitely more than most operators are used to. It looks that way because *there is* a tremendous amount of detail. In its full form, **The Foolproof Foodservice Selection System** is too comprehensive for most operators initially unless they are starting a new venture.

In an ongoing operation the full System may seem overwhelming because a significant amount of time is usually required just to correct and control existing staff, leaving less time to devote to the selection process. In other words, you don't have the time to spend identifying the right people because you are too busy cleaning up the mess made by the *wrong* people you hired in the past! Many foodservice operators spend their entire careers in this counterproductive mode.

All you can do is all you can do, but *anything* you can do to improve the quality of your staff will start to break the cycle. The simplest approach is to carry out as much of **The Foolproof Foodservice Selection System** as you can. Doing so *has* to be more effective than making things up as you go! As the quality of your staff increases, you will find that you have fewer problems to occupy your time. You can use this new-found time to set up more of the System, which will help you further upgrade your staff. A higher-quality crew will give you even more time to spend greeting your guests, coaching your staff, and watching your children grow up.

As a bonus, you can use many parts of the System as an outline for a comprehensive staff training program. In this way, even elements of the System that you cannot use *before* you hire someone can bring you real value *afterward!*

C H A P T E R 2

The Best Employer in Town

The Foolproof Foodservice Selection System will help you improve the quality of your staff selection. It can also help you avoid the labor shortage by becoming the most sought-after employer in town. If you are not already the best employer in your area and would like to earn this distinction, you may have to adjust your thinking.

Consider how different the business environment is now from what it was when we first started working. For one thing, the nature of the work force has changed—workers are more sophisticated, better informed (less educated?), and have more options than ever before. If you can't find people who want to work, maybe it's only that not many people are willing to put up with the way you do business. Think about it. Can you hire someone today who will accept the conditions you endured when *you* first started in foodservice? I surely can't.

For another thing, your guests' expectations have changed. How many of your current guests can you satisfy with the same level of service they would accept even two years ago? Yet how much have your service systems, staff training, and basic business orientation changed to address and keep pace with your guests' new standards?

In spite of these fundamental shifts, most operators, knowingly or unknowingly, still do business the way they always have; they never critically question the way they learned to run a foodservice operation. The problem is that the people who taught us in the 1960s and 1970s were taught in the 1940s and 1950s by people who learned in the 1920s and 1930s. Now, tradition is wonderful, but not everything we learned is still relevant.

It's possible that the dreaded labor shortage may not really be a lack of qualified workers but instead could just be a statement that fewer people are willing to endure the mistreatment they traditionally receive from our industry. Many of our current personnel practices are ineffective, yet we continue to do things the way we do because that is the way we have always done them. And many of these unconscious practices developed when there was an abundance of workers who would eagerly accept minimum wage jobs and repressive working conditions. When we had wrung all we could from workers we simply replaced them with someone else—"Burn 'em and turn 'em" was the accepted attitude. There was little incentive for most operators to question their personnel practices, and the "labor shortage" is the price our industry is finally starting to pay for this insensitivity.

For **The Foolproof Foodservice Selection System** to be most effective, working for you has to be worth the effort the System requires. Even the most clever scheme will not make people want to apply if you have a reputation as a terrible employer.

If you agree that attracting the best available workers is worthwhile, perhaps we should look at what it takes to earn a reputation as the best employer in town.

7

Good Reputation   People with high standards want to work in operations with high standards. This means you have to be known as being serious about providing quality food and service. It may also mean that you support worthwhile causes, participate in recycling programs, and give something back to the community that supports you.

Participatory Climate   Ray Lindstrom, president of Seattle-based Restaurants Unlimited, notes that today's work force grew up in an environment in which they had a voice and a vote in how things were done. "If their parents continually asked for their input at home," he says, "what expectations do you think they have when they come to work?" Lindstrom and his partners quickly realized that today's work force requires a different work environment to be truly effective. "We work very hard to provide an environment where our staff really *is* involved in the daily decisions. It doesn't work if you only try to make them *think* their opinions are important."

Fair Wages   Most managers think that money is the most important consideration to their workers. Surveys show that, in reality, workers place it fifth on their list. Money is a factor, but high wages are not a satisfier as much as low wages are a dissatisfier. Legendary operations pay wages that are at or above the prevailing standards in their market to make a statement about the value they place on their staff. Labor is a profit center. Don't treat it like a cost point.

Appreciative Management   According to surveys, your workers' number-one desire is to receive appreciation for the work they do. This gratitude is a natural consequence of shifting from a "cop-like" management style to a more coach-like one. Remember that people like people who like them.

Extensive Training   If you don't pay the highest wages in town (and even if you do), you *can* usually provide a great vocational training program. For many people, the education is worth more than the salary. Excellent workers are motivated by opportunities to expand their professional skills. Savvy operators recognize that, ultimately, their only real job is to learn as much as they can and pass along as much as they can to their staff.

Meaningful Jobs   The people you are looking for want something more than just eight hours of work and a paycheck. Increasingly, today's workers want jobs with meaningful content. How much more involved might your staff be if they understood why their jobs are important? How much more meaningful would their jobs seem if they knew how their work contributes to the well-being of others? As a further note, meaningful jobs have meaningful job titles, a goal addressed by **The Foolproof Foodservice Selection System**, as you will learn in Chapter 3.

You know that foodservice success comes from designing every element of the operation to properly serve your guests. Becoming the best employer in town requires that same passion and concern for the needs of your staff. Remember, your *crew* creates the experience of your guests. The key to creating a quality staff is to develop the sort of organization that quality people want to become part of.

C H A P T E R   3

Productive Positions

Position descriptions are a road map to your organization; properly constructed, they help workers to better understand the game you are asking them to play. Labor litigation also provides a real incentive for operators to document the content of each position. The problem with most job descriptions is that they are little more than lists of activities. Several times, I worked in operations with activity-based job descriptions, and when I had to conduct performance appraisals for workers who were not meeting my standards, they invariably defended their performance by showing how they had performed every task on their job description. This is akin to claiming to be the world's greatest lover by virtue of having memorized the manual. It is also about as effective!

Marvin's Law of Creative Laziness says that you never do any more work than necessary to accomplish what you want. Why not define positions in terms of *results* rather than *activities*, allowing people to interpret their jobs in ways that work for them? The immediate benefits are increased productivity, enhanced guest service, improved morale, reduced turnover . . . and more constructive performance appraisals!

The Position descriptions in Appendix A (in both English and Spanish) have four sections, which should be self-explanatory:

Position summary, a succinct statement of the reason the position exists.

Essential professional functions, the activities required in the successful performance of the position.

Results upon which performance is evaluated, the results by which successful work will be judged.

Qualification standards, the basic physical requirements of the position in compliance with ADA guidelines.

Position descriptions do not have to be static. For example, when W. C. Wells opened Taylor Vaughn's Old-Fashioned Dinner House in Portland, Oregon, he used position descriptions as an integral part of his staff training. He spent several days reaching a consensus with his new staff on their jobs. They discussed the critical results by which they would evaluate each position, and they agreed on how they could tell if they were achieving those results. "I was gratified to discover that my staff had standards that equaled or exceeded my own," Wells reports.

The ability to define and measure results as the primary means of performance appraisal makes the Position descriptions in **The Foolproof Foodservice Selection System** unique. Review the documents in Appendix A carefully before you use them to be sure they do not call for standards you are not prepared to uphold. Better yet, review them with your staff and come to an agreement on what is possible.

Position Titles

As the structure of jobs change, position titles should change as well. Nevertheless, most foodservice titles have not changed very much in 50 years! The Position descriptions in Appendix A reflect shifting job structures. Here are some traditional job titles and their updated, rough equivalents as suggested in this manual.

CONTEMPORARY TITLE	CONVENTIONAL TITLE
Head Coach	General Manager
Assistant Head Coach	Assistant Manager
Beverage Manager	Bartender
Assistant Beverage Manager	Cocktail Server/Bar Back
Production Manager	Chef/Sous-Chef/Cook
Assistant Production Manager	Dishwasher/Prep Cook
Floor Manager	Greeter/Host/Hostess
Service Manager	Waiter/Waitress/Server
Assistant Service Manager	Busser

Notice that the System eliminates the title of "manager" at the supervisory level. Here is the reason: If you call someone a "manager," they may try to *manage* people; often, this is little more than advanced manipulation. When you think about it, our model of management is closer to law enforcement than it is to enlightened leadership. If you like being a cop, consider applying to the police academy!

In my experience, the only effective way to get others to do things is to *lead* them. Therefore, with a tip of the hat to Don Smith, former football coach, longtime industry leader, and professor at Washington State University, **The Foolproof Foodservice Selection System** uses the title of Coach instead of Manager. The reasoning is simple. Managers look for problems, whereas coaches look for strengths. Coaches think about how they can use their available talent to best accomplish their mission. Approaching your job as a Coach is not only more productive but a lot more fun.

In **The Foolproof Foodservice Selection System**, the "Manager" exists only at the hourly level because it *is* possible to manage activities. And who better to manage activities than the person doing them? Production Managers manage the production in the kitchen, Service Managers manage the service to the guest, and Beverage Managers manage the service of beverages. All act as mentors to their assistants. So, for example, the task of the Assistant Beverage Manager is to learn the Beverage Manager's job, and the Beverage Manager's job is to teach it. Think what *this* will do to create a supportive work environment!

Because we are accustomed to thinking of foodservice jobs in the same old terms, perhaps a brief discussion of the function and content of the System's restructured positions will be helpful.

Production Manager

If you call workers cooks they may think they are doing the job by simply cooking! On the other hand, if they are described as "Production Manager," their job is to manage the production of food. This description involves far more responsibility, and, in most operations, it also sidesteps the controversial distinctions between cooks and chefs. The structure of this position encourages workers to learn all aspects of kitchen operation instead of getting stuck in a slot on the line. Because the Production Manager position requires the ability and willingness to teach, you will be looking for different qualities when considering candidates for it. The Production Managers work under the guidance of an Assistant Head Coach, who, ideally, has a strong kitchen background.

Assistant Production Manager

A common problem in all types of foodservice is finding and keeping dishwashers. The dishwasher position is difficult to fill because few people want to be dishwashers. The first corollary to Marvin's Law of Creative Laziness says never waste time solving a problem you can eliminate. Therefore, why expend energy trying to fill a job that nobody wants? Why not instead create a position people will find interesting? In this spirit, I developed the position of Assistant Production Manager.

Eliminating the dishwasher problem requires more than giving a new title to the same old job. Today's workers are smarter than that, so the solution involves a subtle restructuring of kitchen operation. The Assistant Production Manager still washes dishes and cleans, but does much more.

Assistant Production Managers are in training to be Production Managers. This means they must also learn receiving, storage, and basic food preparation. In the middle of the rush, Assistant Production Managers are on the line helping to get the meal out, and when a Production Manager is off or out sick, an assistant can temporarily fill in.

In many operations there is no real reason, other than force of habit, that dishes have to be washed during the rush. All it takes to break the habit is some additional china, a few more bus tubs, and a few racks. During the rush, load the racks with tubs of soiled servicewear and pack the dishroom full. When the pace slows, have two or three people wash all the dishes in an hour or so and get on with preparation of the next meal! This approach can work for most operators; however, high-volume operations may still have to wash dishes during the meal to keep up with the demands of business. In such situations, Assistant Production Managers can work part of their shift on the line and part in the dishroom without compromising the intent of the position.

Because the job content is greater, the position of Assistant Production Manager merits a higher wage than that of dishwasher. The job also requires a more motivated applicant, and at the same time will be less attractive to people who are just looking for a few dollars before moving on.

Beverage Manager

The traditional bartender's job also takes on more meaning under the System. Besides being responsible for making and serving drinks, Beverage Managers teach their assistants (servers, bar backs) how the bar operates. Beverage Managers are also responsible for teaching their assistants and the service staff about beverages and beverage service. Job responsibilities can also include pouring cost control, ordering, inventory control, merchandising, and other activities usually reserved for management. The teaching content of the position requires you to do more than simply find a good mechanic to fill the post. Beverage Managers work under the guidance of an Assistant Head Coach who, ideally, has a strong beverage background.

Assistant Beverage Manager

Assistant Beverage Managers assist the bartender and serve cocktails. In addition, they are evaluated on how quickly they are learning bar operations. For typical cocktail servers, learning to tend bar is a skill upgrade they can get excited about. So, for example, during slow periods a cocktail server can tend bar with a smile instead of a bartender having to cover the tables and grumbling about it. The structure of the position requires a desire to learn and expand professional skills. A worthy candidate must show more than just basic experience and a desire for a paycheck.

Service Manager

The Service Managers manage the level of service provided to your guests. The position has greater responsibility and authority than a typical server/waiter/waitress job. If workers are managing the service, they must have the latitude to do what you think is necessary to delight the guest. The current buzzword for this is *empowerment*, but it simply means that the person on the scene knows best what to do. As with the other manager positions, exceptional candidates must display not only professional competence but the willingness and ability to share their knowledge with others. Service Managers work under the guidance of an Assistant Head Coach who should have a strong service background.

Assistant Service Manager

Under the System, bussers evolve into Assistant Service Managers, who assist the Service Managers in delivering legendary service to guests. The entire focus of this position changes from doing "grunt work" to becoming an increasingly important part of the guest gratification system. The change in structure may or may not increase the length of time workers remain with your organization, but it will definitely change the level of interest and enthusiasm they bring to the job.

Coaches

Don Smith has always taught that the coach makes the difference. Here are some of his thoughts on coaches and coaching that are worth considering:

> Great coaches are first noticed by their uncanny ability to produce championship teams. However, to be called "coach," a leader must be measured by more than balance sheets, battles won or lifetime win-loss records. Great coaches have one more gift. They change the lives of those they touch. I suggest that great coaches can be measured by the number of success stories they leave in their wake. For once they give their players a taste of sweet success, they will have more. They leave behind a legacy of winning which becomes a lifetime habit. The players ultimately become champions of the coach's values, beliefs and passions for the rest of their lives.

Doesn't that sound like a lot more fun (and productive) than the typical foodservice management job? When the staff starts to look at the person in charge as a coach, that job changes. The measurement criteria shift away from the number of problems identified and solved toward what degree of success the staff is enjoying. Perhaps the coach's job could be defined as "achieving success through the activities of others."

Some people called manager approach their work with a coaching mentality, but many more do not see their jobs in this way. Calling someone a coach instead of a manager sounds like splitting semantic hairs, but language is powerful. When the supervisory positions in your operation carry the title of Coach, I think supervisors approach their work from a fundamentally different direction.

If these position shifts sound a bit radical, I am pleased. Doing more of what you have been doing will only get you more of what you've got! There is an entirely different game going on out there.

C H A P T E R 4

Recruiting Requisites

The world is full of terrific people, and you might be surprised at how many of them are looking for a good offer. The challenge is how to get them to want to work with you! Marketing to prospective staff members is no different (and no less important) than marketing to your guests. If you create a strong magnet, you will pull in more good people than you can believe! As with your guests, job seekers are unlikely to walk through the door if they don't know you are there or what you have to offer. This brings us to the subject of recruiting.

Don't underestimate the value of recruiting. **The Foolproof Foodservice Selection System** will help you identify the best of those who apply, but you still need high-quality raw material to start with. Never forget that the success of your business depends on the quality of your staff.

Recruiting should be an ongoing project. You always need to be on the lookout for what Mike Hurst of Fort Lauderdale's 15th Street Fisheries calls a "sparkler"—that natural talent who instinctively knows how to delight your guests and brighten up your operation. You cannot afford to let "sparklers" get away because by tomorrow they will be making your competitors wealthy. The people you want may not be actively looking for work. They may not even be employed in the foodservice industry right now.

So where are these fabulous folks, and how can you find them? As a start, consider the following list of sources for staff recruitment (taken from a list of over two hundred!) developed by Jim Moffa of Employment Resources Unlimited in Grosse Pointe, Michigan:[1]

1. Present staff members (internal promotion)
2. Door knob hangers
3. Newspaper classified ads
4. Restaurant guests
5. Telemarketing
6. Culinary schools
7. Computer bulletin boards
8. College bars
9. Radio ads
10. Youth groups (e.g., Boy Scouts, Girl Scouts)
11. Workshops and seminars
12. Exchange with competitors
13. Work release programs
14. Police and firefighters (moonlighters)
15. Military bulletin boards
16. Handicapped organizations
17. Fraternities, sororities
18. Referrals from present staff
19. Personnel agencies
20. Direct mail
21. Transit ads
22. Television ads
23. Referrals from barbers and beauticians
24. Open house

[1] Source: *The Restaurant Owner's Idea Book* by James Wm. Moffa, © 1990, pp. 11–17, excerpted with permission of Food for Thought, Grosse Pointe, Michigan.

25. Retiree organizations
26. Returned staff members
27. Employee leasing
28. School-bus drivers
29. Exchange students
30. Day care centers
31. PTA meetings
32. Job fairs

33. Community bulletin boards
34. Apartment managers
35. Trade shows
36. Volunteer agencies
37. Teachers' associations
38. Business cards
39. Weight Watchers
40. Fraternal and service organizations

Jim points out that even the greatest recruiting idea will not work if your execution or follow-up is poor. For example, leaving blank employment applications with a high school guidance counselor is a great idea, but unless you stay in contact with the school to see what interest has been generated, you may miss a potential star. **The Foolproof Foodservice Selection System** can make this job easier. Just attach a copy of the Advice to Applicants letter to the application for employment when you leave it somewhere. This way, potential applicants will know what to expect and exactly what to do if they are interested in a job.

Since this is a manual on staff selection and not a recruiting text, I will not spend much time on ways to attract job seekers. To explore this subject in more detail, I suggest you read Jim Moffa's book (see "Suggested Reading"). I will say, however, that newspaper ads are probably the most common way to find candidates for a vacancy, and thus deserve some attention. In the paragraphs below are some ideas on how to get outrageous results for your classified dollar.

John Chitvanni, president of National Restaurant Search, reports that when the average person is job hunting, he or she looks through a newspaper, selects three or four ads that look good, and calls them first. "Creative and interesting ads stand a better chance of prompting inquiries from prospective staff members," he says. The advantage of intriguing ads is not only the quantity but the quality of the people they attract.

Any money you spend in the newspaper, no matter what for, is advertising for your operation. And when you look at advertising this way, it automatically forces you to think before you place the same old ad. What image do your ads convey? Are you a fun place to work? Are you offering potential staff members something out of the ordinary? Look at the following ads and imagine the sort of response they might bring for you.

BRAVE NEW RESTAURANT

[logo]

EL PUERCO BORDER BBQ, COSMETIC SURGERY & SMALL ENGINE REPAIR™—"The Most Fun You Can Have With Your Mouth Full™"—is an irreverent new restaurant opening near the Citadel in March. El PUERCO will set new standards for guest service in Colorado Springs, and we need a few good people to help us pull it off. We value good experience, but we are more interested in what you can learn than in what you know. People skills are essential. If you believe work should be fun and want to be part of something exciting, attend one of our employment seminars at the Sheraton South on Monday, January 6. Be there at noon or 6pm, dress the part and plan to spend 3 hours. EOE

What kind of people do you think this ad will attract? I first developed this ad copy in 1976 when I was staffing my first restaurant in San Francisco, and we drew the most natural, enthusiastic people I have ever met! Dave Hall, co-owner of The Mustard Seed Restaurants in the Pacific northwest, used a variation of this wording when seeking applicants for a kitchen vacancy. He reports that *everyone* who responded was a potential "keeper."

Perhaps the best thing about this ad is that it clearly sets you apart from your competition. It delivers a clear message to job seekers (and your potential guests) that your operation is different.

WE DON'T HIRE DISHWASHERS

[logo]

We don't hire bussers, either! We wash dishes and clear tables at WADE'S WESTSIDE CAFE, of course, but our jobs involve far more than just that. If you are ambitious and want to learn the restaurant business, we should talk. EOE

If you restructure the jobs in your operation as we discussed earlier, why not get some mileage out of doing it? Attracting entry-level workers is always a challenge, and an ad like this should appeal to those who are looking for a direction in their lives. Eager learners are always a pleasure to have in your organization.

PICKY PETE IS HIRING

[logo]

We wouldn't wait tables for two bucks and tips, why would you? We wouldn't wash dishes for minimum wage, why would you? And we certainly wouldn't cook for $5.00 an hour, why would you? If you want to find out what PETE'S pays for prime people, apply. EOE

Viktor Baker of Proof of the Pudding in Columbus, Ohio, ran an ad like this when he opened a new restaurant called Pete's. Would you be surprised to learn that he had applicants waiting in line to work for him? How do you think this ad would work in *your* market area?

RESTAURANT MANAGEMENT

[logo]

TAYLOR VAUGHN'S OLD-FASHIONED DINNER HOUSE™ is looking for a few professional restaurant managers . . . people who may feel out of step with corporate thinking . . . people who want to be coaches instead of cops . . . people who are frustrated when percentages are emphasized at the expense of guest service . . . people who think there must be a better way to run a restaurant. If you are one of these people, call W. C. at 555-1300. EOE

Attracting qualified management staff is another steady challenge. W. C. Wells opened his new restaurant using an ad like this to draw only the type of people he wanted. "The hacks disqualified themselves before they ever applied," he said. "Practically all those who responded shared my vision of how I wanted the restaurant to run. My biggest challenge was to pick the best of the best from the group of exceptionally talented managers who applied."

These ads are two of my favorites. They were directed toward college students looking for part-time work as pizza delivery drivers. How can you present your jobs to make them more fun and interesting? If you can figure it out, you might find yourself drawing applicants who are more fun and interesting!

Ads like these will cost more than the three-liners your competitors run. If that worries you, ask yourself why you are running the ads at all. If your goal is to attract the best talent in the market, the extra money is well spent. Viktor Baker says, "You have to market for employees just as you market for customers. Pick up any newspaper in any town and turn to the Want Ads. What do you find? 'Wanted: Cook.' 'Help Wanted: Dishwashers.' Would you go after customers that way?"

If you are going to advertise for staff at all, do it right. Spend a little money; use your logo. Perhaps you can run two or three ads on the same day, each building on the others. Have some fun—make your ads unique and worth talking about. Remember, just as with your guests, there is no word-of-mouth without something to talk about. If workers are talking about your ads, the ads will have more impact and more people will hear about you. Just make sure you play as good a game as you talk or you will only succeed in disappointing the hoards arriving at your door.

Start-up Staffing

Start-up staffing is the most important staff selection you will ever do. Your opening crew establishes your first impression in the minds of your market. They also influence the culture of your business for years to come. Selecting staff for a new operation is different from filling one or two openings. First, there are many more applicants to talk with. Second, the last-minute details of finishing construction and readying the new business for opening generate time imperatives you cannot ignore. The only advantage is that without any day-to-day operating demands, there may be more time to devote to staff selection.

You do not have to be starting a new operation to be concerned with large-scale staffing. Many seasonal operations find that gearing up for peak times is quite similar to starting from scratch.

Job seekers arriving one by one to apply requires a tremendous amount of your time. They all ask the same questions, they all need the same information, and they all require the same handling. Human nature being what it is, the first few people receive a thorough briefing with a smile. Those who apply toward the end of the process are lucky to receive their paperwork and a grunt! Your staff just wears down.

Why risk alienating good candidates? Why not make it easy on yourself? If you're planning a major influx of new workers, consider holding a series of employment seminars—group meetings where you introduce the operation, explain your goals, and outline the selection process. Depending on your preferences, you can even conduct some generic foodservice training at these seminars. At the end of the meeting, distribute Advice to Applicants letters and applications to those who are interested. If you conduct the session properly, some attendees will elect not to apply, relieving you of a certain amount of work, and of those who take the material home, an additional percentage will not return it. This self-screening will save you hours of unproductive time.

Saving time is a plus, but the major advantage of employment seminars is that they ensure that all applicants hear the same message and receive the same information. This uniformity is difficult to achieve under any other format. A group meeting also creates an opportunity to build enthusiasm by giving applicants a look at their potential co-workers. If the group gets excited, individuals are more likely to get excited, too, and you can do worse than having a group of excited people who want to work for you!

The owner or other high-ranking company officer should conduct, or at least moderate, the employment seminar. The boss lends credibility to the process and helps job seekers understand that the meeting is important to the company.

System
Summary

C H A P T E R 5

The Advice to Applicants Letter

Ultimately, your staff will treat your guests the same way *you* treat your staff. The best employer in town will therefore take great care to provide the same level of service to prospective staff members as he or she provides to patrons. You must be sure that all applicants receive this quality of attention, no matter when they appear. **The Foolproof Foodservice Selection System** provides this equality. The process begins with the Advice to Applicants letter, copies of which are in Appendix B in both English and Spanish versions.

Train your staff to greet candidates as warmly as they welcome guests. No matter when applicants appear, the response to "Are you accepting applications?" should invariably be "We are always looking for exceptional people" accompanied by a sincere smile. This is a more positive response, it will protect you from the charge of denying anyone access to the application process, and it really ought to be the truth! Give candidates the Advice to Applicants letter along with the job application. This letter contains all the essential information they need to decide if they want to apply for work with your company. It ensures that every applicant is equally informed and provides a self-screening device. Ask candidates to take the material home and follow the instructions in the letter.

Do not allow anyone to fill out an application on the spot. There are several reasons for this:

1. Job seekers will not have all the necessary information with them, as you will realize when you look at the application and see what is required to complete it. It is imperative that candidates complete the application at home and return it only when they have all the requested information. Never accept an incomplete application.
2. The best operators never allow anything to happen in their establishment that does not enhance the guests' experience. Many patrons think it appears unprofessional for someone to be doing paperwork at a table in the dining room, which is exactly what it looks like when someone is filling out an application. Applicants are likely to come in at strange hours and may not be dressed to the same standards as your guests. You will provide them and your guests with a better experience if you require them to take the material home to complete it.
3. If you allow people to submit an application on the spot, you lose the self screening value of the letter and application. Once they see the standards you set for your organization, marginal workers will likely decide not to apply. This will decrease the number of useless applications to wade through and reduce the amount of effort required to fill the position. The fewer people you have to decline, the less chance that one of them will come back at you in the future for some imagined injustice.
4. Some operators point out that permitting the applicants to complete the application at home allows someone else to help them with it. While this is certainly possible, I think there is more to gain from following the recommended approach than there is to lose by not observing the actual completion of the application form. Subsequent tests and interviews will verify the candidates' writing proficiency and ability to work unassisted.

Notes Regarding the
Advice to Applicants Letter

Print the Advice to Applicants letter on your company letterhead, and use good paper, not a photocopy, to create a stronger statement. Above all, don't say anything in the letter that you don't mean. The letter makes an important first statement about the way you conduct your business. If applicants find out that you talk a different game than you play, your credibility will suffer, your turnover will increase, and you will look foolish. To increase the screening potential, you may also want to include a job description with the Advice to Applicants letter.

C H A P T E R 6

The Application

The application for employment in Appendix B (included in both English and Spanish versions) is specifically tailored to the needs of foodservice operators. It provides all the information you need to learn the applicant's credentials, and its questions give you a way to safely disengage from candidates who provide false or misleading information. To illustrate the point and clarify the reason for some questions, here is a brief discussion of the less common questions on the application.

Can you read at a 6th grade level? Reading ability is essential to all positions in foodservice. Even entry-level kitchen workers must read food labels, chemical use instructions, and receiving invoices; and dining room staff must read menus, guest checks, and coupons. It is unlikely that anyone will answer no to this question. If you discover later that workers have substandard reading skills, you may terminate them for making a false statement on the application, not for being unable to read.

Have you been convicted of a felony? Federal law allows you to ask about convictions (not arrests) since the answer is a matter of public record. Individual states may have regulations that are more restrictive. If you plan to ask the question, you must be able to show how the answer bears on the position in question. To protect yourself from a charge of wrongful hiring, be sure to ask the question of all applicants for positions involving driving, security duties, and any others that would be likely to place the individual alone with a member of the opposite sex.

Even when you can ask the question, a positive answer should not automatically disqualify the applicant. However, since you *can* ask the question, you *can* verify the answer. If a police check reveals different information from that provided by candidates, you can drop them for making a false statement on their application, not for having a criminal record.

Can you provide proof (of age)? Federal law requires that a worker be at least 18 years of age to handle certain pieces of kitchen equipment. State law sets a minimum allowable age for people who will prepare or serve alcoholic beverages. The age questions apply to applicants for positions in which age is a bona fide job qualification. If someone is applying for a position in which age is not a factor, just cross the question out.

Are you a smoker? Because there is adequate evidence that smoking increases the danger of passing along foodborne illness, most states allow you to give preference to nonsmokers for foodservice positions. Many operators say that smokers feel their habit entitles them to more breaks than nonsmokers and are therefore often less productive. This may or may not be true. If the issue ever comes up, remember that the public health consideration is your only defensible reason for giving preference to nonsmokers.

Questions relating to driver's license and driving record These questions apply only if the applicant is applying for a driving job or is likely to drive a personal vehicle on company business. If the question does not apply, simply cross it off the application.

Is there any reason why you could not be bonded?   This question is relevant if the position is bonded. It also serves as a self-screening mechanism to discourage applications from those whose history would make them ineligible for bonding. If subsequent research reveals information contrary to the answers provided, a candidate can be terminated for providing misleading information on the application.

Is there any reason you could not perform all the physical requirements of the job?   Again, the obvious answer is no. In the early part of the selection process, you will give applicants a Lifting Test. If they cannot (or will not) meet the physical requirements of the job, you will find out *before* they are a permanent liability on your Workers Comp and can remove them from consideration because they lied on their application, not because they couldn't lift a case of beer.

Describe your use of drugs and alcohol.   You can ask for this information if you declare (as you do in the Advice to Applicants letter) that you operate a drug-free workplace. And because you can ask the question, you can verify the answer. If a subsequent medical test reveals contrary information, the applicant can be terminated for making a false statement on the application, not because of drug or alcohol use.

Availability information   By having applicants make a statement about availability for work, you have a basis to terminate them if they subsequently decide they cannot take a particular shift. This solves the predicament of people who say they can work anytime and suddenly decide to become "religious" on weekends two weeks after starting work.

Work experience information   For each of the applicant's last three positions, the application requests easily verifiable information (dates, salaries, duties) that you can usually get. It also asks for names and telephone numbers of co-workers and subordinates. You will get a different perspective on people's work habits by talking to their peers and those who worked for them. The Advice to Applicants letter states that you will not consider applications from which work experience information (including telephone numbers) is missing. This tests the applicant's seriousness and saves you time.

Education information   It is disturbing how many people list fictitous educational references. By requiring applicants to provide a phone number of the institutions they list, you can verify their educational statements. Of course, if verifying their statements reveals erroneous information, you have a defensible reason for eliminating candidates from further consideration.

Why would you be a good choice for this position?   If applicants do not believe in themselves, why should you? This question allows job seekers to present their case—after all, wouldn't you prefer to staff your operation with people who really *want* to work for you? It also gives you a way to evaluate a candidate's qualifications for positions that require the ability to communicate in writing.

Disclaimer statement   The disclaimer gives you permission to verify all statements the candidate makes on the application. It also provides you with the right to terminate applicants, either during the selection process or after hiring, if you discover they have made false or misleading statements. For these reasons, under no circumstances accept an unsigned application.

Notes Regarding the Application for Employment

To really give your application impact, print it on good-quality 11″ × 17″ paper. Fold it in half to achieve an attractive presentation that will prevent the pages from getting separated (as can happen with attached sheets if the staple gives way). If possible, use the same paper your letterhead is on so that it will match the Advice to Applicants letter. This presents a more professional appearance, particularly if your recruiting plan calls for leaving this material in places where interested applicants can pick it up.

C H A P T E R 7

The Tracking Sheet

The Foolproof Foodservice Selection System has many more checks and cross-checks than most operators are used to dealing with. The Tracking Sheet is the control document for the selection process that monitors each candidate's progress and status. It should be in the possession of the person conducting the screening or interview. Do not give it to the applicant.

A reproducible copy of the Tracking Sheet is in Appendix B. The following paragraphs briefly discuss its principal sections.

Personal Traits   Every time job seekers are in contact with the company, someone is observing their behavior and appearance. Personal traits to be appraised are on the Tracking Sheet. Note them as you observe them. Possible appraisals are Yes (Y), No (N), and Maybe or Not Sure (?).

For the sake of clarification, here is an idea of what the observer should be looking for:

Neat/clean/appearance—is the applicant's appearance crisp and appetizing?

Alert/attentive—are the lights on? Is somebody home?

Punctual—does the person arrive at least five minutes before the agreed-upon appointment time?

Smiling eye contact—does the candidate comfortably look you in the eye while smiling warmly and naturally?

Polite/courteous—does the person's conduct meet common standards of politeness?

Interested—does the applicant listen attentively and show a desire to learn about the company and the job?

Neat/legible—is the candidate's handwriting easy to read? Was the application completed with care?

Availability—is the person available to work when you need someone to work?

Appropriate experience—does the applicant's experience meet the needs of the position?

Appropriate education—does the candidate's education meet the needs of the job?

Desire—does the person's statement on the application make a compelling case for selection?

Complete/signed—were all questions answered and was the application signed?

Presence—is the applicant's attention focused "here" without any obvious distracting thoughts?

Friendly—does the candidate interact easily and pleasantly with others?

Relaxed—does the person appear comfortable and at ease?

Confident—does the applicant show a high level of self-confidence and self-esteem?

Sparkle—does the person display an ability to laugh at themselves? Do they brighten up the room?

Feel good—does being around the applicant make you feel good?

Positive/upbeat—does the candidate seem to take an optimistic view toward things?

Role model—does this person set a good example for others?

Good fit—do you think this person will fit in well with your present staff?

Enthusiastic—is the applicant excited about the company and the job?

Screening   When candidates present applications, the person who conducts the screening interview and administers the screening tests also observes and scores the six personal traits listed on the Tracking Sheet. The screener also notes the scores of the Sanitation and Professional Screening tests, and then, based on the candidate's performance and demonstrated traits, makes a recommendation about whether the person is a good candidate for further consideration.

Details on administering and scoring all employment tests are included in the following chapters. While each operation can set its own standards, a score in the upper quartile usually merits a yes, while a second quartile score earns a maybe.

Application Review   If applicants are worth pursuing, the next step is to review their application. This review is *not* conducted in the applicants' presence. The reviewer should note the areas indicated and make a recommendation about whether to schedule an interview for the individual.

First Demonstrations   The evaluator notes the candidate's scores on the Lifting Test and Demonstration Test 1, appraises the results, and recommends further action.

First Interview   The first interview includes an appraisal of the candidate's personal traits on the Tracking Sheet and completion of the First Interview guide. The score on the First Interview is noted, and the interviewer makes appropriate comments and recommends whether the candidate is worthy of continued attention.

Second Interview   The Second Interview consists of the personal appraisal items on the Tracking Sheet and the Second Interview itself. The evaluator notes the score and appraisal on each section of the interview and notes the total score. This is the time to add any personal comments and recommendations regarding the future of the candidate.

Professional Test   The evaluator notes the test score, the length of time required to complete the test, and the index score (points per minute), which is an indicator of the candidate's certainty. The reviewer then makes a recommendation for future consideration.

Situation Test   Scoring of the Situation Tests follows the evaluation criteria included on the Evaluation Sheet. As usual, the reviewer recommends whether to continue the selection process.

Second Demonstration   A professionally qualified staff member should administer the second Demonstration Test according to the directions given. The procedure is identical to that for the first Demonstration Test.

Third Interview   Documentation for the Third Interview is similar to that for the Second Interview.

Background Research   The personal trait observations represent the consensus of comments received in the reference checks. The law enforcement appraisal is based on the results of the police check (if administered); the medical appraisal is based on the results of a blood test (if administered). The final judgment is the consensus opinion based on reference check interviews with employers, co-workers, and subordinates.

Action Taken   This section documents the decision made on the applicant at whatever point you make that decision.

Notes Regarding the Tracking Sheet

The Tracking Sheet is the coordinating document for **The Foolproof Foodservice Selection System**. Because of the potential number of documents involved in the selection process, be sure to control the Tracking Sheet's whereabouts. I recommend you prepare a folder for each applicant with the Tracking Sheet attached on one side and the various supporting documents attached on the other. This will provide a ready reference on the status of applicants and leave the documents ready for filing whether or not you make an offer.

C H A P T E R 8

The Screening Interview

The Foolproof Foodservice Selection System starts with three screening procedures, copies of which are included in Appendix C:

The **Screening Interview**, which measures general foodservice success potential.

The **Sanitation Screening Test**, which indicates a candidate's basic sanitation awareness.

The **Professional Screening Test**, a preliminary assessment of professional knowledge in each job category.

The Screening Interview

Your guests pay for the value of the experience they receive in your dining operation, not just for the food. The better your staff, the more value they will add to the guest's experience. Hiring good staff is not a matter of luck when you have a way to identify terrific people before you hire them. Imagine the possibilities if you can separate the applicants who will actually add value from the ones who just "give great interviews" and need the money. This is where the Screening Interview gets you off to a great start.

The Screening Interview measures four characteristics that describe the successful, productive staff member—extroverted, proud, responsible, and energetic. Screening for these attributes will help you find candidates who will make every effort to satisfy your guests and who are appropriately sales- and results-oriented.

Extroversion   Extroverts are people-oriented. Their behavior shows a sincere desire to be liked by others, which is particularly important for guest contact staff. Extroverts are generally positive people with good social skills. They are assertive enough to state their opinions clearly and concisely without stepping on anyone's toes.

Pride   People who have pride view their work and other areas of their life as very important. They need to be a part of successful activities. Proud people are very particular about doing their job not only correctly, but in the best possible way. They are significant contributors to the success of any work setting or project. Proud people take a personal investment in your operation. They want you to be successful and to be viewed as the best operation in your community.

Responsibility   Responsible people follow through on commitments within a defined period. They feel accountable for producing a quality effort while they are "on the clock" and thus are likely to provide a quality dining experience and value-added service to every guest and in every job-related task they do.

Energy   Foodservice is extremely fast-paced and requires people with high energy levels and the ability to move quickly and appropriately under pressure. People with a great deal of energy often have varied interests and are involved in several outside activities. With proper direction and guidance, highly active people are likely to accomplish much more in a shorter time and to be more accurate in their work than inactive people.

These qualities are important success factors for all foodservice positions. However, you may choose to give different weight to certain ones for various positions—for example, an outgoing nature may be less critical in production positions where there is little guest contact. In any case, the Screening Interview is extremely effective. Let me relate a personal example to illustrate what I mean.

I was the Foodservice Director for the U.S. Olympic Training Center in Colorado Springs when the World Cycling Championships, one of the world's largest sporting events, came to town. This was the first time this event had ever been held in the United States, so there were no precedents and no idea what to expect. The event organizers asked me to handle the concessions, catering, and hospitality tents for the two weeks of competition. We expected a full house at the Training Center during the event, so I could not use any of my regular foodservice staff.

My challenge was to create an organization of about 150 people from scratch, run it at full speed for two weeks, and then send everyone home! There would be just one opportunity to get the right people, and if they didn't work out, there would be no time to find replacements. I expected about 250 people to apply for jobs, but had no idea how I would have time to go about the selection process. As fortune would have it, I attended a conference two weeks before the event and found my answer.

A major restaurant group had noticed that some of their staff members did a much better job than others. Yet because they hired everyone the same way, the group expected more equal qualifications. In trying to solve this puzzle, they found that the exceptional performers tended to answer questions differently than the mediocre employees, although everyone gave correct replies. They researched this discovery and developed a list of 14 simple questions along with the desired type of answers. The score was all-or-nothing—an applicant received a point only when their response matched the "positive" answer expected from outstanding workers. At the time, I really didn't care if the system was accurate or not—I just wanted a way to make staff selections without spending a lot of time holding interviews!

We held one employment seminar for the entire group and, as expected, we had a huge response to our newspaper ad. When we had presented all the relevant information, we had everyone fill out an application and talk with an interviewer, who simply asked the 14 questions on the Screening Interview. Six people asked the questions (three of whom I had never met before that day!). We screened 265 people in just over an hour, which is about as "quick and dirty" as you can get!

The Screening Interview was the full extent of our selection process for all positions. There were no traditional interviews because there was just no time for them. After totaling the individual scores, we began filling shifts, starting with those who scored highest and working our way down the list until we completed our schedule. The last people assigned were a few who had scored in the middle of the point scale. Once the staff was in place, we promptly forgot the scores and went to work!

The first week of racing started fast and got busier, but my rookie crew handled it beautifully. Just two people failed to report for work. Everyone did a tremendous job, performing their tasks well and keeping a sense of humor in the middle of what was frequently an improvised situation. I couldn't have been more pleased! At the end of that first week, we had a few days off before the final races. Since we didn't need as many staff for the rest of the events, we decided to give the extra hours to our best workers. My supervisors selected their "star performers" based on their demonstrated work performance and positive attitude. When I pulled their applications, I was shocked! *All of our exceptional workers had scored in the top third on the Screening Interview!* There was no bell-shaped curve and not a token lower-scoring person in the bunch!

Administering the Screening Interview

Give the Screening Interview to *all* applicants, no matter what position they seek. A member of your staff asks the questions; the applicant does not see the Screening Interview guide. The process is most effective when you ask the questions without lengthy conversation. Remember, this is a quick way to identify those candidates worthy of more attention, and the idea is to keep it *quick*. Greet the applicants and establish rapport. Then tell them that you have a few quick questions that will help you get a better idea of how they view the foodservice industry. Ask the questions and check off your opinion of how their answers meet the scoring criteria.

The Screening Interview form allows the interviewer to concentrate on the applicant and not be distracted by making notes as the person speaks. Remember that you are only trying to decide how the applicant's response compares with the desired answers. At this stage of the selection process, you are not conducting an interview. Keep the meeting short and focused. Once the questions have been answered, thank candidates for their candor and tell them what to expect next.

The next step depends on the order in which you do the screening tests. You might give the candidate the Sanitation or Professional Screening Test or simply end the session. If you need the position filled immediately, you might ask the candidate to wait in the dining room while you score the Screening Interview. When you know the score, you can decide whether to go on to the First Demonstration tests and the First Interview. Otherwise, make your general observations of the candidate's punctuality, appearance, and general interest level on the Tracking Sheet, and call later in the day if you want to explore the position further.

Scoring the Screening Interview

Scoring in **The Foolproof Foodservice Selection System** makes allowance for answers that are not clearly positive or negative. The possible responses are Yes (Y), No (N), and Maybe (?). Yes is worth two points; Maybe, one point; and No, no points. The highest possible score on the Screening Interview is 28. Scores of 22 or higher suggest prime candidates, while scores of 16 to 21 suggest marginal ones. Different interviewers might give different scores to a particular answer, but personal interpretation is unlikely to yield a score that will materially misrepresent a candidate's potential. *Do not review the questions with the candidate after the interview.*

Notes Regarding the Screening Interview

All other things being equal (which they seldom are), candidates with the highest scores on the Screening Interview are more likely to be successful on the job. Keep in mind, however, that the actual test *score* is less important than what the answers reveal about an applicant's attitude and approach. Except in extreme circumstances, I do not recommend that operators use the Screening Interview as the *sole* hiring criteria.

Still, if you ever face a deadline and have to distinguish people who want to work from ones who just want a job, the Screening Interview can help immeasurably. If you do nothing else but conduct the Screening Interview and interview only those who score in the top third, you will be selecting from a more highly qualified group of applicants.

The Purpose of the Screening Interview

1. **The Screening Interview identifies characteristics essential to success in foodservice.**
   Observation of successful foodservice workers has identified common traits that seem to lead to good performance. The Screening Interview addresses those traits and suggests the extent to which the candidate possesses them.
2. **The Screening Interview saves interview time.**
   The Screening Interview can quickly reduce a large influx of applicants to only those who are most likely to be successful.
3. **The Screening Interview provides documentation and objectivity for the selection process.**
   The Screening Interview sheet is a written record of the applicant's prehire performance. The interview measures job-related factors and is equally (and consistently) administered to all candidates. It provides a basis for staff selection decisions that is difficult for disgruntled candidates to successfully challenge.

C H A P T E R 9

The Sanitation Screening Test

The Sanitation Screening Test makes a statement about the importance of sanitation and proper foodhandling in your operation. Anyone with prior foodservice training or experience should do very well on it; those without prior experience in the industry will get the message that sanitation is not an area they can afford to overlook if they want to work for you. The Sanitation Screening Test is in Appendix C in both English and Spanish versions.

Administering the Sanitation Screening Test

Give the Sanitation Screening Test to *all* applicants, whatever position they are seeking. The candidate receives a copy of the test and an answer sheet, both of which have test instructions. This is a timed test. When the candidate has completed it, the screener notes the elapsed time and the score in the block on the bottom of the answer sheet.

Scoring the Sanitation Screening Test

I suggest you first make a copy of the Answer Sheet Overlay (Appendix C) on a piece of transparency film to make the scoring easier.* Award one point for each correct answer. The maximum score on the test is 20, with scores of 16 or higher suggesting prime candidates and scores of 10 to 15 suggesting marginal ones. *Do* not *review the answers with the candidate after the test.*

The Purpose of the Sanitation Screening Test

1. **The Sanitation Screening Test shows what candidates do (and do not) know.**
   The test suggests the candidates' knowledge of proper sanitation practices and suggests the amount of training that may be required to bring applicants up to your company's professional standards.

---

*Do this for all the tests in **The Foolproof Foodservice Selection System.**

2. **The Sanitation Screening Test shows candidates what they don't know.**
Workers who "know it all" are difficult to train because they don't think they have anything to learn. Even qualified applicants may find questions in this process that will help them see that there is more to know. Once they realize they have something to learn, they are usually more receptive to training.

3. **The Sanitation Screening Test makes a statement about what is important to your business.**
Requiring this testing of every job seeker is a declaration of your seriousness about professional development and standards.

4. **The Sanitation Screening Test provides a framework for future training.**
Having asked the questions, you can discuss the answers in a future training session. The test covers basic areas of concern to your operation, and understanding the reasons for the correct answers will raise the level of your staff's professionalism.

5. **The Sanitation Screening Test saves interview time.**
The time required to ask a candidate all the questions in the test would be prohibitive. Using the test as a way to ask technical questions can save the company time while still covering the topic. The test's simplicity will quickly tell you if applicants have the basic sanitation knowledge required for positions of higher responsibility or if they are more suited to entry-level positions.

6. **The Sanitation Screening Test verifies the applicant's reading ability.**
Reading is important in all foodservice positions. Production staff members need to read recipes, labels, invoices, and guest checks. Service staffers need to read guest checks, menus, and coupons. If a candidate has trouble reading the questions on the test, it may reveal poor reading skills.

7. **The Sanitation Screening Test provides documentation and objectivity for the selection process.**
The test is a written record of the applicant's prehire performance and measures job-related factors. Because it is equally (and consistently) administered to all candidates, it provides a basis for staff selection decisions that is difficult for disgruntled candidates to successfully challenge.

8. **The Sanitation Screening Test provides a measure of applicants' certainty.**
The test is timed. If two applicants score about the same, the one who completed it faster is likely to be most certain of the answers. While completion time is not a factor except as a tiebreaker, workers who are certain of their skills and knowledge are more likely to be effective than workers who are tentative.

Using the Sanitation Screening Test for Training

The Sanitation Screening Test can be an effective outline for future staff training. A training schedule that addresses two to four questions a week is within the ability of most operations. The instructor gives students the questions from the tests and then follows with a discussion of the possible answers for each question based on the material in the answer sheet. At the suggested pace of two to four questions a week, the Sanitation Screening Test can provide five to ten weeks of basic interactive departmental instruction.

C H A P T E R   1 0

The Professional Screening Test

The Professional Screening Test identifies those applicants who have no familiarity with the technical basics of the position they are applying for. A low score on this test does not automatically eliminate someone, but it will alert you to those whose aspirations exceed their experience. These applicants may still be good candidates for entry-level positions. The Professional Screening tests for each department are in Appendix C in English and Spanish versions.

Administering the Professional Screening Test

Give the Professional Screening Test to *all* applicants for a position in the department, whatever the job they seek. The candidate receives a copy of the test and an answer sheet for the department for which they are applying. The instructions are on both. This is a timed test. When the candidate has completed the test, the screener notes the elapsed time and the score in the block at the bottom of the answer sheet.

Scoring the Professional Screening Test

Scoring is the same as for the Sanitation Screening Test: one point for each correct answer, with a maximum score of 20. Scores of 16 or higher suggest prime candidates, while scores of 10 to 15 suggest marginal ones. *Do* not *review the answers with the candidate after the test.*

The Purpose of the Professional Screening Test

1. **The Professional Screening Test shows what candidates do (and do not) know.**
   The test suggests the candidates' knowledge and the amount of training required to meet your company's professional standards. There is never enough time to do all the training you would like to do. The test can give you a head start by identifying those candidates who are farther along in their professional development.
2. **The Professional Screening Test shows candidates what they don't know.**
   Even qualified applicants may find questions in this process that will help them see that there is more to know. Once they realize they have something to learn, they are usually more receptive to training.

3. **The Professional Screening Test makes a statement about what is important to your business.**
Requiring this test of every job seeker is a declaration of your seriousness about professional development and standards. Since the professional knowledge of entry-level staff will be small, the Professional Screening Test helps create an awareness of what it takes to advance to positions of higher responsibility in the operation.

4. **The Professional Screening Test provides a framework for future training.**
The Professional Screening Test covers all the basic areas of concern to your operation. Making it the basis of future training sessions, in which staff will learn the reasons for the correct answers, will raise the level of professionalism.

5. **The Professional Screening Test saves interview time.**
Verbally asking a candidate all the questions on the Professional Screening Test would take too long in a busy operation. Using the test to ask technical questions can save the company time while still thoroughly covering the topic. The test will clearly tell you whether applicants have the professional knowledge required for positions of higher responsibility or are more likely candidates for entry-level jobs.

6. **The Professional Screening Test verifies the applicants' reading ability.**
Recipes, labels, invoices, guest checks, menus, and coupons require reading skills in all staff. Candidates' difficulty in reading the questions on the test will tell you that their skills are poor.

7. **The Professional Screening Test provides documentation and objectivity for the selection process.**
The test is a written record of the applicant's pre-hire performance, measures job-related factors, and is equally (and consistently) administered to all candidates. Thus, it provides a basis for staff selection decisions that will resist legal challenges by disgruntled candidates.

8. **The Professional Screening Test provides a measure of the applicant's certainty.**
If two applicants score about the same on the test, the one who finished faster is likely to be most confident of the answers. Workers who are more certain of their skills and knowledge are more likely to be effective than those who are more tentative.

Using the Professional Screening Tests for Training

The Professional Screening tests can be effective outlines for future staff training. The instructor gives students the questions from the tests. A discussion follows on the possible answers for each question based on the material in the answer sheet. At the suggested pace of two to four questions a week, which is realistic for most operations, each Professional Screening Test can provide five to ten weeks of interactive departmental basic training.

C H A P T E R   1 1

The Lifting Test

Many injuries in foodservice occur as a result of lifting accidents. The hands-on Lifting Test duplicates a job-related situation requiring physical skills and verifies the candidate's ability to meet a major physical requirement of the job. In the test, candidates lift the heaviest object they are likely to encounter on the job. A Lifting Test form is in Appendix E, Appendix F, Appendix G, and Appendix H.

Administering the Lifting Test

Give the Lifting Test to *all* applicants, no matter which job they seek. The test is the same for all positions except for the object to be lifted and where to place it. These details vary according to position but should be the same for all applicants in a department. The object to be used in the test should reflect the tasks typically performed in a particular position and should consider situations a worker is likely to encounter in the normal course of business while helping co-workers. This is not a timed test.

Scoring the Lifting Test

There are ten evaluation factors noted on the test sheet, each requiring a Yes (Y), No (N), or Not Sure (?) by the evaluator based on the evaluation criteria. A Yes is worth two points and a Not Sure one point. The maximum score is 20. Scores of 16 or higher suggest prime candidates, while scores of 10 to 15 suggest marginal ones. Although different interviewers might score an action differently, personal interpretation is unlikely to yield a score that will materially misrepresent a candidate's potential. *Do* not *review the evaluation criteria with the candidate, either before or after the test.*

The Purpose of the Lifting Test

1. **The Lifting Test shows what candidates can (and cannot) do.**
    The Lifting Test is a practical indication of the candidate's physical ability to do the job. Short of putting the applicant to work, it is the most effective way to evaluate physical ability before making a job offer. If candidates have a physical limitation, you can find this out before you accept liability for their injuries by placing them on your payroll.
2. **The Lifting Test makes a statement about what is important to your business.**
    Requiring this test of every job seeker is a declaration of how seriously you take the issue of job safety.
3. **The Lifting Test provides a basis for future training.**
    Having brought up the issue of safe lifting technique, you can use it as the basis for a future training session.

4. **The Lifting Test provides documentation and objectivity for the selection process.**
    Like the other tests, the Lifting Test produces a written record of the applicant's prehire performance and measures job-related factors. It is equally (and consistently) administered to all candidates and so provides legal protection against thwarted job seekers.

Using the Lifting Test for Training

The Lifting Test can be an effective training tool. The instructor presents the lifting situation and opens the floor for questions and ideas. The students' responses are reviewed in light of the evaluation criteria, and each student then has a chance to take part in the demonstration. Afterward the group can discuss each other's performance and help refine techniques. The discussion is likely to generate additional demonstrations for the group to explore.

C H A P T E R   1 2

The Demonstration Tests

The two Demonstration Tests are hands-on situations that identify specific job-related skills and measure the practical aspects of job performance. The first is a short display of basic proficiency; the second is a more extensive performance requiring candidates to show ability to learn. Demonstration Tests are included for the coaching staff (Appendix E), the beverage staff (Appendix F), the production staff (Appendix G), and the service staff (Appendix H).

Administering the Demonstration Tests

Give the Demonstration Tests to *all* applicants for a position in the department, no matter which job they seek. The instruction sheet for each test includes the nature of the demonstration, the materials involved, and any required setup. These details differ between tests for different positions, but should be identical for all applicants for the same job. These tests are not timed.

Scoring the Demonstration Tests

There are 10 evaluation factors noted on the test sheet for Demonstration Test 1 and 20 evaluation factors for Demonstration Test 2. For each factor, the evaluator notes Yes (Y), No (N), or Not Sure (?), depending on how the candidate meets the evaluation criteria. A Yes is worth two points, a Not Sure one. The maximum score on Demonstration Test 1 is 20 points, with 16 or more suggesting prime candidates and 10 to 15 suggesting marginal ones. The maximum score on Demonstration Test 2 is 40 points, with 32 or higher suggesting prime and 20 to 31 suggesting marginal. Again, the evaluator's personal interpretation is unlikely to yield a score that will materially misrepresent a candidate's potential. *Do not review the evaluation criteria with the candidate, either before or after the test.*

The Purpose of the Demonstration Tests

1. **Demonstration Tests show what candidates can (and cannot) do.**
   Demonstration Tests are practical exhibitions of the candidate's physical and professional skill. They

suggest the amount of training that may be required to bring an applicant up to your professional standards. For positions in which the work is performed in view of the public, Demonstration Tests allow you to observe prospective workers' general work habits and the smoothness of their moves. Short of putting the applicant to work, these tests are the best way to evaluate practical ability before making a job offer.

2. **Demonstration Tests make a statement about what is important to your business.**
   Requiring this testing of every job seeker declares your seriousness about professional development and standards. For entry-level staff, whose professional knowledge is minimal, the tests create an appreciation of what it takes to advance to positions of higher responsibility.

3. **Demonstration Tests provide a framework for future training.**
   You can use the Demonstration Tests in future training sessions, since they cover major skills, awareness, and understanding that are of concern to your operation. An understanding of the reasons behind correct procedures will raise the level of your staff's professionalism.

4. **Demonstration Tests provide documentation and objectivity for the selection process.**
   The tests record applicants' prehire performance and measure job-related factors. Because they are equally (and consistently) administered to all candidates, they provide a basis for staff selection decisions that will not be easily challenged by disgruntled candidates.

Using the Demonstration Tests
for Training

Like the Lifting Test, the Demonstration Tests can provide an effective outline for future staff training. The instructor presents the demonstrations and opens the floor for the students' ideas, which can be reviewed in light of the evaluation criteria. Each student can take part in the demonstration, after which the group can discuss each other's performance and help refine techniques. The discussion is likely to generate additional demonstrations for the group to explore.

CHAPTER 13

The Interviews

A common lament among foodservice operators is that we have had to become legal experts just to safely assemble a staff. The growing tangle of regulations covering what you can say is becoming more and more frustrating. Don't worry. We have done all the research for you. If you check with your legal counsel and follow **The Foolproof Foodservice Selection System** exactly, you won't get in trouble. The interview guides for both hourly and coaching staff are included in Appendix D.

The First Interview

The First Interview is *not* conducted to verify the information on the application. Its purpose is to uncover the priorities, patterns, and motives in an individual's past activities as a means to predict their future performance. As with the Screening Interview, the First Interview guide contains a series of standard questions along with suggestions on desirable and undesirable responses. The First Interview follows the format developed by Dr. William S. Swan in his exceptional book, *Swan's How to Hire the Right People Program*.

The Second and Third Interviews

The Second and Third Interviews look at the same qualities, although from different directions. Most interviews try to decide if the applicant can do the job, but in **The Foolproof Foodservice Selection System**, ability is measured by the Demonstration and Professional Tests. The Second and Third Interviews measure five personal and professional areas that define a top candidate—willingness, coachability, approach, professional curiosity, and status. Ability by itself is meaningless without these qualities.

Willingness   No matter how technically qualified, candidates will not be of much use to you unless they are willing to do the job. It is important to find staff members who want to get the job done and can work smoothly as part of the team. You want people who will handle problems calmly and complete tasks efficiently.

Coachability   Even workers who are willing and able can disrupt the organization if they cannot take direction. An example is the stereotypical classically trained chef who will do things only his way. While this person's talent may be commendable, a legendary foodservice operation requires team players. Understanding people's motivations can help you decide if they will fit smoothly into your organization.

Approach   There are dozens of ways to get things done in the foodservice industry. If applicants have a style that is at odds with their supervisor's or with the prevailing climate of the operation, the conflict can hurt productivity and guest service. This section of the interview will give you an indication of how applicants approach their work and their world.

Professional Curiosity   In a legendary foodservice operation, staff members are actively learning and advancing their skills. In such a professional climate, the most successful workers are those who share this goal. On the other hand, individuals who lack professional curiosity are likely to be either self-styled experts or unmotivated. Either condition can work against creating and maintaining the professional climate that fosters excellence and exemplary guest service.

Status   The applicant's job-seeking status suggests whether time constraints and employment priorities are compatible with those of the company. It can also reveal how your company compares with the competition in the candidate's mind.

Conducting the Interviews

A script is included in the First Interview guide to help the interviewer move from one section to another. It is unnecessary (and probably undesirable) to read the script to the applicant. Simply stay close to its intent and you will keep the interview on track. You will also ensure that it is the candidate, not the interviewer, who does most of the talking. The Second and Third Interview guides are for hourly staff and coaching staff. Always stick to the questions on the guides. Avoid "frank discussions" or "thinking aloud."

The First Interview should take 30 to 45 minutes to complete. Interviews for hourly staff should take 20 to 30 minutes, and the coaching staff interviews should take 30 to 45 minutes. To improve your ability to conduct effective interviews, I recommend William Swan's book (see "Suggested Reading").

Scoring the Interviews

Responses to the questions are graded as Yes (Y), No (N), or Maybe (?) depending on how the interviewer compares the candidate's replies against the standards. A Yes is worth two points, a Maybe one point, and a No zero. Score the Second and Third interviews by section (Willingness, Coachability, etc.) on the Tracking Sheet.

Interviewing Outside the Guides

Human resources professionals have reviewed the questions on the interview guides for compliance with existing fair employment regulations. You are free to develop your own questions, but if you choose to improvise, ask yourself if your questions are necessary. That is, do they determine the applicant's ability to satisfactorily discharge the responsibilities of the job? If not, don't ask them. To be safe, I suggest you review the legal summaries in Appendix I, particularly the section on Pre-Employment Inquiries. The material in Appendix I covers federal law. It also notes which states have specific laws covering various elements of fair hiring practice.

Some states' fair-employment laws prohibit certain inquiries that the federal government allows. Readers are warned that guidelines should not substitute for consultation with your legal counsel. Only someone who is knowledgeable on applicable laws (and their interpretations) can assure you that what you do and how you do it—including the elements of **The Foolproof Foodservice Selection System**—complies with all legal requirements.

CHAPTER 14

The Professional Test

The Professional Test is a comprehensive examination of professional knowledge and approach. Its 150 questions cover a wide range of topics related to foodservice. Admittedly, not all of these questions apply to every operation. For example, a hospital foodservice manager might not need an understanding of responsible alcohol service, but what could it hurt? The purpose of the Professional Test is far more than simply measuring knowledge, and even questions that do not relate directly to the operation are significant. The test is divided into sections. This makes it easy to disregard any areas that do not relate to your operation, allowing more equitable comparisons between candidates.

Professional Tests are included for the coaching staff (Appendix E), the beverage staff (Appendix F), the production staff (Appendix G), and the service staff (Appendix H). They are presented in both English and Spanish versions.

Administering the Professional Test

Give the Professional Test to *all* applicants for any position in the department. The candidate receives a copy of the test for the department in which he is applying and an answer sheet, both of which contain instructions. This is a timed test. Be sure to have someone supervise a group test to ensure that applicants do only their own work. The math required on the test is quite basic. If you do not allow the use of electronic calculators, you will learn more about the candidate's mathematical skills. Moreover, where there are questions of interpretation, applicants should use their own perspective, *not* make a guess about the perspective they think the test designers had in mind. Once the Professional Test is corrected, the screener notes the score by sections in the block at the bottom of the answer sheet, along with the time taken to complete the test.

Scoring the Professional Test

Award one point for each correct answer. The maximum score on the test is 20. Scores of 16 or higher suggest prime candidates, while scores of 10 to 15 suggest those who are marginal. *Do not review the answers with the candidate after the test.*

Purpose of the Professional Test

1. **The Professional Test shows what candidates do (and do not) know.**
   Above all, the Professional Test shows the candidates' professional knowledge and suggests the amount of training that may be required to bring them up to your standards. There is never enough time to do all the training you would like to do. Professional tests can help you get a head start by identifying how far along candidates are in their professional development. Since teaching is an important element of all senior-level positions, the Professional Test will also show you what knowledge an applicant brings to the company.

2. **The Professional Test saves interview time.**
   Using the Professional Test to ask technical questions can save the company countless hours while still covering all the technical topics. Since time is always an issue in hiring, the Professional Test enables a more complete evaluation of what an applicant can bring to the job.

3. **The Professional Test shows candidates what they don't know.**
   As I said before, workers who "know it all" are difficult to teach. The Professional Test will give even the most qualified applicants pause and help them see that there is always more to learn. And once they realize this, they usually become more receptive to training. Entry-level applicants will be totally overwhelmed by the Professional Test, but the test will show them what they will learn if they come to work for you and apply themselves professionally. This awareness may get them excited about learning. You could do worse.

4. **The Professional Test makes a statement about what is important to your business.**
   Several questions on the Professional Test are included just to remind applicants about certain points, not because applicants are likely to know (or not know) the answers. The simple fact that you require this test of every job seeker is a declaration of your seriousness about professional development and standards.

5. **The Professional Test provides a framework for future training.**
   Having asked the questions, you can then use a discussion of the answers as a basis for future training sessions. The Professional Test covers all principal areas of professional concern. Understanding the reasons behind the correct answers will raise the level of your staff's professionalism.

6. **The Professional Test verifies the applicants' reading ability.**
   Production staff members need to read recipes, labels, invoices, and guest checks; service staffers need to read guest checks, menus, and coupons. The Professional Test will reveal poor reading skills if a candidate is having trouble understanding the questions.

7. **The Professional Test provides documentation and objectivity for the selection process.**
   The test is a written record of applicants' prehire performance and measures job-related factors. It is administered to all candidates equally and consistently and thus discourages charges of unfair hiring.

8. **The Professional Test identifies compatible perspectives in the applicant.**
   Portions of the Professional Test are designed to reveal an applicant's approach to various situations. A candidate whose answers are similar to those of supervisors is more likely to see the job in the same way. This compatibility may make for a more productive working relationship.

9. **The Professional Test provides a measure of applicants' certainty.**
   If two applicants score about the same on the Professional Test, which is timed, the one who completed it faster is probably the more certain of the answers. In the real world of foodservice, events happen quickly and workers often have to respond instantly. Those who are more certain of their skills and knowledge are likely to be the most effective.

Using the Professional Test for Training

Using the Professional Test, the instructor asks students the questions, then leads a discussion of the possible answers based on the material in the answer sheet. At the suggested pace of two to three questions a week (which should be feasible for most operations), each Professional Test can provide 50 to 75 weeks of interactive departmental training.

The Situation Tests

Situation tests are plausible foodservice scenarios that require the applicant to handle a sticky situation. They give you an idea of how candidates think, provide an insight into their perspective on the industry, and help you gauge the applicant's priorities. The diversity of operating styles in the foodservice industry virtually guarantees that particular test situations will not arise in some operations. However, the examples in the System should provide enough models to allow operators to create cases that more closely match their unique needs.

Two situations each are included for the coaching staff (Appendix E), the beverage staff (Appendix F), the production staff (Appendix G), and the service staff (Appendix H). They are presented in both English and Spanish versions.

Administering the Situation Tests

Give the Situation Tests to *all* applicants for all positions within the department. Have them read the first situation and verbally answer the questions that follow. The evaluator must be knowledgeable in the professional area under review and must remain neutral during the test. Resist the urge to prompt or coach candidates—there will be plenty of opportunity for that if they are good enough to join your staff. When the candidate completes the first test, go on to the second situation and repeat the process.

Scoring the Situation Tests

More than any other element of the System, the Situation tests are subjective—there is no "right" answer. To help the evaluation, ten evaluation factors are noted on the Situation Test Evaluation Sheet for each situation. For each factor, the evaluator notes Yes (Y), No (N), or Not Sure (?) depending on his or her reading of how well the candidate's answers met the criteria. A Yes is worth two points and a Not Sure one point; the maximum score on each situation is 20 points. Scores of 16 or higher suggest prime candidates, while scores of 10 to 15 suggest those who are marginal. The evaluator's personal interpretation is unlikely to yield a score that will materially misrepresent a candidate's potential. *Do not review the evaluation criteria with the candidate.*

Purpose of the Situation Tests

1. **Situation Tests show how candidates are likely to act.**
    Situation Tests suggest candidates' probable performance in real-life situations, as well as the amount of training required for them to meet your professional standards. Since there is never enough time to do all the training you would like to do, Situation Tests can help you identify those candidates whose professional perspective is more developed.

2. **Situation Tests show candidates what they don't know.**
    Since workers who "know it all" don't think they have anything to learn, they are difficult to train. Yet even the most qualified applicants will find some interesting questions in the Situation Tests. Once they realize there is more to know, many people welcome the opportunity to learn.

3. **Situation Tests provide documentation and objectivity for the selection process.**
    Like all the other tests, the Situation Tests are a written record of applicants' prehire performance and measure only job-related factors. They are equally and consistently administered to all candidates and thus protect you from charges of unfair hiring practices.

4. **Situation Tests make a statement about what is important to your business.**
    Requiring this testing of every job seeker declares your seriousness about professional development and standards. Entry-level staff will have minimal professional experience. These tests help give them an appreciation of what it takes to advance to positions of greater responsibility.

5. **Situation Tests identify compatible perspectives in the applicant.**
    Applicants who approach a situation similarly to their supervisors are more likely to see the job in the same way, and thus they are more likely to develop productive working relationships within the operation.

6. **Situation Tests provide a measure of applicants' certainty.**
    The tests show the extent to which candidates will take charge of a situation. In the real world of foodservice, things happen quickly and workers often have to respond instantly. The confident workers are more likely to be effective than workers who are unsure of themselves.

7. **Situation Tests verify the applicant's reading ability.**
    If candidates have difficulty understanding the Situation Test, you will be alerted that they may not have the reading skills that are critical in any foodservice position.

Using the Situation Tests for Training

The Situation Test can be an effective staff training tool. Students can present their ideas on the situations, which you can review in light of the evaluation criteria. Each situation can easily be discussed over several weeks. The discussion is likely to generate additional situations for the group to explore.

C H A P T E R   1 6

Background Research

There are three major areas of background research you may want to explore on each applicant:

Reference checks from supervisors, co-workers, and subordinates to determine work patterns.

A **law enforcement report** that provides information to verify statements on the application.

A **medical exam** to verify information regarding drug and alcohol use.

Reference Checks

If you ask for references, you must check them. Apart from the due diligence aspect of reference checks, failure to check applicants' statements is a breach of trust. You *told* the candidates that you would check all references. Following through on this promise sets a precedent for your future business relationship with them. When you check references, you deliver the message that you do what you say you will do, which gives you permission to hold staff members to the same standard. If you ask for references and don't check them, a court may consider this as an effort to discriminate.

Here are a few points about reference checks that you may find helpful. They were compiled by the personnel firm of Robert Half International, Inc.

1. **Ignore written references handed directly to you by the candidate.**
   The reference letters some candidates carry with them into an interview were often written on the day of termination and consequently may be a response to guilt feelings. Sometimes the candidates write such letters themselves.
2. **Seek references not mentioned by the candidate.**
   When you call a previous employer, ask for somebody other than the individual whose name you have been given. Ask a person whose name was supplied as a reference for the name of somebody who knows the candidate. Pyramid references this way until you have enough information.
3. **Call most former employers.**
   The most recent employer may not have bad things to say about a candidate, but this does not mean that *previous* employers did not have problems you want to hear about. This is even more reason to call as many of the candidate's former employers as possible.
4. **Get references by phone, not by mail.**
   People tend to be reluctant to put derogatory remarks on paper. Also, you are in a better position to judge the sincerity and enthusiasm of the reference when talking directly with the person who provided it.

5. When filling a key position, make a personal visit to the person giving the reference.

People are generally more candid in face-to-face situations than they might be over the phone or in a letter.

You will receive names and numbers of superiors, supervisors, co-workers, and subordinates on the application, and each will give you a different perspective on the applicant's attitudes and abilities. In the litigious climate we live in, companies are often reluctant to provide more than "name, rank, and service number." However, there is information that almost everyone will provide most of the time. The Reference Check forms in Appendix B include the relevant questions. Following them will save time and keep the interview on track.

You might want to ask for names and phone numbers of people who worked with the candidate in the past and are now working for another company. Often you can get more complete and accurate information from people who no longer work for the candidate's former employer. Once they are free from the organizational structure, people often feel less reluctant to share candid impressions of former business associates.

If you cannot get sufficient information from the names and numbers provided by the applicant, request additional references. Explain that without checking prior references you cannot offer a position. Put the burden on the applicants to give you what you need to make an offer—after all, it is to their benefit. If you are unable to get any historical information, eliminate the applicant from further consideration.

Reference-checking Procedure

Unless you are seriously pressed for time in filling a vacancy, don't invest the time in reference checks until the candidate starts to look good enough to be a finalist. At that point, ask applicants to contact their references and give them permission to talk with you. This will save time and make it easier when you call them.

When you reach the reference on the phone, introduce yourself, explain why you are calling, and let the person know that the applicant has requested that you call. Reference Check forms for employers, co-workers, and personal references are included in Appendix B. Following the format on the appropriate form will keep the conversation brief and focused. If you are not getting the information you need, or if you suspect there is more to the story, don't be afraid to ask the reference to suggest the names of others you can call. Continue this process until you have a consistent picture of the candidate.

Recording the Results

When you have finished, summarize the consensus from the reference checks on the Tracking Sheet and file the Reference Check worksheets in the candidate's file.

Law Enforcement Report

In most parts of the country (with the permission of the person involved) you can conduct a police check. In Colorado Springs, at least, this report comes back in about 10 working days, and the cost is very reasonable. The report will give you information on convictions (felony and misdemeanor) and moving vehicle violations.

The law enforcement report is very important for positions involving driving, security duties, or work that would place the worker in an isolated setting with a member of the opposite sex. It will provide essential information that can protect you from a charge of wrongful and negligent hiring, which means that you should have known not to hire a person. An example would be hiring a driver with a history of DWI convictions. If this person subsequently drove your company van into a crowd of people while drunk, you could easily be liable. Or consider a situation where a female manager closes the operation alone late at night and, unknown to you, your evening cleaning man has a history of sex offenses. If there is an incident, you can be held liable for wrongful and negligent hiring because you should have discovered his criminal history before you hired him.

Another benefit of the law enforcement report is that it allows you to verify the statements made on the application regarding prior convictions. The point is not whether applicants have a prior police record. Many candidates may have made mistakes in the past. The question is whether they told the truth on their applications. Run-ins with the law are history, but lying is a current character flaw. Wrong or misleading statements on the application are defensible grounds for dismissal.

Medical Exam

If you follow **The Foolproof Foodservice Selection System**, you will have written permission from the applicant to conduct a medical examination for the presence of drugs and alcohol. Because candidates know you can do such a test (and because you have verified all their other statements), some abusers may self-screen themselves out of consideration. Whether you choose to administer the medical exam or not is your choice, but as with all personnel policies, be sure you handle it the same way for all applicants. The purpose of the medical exam is to determine if candidates are medically qualified to perform the job functions and to verify the statements they made on their application. The consequences for false or erroneous statements still apply.

Making the Offer

The goal of **The Foolproof Foodservice Selection System** is to select and hire top-quality staff. If you followed the System, or even used just *parts* of it, you should have a clear idea of which applicants you want to join your staff. Now you have to sign them up!

The Mercy Hire

Being a compassionate person, you will undoubtedly be touched at one time or another by an applicant who does not really meet your standards but whom you *know* will be a great worker if given the chance. Remember that while everybody *can* be great, not everybody *will* be great. I might remind you that you are in the foodservice business, not the rehabilitation business, but this warning will not carry much weight when you are dealing with a misfit who has touched your heart.

    The Foolproof Foodservice Selection System helps reduce the temptation to make a "mercy hire" by providing for several other staff members to be involved in the selection process. In a participatory company, the selection team must reach consensus before a job offer can be made.

    If you insist upon circumventing the System, then allow yourself *one, and only one*, mercy hire a year! And keep in mind that if you give yourself this latitude, you must also give it to every member of the selection team. As an extra incentive you might tie the performance of the special hire to the performance appraisal of the sponsor. If giving yourself permission for a mercy hire means opening up the possibility of six to ten such hires a year (one per team member), you might decide simply to trust the System and make no exceptions. You will thank yourself later.

The Offer Letter

As a logical extension of the employment documentation started in the selection process, make all job offers in writing. A suggested format for an Offer of Employment letter follows. The offer letter provides a basis of understanding between the employer and the new hire that is defensible should there be a dispute in the future. It documents and clarifies the following elements of the job offer:

- The position offered
- Whether the position is exempt or nonexempt
- The rate of pay
- The overtime rate of pay

- The frequency of paychecks
- Whether the position is full-time or part-time
- The projected starting date
- The procedure for completing INS Form I-9 documentation
- The requirements for a medical examination (if necessary)

Exempt Position

If the position offered is exempt under the FLSA, use this paragraph in place of the current Paragraph 2 of the offer letter:

> This position is exempt under the FLSA; therefore, overtime pay is not applicable. The base rate of pay for this position is $_____ (per hour, biweekly, semimonthly, monthly). Our pay days are (every Friday, the first and fifteenth day of the month, every other Friday, etc.). This position is (part-time, full-time, forty hours per week).

Tipped Position

If the position offered customarily receives tips, add the following sentence at the end of Paragraph 2:

> This is a tipped position.

If you intend to take tip credit, add the following sentence after the one above:

> As permitted by the federal Fair Labor Standards Act, we will take a tip credit of up to 50% of the applicable minimum wage to help meet the federal minimum wage obligation for tipped employees.

Medical Exam

This paragraph is optional. Include it if you require medical exams of all other new hires for the position.

> Your starting work is further conditioned upon the results of a pre-employment medical examination, which we require of everyone accepting employment with us. The medical examination will determine whether you are medically qualified to perform the job functions described in the enclosed position description. The examination will also verify the medical statements made on your employment application. We will hold the information received as a confidential medical record except on a "need to know" basis. We may inform your supervisors and/or coaches about necessary restrictions to your work, necessary accommodations, etc. Once you have accepted our employment offer, we will schedule the medical examination. Time spent taking the medical examination will not be paid time; however, we will pay all costs associated with the examination.

INS Documentation

You will notice that the letter requests applicants to bring in their I-9 identification and complete the form in your office. This is because the employer is required to inspect the original identification documents and witness preparation of INS Form I-9. If candidates complete the form at home, they will have to repeat the process in your presence.

Offer of Employment Letter

(Company Letterhead)

Date:

Applicant's Name:
Applicant's Address:
Applicant's City, State, Zip

Subject: Employment Offer

Dear _____:

We are pleased to extend to you an offer to join our staff as a ____(job title)____. A copy of the job description for this position is enclosed for your review.

This position is nonexempt under the FLSA, which means that any time worked in excess of forty hours worked will be paid at 1½ times the regular base rate of pay. The base rate of pay for this position is $_____ (per hour, biweekly, semimonthly, monthly). Our pay days are (every Friday, the first and fifteenth day of the month, every other Friday, etc.). This position is (part-time, full-time, forty hours per week).

Your starting date will be ____(date)____. This offer will be conditional upon completion of the enclosed Employment Eligibility Verification, INS Form I-9. Please read through this document and bring the appropriate forms of identification with you. We will complete this form on your first day of employment.

Please acknowledge your acceptance or declination of this position by signing the enclosed copy of this letter and return it to us no later than ____(date)____. We look forward to hearing from you regarding this employment offer.

With best regards,

Your Name
Your Title

Enclosures: Position Description
              INS Form I-9

_____ I accept your offer   _____ I decline your offer

Signature _____ Date _____

At-will Employment

You (or your legal counsel) may notice that the letter makes no reference to an "at-will" employment relationship. While the at-will provision has been with us for years, there is some doubt as to whether it will work in today's climate. Writing in *The Cornell Hotel and Restaurant Administration Quarterly*, Jeffrey Pellissier of California State Polytechnic University at Pomona, offers some interesting thoughts on the subject. He starts by discussing the notion of an at-will employment agreement:

> Such a document would state that the employment arrangement is strictly at-will and may be terminated by either party at any time; that the employment arrangement may be altered in writing only by a top company official; and that the contract is made by offering the employee some kind of consideration for entering this contract, say, a bonus. With such a policy, the company must make sure that none of its documents even imply that jobs are guaranteed in any way. Moreover, the company must follow the at-will employment policy consistently with all employees in a given work classification. Termination must be at will, with no cause given, or the courts will determine that termination has really been for cause.
>
> While this procedure sounds good in theory, many courts will not accept it (others will do so, however). As a result, an employer can use the same at-will argument in different courts and get different results. Many judges are suspicious of at-will agreements, because they believe at-will agreements are used to cover up the "real" reason for termination.
>
> The at-will agreement can be nullified if the employer even hints orally that the employee's job is in any way protected. Technically known as "promissory estoppel," this doctrine can be used by an employee who claims to have relied upon an employer's spoken promise that he or she was protected.

You can see the difficulties. For one, if you ever counsel staff members about their work performance, as all good coaches do, you have effectively voided an at-will relationship. You have also made the at-will argument undefensible if you even hint at the possibility of long-term employment. My suggestion is that even if it were possible to create true at-will employment, it is too damaging to staff morale and team-building to be a good idea.

Post-hire Documentation

This manual leaves you at the point where the candidate accepts your offer. You are familiar with the requirements for verifying employment eligibility for the INS. The summary of the FLSA in Appendix I outlines the recordkeeping requirements for your staff members. I urge you to be sure you complete and maintain this documentation for everyone in your employ since the penalties for noncompliance are severe.

Closing
Comments

Selection Is Just the Start

Once you find the best of the best, you have to keep them—staff turnover is the bane of the foodservice industry. If we are to achieve our goals, as individuals and as an industry, we must do a better job of keeping the wonderful people we spend so much time selecting. It sounds simplistic, but *your staff leaves because they do not want to stay!* Success at staff retention requires paying attention to the climate you create in your operation.

To slow the revolving door, start thinking in terms of retention instead of turnover. (Of course, if you want to be able to measure retention you have to get turnover below 100 percent a year!) But what is legitimately turnover and what isn't? To start with, a certain amount of turnover is normal and healthy. Without some influx of new talent and ideas, it is easy for an operation to get stale. Then, too, not every departure should count as turnover since everyone leaves eventually. Would you be bothered if someone left after working with you for six years? Are you surprised when students leave after graduation? What about the serviceman's wife who leaves when her husband gets new orders? These are just facts of life, not turnover problems. The statistic to track is unplanned vacancies—people who leave without giving at least two weeks' notice.

As I complete work on this manual, the next book in the series, *From Turnover to Teamwork: How to Build and Retain a Service-Oriented Staff*, is already taking shape. This will be a detailed exploration of why people leave and what you can do about it. For now I will briefly outline the elements of a staff retention system by giving *you* a quiz for a change.

Care and feeding of the working climate involves addressing a number of questions, the answers to which will help you understand what is happening in your organization. To assess your retention climate in your operation, answer the following questions honestly, avoiding wishful thinking. If you really want a precise picture, ask your staff members to complete this quiz (anonymously, of course).

Evaluate Your Retention Climate

For each question, mark Yes (Y) if the statement is always true, No (N) if the answer is not indicative of your operation, and Maybe or Not Sure (?) if your results in this area are inconsistent.

Y N ?

☐ ☐ ☐ 1. *Are* you the best employer in town?

☐ ☐ ☐ 2. Does your operation have a reputation for professional excellence?

☐ ☐ ☐ 3. Are your wages at or above prevailing rates in your area?

☐ ☐ ☐ 4. Have you created meaningful jobs?

☐ ☐ ☐ 5. Do you see labor hours primarily as an investment in building sales and guest gratification?

☐ ☐ ☐ 6. Does your crew participate in the decisions that affect their careers?

☐ ☐ ☐ 7. Do you treat your staff the same way you treat your guests?

☐ ☐ ☐ 8. Do you measure your success by the success of your staff?

☐ ☐ ☐ 9. Are you more of a coach than a cop?

☐ ☐ ☐ 10. Do you keep statistics on turnover?

☐ ☐ ☐ 11. Is the retention rate part of the performance appraisal for your coaching staff?

☐ ☐ ☐ 12. Are the performance appraisals of your staff based on results instead of activities?

☐ ☐ ☐ 13. Do you provide a benefit program for your coaching staff?

☐ ☐ ☐ 14. Do you provide a benefit program for full-time workers?

☐ ☐ ☐ 15. Do you provide a benefit program for part-time workers?

☐ ☐ ☐ 16. Do you require that you and your staff take paid vacations at least once a year?

☐ ☐ ☐ 17. Do you reward staff members for going beyond the norm to delight guests?

☐ ☐ ☐ 18. Do you consistently reinforce your crew's feelings of self-worth?

☐ ☐ ☐ 19. Do you consistently and effectively convey your gratitude to your staff for their work?

☐ ☐ ☐ 20. Do you place more value on avoiding problems than on solving them?

☐ ☐ ☐ 21. Do you have a written staff manual or handbook?

☐ ☐ ☐ 22. Do you have written human resources policies?

☐ ☐ ☐ 23. If you have an operations manual, is it limited to no more than ten key points?

☐ ☐ ☐ 24. Is your procedures manual minimal?

☐ ☐ ☐ 25. Do you conduct regular performance appraisals?

☐ ☐ ☐ 26. Do you provide uniforms your staff is proud to wear?

☐ ☐ ☐ 27. Do you want to hear "bad news" quickly?

☐ ☐ ☐ 28. Do you treat all your staff equally?

☐ ☐ ☐ 29. Do you see behavior as a symptom instead of as the problem?

☐ ☐ ☐ 30. Do you take a benefit-of-the-doubt stance toward your staff?

☐ ☐ ☐ 31. Do you and your coaching staff have a satisfying life *outside* the operation?

☐ ☐ ☐ 32. Does everyone in your employ know that you have a sense of humor?

☐ ☐ ☐ 33. Do you have a profit-sharing plan or a bonus plan based on profitability?

☐ ☐ ☐ 34. Do you know the personal and professional goals of each member of your staff?

Y N ?

☐ ☐ ☐ 35. Are you actively helping staff members achieve their goals?

☐ ☐ ☐ 36. Do you praise your staff members at least twice as often as you criticize them?

☐ ☐ ☐ 37. Do you know the names of everyone on your staff?

☐ ☐ ☐ 38. Do you conduct a formal orientation program for all new staff members?

☐ ☐ ☐ 39. Do you encourage your staff to experiment and try new ideas?

☐ ☐ ☐ 40. Do you support your staff if they fail?

☐ ☐ ☐ 41. Does your crew always know how well they are meeting your expectations?

☐ ☐ ☐ 42. Do you have a regular, effective means of communication within the company?

☐ ☐ ☐ 43. Do you have an active, ongoing training program for all staff levels?

☐ ☐ ☐ 44. Do you have periodic company gatherings strictly for the fun of it?

☐ ☐ ☐ 45. Do you truly expect the best from each member of your staff?

☐ ☐ ☐ 46. Do you encourage (and financially support) attendance at professional seminars?

☐ ☐ ☐ 47. Do you prohibit yourself and your coaching staff from working over 45 hours a week?

☐ ☐ ☐ 48. Do you always play as good a game as you talk?

☐ ☐ ☐ 49. Do you go out of your way to accommodate special requests from your staff?

☐ ☐ ☐ 50. Are you having fun yet?

Score the test as you score the tests in the System—two points for a Yes, one point for a Maybe, and no points for a No. Here is an idea of what your score means:

90–100   Give yourself an A! You are a super climate builder and your success is no accident.

80–89   Excellent. You are well on your way to becoming the best employer in town.

70–79   Very good. Your heart is in the right place. Keep working on it.

60–69   Good . . . and you know you can do better. The rewards are worth it.

50–59   Okay . . . and you need to make some adjustments to stay ahead of the competition.

Below 50   Time to take a serious look at your business and make that self-improvement action plan.

Implementing the ideas in this manual is an effective first step toward improving your retention rate. As a second step, consider the points raised in the quiz questions and see what you can do to improve your score. There are many innovations you can introduce that will improve your retention climate and make your work easier and your staff happier. It is all money in your pocket. You just have to want to do it and be willing to start somewhere. It is never too late to become a legend!

SUGGESTED READINGS

I designed this manual to give foodservice operators ready-to-use tools that will enable them to do a better job of creating the work force they deserve. Of necessity, this approach required that a large body of information be reduced to a workable system. For readers who wish to examine some of these ideas more deeply, I recommend the following books. If you have trouble finding any of them, please give me a call.

Gross, T. Scott. *Positively Outrageous Service*, 1991. MasterMedia Limited, 16 East 72nd Street, New York, NY 10021.

Kausen, Robert. *Customer Satisfaction Guaranteed: A New Approach to Customer Service, Bedside Manner and Relationship Ease*, 1988. Life Education, Inc., Star Route 2-3969G, Trinity Center, CA 96091.

Marvin, Bill. *Restaurant Basics: Why Guests Don't Come Back and What You Can Do About It*, 1992. John Wiley & Sons, Inc., 605 Third Avenue, New York, NY 10158.

Moffa, James. *The Restaurant Owner's Idea Book*, 1990. Food for Thought!, P.O. Box 36575, Grosse Pointe, MI 48236.

National Restaurant Association. *A Primer on How to Recruit, Hire & Retain Employees*, 1987. Educational Foundation of the National Restaurant Association, 250 South Wacker Drive, Chicago, IL 60606.

————. *Food Management Professional (FMP) Program–Review Notebook*, 1991. Educational Foundation of the National Restaurant Association, 250 South Wacker Drive, Chicago, IL 60606.

Rinke, Wolf J. *The Winning Foodservice Manager: Strategies for Doing More With Less*, 1990. Achievement Press, 4412 Cherry Valley Drive, Rockville, MD 20853.

Swan, William S. *Swan's How to Pick the Right People Program*, 1989. John Wiley & Sons, Inc., 605 Third Avenue, New York, NY 10158.

Zaccarelli, Herman. *Foodservice Management by Checklist*, 1991. John Wiley & Sons, Inc., 605 Third Avenue, New York, NY 10158.

APPENDIX A

Position
Descriptions

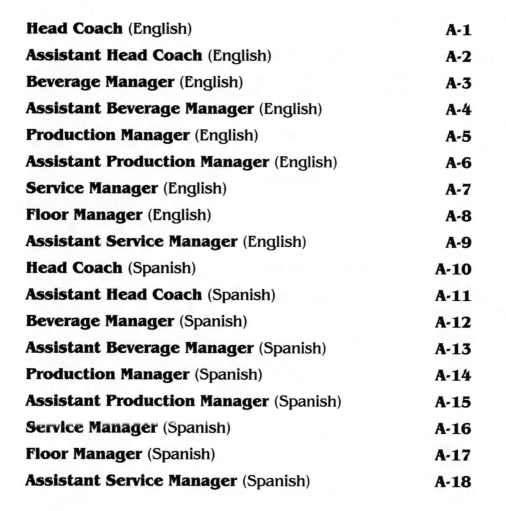

Head Coach (English)   **A-1**

Assistant Head Coach (English)   **A-2**

Beverage Manager (English)   **A-3**

Assistant Beverage Manager (English)   **A-4**

Production Manager (English)   **A-5**

Assistant Production Manager (English)   **A-6**

Service Manager (English)   **A-7**

Floor Manager (English)   **A-8**

Assistant Service Manager (English)   **A-9**

Head Coach (Spanish)   **A-10**

Assistant Head Coach (Spanish)   **A-11**

Beverage Manager (Spanish)   **A-12**

Assistant Beverage Manager (Spanish)   **A-13**

Production Manager (Spanish)   **A-14**

Assistant Production Manager (Spanish)   **A-15**

Service Manager (Spanish)   **A-16**

Floor Manager (Spanish)   **A-17**

Assistant Service Manager (Spanish)   **A-18**

Position Description

Position: Head Coach
Mentor: Managing Director
Trains: Assistant Head Coaches

POSITION SUMMARY:

Supports the restaurant staff in delivering legendary guest service.

ESSENTIAL PROFESSIONAL FUNCTIONS:

- Talks with all restaurant guests to ensure their delight with the dining experience.
- Creates effective staff training programs.
- Maintains the physical integrity of the restaurant.
- Prepares management reports, budgets, and forecasts.
- Oversees preparation of staff schedules.
- Plans and conducts staff meetings.
- Maintains the profitability of the restaurant.
- Conducts daily inspections of all areas of the restaurant.
- Prepares regular performance appraisals for restaurant staff.
- Oversees staff coaching, counseling, and discipline.
- Makes employment and termination decisions.
- Fills in where needed to ensure efficient operations.
- Implements improvements to the operating format.

RESULTS UPON WHICH PERFORMANCE IS EVALUATED:

- Health department scores exceed 90 with no major violations.
- Assistants are steadily improving their skills as measured by quarterly tests.
- Vacancies are filled by internal promotions.
- Stories of legendary guest service abound.
- Contributions are recognized by co-workers on peer appraisals.
- Restaurant is always neat and clean.
- Guests have a great time every time as measured by repeat patronage of 80 to 85 percent.
- Resolves guest problems (in favor of the guest) immediately.
- Knowledgeable on menu items, drinks, and wines.
- Keeps the staff out of "the weeds."
- Annual staff retention rate exceeds 75 percent.
- Departing staff members give two to four weeks' notice.
- Restaurant wins best of category in local polls.
- Guests regularly ask "where do you find all those nice employees?"
- Meets the financial goals of the restaurant.
- Knows the personal and professional status of all restaurant staff.
- Leads by personal example.
- Continually develops professional skills (attends seminars, etc.).
- All discipline and terminations are properly documented.
- Staff performance appraisals are completed accurately and on time.
- Written guest complaints are resolved (in favor of the guest) within 24 hours.

QUALIFICATION STANDARDS:

- Able to operate a cash register or electronic POS system.
- Walks and stands during 90 percent of the shift.
- Reading and writing skills required.
- Reaches, bends, stoops, and wipes.
- Interacts verbally with patrons.
- Hazards may include, but are not limited to, cuts, burns, slipping, and tripping.

Position Description

Position: Assistant Head Coach
Mentor: Head Coach
Trains: Production Manager, Beverage Manager, Service Manager, Floor Manager

POSITION SUMMARY:

Supports the restaurant staff in delivering legendary guest service.

ESSENTIAL PROFESSIONAL FUNCTIONS:

- Talks with all restaurant guests to ensure their delight with the dining experience.
- Creates effective training programs.
- Maintains the physical integrity of the restaurant.
- Prepares management reports, budgets, and forecasts.
- Prepares staff schedules.
- Plans and conducts staff meetings.
- Maintains the profitability of the restaurant.
- Conducts daily inspections of all areas of the restaurant.
- Prepares regular performance appraisals for restaurant staff.
- Coaches, counsels, and disciplines staff members.
- Consults on employment and termination decisions.
- Learns the skills required to advance to the position of Head Coach.
- Fills in where needed to ensure efficient operations.
- Implements improvements to the operating format.

RESULTS UPON WHICH PERFORMANCE IS EVALUATED:

- Health department scores exceed 90 with no major violations.
- Trainees are steadily improving their skills as measured by quarterly tests.
- Vacancies are filled by internal promotions.
- Stories of legendary guest service abound.
- Contributions are recognized by co-workers on peer appraisals.
- Restaurant is always neat and clean.
- Guests have a great time every time as measured by repeat patronage of 80 to 85 percent.
- Resolves guest problems (in favor of the guest) immediately.
- Knowledgeable on menu items, drinks, and wines.
- Keeps the staff out of "the weeds."
- Annual staff retention rate exceeds 75 percent.
- Departing staff members give two to four weeks' notice.
- Restaurant wins best of category in local polls.
- Guests regularly ask "where do you find all those nice employees?"
- Meets the financial goals of the restaurant.
- Knows the personal and professional status of all restaurant staff.
- Leads by personal example.
- Continually develops professional skills (attends seminars, etc.).
- All discipline and terminations are properly documented.
- Staff performance appraisals are completed accurately and on time.
- Written guest complaints are resolved (in favor of the guest) within 24 hours.

QUALIFICATION STANDARDS:

- Able to operate a cash register or electronic POS system.
- Walks and stands during 90 percent of the shift.
- Reading and writing skills required.
- Reaches, bends, stoops, and wipes.
- Interacts verbally with patrons.
- Hazards may include, but are not limited to, cuts, burns, slipping, and tripping.

Position Description

Position: Beverage Manager
Mentor: Assistant Head Coach
Trains: Assistant Beverage Managers, Service Managers

POSITION SUMMARY:

Delights restaurant patrons with quality beverage preparation and service.

ESSENTIAL PROFESSIONAL FUNCTIONS:

- Sells, mixes, and serves alcoholic and alcohol-free beverages.
- Follows standardized recipes consistently from memory.
- Serves wine, draft beer, and bottled beer.
- Creates signature and daily special beverages.
- Manages pouring cost control procedures.
- Collects money for food and beverages served.
- Orders liquor and supplies.
- Arranges glassware and bottles to make an attractive display.
- Washes glassware and bar utensils.
- Cleans draft beer lines.
- Creates and conducts classes on beverages and responsible beverage service.
- Conducts daily inspections of beverage areas.
- Creates effective training program for assistants.
- Recognizes and reports all necessary maintenance promptly.
- Conducts daily beverage inventories.
- Fills in where needed to ensure efficient operations.
- Suggests improvements to the operating format.

RESULTS UPON WHICH PERFORMANCE IS EVALUATED:

- Guests comment favorably on the tastiness and presentation of drinks.
- Drink orders are completed within two minutes of ordering.
- Restaurant operates within ½ percent of theoretical beverage cost.
- Monthly inventory turns over at least six times.
- Assistants are steadily improving their skills as measured by quarterly tests.
- Beverage staff vacancies are filled by internal promotions.
- Regularly attends training seminars.
- Resolves guest problems on the spot.
- Knowledgeable on menu items, drinks, and wines.
- Stories of legendary beverage service abound.
- Bar area is always neat and clean.
- Health department scores exceed 90 with no major violations in the beverage department.
- Contributions are recognized by co-workers on peer appraisals.

QUALIFICATION STANDARDS:

- Able to operate a cash register or electronic POS system.
- Able to accurately add guest checks and make change.
- Stands during the entire shift.
- Reaches, bends, stoops, shakes, stirs, and wipes.
- Reading and writing skills required.
- Interacts verbally with patrons.
- With the assistance of another staff member, lifts 120-pound barrels of beer to a height of 30 inches several times a day.
- Lifts 30-pound cases to a maximum height of 72 inches about ten times per shift.
- Immerses hands in water frequently (every five minutes).
- Hazards may include, but are not limited to, cuts, burns, slipping, tripping, and exposure to secondary smoke.

Position Description

Position: Assistant Beverage Manager
Mentor: Beverage Manager

POSITION SUMMARY:

Delights restaurant patrons with quality beverage preparation and service.

ESSENTIAL PROFESSIONAL FUNCTIONS:

- Sells and serves beverages to guests in the dining room and bar.
- Presents menus, answers questions, makes suggestions regarding beverages.
- Writes orders on guest checks.
- Relays orders to service bar and kitchen.
- Serves courses from service bar and kitchen.
- Observes guests, anticipates needs, and responds to additional requests.
- Accurately totals guest checks, accepts payment, and makes change.
- Clears and resets tables.
- Assists the Beverage Manager in bar operations.
- Washes glassware and bar utensils.
- Cuts fruit and replenishes bar stocks.
- Learns the skills required to advance to the position of Beverage Manager.
- Recognizes and reports all necessary maintenance promptly.
- Assists with daily beverage inventories.
- Fills in where needed to ensure efficient operations.
- Suggests improvements to the operating format.

RESULTS UPON WHICH PERFORMANCE IS EVALUATED:

- Bar is continually stocked with clean glassware, equipment, and supplies.
- Drink orders are delivered within one minute of the order being completed.
- Testing shows a steady improvement of professional skills.
- Regularly attends training seminars.
- Resolves guest problems on the spot.
- Knowledgeable on menu items, drinks, and wines.
- Stories of legendary beverage service abound.
- Bar area is always neat and clean.
- Health department scores exceed 90 with no major violations in the beverage department.
- Contributions are recognized by co-workers on peer appraisals.

QUALIFICATION STANDARDS:

- Able to operate a cash register or electronic POS system.
- Able to accurately add guest checks and make change.
- Stands during the entire shift.
- Reaches, bends, stoops, shakes, stirs, and wipes.
- Reading and writing skills required.
- Interacts verbally with patrons.
- With the assistance of another staff member, lifts 120-pound barrels of beer to a height of 30 inches several times a day.
- Lifts 30-pound cases to a maximum height of 72 inches about ten times per shift.
- Immerses hands in water frequently (every five minutes).
- Hazards may include, but are not limited to, cuts, burns, slipping, tripping, and exposure to secondary smoke.

Position Description

Position: Production Manager
Mentor: Assistant Head Coach
Trains: Assistant Production Managers, Service Managers

POSITION SUMMARY:

Delights restaurant patrons with quality food preparation and presentation.

ESSENTIAL PROFESSIONAL FUNCTIONS:

- Prepares hot and cold food items following standardized recipes.
- Creates signature and daily special appetizers, entrees, and desserts.
- Manages food cost control procedures.
- Washes kitchen utensils.
- Cleans the production areas as necessary.
- Orders food and supplies.
- Creates and conducts classes on food sanitation, food preparation, and food presentation.
- Conducts daily inspections of production areas.
- Creates effective training program for assistants.
- Recognizes and reports all necessary maintenance promptly.
- Conducts weekly food inventories.
- Fills in where needed to ensure efficient operations.
- Suggests improvements to the operating format.

RESULTS UPON WHICH PERFORMANCE IS EVALUATED:

- Hot food is consistently served hot and cold food is consistently served cold.
- Guests have a spontaneous positive reaction when the plate is presented.
- Restaurant operates within ½ percent of theoretical food cost.
- Health department scores exceed 90 with no major violations in the production department.
- Monthly inventory turns over at least six times.
- Assistants are steadily improving their skills as measured by quarterly tests.
- Production staff vacancies are filled by internal promotions.
- Regularly attends training seminars.
- Stories of legendary food service abound.
- Contributions are recognized by co-workers on peer appraisals.
- Guests comment favorably on the tastiness and presentation of meals.
- Food orders are completed within 15 minutes of ordering.
- Production areas are always neat and clean.

QUALIFICATION STANDARDS:

- Stands during the entire shift.
- Works frequently in a hot and damp environment.
- Reaches, bends, stoops, shakes, stirs, and wipes.
- Lifts and carries sacks and cases weighing up to 70 pounds up to 20 times per shift.
- Reading and writing skills required.
- Immerses hands in water frequently.
- Hazards may include, but are not limited to, cuts, burns, slipping, and tripping.

Position Description

Position: Assistant Production Manager
Mentor: Production Manager

POSITION SUMMARY:

Delights restaurant patrons with quality food preparation and presentation.

ESSENTIAL PROFESSIONAL FUNCTIONS:

- Prepares hot and cold food items following standardized recipes.
- Washes serviceware and kitchen utensils.
- Receives and stores food.
- Cleans the production areas as necessary.
- Creates and conducts sanitation classes and inspections.
- Recognizes and reports all necessary maintenance promptly.
- Assists the Production Manager with weekly food inventories.
- Learns the skills required to advance to the position of Production Manager.
- Fills in where needed to ensure efficient operations.
- Suggests improvements to the operating format.

RESULTS UPON WHICH PERFORMANCE IS EVALUATED:

- Hot food is consistently served hot and cold food is consistently served cold.
- Guests have a spontaneous positive reaction when the plate is presented.
- All serviceware is spotless.
- All necessary maintenance is promptly reported.
- Food production is never delayed due to incomplete preparation.
- Health department scores exceed 90 with no major violations in the production department.
- Regularly attends training seminars.
- Stories of legendary food service abound.
- Contributions are recognized by co-workers on peer appraisals.
- Guests comment favorably on the tastiness and presentation of meals.
- Food orders are completed within 15 minutes of ordering.
- Production areas are always neat and clean.

QUALIFICATION STANDARDS:

- Stands during the entire shift.
- Works frequently in a hot and damp environment.
- Reaches, bends, stoops, shakes, stirs, and wipes.
- Lifts and carries sacks and cases weighing up to 70 pounds up to 20 times per shift.
- Reading and writing skills required.
- Immerses hands in water frequently.
- Hazards may include, but are not limited to, cuts, burns, slipping, and tripping.

Position Description

Position: Service Manager
Mentor: Assistant Head Coach
Trains: Assistant Service Managers, Floor Managers

POSITION SUMMARY:

Delights restaurant patrons with responsive food and beverage service.

ESSENTIAL PROFESSIONAL FUNCTIONS:

- Sells and serves food and beverages to guests in the dining room and bar.
- Presents menus, answers questions, makes suggestions regarding food and beverages.
- Writes orders on guest checks.
- Relays orders to the service bar and kitchen.
- Serves courses from service bar and kitchen.
- Observes guests, anticipates needs, and responds to additional requests.
- Accurately totals guest checks, accepts payment, and makes change.
- Clears and resets tables.
- Cleans the service areas as necessary.
- Inspects restrooms every 30 minutes and cleans as necessary.
- Conducts daily inspections of service areas.
- Creates effective training program for assistants.
- Recognizes and reports all necessary maintenance promptly.
- Fills in where needed to ensure efficient operations.
- Suggests improvements to the operating format.

RESULTS UPON WHICH PERFORMANCE IS EVALUATED:

- Guests are acknowledged within one minute of being seated.
- Food orders are delivered within one minute of completion.
- Average check meets or exceeds posted goals.
- Hot food is consistently served hot and cold food is consistently served cold.
- Guests have a spontaneous positive reaction when the plate is presented.
- Health department scores exceed 90 with no major violations in the service department.
- Assistants are steadily improving their skills as measured by quarterly tests.
- Service staff vacancies are filled by internal promotions.
- Regularly attends training seminars.
- Stories of legendary guest service abound.
- Contributions are recognized by co-workers on peer appraisals.
- Guests comment favorably on the tastiness and presentation of meals.
- Service areas are always neat and clean.
- Guests have a great time every time as measured by repeat patronage of 80 to 85 percent.
- Resolves guest problems (in favor of the guest) immediately.
- Knowledgeable on menu items, drinks, and wines.
- Guests regularly ask for this staff member to serve them.
- Guests make unsolicited comments on the cleanliness of the restrooms.

QUALIFICATION STANDARDS:

- Able to operate a cash register or electronic POS system.
- Walks and stands during the entire shift.
- Reading and writing skills required.
- Reaches, bends, stoops, and wipes.
- Carries service tray weighing up to 30 pounds from the kitchen to the dining room about 24 times per shift.
- Interacts verbally with patrons.
- Hazards may include, but are not limited to, cuts, burns, slipping, and tripping.

Position Description

Position: Floor Manager
Mentor: Assistant Head Coach

POSITION SUMMARY:

Creates a positive first and last impression for the guest and controls the flow of service in the dining room.

ESSENTIAL PROFESSIONAL FUNCTIONS:

- Greets arriving guests and thanks departing guests.
- Manages the guests' wait.
- Keeps guests informed of the status of their wait.
- Observes guests, anticipates needs, and responds to additional requests.
- Anticipates the special needs of waiting guests.
- Escorts guests to a table they will enjoy.
- Balances the loading of the dining room stations.
- Presents menus, answers questions, makes suggestions regarding food and beverages.
- Answers the telephone and answers questions from callers.
- Takes reservations for tables and special functions.
- Inspects the restaurant exterior and reception areas and cleans them as necessary.
- Recognizes and reports all necessary maintenance promptly.
- Fills in where needed to ensure efficient operations.
- Suggests improvements to the operating format.

RESULTS UPON WHICH PERFORMANCE IS EVALUATED:

- Guests are acknowledged warmly within 30 seconds of entering the restaurant.
- Quotes of waiting time are three to five minutes *longer* than actual waiting time.
- Keeps guests informed of the status of their wait; manages the wait.
- Guests are thanked warmly as they leave the restaurant.
- Guests always receive clean menus.
- Stories of legendary guest service abound.
- Contributions are recognized by co-workers on peer appraisals.
- Restaurant exterior and reception areas are always neat and clean.
- Guests have a great time every time as measured by repeat patronage of 80 to 85 percent.
- Resolves guest problems (in favor of the guest) immediately.
- Knowledgeable on menu items, drinks, and wines.

QUALIFICATION STANDARDS:

- Walks and stands during the entire shift.
- Reading and writing skills required.
- Reaches, bends, stoops, and wipes.
- Interacts verbally with patrons.
- Hazards may include, but are not limited to, slipping and tripping.

Position Description

Position: Assistant Service Manager
Mentor: Service Manager

POSITION SUMMARY:

Delights restaurant patrons with responsive food and beverage service.

ESSENTIAL PROFESSIONAL FUNCTIONS:

• Serves food and beverages to guests in the dining room.
• Carries food from the kitchen and service bar to the dining room.
• Carries soiled serviceware from the dining room to the kitchen and service bar.
• Relays orders to the service bar and kitchen.
• Responds to guests' requests.
• Clears and resets tables.
• Cleans the service areas as necessary.
• Inspects restrooms every 30 minutes and cleans as necessary.
• Recognizes and reports all necessary maintenance promptly.
• Learns the skills required to advance to the position of Service Manager.
• Fills in where needed to ensure efficient operations
• Suggests improvements to the operating format.

RESULTS UPON WHICH PERFORMANCE IS EVALUATED:

• Food orders are delivered within one minute of completion.
• Hot food is consistently served hot and cold food is consistently served cold.
• Tables are cleared and reset within three minutes after the guest leaves the dining room.
• Health department scores exceed 90 with no major violations in the service department.
• Regularly attends training seminars.
• Stories of legendary guest service abound.
• Contributions are recognized by co-workers on peer appraisals.
• Service areas are always neat and clean.
• Knowledgeable on menu items, drinks, and wines.
• Guests make unsolicited comments on the cleanliness of the restrooms.

QUALIFICATION STANDARDS:

• Able to operate a cash register or electronic POS system.
• Walks and stands during the entire shift.
• Reading and writing skills required.
• Reaches, bends, stoops, and wipes.
• Carries service tray weighing up to 30 pounds from the kitchen to the dining room about 24 times per shift.
• Interacts verbally with patrons.
• Hazards may include, but are not limited to, cuts, burns, slipping, and tripping.

Descripción de la Posición

Posición: Jefe de Entrenamiento
Mentor: Director de la Administración
Entrena: Jefes Auxiliares

RESUMEN DE LA POSICIÓN:

Apoya al equipo técnico del restaurante con el servicio superior de los clientes.

FUNCIONES PROFESIONALES ESENCIALES:

- Habla con todos los clientes del restaurante para asegurarse que estén disfrutando de la comida.
- Crea programas efectivos de entrenamiento para el equipo técnico.
- Mantiene la integridad física del restaurante.
- Prepara informes sobre la administración, presupuesto y planes.
- Supervisa la preparación del horario del equipo técnico.
- Planifica y conduce reuniones del equipo técnico.
- Mantiene las ganancias del restaurante.
- Conduce inspecciones diarias de todas las áreas del restaurante.
- Prepara evaluaciones regulares de desempeño de trabajo para el equipo técnico del restaurante.
- Supervisa entrenamientos, sesiones consejeras y disciplinarias del equipo técnico.
- Toma decisiones de empleo y despido.
- Reemplaza cuando sea necesario a quien falte para asegurarse que las operaciones sean eficientes.
- Instrumenta mejoras en el formato operativo.

RESULTADOS EN LOS QUE SE BASA LA EVALUACIÓN DEL DESEMPEÑO DEL TRABAJO:

- El puntaje del Departamento de Salud excede 90 sin ninguna violación mayor.
- Los ayudantes constantemente mejoran sus habilidades.
- Las vacantes se llenan con promociones internas.
- Abundan historias legendarias de servicio a los clientes.
- Sus contribuciones son reconocidas por los colegas en las evaluciones de los empleados.
- El restaurante siempre está ordenado y limpio.
- Los clientes siempre pasan un buen rato tal y como lo indica una clientela que regresa del 80–85% de las veces.
- Resuelve problemas de los clientes (a favor de los clientes) inmediatamente.
- Conoce detalles del menú, bebidas y vinos.
- Mantiene al equipo técnico fuera de "apretujones en el trabajo."
- La tasa anual de retención del equipo técnico excede el 75%.
- Miembros del equipo técnico que se van a ir dan aviso de 2 a 4 semanas antes de partir.
- El restaurante gana la mejor categoría en las encuestas locales.
- Los clientes preguntan regularmente "¿Dónde encuentran ustedes estos empleados tan buenos?"
- Alcanza las metas financieras del restaurante.
- Conoce el estado personal y profesional de todo el equipo técnico del restaurante.
- Guía a traves del ejemplo personal.
- Desarrolla continuamente habilidades profesionales (asiste a seminarios, etc.).
- Todos los despidos y procedimientos disciplinarios son documentados apropiadamente.
- Las evaluaciones de desempeño del trabajo por el equipo técnico son completadas exactamente y a tiempo.
- Las quejas escritas de los clientes son resueltas (a favor del cliente) en un plazo de 24 horas.

REQUISITOS:

- Capaz de operar una caja registradora o sistema electrónico de POS.
- Poder estar de pie ó caminando durante el 90% del turno.
- Se necesita saber leer y escribir.
- Poder alcanzar, doblarse, inclinarse y limpiar.
- Poder relacionarse verbalmente con los clientes.
- Los peligros pueden incluir, pero no están limitados a, cortadas, quemaduras, resbalones y tropezones.

Descripción de la Posición

Posición: Jefe Auxiliar
Mentor: Jefe de Entrenamiento
Entrena: Administrador de Producción, Administrador de Bebidas, Administrador de Servicio, Administrador de Piso.

RESUMEN DE LA POSICIÓN:

Apoya al equipo técnico del restaurante con el servicio superior de los clientes.

FUNCIONES PROFESIONALES ESENCIALES:

- Habla con todos los clientes del restaurante para asegurarse que estén disfrutando de la comida.
- Crea programas efectivos de entrenamiento.
- Mantiene la integridad física del restaurante.
- Prepara informes de la administración, presupuestos y planes.
- Prepara los horarios del equipo técnico.
- Planifica y conduce reuniones con el equipo técnico.
- Mantiene las ganancias del restaurante.
- Conduce inspecciones diarias de todas las áreas del restaurante.
- Prepara evaluaciones regulares de desempeño de trabajo para el equipo técnico del restaurante.
- Entrena, aconseja e impone disciplina a los miembros del equipo técnico.
- Consulta en las decisiones de empleo y terminación.
- Aprende las habilidades requeridas para avanzar a la posición de Jefe de Entrenamiento.
- Reemplaza a quien falte cuando sea necesario para asegurarse que las operaciones sean eficientes.
- Implementa mejoramientos en el formato operativo.

RESULTADOS EN LOS QUE SE BASA LA EVALUACIÓN DEL DESEMPEÑO DEL TRABAJO:

- El puntaje del Departamento de Salud excede 90 sin ninguna violación mayor.
- La gente en entrenamiento mejora constantemente sus habilidades.
- Las vacantes se llenan con promociones internas.
- Abundan historias legendarias de servicio a los clientes.
- Sus contribuciones son reconocidas por los colegas en las evaluaciones de los empleados.
- El restaurante siempre está ordenado y limpio.
- Los clientes siempre pasan un buen rato tal y como lo indica una clientela que regresa del 80–85% de las veces.
- Resuelve problemas de los clientes (a favor del cliente) inmediatamente.
- Conoce detalles del menú, bebidas y vinos.
- Mantiene el equipo técnico fuera de "apretujones en el trabajo."
- La tasa anual de retención del equipo técnico excede el 75%.
- Miembros del equipo técnico que se van a ir dan aviso de 2 a 4 semanas antes de partir.
- El restaurante gana la mejor categoría en las encuestas locales.
- Los clientes preguntan regularmente "¿Dónde encuentran ustedes estos empleados tan buenos?"
- Alcanza las metas financieras del restaurante.
- Conoce el estado personal y profesional de todo el equipo técnico del restaurante.
- Guía a traves del ejemplo personal.
- Desarrolla continuamente habilidades profesionales (asiste a seminarios, etc.).
- Todos los despidos y procedimientos disciplinarios son documentados apropiadamente.
- Las evaluaciones de desempeño del trabajo por el equipo técnico son completadas exactamente y a tiempo.
- Las quejas escritas de los clientes son resueltas (a favor del cliente) en un plazo de 24 horas.

REQUISITOS:

- Capaz de operar una caja registradora o sistema electrónico de POS.
- Poder estar de pie o caminando durante el 90% del turno.
- Se necesita saber leer y escribir.
- Poder alcanzar, doblarse, inclinarse y limpiar.
- Poder relacionarse verbalmente con los clientes.
- Los peligros pueden incluir, pero no están limitados a, cortadas, quemaduras, resbalones y tropezones.

Descripcíon de la Posicíon

Posición: Administrador de Bebidas
Mentor: Jefe Auxiliar de Entrenamiento
Entrena: Administradores Auxiliares de Bebidas, Administradores de Servicio

RESUMEN DE LA POSICIÓN:

Deleita a los clientes de los restaurantes con la calidad de la preparación de las bebidas y del servicio.

FUNCIONES PROFESIONALES ESENCIALES:

- Vende, mezcla y sirve bebidas alcohólicas y sin alcohol.
- Sigue las recetas de memoria dadas por el restaurante consistentemente.
- Sirve vino, cerveza de barril y cerveza en botella.
- Crea bebidas especiales y de la casa diariamente.
- Administra el control de costo por bebida.
- Cobra dinero por alimentos y bebidas servidos.
- Ordena licor y provisiones.
- Organiza la cristalería y las botellas para mantener el mostrador atractivo.
- Lava la cristalería y utensilios del bar.
- Limpia la cañeria de la cerveza de barril.
- Crea y conduce clases acerca de bebidas y servicio de bebidas responsable.
- Conduce inspecciones diarias en las áreas de bebida.
- Crea programas efectivos para el entrenamiento de los ayudantes.
- Reconoce e informa rápidamente de todo el mantenimiento necesario.
- Conduce inventarios diarios de bebidas.
- Reemplaza donde sea necesario a quien falte para asegurarse que las operaciones sean eficientes.
- Sugiere mejoramientos para el formato operativo.

RESULTADOS EN LOS QUE SE BASA LA EVALUACIÓN DEL DESEMPEÑO DEL TRABAJO:

- Los clientes comentan a favor del sabor y presentación de las bebidas.
- Las órdenes de las bebidas son entregadas en un plazo de 2 minutos.
- El restaurante opera dentro del ½ por ciento del costo teórico de bebidas.
- El inventario mensual se rota al menos seis veces.
- Los ayudantes mejoran constantemente sus habilidades.
- Las vacantes en el equipo técnico de bebidas son llenadas con promociones internas.
- Asiste a seminarios de entrenamiento regularmente.
- Resuelve problemas de los clientes en el momento que suceden.
- Conoce detalles del menú, bebidas y vinos.
- Abundan la historias legendarias del servicio de bebidas.
- El área del bar siempre está ordenada y limpia.
- El puntaje del Departamento de Salud excede de 90 sin violaciones mayores en el Departamento de Bebidas.
- Las contribuciones son reconocidas por colegas en las evaluaciones de los empleados.

REQUISITOS:

- Capaz de operar una caja registradora o un sistema electrónico de POS.
- Capaz de sumar con exactitud las cuentas de los clientes y dar cambio.
- Poder estar de pie durante el turno completo.
- Poder alcanzar, doblarse, inclinarse, sacudir, agitar y limpiar.
- Se necesita saber leer y escribir.
  relacionarse verbalmente con los clientes.
- Con la ayuda de otro miembro del equipo técnico, poder cargar barriles de cerveza de 120 lbs. a una altura de 30″ varias veces al día.
- Poder cargar cajas de 30 lbs. a una altura máxima de 72″ cerca de. 10 veces por turno.
- Poder sumergir frecuentemente las manos en agua (cada 5 minutos).
- Los peligros pueden incluir, pero no están limitados a, cortadas, quemaduras, resbaladas, tropezones y exposición a humo indirecto.

Descripción de la Posición

Posición: Administrador Auxiliar de Bebidas
Mentor: Administrador de Bebidas

RESUMEN DE LA POSICIÓN:

Deleita a los clientes del restaurante con la calidad de la preparación de las bebidas y del servicio.

FUNCIONES PROFESIONALES ESENCIALES:

* Sirve bebidas a los clientes en el restaurante y el bar.
* Presenta menúes, contesta preguntas, hace sugerencias sobre las bebidas.
* Escribe órdenes en las cuentas de los clientes.
* Hace llegar las órdenes al bar de servicio y a la cocina.
* Sirve comidas del bar de servicio y de la cocina.
* Observa a los clientes, anticipa sus necesidades y responde a solicitudes adicionales.
* Suma con exactitud las cuentas de los clientes, acepta pago y da cambio.
* Limpia y reorganiza las mesas.
* Ayuda al Administrador de Bebidas con las operaciones del bar.
* Lava la cristalería y utensilios del bar.
* Corta la fruta y llena el bar de provisiones
* Aprende las cualidades requeridas para avanzar a la posición de Administrador de Bebidas.
* Identifica e informa rápidamente de todo el mantenimiento necesario.
* Ayuda con los inventarios de bebida diarios.
* Reemplaza cuando sea necesario a quien falte para asegurarse que las operaciones sean eficientes.
* Sugiere mejoramientos en el formato operativo.

RESULTADOS EN LOS QUE SE BASA LA EVALUACIÓN DEL DESEMPEÑO DEL TRABAJO:

* Continuamente se suministra al bar con cristalería limpia, equipo y provisiones.
* Las órdenes de las bebidas son entregadas en un plazo de 1 minuto.
* Las pruebas demuestran un mejoramiento constante en las habilidades profesionales.
* Asiste a seminarios de entrenamiento regularmente.
* Resuelve problemas de los clientes en el momento que suceden.
* Conoce detalles del menú, bebidas y vinos.
* Abundan las historias legendarias de servicio de bebidas.
* El área del bar siempre está ordenada y limpia.
* El puntaje del Departamento de Salud excede de 90 sin violaciones mayores en el Departamento de Bebidas.
* Las contribuciones son reconocidas por colegas en las evaluaciones de los empleados.

REQUISITOS:

* Capaz de operar una caja registradora o sistema electrónico de POS.
* Capaz de sumar con exactitud las cuentas de los clientes y dar cambio.
* Poder estar de pie durante el turno completo.
* Poder alcanzar, doblarse, inclinarse, sacudir, agitar y limpiar.
* Se necesita saber leer y escribir.
* Relacionarse verbalmente con los clientes.
* Con la ayuda de otro miembro del equipo técnico, poder cargar barriles de cerveza de 120 lbs. a una altura de 30″ varias veces al día.
* Cargar cajas de 30 lbs. a una altura máxima de 72″ cerca de 10 veces por turno.
* Poder sumergir frecuentemente las manos en agua (cada 5 minutos).
* Los peligros pueden incluir, pero no están limitados a, cortadas, quemaduras, resbaladas, tropezones y exposición a humo indirecto.

Descripción de la Posición

Posición:	Administrador de Producción
Mentor:	Jefe Auxiliar de Entrenamiento
Entrena:	Administrador Auxiliar de Producción, Administradores de Servicio

RESUMEN DE LA POSICIÓN:

Deleita a los clientes de los restaurantes con la calidad de la preparación y presentación de las comidas.

FUNCIONES PROFESIONALES ESENCIALES:

* Prepara comidas frías y calientes siguiendo las recetas dadas por el restaurante.
* Crea especiales de la casa, aperitivos especiales diarios, platos principales y postres.
* Maneja los procedimientos de control de costo de comida.
* Lava los utensilios de la cocina.
* Limpia las áreas de producción cuando es necesario.
* Ordena alimentos y provisiones.
* Crea y conduce clases de sanidad, preparación y presentación de las comidas.
* Conduce inspecciones diarias de las áreas de producción.
* Crea programas de entrenamiento efectivos para los auxiliares.
* Reconoce e informa rápidamente de todo el mantenimiento necesario.
* Conduce inventarios semanales de los alimentos.
* Reemplaza cuando sea necesario a quien falte para asegurarse que las operaciones sean eficientes.
* Sugiere mejoramientos para el formato operativo.

RESULTADOS EN LOS QUE SE BASA LA EVALUACIÓN DEL DESEMPEÑO DEL TRABAJO:

* Las comidas calientes son servidas consistentemente calientes y las frías son servidas consistentemente frías.
* Los clientes tienen una reacción positiva espontánea cuando el plato es presentado.
* El restaurante opera dentro del ½ por ciento de costo teórico de la comida.
* El puntaje del Departamento de Salud excede de 90 sin violaciones mayores en el Departamento de Producción.
* El inventario mensual se rota al menos seis veces.
* Los ayudantes constantemente mejoran sus habilidades.
* Las vacantes en el equipo técnico de producción son llenadas con promociones internas.
* Asiste a seminarios de entrenamiento regularmente.
* Abundan las historias legendarias de servicio de alimento.
* Sus contribuciones son reconocidas por los colegas en evaluaciones de los empleados.
* Los clientes hacen comentarios favorables sobre el sabor y presentación de las comidas.
* Las órdenes de las comidas son completadas en un plazo de 15 minutos.
* Las áreas de producción siempre están ordenadas y limpias.

REQUISITOS:

* Poder estar de pie durante el turno completo.
* Frecuentemente trabajará en un ambiente húmedo y caliente.
* Poder alcanzar, doblarse, inclinarse, sacudir, agitar y limpiar.
* Poder alzar y mover sacos y cajas de 70 lbs. hasta 20 veces por turno.
* Se necesita saber leer y escribir.
* Sumergir frecuentemente las manos en agua.
* Los peligros pueden incluir, pero no están limitados a, cortadas, quemaduras, resbaladas y tropezones.

Descripción de la Posición

Posición: Administrador de Producción Auxiliar
Mentor: Administrador de Producción

RESUMEN DE LA POSICIÓN:

Deleita a los clientes de los restaurantes con la calidad de la preparación y la presentación de las comidas.

FUNCIONES PROFESIONALES ESENCIALES:

- Prepara alimentos calientes y fríos siguiendo las recetas establecidas de antemano.
- Lava los cubiertos y utensilios de la cocina.
- Recibe y abastece los alimentos.
- Limpia las áreas de producción cuando sea necesario.
- Crea y conduce clases de sanidad e inspecciones.
- Reconoce e informa rápidamente de todo el mantenimiento necesario.
- Ayuda al Administrador de Producción con los inventarios semanales de alimentos.
- Aprende las habilidades requeridas para avanzar a la posición de Administrador de Producción.
- Reemplaza cuando sea necesario a quien falte para asegurarse que las operaciones sean eficientes.
- Sugiere mejoramientos en el formato operativo.

RESULTADOS EN LOS QUE SE BASA LA EVALUACIÓN DEL DESEMPEÑO DEL TRABAJO:

- Las comidas calientes son servidas consistentemente calientes y las frías son servidas frías consistentemente.
- Los clientes tienen una reacción positiva espontánea cuando el plato es presentado.
- Todo los cubiertos deben estar limpios.
- Reporta rápidamente de todo el mantenimiento necesario.
- La producción de la comida nunca es retrasada por actividades de preparación incompletas.
- El puntaje del Departamento de Salud excede de 90 sin violaciones mayores en el Departamento de Producción.
- Asiste a seminarios de entrenamiento regularmente.
- Abundan las historias legendarios de servicio de alimento.
- Sus contribuciones son reconocidas por colegas en evaluaciones de los empleados.
- Los clientes hacen comentarios favorables sobre el sabor y la presentación de las comidas.
- Las órdenes de las comidas son completadas en un plazo de 15 minutos.
- Las áreas de producción siempre están ordenadas y limpias.

REQUISITOS:

- Poder estar de pie durante el turno completo.
- Frecuentemente trabajará en un ambiente húmedo y caliente.
- Poder alcanzar, doblarse, inclinarse, sacudir, agitar y limpiar.
- Poder alzar y mover sacos y cajas de 70 lbs. hasta 20 veces por turno.
- Se necesita saber leer y escribir.
- Sumergir frecuentemente las manos en agua.
- Los peligros pueden incluir, pero no están limitados a, cortadas, quemaduras, resbaladas y tropezones.

Descripción de la Posición

Posición: Administrador de Servicio
Mentor: Jefe Auxiliar de Entrenamiento
Entrena: Administrador de Servicio Auxiliar, Administrador de Piso

---

RESUMEN DE LA POSICIÓN:

Deleita a los clientes de los restaurantes con un servicio sensible de comidas y bebidas.

FUNCIONES PROFESIONALES ESENCIALES:

- Vende y sirve comidas y bebidas a los clientes en el restaurante y bar.
- Presenta menúes, contesta preguntas, hace sugerencias acerca de las comidas y bebidas.
- Toma la orden en la cuenta del cliente.
- Da las órdenes a la cocina y al bar de servicio.
- Sirve las comidas del bar de servicio y de la cocina.
- Observa a los clientes, anticipa sus necesidades y responde a solicitudes adicionales.
- Suma con exactitud las cuentas de los clientes, acepta pagos y da cambio.
- Limpia y reorganiza las mesas.
- Limpia las áreas de servicio cuando sea necesario.
- Inspecciona los baños cada 30 minutos y los limpia cuando sea necesario.
- Conduce inspecciones diarias en las áreas de servicio.
- Crea programas de entrenamiento efectivos para los auxiliares.
- Reconoce e informa rápidamente de todo el mantenimiento necesario.
- Reemplaza cuando sea necesario a quien falte para asegurarse que las operaciones sean eficientes.
- Sugiere mejoramientos en el formato operativo.

RESULTADOS EN LOS QUE SE BASA LA EVALUACIÓN DEL DESEMPEÑO DEL TRABAJO:

- Las comidas calientes son servidas calientes consistentemente y las frías son servidas frías consistentemente.
- Los clientes tienen una reacción positiva espontánea cuando el plato es presentado.
- Los clientes son tomados en cuenta al minuto de haber sido sentados.
- El puntaje del Departamento de Salud excede de 90 sin violaciones mayores en el Departamento de Servicio.
- Los ayudantes mejoran constantemente sus habilidades.
- Las vacantes en el equipo técnico de servicio son llenadas con promociones internas.
- Asiste a seminarios de entrenamiento regularmente.
- Abundan las historias legendarias de servicio de clientes.
- Sus contribuciones son reconocidas por colegas en las evaluaciones de los empleados.
- Los clientes hacen comentarios favorables sobre el sabor y la presentación de las comidas.
- Las órdenes de comida son entregadas en un plazo de 1 minuto después de completadas.
- Las áreas de servicio siempre están ordenadas y limpias.
- Los clientes pasan un buen rato tal y como lo indica la clientela que regresa de un 80–85% de las veces.
- Resuelve problemas de los clientes (a favor de los clientes) inmediatamente.
- Conoce los detalles del menú, bebidas y vinos.
- Los clientes piden regularmente a un miembro del equipo técnico que les sirva.
- Los clientes hacen comentarios no solicitados sobre la limpieza de los baños.

REQUISITOS:

- Capaz de operar una caja registradora o sistema electrónico de POS.
- Poder estar de pie caminando durante el turno completo.
- Se necesita saber leer y escribir.
- Poder alcanzar, doblarse, inclinarse y limpiar.
- Poder cargar bandejas de servicio de 30 lbs. de peso de la cocina al comedor por lo menos 24 veces por turno.
- Poder relacionarse verbalmente con los clientes.
- Los peligros pueden incluir, pero no están limitados a, cortadas, quemaduras, resbalones y tropezones.

Descripción de la Posición

Posición: Administrador de Piso
Mentor: Jefe Auxiliar de Entrenamiento

RESUMEN DE LA POSICIÓN:

Crea una primera y última impresión positiva en los clientes y controla el flujo de servicio en el comedor.

FUNCIONES PROFESIONALES ESENCIALES:

- Saluda a los clientes que van llegando y les da las gracias a los clientes que van de salida.
- Maneja la espera de los huéspedes.
- Mantiene a los clientes informados de la condición de la espera.
- Observa a los clientes, anticipa sus necesidades y responde a solicitudes adicionales.
- Anticipa las necesidades especiales de los clientes que esperan.
- Escolta a los clientes a una mesa que disfrutarán.
- Hace un balance de como se van llenando las estaciones del comedor.
- Presenta el menú, contesta preguntas, hace sugerencias acerca de la comida y bebidas.
- Contesta el teléfono y responde a las preguntas de los que llaman.
- Toma las reservaciones de mesas y funciones especiales.
- Inspecciona el exterior del restaurante y las áreas de recepción y las limpia cuando sea necesario.
- Reconoce e informa rápidamente de todo el mantenimiento necesario.
- Reemplaza cuando sea necesario a quien falta para asegurarse que las operaciones sean eficientes.
- Sugiere mejoramientos en el formato operativo.

RESULTADOS EN LOS QUE SE BASA LA EVALUACIÓN DEL DESEMPEÑO DEL TRABAJO:

- Los clientes son reconocidos calurosamente en los primeros 30 segundos de haber entrado al restaurante.
- Estimaciones del tiempo de espera son 5 minutos más de lo que realmente es la espera.
- Los clientes son agradecidos calurosamente cuando salen del restaurante.
- Los clientes siempre reciben menúes limpios.
- Abundan las historias legendarias de servicio de clientes.
- Sus contribuciones son reconocidas por colegas en las evaluaciones de los empleados.
- Las áreas exteriores y de recepción siempre están ordenadas y limpias.
- Los clientes pasan un buen rato tal y como lo indica la clientela que regresa de un 80–85% de las veces.
- Resuelve problemas de los clientes (a favor de los clientes) inmediatamente.
- Conoce detalles del menú, bebidas y vinos.

REQUISITOS:

- Poder estar de pie y caminando durante el turno completo.
- Se necesita saber leer y escribir.
- Poder alcanzar, doblarse, inclinarse y limpiar.
- Poder relacionarse verbalmente con los clientes.
- Los peligros pueden incluir, pero no están limitados a, resbalones y tropezones.

Descripción de la Posición

Posición: Administrador de Servicio Auxiliar
Mentor: Administrador de Servicio

RESUMEN DE LA POSICIÓN:

Deleita a los clientes del restaurante con un servicio sensible de comidas y bebidas.

FUNCIONES PROFESIONALES ESENCIALES:

- Sirve comida y bebidas a los clientes en el comedor.
- Lleva comidas de la cocina y del bar de servicio al comedor.
- Lleva los cubiertos sucios del comedor a la cocina y al bar de servicio.
- Da las órdenes al bar del servicio y a la cocina.
- Responde a las solicitudes de los clientes.
- Limpia y reorganiza las mesas.
- Limpia las áreas de servicio cuando sea necesario.
- Inspecciona los baños cada 30 minutos y los limpia cuando sea necesario.
- Reconoce e informa rápidamente de todo el mantenimiento necesario.
- Aprende las habilidades requeridas para avanzar a la posición de Administrador de Servicio.
- Reemplaza cuando sea necesario a quien falte para asegurarse que las operaciones sean eficientes.
- Sugiere mejoramientos en el formato operativo.

RESULTADOS EN LOS QUE SE BASA LA EVALUACIÓN DEL DESEMPEÑO DEL TRABAJO:

- Las comidas calientes son servidas calientes consistentemente y las frías son servidas frías consistentemente.
- Las mesas son despejadas y reorganizadas en un plazo de 3 minutos después de que el cliente se haya ido del restaurante.
- El puntaje del Departamento de Salud excede de 90 sin violaciones mayores en el Departamento de Servicio.
- Asiste a seminarios de entrenamiento regularmente.
- Abundan las historias legendarias de servicio de clientes.
- Sus contribuciones son reconocidas por colegas en las evaluaciones de los empleados.
- Las órdenes de las comidas son entregadas en un plazo de 1 minuto después de completadas.
- Las áreas de servicio siempre están ordenadas y limpias.
- Conoce detalles del menú, bebidas y vinos.
- Los clientes hacen comentarios no solicitados sobre la limpieza de los baños.

REQUISITOS:

- Capaz de operar una caja registradora o sistema electrónico de POS.
- Poder estar de pie y caminando durante el turno completo.
- Se necesita saber leer y escribir.
- Poder alcanzar, doblarse, inclinarse y limpiar.
- Poder cargar bandejas de servicio de 30 lbs. de peso de la cocina al comedor por lo menos 24 veces por turno.
- Poder relacionarse verbalmente con los clientes.
- Los peligros pueden incluir, pero no están limitados a, cortadas, quemaduras, resbalones y tropezones.

A P P E N D I X   B

Selection
Documents

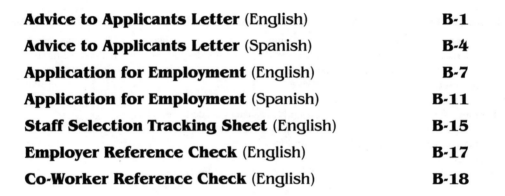

Advice to Applicants Letter (English)   **B-1**

Advice to Applicants Letter (Spanish)   **B-4**

Application for Employment (English)   **B-7**

Application for Employment (Spanish)   **B-11**

Staff Selection Tracking Sheet (English)   **B-15**

Employer Reference Check (English)   **B-17**

Co-Worker Reference Check (English)   **B-18**

Advice to Applicants

Thank you for your interest in working with us. I think you will find our approach to hospitality to be different from that of most other operators in the market, and we think this is the secret of our success. Our company has several significant goals:

1. TO EARN A REPUTATION AS THE BEST EMPLOYER IN THE AREA

To achieve this goal we will hire the most qualified people we can find. We will support their development both within and outside the organization. We will talk to them, listen to them, learn from them, pay them well, and demand a lot from them. We will enjoy a high retention rate (over 80%). We will have a waiting list of people who want to join the company. We believe that only happy and professional staff can give the level of personal service we demand. We see an investment in people to be a worthy investment in the future of the company.

2. TO OPERATE THE MOST SUCCESSFUL OPERATIONS IN THE MARKET

Our operations will be exciting, diverse, and profitable. We will consistently deliver on our service guarantee of "a great time every time" and foster high professional standards. We will provide legendary service—the unique and powerful sort of personal care and attention that our guests tell stories about. We will win the various local polls that are a measure of our position and regard in the market. We will consistently achieve the highest volumes in our market and have a waiting line when our competitors are half full. We will develop a loyal repeat trade. We will find out what our guests want and be sure they are getting it. We will maintain rigid sanitation standards. We will take the lead in addressing the nutritional concerns of our guests. We will continuously re-examine our operations to stay fresh and responsive to our market while being stimulating to our staff.

3. TO BE A GOOD CITIZEN OF THE COMMUNITY AND THE PLANET

We will support worthy local charities with money, resources, and volunteers. We will maintain a high visibility in local activities. We will be environmentally responsible. We will recycle, conserve water and utilities, and reduce our use of chemicals. Whenever possible, we will select supplies and suppliers who are environmentally friendly.

4. TO BE A MODEL FOR OPEN, PARTICIPATORY BUSINESS

Our industry cannot get where it needs to go doing business the way we've always done it. The industry needs a new model and we are willing to be that model. We will maintain open books with our staff and investors. We will innovate in the areas of compensation, profit-sharing, rewards, and recognition. We will involve our staff in all areas of policy-making. We will always move in the direction of less structure, greater professionalism and more fun! We will be judged on our results.

5. TO MAINTAIN A PERSONAL WORKING RELATIONSHIP WITH OUR STAFF

We are not anti-union. However, regardless of what image it tries to project, a union is a profit-making business that can only get money from its own members. A union must justify its position by creating and maintaining a "them and us" relationship between the company and staff. We do not believe such a polarity exists in our organization and we do not think our staff should pay for any such disruptive force. We believe the way to achieve the kind of business environment we want is to create a trusting relationship with our staff. In this atmosphere, both staff and the company can work out difficulties and make decisions together. In this environment, a union is unnecessary and is likely to be destructive to operational flexibility and personal well-being. We cannot imagine a problem that we cannot effectively resolve among ourselves without the need for a self-serving third party.

6. TO HAVE A GOOD TIME

We recognize that people go out to eat because they are looking for a good time, not just a good meal. We will build fun and lightness into our company in the interest of our collective mental health and peace of mind.

We are not just another foodservice company, and we are not looking for just another job applicant. This letter will give you some ideas of what to expect and how to proceed from here:

1. Do not try to complete this application now. Please take it home, give it some thought, and take your time with it. Be sure to fill it out *completely*, even if you enclose a resume. If a question does not apply to you, mark it "NA" so we know you didn't avoid the answer. Foodservice is a business of details, and we will only consider people who share our concern about the importance of handling all the small points.

2. We will verify *all* information you give us on the application. *Any* false or misleading statements will disqualify you from consideration, no matter how talented you may be. Please understand that we are not as concerned with *what* you tell us as we are that you give us the truth. Honesty is always the best policy . . . especially if you hope to become part of our team.

3. We are committed to maintaining a drug-free workplace. This means that we do not tolerate the possession of drugs or alcohol on the premises, nor do we permit our staff to work under the influence of drugs or alcohol.

4. All our operations are completely nonsmoking establishments. This means there are no cigarette breaks and we do not permit staff to smoke while on duty or while in uniform.

5. If an offer of employment is made to you, we may require that you pass a physical examination. The company will pay all expenses of this examination although we do not pay for the time required to take it.

6. We will verify *all* your references. In addition to your supervisors, we want to talk with your co-workers and anyone who may have worked for you in your past positions. If we cannot check your references, we cannot consider you for employment, so be sure you list valid names and phone numbers. It does not matter if they still work for your old company or not. In fact, we often get better information from people who have taken other jobs. Please be sure that everyone you list knows to expect a call from us and has your permission to talk with us. It will require some work on your part, but, then, it takes a little extra effort to succeed in this business!

7. Be sure to include the correct telephone number for the registrar's office of your college or university and the records department of your school district so we can verify your education. This may involve a long distance call or two to get the numbers, but we will not consider applications that do not have this information.

8. On the last page of the application, we give you the opportunity to make a personal "sales pitch." We suggest you give it some thought and present a case for yourself. After all, if *you* don't believe in you, why should we?

9. Read the final statement on the application carefully before you sign it. If you have any questions, please ask them before you give us your application. We will not consider unsigned applications.

10. When you have completed the application, call _____ at _____ to set up an appointment to submit your application and take some short screening tests. This appointment should last no longer than 30 minutes. Be aware that what you do and how you do it are being evaluated throughout the selection process, so dress the part, be on time, and show us your best. Remember the saying about first impressions!

11. Based on our observations, your test results, and a review of your application, we will notify you within five *working* days (weekdays) from the date of your initial screening about the status of your application. We will either call or send you a letter. If by some chance the five working days pass without your hearing from us, call the number above.

12. We take staff selection very seriously. If you are a final candidate, you can expect up to three interviews and perhaps several written tests. We may ask you to demonstrate your skills and tell us how you would handle some "sticky situations." We will not take a "warm body" just to fill a vacancy quickly. Please be patient. We go to this trouble because our goals and standards are very high. If you are good enough to become part of our staff, you are truly an outstanding individual. With rare exceptions, if you need a job *today*, you should not count on us to provide it. If you need a job right away, we suggest you find something else that will work while we process your application.

13. Because our staff is actively involved in the operation of our company, do not be surprised to have portions of the selection process conducted by persons other than our managers. We give our staff a voice in the selection of their coaches and believe that co-workers are excellent judges of the talents of their peers.

14. We are an equal opportunity employer, and we will select only qualified applicants for every position. Period. We will not discourage you from applying for any position you feel qualified for. We will make selections based on what strengths you bring to our team and how you fit into our operating style. We are looking for people committed to professional excellence and legendary guest service who will make a positive contribution to our company for as long as we choose to work together.

15. We often bring new people into our company as part-time staff, moving them to full-time (if they want it) or changing their duties when the opportunity for more hours arises and their work performance justifies additional responsibility.

16. We expect you to take an active role in your own success and the success of your co-workers. Toward this end, it will be part of your job responsibilities to help train your co-workers for positions of higher skill and responsibility. Because of this focus, we will evaluate your performance based not only on your own professional development, but by the advancement of your trainees.

17. We will regularly evaluate your performance so you know where you stand and how you are doing. The purpose of the appraisals is to assist with your personal and professional development. Much of the responsibility for performance appraisal rests with your coaches, but we will also ask your co-workers to give us their impressions of your work and ask you to do the same of theirs. Their comments will be part of your performance appraisal. We will also ask you to evaluate the effectiveness of your coaches, and that will become part of *their* performance appraisal. We do not keep secrets from each other or ignore unproductive behavior.

18. Our success comes from delighting our guests and earning their regular patronage. Everything in our company is focused on achieving this goal. We do not believe in creating any more rules or structure than is necessary to ensure that our guests have a great time every time they dine with us. This means that there are no procedures to hide behind and that success is measured by your results rather than by your activities. There is nothing to "get away with."

19. If you are not offered a position, we will return your application. We encourage you to apply again later if you are still interested in working with us. Many of our most successful staff members were not selected until their second or third try. You must decide if what we offer is worth your effort to meet our high standards. Whatever your choice, we hope you will visit us often as a guest and let us know how we are doing.

Thank you again for your interest and your time. We wish you all the best luck in the future, whatever direction your career may take you.

With best regards,

Consejo para los solicitantes

Gracias por su interés de trabajar con nosotros. Creo que usted encontrará que nuestro enfoque de hospitalidad es diferente al ofrecido por la mayoría de los operadores en el mercado y creemos que este es el secreto de nuestro éxito. Nuestra compañía tiene varias metas importantes:

1. GANARSE LA REPUTACIÓN DE SER EL MEJOR EMPLEADOR EN EL ÁREA.

Para alcanzar esta meta, contrataremos a las personas más calificadas que podamos encontrar. Apoyaremos su desarrollo dentro y fuera de la organización. Les hablaremos, los escucharemos, aprenderemos de ellos, les pagaremos bien y exigiremos mucho de ellos. Disfrutaremos un alto porcentaje de retención (más del 80%). Tendremos una lista de espera de personas que quieren ser parte de esta compañía. Creemos que solo miembros del equipo técnico que sean profesionales y esten satisfechos pueden ofrecer el nivel de servicio personal que nosotros exigimos. Vemos que una inversión en nuestro equipo humano es una inversión que vale la pena para el futuro de la compañía.

2. ESTAR ENCARGADO DE LAS OPERACIONES DE MAYOR ÉXITO EN EL MERCADO.

Nuestras operaciones serán emocionantes, diversas y de muchas ganancias. Ofrecemos consistentemente nuestro servicio garantizado de "siempre pasarla muy bien" y de cultivar normas profesionales muy altas. Proveeremos servicio legendario—la única y poderosa atención personal que nuestros clientes utilizan son las historias legendarias que pueden contar. Ganaremos varias encuestas locales, que son la forma de medir nuestra posición y reconocimiento en el mercado. Consistentemente alcanzaremos los volúmenes más altos en el mercado y tendremos una lista de espera mientras que nuestros competidores estén a medio llenar. Desarrollaremos un negocio repetido fiel. Nos enteraremos de lo que nuestros amigos clientes quieren y nos aseguraremos de que lo estén recibiendo. Mantendremos los reglamentos sanitarios estrictamente. Tomaremos la delantera en referirnos e interesarnos en las preocupaciones nutricionales de nuestros clientes. Constantemente re-evaluaremos nuestras operaciones para mantenernos al día y responderemos al mercado sin dejar de estimular al equipo técnico.

3. SER UN BUEN CIUDADANO DE LA COMUNIDAD Y DEL PLANETA.

Apoyaremos con dinero, recursos y voluntarios a grupos de caridad que tengan impacto positivo. Mantendremos un grado de visibilidad muy alto en todas las actividades locales. Seremos responsables con el medio ambiente. Reciclaremos, conservaremos el agua y las facilidades y reduciremos el uso de químicos. Cuando sea posible, seleccionaremos materiales y abastecedores que tienen consideración por el medio ambiente.

4. SER UN NEGOCIO MODELO EN TÉRMINOS DE LA APERTURA Y PARTICIPACIÓN.

Nuestra industria no puede llegar a donde necesita llegar conduciendo los negocios de la manera en la que siempre lo ha hecho. La industria necesita un modelo nuevo y nosotros estamos dispuestos a ser ese modelo. Mantendremos los libros abiertos a nuestro equipo técnico e inversionistas. Innovaremos en las áreas de compensación, compartiremos ganancias, recompensas y reconocimiento. Envolveremos a nuestros equipo técnico en todas las áreas del proceso de diseñar políticas. ¡Siempre nos moveremos en la dirección que tenga menos estructura, más profesionalismo y más diversión! Seremos juzgados por nuestros resultados.

5. MANTENER UNA RELACIÓN DE TRABAJO PERSONAL CON NUESTRO EQUIPO TÉCNICO.

No estamos en contra de los sindicatos. Sin embargo, sin importar de qué imagen se trate de proyectar, un sindicato es un negocio orientado hacia ganancias que solamente pueden obtener sus propios miembros. Un sindicato debe justificar su posición creando y manteniendo una relación de "ellos y nosotros" entre la compañía y el equipo técnico. No creemos que dicha polarización deba existir en nuestra organización y no creemos que nuestro equipo técnico tenga que pagar por cualquiera de estas fuerzas interruptoras. Creemos que la forma de alcanzar la clase de ambiente de negocio que queremos es a través de la creación de una relación de confianza con nuestro equipo técnico. En este medio, tanto el equipo técnico como la compañía pueden resolver sus dificultades y hacer decisiones en conjunto. En este ambiente, un sindicato es innecesario y es probable que sea destructivo de la flexibilidad operacional y del bienestar personal. No podemos imaginarnos un problema que no podamos resolver entre nosotros sin la necesidad de tener que recurrir a un tercer miembro.

6. PASARLA MUY BIEN.

Reconocemos que la gente sale a comer porque está buscando como pasarla bien, no solo para comer bien. Crearemos diversión y comodidad en nuestra compañía con el fin de proporcionar salud mental colectiva y paz.

No somos solamente otra compañía de servicio de comida y no estamos buscando solamente a otro aplicante del trabajo. Esta carta le dará algunas ideas de qué esperar y de cómo seguir de aquí en adelante:

1. No intente completar esta solicitud ahora. Por favor llévela a su casa, piénselo un poco y tome su tiempo. Asegúrese de llenarla *completamente*, aunque adjunte su currículo (résumé). Si una pregunta no se aplica a usted, márquela "NA" de modo que sepamos que usted no estaba evadiendo la respuesta. Nuestro negocio es un negocio de muchos detalles y solamente consideraremos gente que comparta nuestra preocupación acerca de la importancia del manejo de pequeños detalles.

2. Verificaremos toda la información que usted nos dé en la solicitud y *cualquier* declaración falsa o información tergiversada

lo descalificará de ser empleado por nosotros en el momento o en el futuro, sin importar los talentos que usted pueda tener. Honestidad siempre será la mejor política … especialmente si usted espera ser parte de nuestro equipo.

3. Nos comprometemos a mantener un ambiente libre de drogas. Esto significa que no toleraremos la posesión de drogas o alcohol dentro del establecimiento; tampoco permitiremos que los empleados trabajen bajo la influencia de drogas o del alcohol.

4. En nuestros establecimientos no se permite fumar. Esto significa que no hay recreos para ir a fumar y que no permitimos que nuestros empleados fumen durante las horas de trabajo o con el uniforme puesto.

5. Si una oferta de empleo le es hecha a usted, será bajo la condición de que usted pase el examen físico prescrito. Nosotros lo pagamos; sin embargo, no pagaremos por el tiempo perdido mientras se hace tal examen.

6. Verificaremos todas sus referencias. Aparte de sus supervisores, nos gustaría hablar con sus colegas y sus subalternos (si ha habido) en trabajos anteriores. Si no podemos verificar sus referencias, no podremos considerarlo para el empleo, así que asegúrese de darnos nombres y números de teléfonos válidos. No importa si todavía trabajan para la compañía en donde usted trabajó. De hecho, frecuentemente nos proporcionan mayor información la gente que ha tomado otros trabajos. Por favor asegúrese que todas las personas en la lista sepan que recibirán una llamada de nosotros y que tienen su permiso de hablar con nosotros. Va a tomar un poquito de esfeurzo extra de su parte, pero *toma* un poquito extra triunfar en este negocio.

7. Asegúrese de incluir el número de teléfono correcto de la oficina de registro de su colegio o de su universidad y el departamento de registro de su distrito escolar para que podamos verificar su educación. Esto puede involucrar una o dos llamadas de larga distancia de su parte para obtener los números, no consideraremos solicitudes que no tengan esta información.

8. En la ultima página de la solicitud, le damos la oportunidad de hacer una "venta personal." Le sugerimos que usted tome su tiempo para pensarlo y presente su propio caso. Total, si usted no cree en usted mismo, ¿por qué debemos nosotros?

9. Lea la última sección de la solicitud cuidadosamente antes de firmarla. Si usted tiene preguntas, por favor hágalas antes de que usted nos dé su solicitud. No consideraremos solicitudes sin firma.

10. Cuando usted haya completado la solicitud, llame a _____ al _____ para hacer una cita en la que presente su solicitud y tome tres pruebas de eliminación cortas. Esta cita no deberá tomar más de 30 minutos. Esté conciente de lo que hace y cómo lo hace, se evaluará a través del proceso de selección, así que desempeñe el papel, llegue a tiempo y muestrenos lo mejor de usted. Recuerde lo que se dice de las primeras impresiones.

11. Basados en nuestras observaciones, los resultados de sus pruebas y la evaluación de su solicitud, le notificaremos en un plazo de 5 *días laborales* después de la fecha de sus pruebas de eliminación del estado de la solicitud. Le notificaremos por teléfono o por correspondencia. Si después de 5 días laborales no ha sabido de nosotros, llame al número de telefono indicado arriba.

12. Nosotros tratamos seriamente la selección del equipo técnico y puede tomar varias semanas. Si usted fuera un candidato finalista, usted debe esperar otras tres entrevistas y varias pruebas escritas profesionales. Le pediremos que nos demuestre sus habilidades y que nos diga cómo es que usted manejaría algunas "situaciones difíciles." No tomamos un "cuerpo vivo" solamente para llenar una vacante. Sea paciente. Comprenda que nosotros nos molestamos porque nuestros objetivos y normas son muy altas. Si usted es lo suficientemente bueno como para ser parte de nuestro equipo técnico, usted sinceramente es una persona excepcional. Con raras excepciones, si usted necesitara un trabajo *hoy*, usted no debe contar con nosotros para esto. Si su necesidad es inmediata, sugerimos que usted busque otra cosa que le ayude mientras procesamos su aplicación.

13. Porque todo nuestro equipo técnico está involucrado activamente en la operación de nuestros restaurantes, no se sorprenda de que haya partes del proceso de selección conducidas por personas que no son de la administración. Nosotros damos voz a nuestro equipo técnico en la selección de sus entrenadores y creemos que los colegas son excelentes jueces del talento de sus compañeros.

14. Somos una compañía que da las mismas oportunidades de empleo y solamente seleccionaremos candidatos calificados para cada posición. Punto. No desanimaremos al candidato de solicitar por cualquier posición que desee. Basaremos nuestra decisión en las fortalezas que pueda proporcionar a nuestro equipo y como se acomode a nuestro estilo de operación. No adivinaremos lo que usted puede o no decidir acerca de su futuro y no pretendemos que cada uno de ustedes siga con nosotros siempre. Buscamos gente comprometida a la excelencia profesional y al servicio de huéspedes legendario, que haga una contribución positiva para nuestra compañía por el tiempo que escojamos trabajar juntos.

15. Frecuentemente contratamos gente nueva en nuestra compañía como equipo técnico de medio tiempo, cambiándolas a jornada completa (si lo quieren) o cambiando sus deberes cuando la oportunidad de trabajar más horas surga y la ejecucion de su trabajo justifique responsabilidad adicional y la oportunidad exista.

16. Nosotros promovemos dentro de la compañía siempre que sea posible. Con ese fin, será parte de sus responsabilidades en el trabajo el ayudar a entrenar a sus colegas (si hubiera) para posiciones de habilidad y responsabilidad más altas. Debido a este enfoque, evaluaremos el desempeño de su trabajo basado no solamente en el trabajo que usted mismo hace y su propio avance profesional, pero también en el desarrollo de sus subalternos.

17. Evaluaremos su trabajo formalmente para que usted sepa su posición y cómo se está desempeñando. El propósito de las evaluaciones es ayudarle con su desarrollo personal y profesional. Gran parte de la responsabilidad de las evaluaciones cae en sus entrenadores pero también le pediremos a sus colegas de darnos opiniones de su trabajo y pedirle a usted que haga

lo mismo para con ellos. Sus comentarios serán parte de su evaluación. También le pediremos que evalúe la efectividad de sus entrenadores y que eso formará parte de la evaluación de ellos. No mantenemos secretos de unos a otros o ignoramos comportamiento de baja productividad.

18. Nuestro éxito viene de deleitar a nuestros huéspedes y de ganar su clientela regular. Todo en nuestra compañía se basa en el logro de este objetivo. No creemos en crear más reglas o estructuras de las que son necesarias para asegurar que nuestros huéspedes pasen un buen rato cada vez que comen con nosotros. Esto signifca que no hay que ocultar procedimientos y que el éxito está medido por sus resultados más que por sus actividades. No hay nada con lo que usted pueda "salirse con la suya."

19. Si usted decide no hacer la solicitud en este momento, o si a ud. no le ofrecen una posición, le sugerimos intentar otra vez. Muchos de nuestros miembros del equipo técnico de más éxito no fueron aceptados sino que hasta su segundo o tercer intento. Usted tiene que decidir si lo que le ofrecemos vale el esfuerzo y si usted está dispuesto a hacer lo que sea necesario para cumplir con nuestras normas. Cualquiera que sea su preferencia, esperamos que usted visite nuestros restaurantes frecuentemente cómo cliente y nos informe cómo nos estamos desempeñando.

De nuevo, gracias por su interés y su tiempo. Le deseo la mejor de las suertes en el futuro, en cualquier dirección que tome.

Son mis mejores deseos,

Application for Employment

ABOUT YOU

Name_____ Nickname_____

Social Security No._____-_____-_____ Home Phone_____ Message Phone_____

Street Address_____ City_____ State_____ Zip_____

Mailing Address_____ City_____ State_____ Zip_____

If you listed a message phone above, how often do you check for messages?_____

Do you have reliable transportation to meet any scheduled shift?_____

Can you read at a 6th-grade level?_____ Have you been convicted of a felony?_____ If yes, please give details on last page.

Have you ever worked for us before?_____ If so, under what name?_____

Do you have any friends or relatives working for us?_____ Who?_____

Can you provide proof that you are over 18 years old?_____ . . . over 21 years old?_____ Are you a smoker?_____

Do you have a valid driver's license?_____ Class_____ State_____ License No._____

Have you had any accidents or moving violations in the past three years?_____ If yes, please provide details on last page.

Have you ever been bonded?_____ Is there any reason why you could *not* be bonded?_____ If yes, please give details on last page.

Do you have a legal right to work in the U.S.?_____ Can you provide documentation of your legal right to work?_____

Is there any reason you could not perform all physical aspects of this job (including being able to lift up to 50 pounds)?_____ If yes, please provide details on last page.

Is additional information concerning change of name necessary to check work or education records?_____ If yes, please explain (continue on last page if necessary).

Describe your use of drugs and alcohol (please continue on last page if necessary):

ABOUT THE JOB

For what position are you applying?_____ Salary Requirement: $_____ per_____

Would you accept another position?_____ If so, which one?_____

Which do you *prefer*? ☐ full-time work ☐ part-time work. If part-time, about how many hours per week?_____

Which will you *accept*? ☐ full-time work ☐ part-time work

When could you start working for us **full-time**?_____ When are you **NOT** available to work for us full-time?

MON	TUE	WED	THU	FRI	SAT	SUN
☐ morning	☐ morning	☐ morning	☐ morning	☐ morning	☐ morning	☐ morning
☐ afternoon	☐ afternoon	☐ afternoon	☐ afternoon	☐ afternoon	☐ afternoon	☐ afternoon
☐ evening	☐ evening	☐ evening	☐ evening	☐ evening	☐ evening	☐ evening
☐ can work anytime	☐ can work anytime	☐ can work anytime	☐ can work anytime	☐ can work anytime	☐ can work anytime	☐ can work anytime

When could you start working for us **part-time**?_____ When are you **NOT** available to work for us part-time?

MON	TUE	WED	THU	FRI	SAT	SUN
☐ morning	☐ morning	☐ morning	☐ morning	☐ morning	☐ morning	☐ morning
☐ afternoon	☐ afternoon	☐ afternoon	☐ afternoon	☐ afternoon	☐ afternoon	☐ afternoon
☐ evening	☐ evening	☐ evening	☐ evening	☐ evening	☐ evening	☐ evening
☐ can work anytime	☐ can work anytime	☐ can work anytime	☐ can work anytime	☐ can work anytime	☐ can work anytime	☐ can work anytime

ABOUT YOUR WORK EXPERIENCE

(PLEASE START WITH YOUR MOST RECENT POSITION)   **Resume Attached?** ☐ YES ☐ NO

COMPANY_____ Mo./Yr. Hired_____ Mo./Yr. Left_____

Job Title_____ Reason for Leaving_____

_____

No. Supervised: Starting_____ Ending_____ Starting Salary: $_____ per _____ Final Salary: $_____ per _____

Supervisor's Name_____ Position_____ Phone_____

Superior's Name_____ Position_____ Phone_____

Co-worker's Name_____ Position_____ Phone_____

Co-worker's Name_____ Position_____ Phone_____

Subordinate's Name_____ Position_____ Phone_____

Subordinate's Name_____ Position_____ Phone_____

Major Responsibilities and Accomplishments:

COMPANY_____ Mo./Yr. Hired_____ Mo./Yr. Left_____

Job Title_____ Reason for Leaving_____

_____

No. Supervised: Starting_____ Ending_____ Starting Salary: $_____ per _____ Final Salary: $_____ per _____

Supervisor's Name_____ Position_____ Phone_____

Superior's Name_____ Position_____ Phone_____

Co-worker's Name_____ Position_____ Phone_____

Co-worker's Name_____ Position_____ Phone_____

Subordinate's Name_____ Position_____ Phone_____

Subordinate's Name_____ Position_____ Phone_____

Major Responsibilities and Accomplishments:

MORE ABOUT YOUR WORK EXPERIENCE

COMPANY_____ Mo./Yr. Hired_____ Mo./Yr. Left_____

Job Title_____ Reason for Leaving_____

_____

No. Supervised: Starting_____ Ending_____ Starting Salary: $_____ per _____ Final Salary: $_____ per _____

Supervisor's Name_____ Position_____ Phone_____

Superior's Name_____ Position_____ Phone_____

Co-worker's Name_____ Position_____ Phone_____

Co-worker's Name_____ Position_____ Phone_____

Subordinate's Name_____ Position_____ Phone_____

Subordinate's Name_____ Position_____ Phone_____

Major Responsibilities and Accomplishments:

ABOUT YOUR EDUCATION

HIGH SCHOOL_____ City_____ State_____ Graduated?_____

No. Yrs. Completed_____ Major_____ Verification Phone (_____)_____

COLLEGE_____ City_____ State_____ Degree_____

No. Yrs. Completed_____ Major_____ Verification Phone (_____)_____

GRAD SCHOOL_____ City_____ State_____ Degree_____

No. Yrs. Completed_____ Major_____ Verification Phone (_____)_____

Extracurricular activities:

Other training programs completed:

Professional memberships and certifications:

OTHER COMMENTS

Why would you be a good choice for this position?

I certify that the information above is complete and accurate to the best of my knowledge. I authorize the individuals, companies, and agencies concerned to provide this company and its agents with all information necessary to verify the statements I have made in this application, and I release them from any liability for so doing. I understand I must receive satisfactory references from previous employers, co-workers, and subordinates (if any) before an offer of employment can be made. I understand that incomplete or unsigned applications will not be considered and that false, incomplete, or misleading statements are grounds for my immediate discharge. I understand that any offer of employment is contingent upon my passing a prescribed physical examination, proving my identity, and documenting my right to work. I understand that these policies cannot be changed except in writing.

Signature_____ Print Name_____ Date_____

Aplicación de Empleo

SOBRE USTED

Nombre_____ Sobrenombre_____

Número de seguridad social_____ - _____ - _____ Teléfono_____ Teléfono donde dejar mensajes_____

Dirección_____ Ciudad_____ Estado_____ Zip_____

Dirección de correo_____ Ciudad_____ Estado_____ Zip_____

Si usted incluyó un teléfono para mensajes, ¿cada cuánto oye sus mensajes?_____

¿Tiene usted transportación segura para asistir a cualquier turno programado?_____

¿Puede usted leer a un nivel escolar de 6to?_____ ¿Ha sido usted condenado por un crimen?_____ Descríbalo en la última página.

¿Ha trabajado alguna vez con nosotros?_____ Si es así, ¿bajo qué nombre?_____

¿Tiene usted algún amigo o familiar que trabaja con nosotros?_____ ¿Quién?_____

¿Puede usted demostrar que usted es mayor de 18 años de edad?_____ . . . mayor de 21 años?_____ ¿Fuma?_____

¿Tiene usted licencia de conducir?_____ ¿Clase?_____ ¿Estado?_____ ¿Número?_____

¿Ha tenido accidentes o violaciones automobilísticas en los últimos tres años? Si es así, por favor descríbalo en la última página.

¿Alguna vez lo han sacado bajo fianza?_____ ¿Existe alguna razón por la que usted *no* pueda salir con fianza?_____ Si es así, descríbalo en la última página.

¿Tiene usted el derecho legal de trabajar en los Estados Unidos?_____ ¿Puede usted proveer documentación legal que le permita trabajar?_____

¿Existe algúna razón por la cual usted no pueda desempeñar los aspectos físicos del trabajo (incluyendo la habilidad de levantar hasta 50 lbs.)?_____ Si es así, por favor descríbalo en la última página.

¿Si necesita información adicional acerca del cambio de su nombre a la hora de revisar sus registros de trabajo o educación?

_____ Si es así, por favor descríbalo en la última página.

Describa su uso de drogas y alcohol: (continúe en la última página si es necesario)

ACERCA DEL TRABAJO

¿Para cuál posición está usted solicitando?_____ Salario requerido: $_____ por _____

¿Aceptaría otra posición?_____ Si es así, ¿cuál?_____

¿Qué *prefiere* usted? ☐ Tiempo Completo ☐ Medio Tiempo. Si prefiere medio tiempo, ¿cuántas horas a la semana?_____

¿Cuál *aceptaría* usted? ☐ Tiempo Completo ☐ Medio Tiempo.

¿Cuándo podría comenzar a trabajar para nosotros tiempo completo?_____ ¿Cuándo **NO** estará diponible para trabajar con nosotros tiempo completo?

LUN	MAR	MIE	JUE	VIE	SAB	DOM
☐ mañana	☐ mañana	☐ mañana	☐ mañana	☐ mañana	☐ mañana	☐ mañana
☐ tarde	☐ tarde	☐ tarde	☐ tarde	☐ tarde	☐ tarde	☐ tarde
☐ noche	☐ noche	☐ noche	☐ noche	☐ noche	☐ noche	☐ noche
☐ cualquier hora	☐ cualquier hora	☐ cualquier hora	☐ cualquier hora	☐ cualquier hora	☐ cualquier hora	☐ cualquier hora

¿Cuándo podría comenzar a trabajar para nosotros medio tiempo?_____ ¿Cuándo **NO** estará diponible para trabajar con nosotros medio tiempo?

LUN	MAR	MIE	JUE	VIE	SAB	DOM
☐ mañana	☐ mañana	☐ mañana	☐ mañana	☐ mañana	☐ mañana	☐ mañana
☐ tarde	☐ tarde	☐ tarde	☐ tarde	☐ tarde	☐ tarde	☐ tarde
☐ noche	☐ noche	☐ noche	☐ noche	☐ noche	☐ noche	☐ noche
☐ cualquier hora	☐ cualquier hora	☐ cualquier hora	☐ cualquier hora	☐ cualquier hora	☐ cualquier hora	☐ cualquier hora

ACERCA DE SU EXPERIENCIA

(POR FAVOR COMIENZE CON SU POSICIÓN MÁS RECIENTE)   **Currículo adjunto?** ☐ SI ☐ NO

COMPAÑIA_____ Mes/Año en que entró_____ Mes/Año en que salió_____

Cargo_____ Razón de salida_____

_____

Nº de supervisados: Principio_____ Final_____ Primer salario: $_____ por _____ Ultimo salario: $_____ por _____

Nombre del supervisor_____ Cargo_____ Teléfono_____

Nombre del supervisor_____ Cargo_____ Teléfono_____

Nombre de colegas_____ Cargo_____ Teléfono_____

Nombre de colegas_____ Cargo_____ Teléfono_____

Nombre de subalternos_____ Cargo_____ Teléfono_____

Nombre de subalternos_____ Cargo_____ Teléfono_____

Mayores responsabilidades y logros:

COMPAÑIA_____ Mes/Año en que entró_____ Mes/Año en que salió_____

Cargo_____ Razón de salida_____

_____

Nº de supervisados: Principio_____ Final_____ Primer salario: $_____ por _____ Ultimo salario: $_____ por _____

Nombre del supervisor_____ Cargo_____ Teléfono_____

Nombre del supervisor_____ Cargo_____ Teléfono_____

Nombre de colegas_____ Cargo_____ Teléfono_____

Nombre de colegas_____ Cargo_____ Teléfono_____

Nombre de subalternos_____ Cargo_____ Teléfono_____

Nombre de subalternos_____ Cargo_____ Teléfono_____

Mayores responsabilidades y logros:

MÁS ACERCA DE SU EXPERIENCIA DE TRABAJO

COMPAÑIA_____ Mes/Año en que entró_____ Mes/Año en que salió_____

Cargo_____ Razón de salida_____

_____

Nº de supervisados: Principio_____ Final_____ Primer salario: $_____ por _____ Ultimo salario: $_____ por _____

Nombre del supervisor_____ Cargo_____ Teléfono_____

Nombre del supervisor_____ Cargo_____ Teléfono_____

Nombre de colegas_____ Cargo_____ Teléfono_____

Nombre de colegas_____ Cargo_____ Teléfono_____

Nombre de subalternos_____ Cargo_____ Teléfono_____

Nombre de subalternos_____ Cargo_____ Teléfono_____

Mayores responsabilidades y logros:

ACERCA DE SU EDUCACIÓN

ESCUELA SECUNDARIA_____ Ciudad_____ Estado_____ ¿Graduado?_____

Años asistidos_____ Grado_____ Teléfono de verificación (_____)_____

UNIVERSIDAD_____ Ciudad_____ Estado_____ ¿Grado?_____

Años asistidos_____ Carrera_____ Teléfono de verificación (_____)_____

POST-GRADO_____ Ciudad_____ Estado_____ ¿Grado?_____

Años asistidos_____ Carrera_____ Teléfono de verificación (_____)_____

Actividades extracurriculares:

Otros programas de entrenamiento completados:

Membrecías profesionales y certificados:

OTROS COMENTARIOS

¿Por qué sería usted una buena opción para esta posición?

Certifico que la información dada anteriomente es completa y exacta en lo mejor de mis conocimientos. Autorizo a las personas, compañías y agencias interesadas de proveer a esta compañía y a sus agentes de toda la información necesaria para verificar las declaraciones que he hecho en esta solicitud y los libero de cualquier responsabilidad al hacer esto. Entiendo que debo recibir referencias satisfactorias de los supervisores de las compañías anteriores, colegas y subalternos (si hubo) antes que una oferta de empleo sea hecha. Entiendo que solicitudes incompletas o sin firma no serán consideradas y que declaraciones falsas, incompletas o tergiversadas serán motivo de mi despido inmediato. Entiendo que cualquier oferta de empleo será bajo la condición de pasar un examen físico prescrito, provar mi identidad y proveer documentos legales que me permitan trabajar. Entiendo que estas declaraciones no pueden ser cambiadas excepto por escrito.

Firma_____ Nombre_____ Fecha_____

Staff Selection Tracking Sheet

GENERAL INFORMATION

APPLICANT_____ Social Security No._____ - _____ - _____

Position Applied for_____ ☐ Full-Time ☐ Part-Time

SCREENING

	Y N ?		Y N ?		Y N ?
Neat/Clean/Appearance	☐ ☐ ☐	Alert/Attentive	☐ ☐ ☐	Punctual	☐ ☐ ☐
Smiling Eye Contact	☐ ☐ ☐	Polite/Courteous	☐ ☐ ☐	Interested	☐ ☐ ☐
INTERVIEW _____	☐ ☐ ☐	SANITATION _____	☐ ☐ ☐	PROFESSIONAL _____	☐ ☐ ☐

COMMENTS:

Screened by_____ Date_____ **GOOD CANDIDATE?** ☐ ☐ ☐

APPLICATION REVIEW

	Y N ?		Y N ?		Y N ?
Neat/Legible	☐ ☐ ☐	Availability	☐ ☐ ☐	Appropriate Experience	☐ ☐ ☐
Appropriate Education	☐ ☐ ☐	Desire	☐ ☐ ☐	Complete/Signed	☐ ☐

Reviewed by_____ Date_____ **GOOD CANDIDATE?** ☐ ☐ ☐

FIRST DEMONSTRATIONS

COMMENTS:

	Y N ?
Lifting Test_____	☐ ☐ ☐
Demo Test 1_____	☐ ☐ ☐

Evaluated by_____ Date_____ **GOOD CANDIDATE?** ☐ ☐ ☐

FIRST INTERVIEW

	Y N ?		Y N ?		Y N ?
Punctual	☐ ☐ ☐	Smiling Eye Contact	☐ ☐ ☐	Presence	☐ ☐ ☐
Friendly	☐ ☐ ☐	Relaxed	☐ ☐ ☐	Neat/Clean/Appearance	☐ ☐ ☐
Confident	☐ ☐ ☐	Sparkle	☐ ☐ ☐	Feel Good	☐ ☐ ☐
COMMENTS:				1ST INTERVIEW _____	☐ ☐ ☐

Interviewed by_____ Date_____ **GOOD CANDIDATE?** ☐ ☐ ☐

SECOND INTERVIEW

	Y N ?		Y N ?		Y N ?
Punctual	☐ ☐ ☐	Smiling Eye Contact	☐ ☐ ☐	Positive/Upbeat	☐ ☐ ☐
Presence	☐ ☐ ☐	Feel Good	☐ ☐ ☐	Relaxed	☐ ☐ ☐
Friendly	☐ ☐ ☐	Sparkle	☐ ☐ ☐	Neat/Clean Appearance	☐ ☐ ☐
WILLINGNESS _____	☐ ☐ ☐	APPROACH _____	☐ ☐ ☐	COACHABILITY _____	☐ ☐ ☐
PRO. CURIOSITY _____	☐ ☐ ☐	STATUS _____	☐ ☐ ☐	2ND INTERVIEW_____	☐ ☐ ☐

COMMENTS:

Interviewed by_____ Date_____ **GOOD CANDIDATE?** ☐ ☐ ☐

PROFESSIONAL TEST

COMMENTS:

Score: _____
Time: _____
Index: _____

Evaluated by_____ Date_____ **GOOD CANDIDATE?** ☐ ☐ ☐

SITUATION TEST

COMMENTS:

	Y	**N**	**?**
No. 1: Score:_____	☐	☐	☐
No. 2: Score:_____	☐	☐	☐

Evaluated by_____ Date_____ **GOOD CANDIDATE?** ☐ ☐ ☐

SECOND DEMONSTRATION

COMMENTS:

	Y	**N**	**?**
Score:_____	☐	☐	☐

Evaluated by_____ Date_____ **GOOD CANDIDATE?** ☐ ☐ ☐

THIRD INTERVIEW

	Y N ?		Y N ?		Y N ?
Punctual	☐ ☐ ☐	Smiling Eye Contact	☐ ☐ ☐	Feel Good	☐ ☐ ☐
Presence	☐ ☐ ☐	Role Model	☐ ☐ ☐	Relaxed	☐ ☐ ☐
Friendly	☐ ☐ ☐	Good Fit	☐ ☐ ☐	Neat/Clean/Appearance	☐ ☐ ☐
Confident	☐ ☐ ☐	Positive	☐ ☐ ☐	Enthusiastic	☐ ☐ ☐
WILLINGNESS _____	☐ ☐ ☐	APPROACH _____	☐ ☐ ☐	COACHABILITY _____	☐ ☐ ☐
PRO. CURIOSITY _____	☐ ☐ ☐	STATUS _____	☐ ☐ ☐	3RD INTERVIEW _____	☐ ☐ ☐

COMMENTS:

Interviewed by_____ Date_____ **GOOD CANDIDATE?** ☐ ☐ ☐

BACKGROUND RESEARCH

	Y N ?		Y N ?		Y N ?
Punctual	☐ ☐ ☐	Reliable	☐ ☐ ☐	Disruptive	☐ ☐ ☐
Even-Tempered	☐ ☐ ☐	Good Role Model	☐ ☐ ☐	Inconsistent	☐ ☐ ☐
Honest	☐ ☐ ☐	Competent	☐ ☐ ☐	Careless	☐ ☐ ☐
Open-Minded	☐ ☐ ☐	Professional	☐ ☐ ☐	Moody	☐ ☐ ☐
Organized	☐ ☐ ☐	Safe Worker	☐ ☐ ☐	Negative	☐ ☐ ☐
SUPERVISOR	☐ ☐ ☐	SUBORDINATE	☐ ☐ ☐	MEDICAL	☐ ☐ ☐
CO-WORKER	☐ ☐ ☐	LAW ENFORCEMENT	☐ ☐ ☐	**GOOD CANDIDATE?**	☐ ☐ ☐

ACTION

Action_____ Date_____

Approved by_____ Notified by_____ ☐ Phone ☐ Letter

Position Offered_____ Starting Salary $_____ per _____ ☐ Full-Time ☐ Part-Time

COMMENTS:

Employer Reference Check

APPLICANT: _____ **POSITION:** _____

Reference_____ **Position**_____

Company_____ **Phone**_____

Dates of Employment_____ Job Title_____

Principal Duties_____

What reasons were given for leaving?_____

This individual is applying for the position of _____ . From the brief description of the job, do you think the applicant could fulfill the job requirements? Why or why not?

_____

What job skills were outstanding?_____

_____

In what areas was more training needed?_____

_____

How did the applicant get along with peers and supervisors?_____

_____

How did the applicant compare to others holding the same position?_____

_____

I am going to give you a list of personal qualities. For each one, please tell me if you would use the term to describe this person, based on your experience of working with them. To keep it easy, please respond with Y (Yes), N (No), or ? (Not Sure).

	Y N ?		Y N ?		Y N ?
Punctual	☐ ☐ ☐	Reliable	☐ ☐ ☐	Disruptive	☐ ☐ ☐
Even-Tempered	☐ ☐ ☐	Good Role Model	☐ ☐ ☐	Inconsistent	☐ ☐ ☐
Honest	☐ ☐ ☐	Competent	☐ ☐ ☐	Careless	☐ ☐ ☐
Open-Minded	☐ ☐ ☐	Professional	☐ ☐ ☐	Moody	☐ ☐ ☐
Organized	☐ ☐ ☐	Safe Worker	☐ ☐ ☐	Negative	☐ ☐ ☐

Would you rehire?_____ Why or why not?_____

_____

What other observations can you offer on this individual's qualifications and work habits?_____

_____

_____

Reference checked by:_____ **Date:**_____ **GOOD CANDIDATE?** ☐ Yes ☐ No ☐ ?

Co-Worker Reference Check

APPLICANT: _____ **POSITION:** _____

Reference_____ **Position**_____

Company_____ **Phone**_____

How long did you work with this person?_____ What was your job title?_____

What was this person's job title?_____ What were this person's principal duties?_____

_____

What was the best part about working with this person?_____

_____

If you could have changed anything about this person, what would it have been?_____

_____

How did this person get along with others?_____

_____

How did this person compare to others holding the same position?_____

_____

_____

I am going to give you a list of personal qualities. For each one, please tell me if you would use the term to describe this person, based on your experience of working with them. To keep it easy, please respond with Y (Yes), N (No), or ? (Not Sure).

	Y N ?		Y N ?		Y N ?
Punctual	☐ ☐ ☐	Reliable	☐ ☐ ☐	Disruptive	☐ ☐ ☐
Even-Tempered	☐ ☐ ☐	Good Role Model	☐ ☐ ☐	Inconsistent	☐ ☐ ☐
Honest	☐ ☐ ☐	Competent	☐ ☐ ☐	Careless	☐ ☐ ☐
Open-Minded	☐ ☐ ☐	Professional	☐ ☐ ☐	Moody	☐ ☐ ☐
Organized	☐ ☐ ☐	Safe Worker	☐ ☐ ☐	Negative	☐ ☐ ☐

Would you like to work with this person again?_____ Why or why not?_____

_____

_____

What other observations can you offer on this person's qualifications and work habits?_____

_____

_____

Reference checked by:_____ **Date:**_____ **GOOD CANDIDATE?** ☐ Yes ☐ No ☐ ?

A P P E N D I X C

Screening Tests

Answer Sheet (English)   C-1

Answer Sheet (Spanish)   C-2

Answer Sheet Overlay (English)   C-3

Screening Interview (English)   C-4

Sanitation Screening Test (English)   C-5

Sanitation Screening Test (Spanish)   C-6

Service Screening Test (English)   C-7

Service Screening Test (Spanish)   C-8

Production Screening Test (English)   C-9

Production Screening Test (Spanish)   C-10

Beverage Screening Test (English)   C-11

Beverage Screening Test (Spanish)   C-12

Coaching Screening Test (English)   C-13

Coaching Screening Test (Spanish)   C-14

Sanitation Screening Test Answers (English)   C-15

Service Screening Test Answers (English)   C-16

Production Screening Test Answers (English)   C-17

Beverage Screening Test Answers (English)   C-18

Coaching Screening Test Answers (English)   C-19

Staff Screening Tests

Answer Sheet

NAME: _____   SSN: _____

These tests are designed to provide a sense of how you view the foodservice industry. As a result, you will find that questions may have more than one correct answer. Check the single answer you think is *MOST CORRECT* based on your point of view. Time is of the essence. The faster you complete the test, the better your index score.

SANITATION	SERVICE	PRODUCTION	BEVERAGE	COACHING
T F	T F	T F	T F	1 2 3 4 5

SANITATION
T F
1. ☐ ☐
2. ☐ ☐
3. ☐ ☐
4. ☐ ☐
5. ☐ ☐
6. ☐ ☐
7. ☐ ☐
8. ☐ ☐
9. ☐ ☐
10. ☐ ☐
11. ☐ ☐
12. ☐ ☐
13. ☐ ☐
14. ☐ ☐
15. ☐ ☐
16. ☐ ☐

A B C D
17. ☐ ☐ ☐ ☐
18. ☐ ☐ ☐ ☐
19. ☐ ☐ ☐ ☐
20. ☐ ☐ ☐ ☐

SERVICE
T F
1. ☐ ☐
2. ☐ ☐
3. ☐ ☐
4. ☐ ☐
5. ☐ ☐
6. ☐ ☐
7. ☐ ☐
8. ☐ ☐
9. ☐ ☐
10. ☐ ☐
11. ☐ ☐
12. ☐ ☐
13. ☐ ☐
14. ☐ ☐
15. ☐ ☐
16. ☐ ☐

A B C D
17. ☐ ☐ ☐ ☐
18. ☐ ☐ ☐ ☐
19. ☐ ☐ ☐ ☐
20. ☐ ☐ ☐ ☐

PRODUCTION
T F
1. ☐ ☐
2. ☐ ☐
3. ☐ ☐
4. ☐ ☐
5. ☐ ☐
6. ☐ ☐
7. ☐ ☐
8. ☐ ☐
9. ☐ ☐
10. ☐ ☐
11. ☐ ☐
12. ☐ ☐
13. ☐ ☐
14. ☐ ☐
15. ☐ ☐
16. ☐ ☐

A B C D E F
17. ☐ ☐ ☐ ☐ ☐ ☐
18. ☐ ☐ ☐ ☐ ☐ ☐
19. ☐ ☐ ☐ ☐ ☐ ☐
20. ☐ ☐ ☐ ☐ ☐ ☐

BEVERAGE
T F
1. ☐ ☐
2. ☐ ☐
3. ☐ ☐
4. ☐ ☐
5. ☐ ☐
6. ☐ ☐
7. ☐ ☐
8. ☐ ☐
9. ☐ ☐
10. ☐ ☐
11. ☐ ☐
12. ☐ ☐
13. ☐ ☐
14. ☐ ☐
15. ☐ ☐
16. ☐ ☐

A B C D
17. ☐ ☐ ☐ ☐
18. ☐ ☐ ☐ ☐
19. ☐ ☐ ☐ ☐
20. ☐ ☐ ☐ ☐

COACHING
1 2 3 4 5
1. ☐ ☐ ☐ ☐ ☐
2. ☐ ☐ ☐ ☐ ☐
3. ☐ ☐ ☐ ☐ ☐
4. ☐ ☐ ☐ ☐ ☐
5. ☐ ☐ ☐ ☐ ☐
6. ☐ ☐ ☐ ☐ ☐
7. ☐ ☐ ☐ ☐ ☐
8. ☐ ☐ ☐ ☐ ☐
9. ☐ ☐ ☐ ☐ ☐
10. ☐ ☐ ☐ ☐ ☐
11. ☐ ☐ ☐ ☐ ☐
12. ☐ ☐ ☐ ☐ ☐
13. ☐ ☐ ☐ ☐ ☐
14. ☐ ☐ ☐ ☐ ☐
15. ☐ ☐ ☐ ☐ ☐
16. ☐ ☐ ☐ ☐ ☐
17. ☐ ☐ ☐ ☐ ☐
18. ☐ ☐ ☐ ☐ ☐
19. ☐ ☐ ☐ ☐ ☐
20. ☐ ☐ ☐ ☐ ☐

FOR OFFICE USE:

SAN: _____	SVC: _____	PROD: _____	BEV: _____	COACH:_____
TIME: _____	TIME: _____	TIME: _____	TIME: _____	TIME: _____
INDEX: _____	INDEX: _____	INDEX: _____	INDEX: _____	INDEX: _____

Exámenes Para Seleccionar Al Equipo Técnico

Hoja de Respuestas

NOMBRE: **NUMERO DE SEGURIDAD SOCIAL:**

Estas pruebas están diseñadas para formar una opinión de cómo ve usted a la industria de los restaurantes. Por lo tanto, usted encontrará que estas preguntas pueden tener más de una respuesta correcta. Marque la única respuesta que usted piense es la *MÁS CORRECTA* basándolo en su punto de vista. El tiempo es esencial. Entre más rápido complete usted el examen, mejor será su índice de puntuación.

SANIDAD	SERVICIO	PRODUCCIÓN	BEBIDAS	ENTRENAMIENTO
V F	V F	V F	V F	1 2 3 4 5
1. ☐ ☐	1. ☐ ☐	1. ☐ ☐	1. ☐ ☐	1. ☐ ☐ ☐ ☐ ☐
2. ☐ ☐	2. ☐ ☐	2. ☐ ☐	2. ☐ ☐	2. ☐ ☐ ☐ ☐ ☐
3. ☐ ☐	3. ☐ ☐	3. ☐ ☐	3. ☐ ☐	3. ☐ ☐ ☐ ☐ ☐
4. ☐ ☐	4. ☐ ☐	4. ☐ ☐	4. ☐ ☐	4. ☐ ☐ ☐ ☐ ☐
5. ☐ ☐	5. ☐ ☐	5. ☐ ☐	5. ☐ ☐	5. ☐ ☐ ☐ ☐ ☐
6. ☐ ☐	6. ☐ ☐	6. ☐ ☐	6. ☐ ☐	6. ☐ ☐ ☐ ☐ ☐
7. ☐ ☐	7. ☐ ☐	7. ☐ ☐	7. ☐ ☐	7. ☐ ☐ ☐ ☐ ☐
8. ☐ ☐	8. ☐ ☐	8. ☐ ☐	8. ☐ ☐	8. ☐ ☐ ☐ ☐ ☐
9. ☐ ☐	9. ☐ ☐	9. ☐ ☐	9. ☐ ☐	9. ☐ ☐ ☐ ☐ ☐
10. ☐ ☐	10. ☐ ☐	10. ☐ ☐	10. ☐ ☐	10. ☐ ☐ ☐ ☐ ☐
11. ☐ ☐	11. ☐ ☐	11. ☐ ☐	11. ☐ ☐	11. ☐ ☐ ☐ ☐ ☐
12. ☐ ☐	12. ☐ ☐	12. ☐ ☐	12. ☐ ☐	12. ☐ ☐ ☐ ☐ ☐
13. ☐ ☐	13. ☐ ☐	13. ☐ ☐	13. ☐ ☐	13. ☐ ☐ ☐ ☐ ☐
14. ☐ ☐	14. ☐ ☐	14. ☐ ☐	14. ☐ ☐	14. ☐ ☐ ☐ ☐ ☐
15. ☐ ☐	15. ☐ ☐	15. ☐ ☐	15. ☐ ☐	15. ☐ ☐ ☐ ☐ ☐
16. ☐ ☐	16. ☐ ☐	16. ☐ ☐	16. ☐ ☐	16. ☐ ☐ ☐ ☐ ☐
				17. ☐ ☐ ☐ ☐ ☐
A B C D	A B C D	A B C D E F	A B C D	18. ☐ ☐ ☐ ☐ ☐
17. ☐ ☐ ☐ ☐	17. ☐ ☐ ☐ ☐	17. ☐ ☐ ☐ ☐ ☐ ☐	17. ☐ ☐ ☐ ☐	19. ☐ ☐ ☐ ☐ ☐
18. ☐ ☐ ☐ ☐	18. ☐ ☐ ☐ ☐	18. ☐ ☐ ☐ ☐ ☐ ☐	18. ☐ ☐ ☐ ☐	20. ☐ ☐ ☐ ☐ ☐
19. ☐ ☐ ☐ ☐	19. ☐ ☐ ☐ ☐	19. ☐ ☐ ☐ ☐ ☐ ☐	19. ☐ ☐ ☐ ☐	
20. ☐ ☐ ☐ ☐	20. ☐ ☐ ☐ ☐	20. ☐ ☐ ☐ ☐ ☐ ☐	20. ☐ ☐ ☐ ☐	

FOR OFFICE USE:

SAN: _____	SVC: _____	PROD: _____	BEV: _____	COACH: _____
TIME: _____	TIME: _____	TIME: _____	TIME: _____	TIME: _____
INDEX: _____	INDEX: _____	INDEX: _____	INDEX: _____	INDEX: _____

Staff Screening Tests
Answer Sheet Overlay

NOTE: To save time when grading the screening tests, make a copy of this sheet on clear transparency film and lay it over the candidate's completed test. This should enable you to easily note the number of questions marked correctly and incorrectly, and you can simply transfer the score to the blocks on the bottom of the answer sheet. The answer sheet and tests are not returned to the applicant, so it is your choice to physically mark the answer to a specific question as correct or incorrect.

SANITATION	SERVICE	PRODUCTION	BEVERAGE	COACHING
T F	T F	T F	T F	
1. □ ■	1. □ ■	1. ■ □	1. □ ■	1. 5 4 3 2 1
2. ■ □	2. □ ■	2. □ ■	2. □ ■	2. 1 2 3 4 5
3. □ ■	3. □ ■	3. □ ■	3. □ ■	3. 1 2 3 4 5
4. ■ □	4. □ ■	4. □ ■	4. □ ■	4. 5 4 3 2 1
5. □ ■	5. □ ■	5. ■ □	5. □ ■	5. 5 4 3 2 1
6. ■ □	6. ■ □	6. ■ □	6. ■ □	6. 5 4 3 2 1
7. □ ■	7. □ ■	7. ■ □	7. □ ■	7. 1 2 3 4 5
8. ■ □	8. □ ■	8. ■ □	8. □ ■	8. 1 2 3 4 5
9. □ ■	9. ■ □	9. ■ □	9. ■ □	9. 5 4 3 2 1
10. □ ■	10. □ ■	10. ■ □	10. ■ □	10. 1 2 3 4 5
11. ■ □	11. □ ■	11. □ ■	11. □ ■	11. 5 4 3 2 1
12. ■ □	12. ■ □	12. ■ □	12. ■ □	12. 1 2 3 4 5
13. ■ □	13. □ ■	13. ■ □	13. □ ■	13. 5 4 3 2 1
14. □ ■	14. ■ □	14. □ ■	14. □ ■	14. 1 2 3 4 5
15. □ ■	15. □ ■	15. ■ □	15. □ ■	15. 1 2 3 4 5
16. □ ■	16. □ ■	16. □ ■	16. □ ■	16. 1 2 3 4 5
A B C D	**A B C D**	**A B C D E F**	**A B C D**	17. 1 2 3 4 5
17. □ □ □ ■	17. □ ■ □ □	17. □ □ □ □ ■ □	17. □ ■ □ □	18. 5 4 3 2 1
18. □ ■ □ □	18. □ ■ □ □	18. □ ■ □ □ □ □	18. □ ■ □ □	19. 1 2 3 4 5
19. □ □ ■ □	19. □ □ □ ■	19. □ □ □ □ ■ □	19. □ □ ■ □	20. 5 4 3 2 1
20. □ □ ■ □	20. ■ □ □ □	20. □ □ □ ■ □ □	20. ■ □ □ □	

Screening Interview

NAME: _____   POSITION: _____

EXTROVERSION	Yes Response	No Response
Y N ?		
☐ ☐ ☐ As a member of the restaurant staff, how would you help develop repeat business?	Specific answer that shows personal action or interaction, e.g., learn and use their names, ask questions, make suggestions, make sure food always looks and tastes great	Be friendly, give good service
☐ ☐ ☐ If I asked your best friend to describe you, what would he/she say?	People-oriented answers, e.g., outgoing, lots of fun, friendly, positive	Nice person, good worker
☐ ☐ ☐ If you saw someone you thought you recognized but weren't quite sure, what would you do?	Go up and ask—make an effort to talk to them	Just keep walking—wait until I was sure

PRIDE		
☐ ☐ ☐ What qualities do you need to be a great (position) in a restaurant?	Like people; work hard; do more than expected; smile, be flexible, patient; have lots of stamina, good work habits; pay attention to detail; be good communicator	Be nice
☐ ☐ ☐ Is it difficult for you to carry on "small talk" with people?	No, not at all	Sometimes, depending on the situation
☐ ☐ ☐ What recent accomplishments do you take great pride in?	Specific advancement toward a goal, e.g., completed courses, finished a difficult project; job advancement; family success	Don't have any specific goals
☐ ☐ ☐ What are some reasons for your successes?	My personality, optimism, positive self-image, desire to succeed	Just lucky, I don't know

RESPONSIBILITY		
☐ ☐ ☐ What would your previous employers say about your work?	Hard worker, dependable, valuable, ideal employee, would rehire	Did a good job
☐ ☐ ☐ What would you do to make a negative situation positive?	Find out what the problem is and fix it	Get a manager, stay calm
☐ ☐ ☐ What kinds of people irritate you?	Lazy, negative, complainers	I like everyone; I don't pay attention to them
☐ ☐ ☐ How do you decide what to do with your time off?	Make lists, organize, get right at things	Don't do it very well, go with the flow

ENERGY		
☐ ☐ ☐ What activities have you been involved in during the past two years?	Participative activities, e.g., aerobics, sports, volunteer work, charities	Not many, I just work
☐ ☐ ☐ What motivates you to get your job done?	Money, recognition, pride in my work	Making people happy, giving good service
☐ ☐ ☐ How do you feel about doing more than one activity at a time?	Like it; it's a challenge	Want to do one thing at a time; it doesn't bother me

Sanitation Screening Test

ALL APPLICANTS

Pick the *MOST CORRECT* answer and mark your choice on the answer sheet. Please do not write on this test.

TRUE OR FALSE

1. Harmful bacteria are killed by temperatures below freezing.
2. You *must* wash your hands before starting your shift.
3. Increasing the amount of detergent will increase the cleaning power of a solution.
4. You *must* wash your hands after using the restroom.
5. It's OK to break some of the sanitation rules as long as you don't do it too often.
6. You *must* wash your hands before returning to work after a break.
7. Coats worn to work may be hung in the work areas.
8. You *must* wash your hands periodically during the shift.
9. If you are out of sight of restaurant guests, it is OK to eat or drink at your workstation.
10. You *must* wash your hands after filling the silverware container before you can handle food.
11. It is a major health department violation for spray bottles to be unlabeled.
12. You *must* wash your hands before handling food if you have just handled money.
13. Dairy products must be stored under refrigeration.
14. You never *have* to wash your hands unless you want to.
15. All food in refrigerators must be covered unless it is on the top shelf.
16. When washing your hands on the job, use the closest sink to your work area.

17. Which of the following is the most common source of food contamination?
    A. Flies.
    B. Rats and mice.
    C. Roaches.
    D. People.

18. What is sanitizing solution?
    A. The chemical injected into the dish machine wash cycle to kill germs.
    B. A mixture of bleach and water that cleaning cloths are stored in to kill germs.
    C. A solution of detergent and water used in the mop bucket to clean the floor.

19. What is the "danger zone" for food?
    A. Between freezing and boiling.
    B. Between 32°F and 120°F.
    C. Between 45°F and 140°F.
    D. Between 60°F and 165°F.

20. What should you do when you have a cold?
    A. Call in sick and don't come to work.
    B. Contact your supervisor to file a Workers' Compensation claim.
    C. Report to work but do a job that does not involve handling food.
    D. Come to work and do your regular job.

Examen Sobre Sanidad

PARA TODOS LOS SOLICITANTES

Escoja la respuesta *MÁS CORRECTA* y márquela en la hoja de respuestas. Por favor no escriba en este examen.

FALSO O VERDADERO

1. Las bacterias dañinas pueden ser matadas con temperaturas más bajas del punto de congelación.
2. Usted *TIENE* que lavarse las manos antes de comenzar su turno.
3. El aumentar la cantidad de detergente incrementará el poder limpiador de la solución.
4. Usted *TIENE* que lavarse las manos después de utilizar el baño.
5. Está bien no obedecer parte de las reglas de salubridad, con tal que usted no lo haga con demasiada frecuencia.
6. Usted *TIENE* que lavarse las manos antes de regresar al trabajo después de su descanso.
7. Los abrigos que se ponga para ir a trabajar podrán ser colgados en las zonas de trabajo.
8. Usted *TIENE* que lavarse las manos periódicamente durante su turno.
9. Si usted está fuera de la vista de los clientes del restaurante, está bien que coma o beba en su estación de trabajo.
10. Usted *TIENE* que lavarse las manos después de haber llenado el recipiente de los cubiertos y antes de tocar cualquier comida.
11. Es una violación muy grande del Departamento de Salud el tener botellas de aerosol sin etiquetas.
12. Usted *TIENE* que lavarse las manos antes de tocar cualquier alimento si usted ha manejado dinero anteriormente.
13. Los productos lácteos almacenados tienen que mantenerse refrigerados.
14. Usted nunca *TIENE* que lavarse las manos a menos que usted quiera.
15. Todos los alimentos en el refrigerador deben ser cubiertos a menos que estén en el primer estante.
16. Cuando se lave sus manos en el trabajo, utilice el cuarto de baño más cercano a su estación.

17. ¿Cuál de las siguientes es la fuente más común de contaminación de alimentos?
   A. Las moscas.
   B. Las ratas y ratones.
   C. Las cucarachas.
   D. La gente.

18. ¿Qué es una solución sanitante?
   A. El químico inyectado en el ciclo de la lavadora de platos para matar gérmenes.
   B. Una mezcla de blanqueador y agua donde los paños de limpieza se colocan para matar los gérmenes.
   C. Una solución de detergente y agua utilizado en el balde del trapeador para limpiar el piso.

19. ¿Cuál es la "zona de peligro" del alimento?
   A. Entre el punto de congelación y el punto de ebullición.
   B. Entre 32°F y 120°F.
   C. Entre 45°F y 140°F.
   D. Entre 60°F y 165°F.

20. ¿Qué deberá hacer usted cuando tenga un catarro?
   A. Llamar para informar que está enfermo y no ir a trabajar.
   B. Contactar a su supervisor para que mande un reclamo a la Compensación de Trabajadores.
   C. Ir a trabajar pero hacer deberes que no involucren el manejo de alimentos.
   D. Ir a trabajar y hacer su trabajo normal.

Professional Screening Test

SERVICE STAFF

Pick the *MOST CORRECT* answer and mark your choice on the answer sheet. Please do not write on this test.

TRUE OR FALSE

1. It is OK to place fingers in glasses to clear a table, provided the guests have already left.
2. When filling a glass with ice, it is OK to use the glass as a scoop because it speeds up service.
3. Glasses should be handled by the rims so you can easily check to be sure they are clean.
4. It is nearly impossible to give good service during the rush.
5. Dinner rolls may be re-served if they haven't been touched by the guests.
6. People always have good reasons for the requests they make.
7. Garbage may be stored outside the restaurant in plastic bags.
8. Clean cans of tomato juice may be chilled in the ice used for drinks.
9. It is not OK to use the same cloth to wipe tabletops and the seats of booths or chairs.
10. Sanitizing solution kills bacteria on contact.
11. Open-toed shoes are acceptable for work provided they are clean and polished.
12. The best way to keep your cool is not to take things personally.
13. Boxes may be placed on the floor of walk-in coolers.
14. Uniforms should not be changed in the dining room.
15. As an hourly worker, there is little you can do to make a restaurant profitable.
16. Knives are typically set to the guest's left.

17. What is the correct way to carry something to the table?
   A. In your hand.
   B. On a tray.
   C. Either method is correct.

18. To which side of the guest are glasses typically placed?
   A. Left.
   B. Right.
   C. Either side is OK.

19. When a guest is choking on a piece of food and coughing violently, what first aid procedure is urgently needed to save the person's life?
   A. CPR.
   B. The Heimlich maneuver.
   C. Artificial respiration.
   D. No first aid procedure is necessary.

20. What is the correct procedure for clearing a table?
   A. Move around the table to clear it.
   B. Stay in one spot when clearing plates to save time and avoid unnecessary movement in the dining room.
   C. Both procedures are correct.
   D. Neither procedure is correct.

Examen Profesional

EQUIPO TÉCNICO DE SERVICIO

Escoja la respuesta *MÁS CORRECTA* y márquela en la hoja de respuestas. Por favor no escriba en este examen.

FALSO O VERDADERO

1. Está BIEN colocar los dedos en los vasos al despejar una mesa, proveyendo que los clientes se hayan ido.
2. Al llenar un vaso con hielo, es correcto utilizar el vaso como una cuchara porque acelera el servicio.
3. Los vasos deben ser manejados por los aros de modo que usted pueda asegurarse fácilmente si están limpios.
4. Es casi imposible dar buen servicio durante la hora cumbre.
5. Los panes de la cena pueden ser servidos otra vez si no fueron tocados por los clientes.
6. La gente siempre tiene buenas razones de hacer las solicitudes que hacen.
7. La basura puede estar almacenada afuera del restaurante en bolsas plásticas.
8. Las latas de jugo de tomate limpias pueden ser enfriadas en el hielo y utilizadas para beber.
9. No es correcto utilizar el mismo paño para limpiar las mesas y las sillas.
10. La solución sanitante mata las bacterias al contacto.
11. Zapatos con la punta del pie abierta son aceptables para el trabajo proveyendo que estén limpios y pulidos.
12. La mejor manera de mantenerse tranquilo es no tomar las cosas personalmente.
13. Las cajas pueden ser situadas en el piso de los cuartos de refrigeración.
14. Los uniformes no se deben cambiar en el comedor.
15. Como trabajador por hora, es poco lo que usted puede hacer para que el restaurante sea lucrativo.
16. Los cuchillos típicamente son colocados a la izquierda del cliente.

17. ¿Cuál es el modo más correcto de llevar algo a la mesa?
   A. Llevarlo en su mano.
   B. Llevarlo en una bandeja.
   C. Cualquier método es correcto.

18. ¿A cuál lado del cliente son típicamente colocados los vasos?
   A. Izquierdo.
   B. Derecho.
   C. Cualquier lado es correcto.

19. Cuando un cliente se está ahogando con un pedazo de alimento y tociendo violentamente, ¿cuáles procedimientos de primeros auxilios serán necesitados urgentemente para salvarle la vida a la persona?
   A. CPR.
   B. La maniobra de Heimlich.
   C. Respiración artificial.
   D. No serán necesarios procedimientos de primeros auxilios.

20. ¿Cuál es el procedimiento correcto para limpiar una mesa?
   A. Moverse alrededor de la mesa para despejarla.
   B. Quedarse en un solo lugar al limpiar los platos para ahorrar tiempo y evitar el movimiento innecesario en el comedor.
   C. Ambos procedimientos son correctos.
   D. Ningún procedimiento es correcto.

Professional Screening Test

PRODUCTION STAFF

Pick the *MOST CORRECT* answer and mark your choice on the answer sheet. Please do not write on this test.

TRUE OR FALSE

1. Cups and glasses should be stored upside down.
2. Sanitizing solution kills bacteria on contact.
3. After each use, mops should be washed in the pot sink.
4. Frozen foods may be thawed on the counter as long as the center of the item stays below 45°F.
5. Mops should be rinsed and hung up to dry after each use.
6. Sharp knives are safer than dull knives.
7. Garbage may be stored outside the restaurant in plastic bags.
8. Food preparation staff must wear hair restraints like hats or hair nets at all times.
9. Required operating temperatures for dish machines may be found on the machine's data plate.
10. Knives and cutting boards *must* be cleaned and sanitized when switching from one product to another.
11. Steam tables may be used to reheat previously prepared foods.
12. The best way to keep your cool is not to take things personally.
13. It is a health department requirement to keep dumpster lids closed.
14. Cleaning chemicals may be stored in the same room with food products.
15. Eating or drinking is not allowed in food prep areas because it creates a safety hazard.
16. Damp cleaning cloths should be kept on the counter, out of the way of your work.

17. **Which of the following is an *incorrect* storage procedure?**
    A. Boxes of cereal stacked to the ceiling to maximize storage.
    B. A plastic pail of pickles on the floor of the walk-in.
    C. Covered food pans stacked on top of each other in the refrigerators.
    D. A thawing turkey placed on an upper wire shelf of the walk-in.
    E. All of the above are incorrect storage procedures.

18. **What is in the second compartment of a three-compartment sink?**
    A. Hot water with a chemical solution used for sanitizing.
    B. Clean hot water used for rinsing.
    C. Hot water with a chemical solution used for rinsing.
    D. Hot detergent solution used for washing.
    E. Lukewarm water with a chemical solution used for sanitizing.
    F. Hot water with a chemical solution used for washing.

19. **What is in the third compartment of a three-compartment sink?**
    A. Hot water with a chemical solution used for sanitizing.
    B. Clean hot water used for rinsing.
    C. Hot water with a chemical solution used for rinsing.
    D. Hot detergent solution used for washing.
    E. Lukewarm water with a chemical solution used for sanitizing.
    F. Hot water with a chemical solution used for washing.

20. **What is in the first compartment of a three-compartment sink?**
    A. Hot water with a chemical solution used for sanitizing.
    B. Clean hot water used for rinsing.
    C. Hot water with a chemical solution used for rinsing.
    D. Hot detergent solution used for washing.
    E. Lukewarm water with a chemical solution used for sanitizing.
    F. Hot water with a chemical solution used for washing.

Examen Profesional

EQUIPO TÉCNICO DE PRODUCCIÓN

Escoja la respuesta *MÁS CORRECTA* y márquela en la hoja de respuestas. Por favor no escriba en este examen.

FALSO O VERDADERO

1. Las tazas y los vasos deberán ser almacenados en forma invertida.
2. La solución sanitante mata las bacterias al contacto.
3. Después de cada uso, los trapeadores deben ser lavados en los lavaplatos.
4. Los alimentos congelados pueden ser descongelados en el mueble de la cocina siempre y cuando el centro del producto permanezca bajo los 45°F.
5. Los trapeadores deben ser lavados y colgados para que se sequen después de cada uso.
6. Los cuchillos afilados son más seguros que los cuchillos sin filo.
7. La basura puede ser almacenada fuera del restaurante en bolsas plásticas.
8. El equipo técnico de preparación de alimentos debe protegerse el pelo con sombreros o mallas en todo momento.
9. Las temperaturas de operación requeridas por las máquinas lavadoras de platos podrán ser encontradas en la placa con las instrucciones de la máquina.
10. Los cuchillos y las tablas de cortar tienen que ser limpiadas y desinfectadas al cambiar de un producto a otro.
11. Las mesas de vapor pueden ser utilizadas para recalentar alimentos previamente preparados.
12. La mejor manera de mantenerse tranquilo es no tomar las cosas personalmente.
13. Es un requisito del Departamento de Salud mantener las tapas de los basureros cerradas.
14. Los productos químicos de limpieza pueden ser almacenados en el mismo cuarto con los productos alimenticios.
15. Comer o beber no está permitido en las áreas de preparación de alimentos porque crea un riesgo a la seguridad.
16. Los paños de limpieza que estén húmedos deberán permanecer en el mostrador, lejos del área de trabajo.

17. **¿Cuál de los siguientes es un procedimiento de almacenamiento incorrecto?**
    A. Cajas de cereal amontonadas hasta el techo para aumentar el área de almacenamiento.
    B. Un balde plástico de encurtido en el piso del corredor.
    C. Ollas de alimento cubiertas amontonadas, una encima de la otra en los refrigeradores.
    D. Un pavo descongelado situado en un estante superior de alambre en el corredor.
    E. Todos los procedimientos anteriores son formas de almacenamiento incorrectos.

18. **¿Qué hay en el segundo compartimiento de un lavaplatos de (3) tres compartimientos?**
    A. Agua caliente con una solución química utilizada para desinfectar.
    B. Agua caliente limpia utilizada para lavar.
    C. Agua caliente con una solución química utilizada para lavar.
    D. Una solución de detergente caliente utilizada para lavar.
    E. Agua tibia con una solución química utilizada para desinfectar.
    F. Agua caliente con una solución química utilizada para lavar.

19. **¿Qué hay en el tercer compartimiento de un lavaplatos de (3) tres compartimientos?**
    A. Agua caliente con una solución química utilizada para desinfectar.
    B. Agua caliente limpia utilizada para lavar.
    C. Agua caliente con una solución química utilizada para lavar.
    D. Una solución de detergente caliente utilizada para lavar.
    E. Agua tibia con una solución química utilizada para desinfectar.
    F. Agua caliente con una solución química utilizada para lavar.

20. **¿Qué hay en el primer compartimiento de un lavaplatos de (3) tres compartimientos?**
    A. Agua caliente con una solución química utilizada para desinfectar.
    B. Agua caliente limpia utilizada para lavar.
    C. Agua caliente con una solución química utilizada para lavar.
    D. Una solución de detergente caliente utilizada para lavar.
    E. Agua tibia con una solución química utilizada para desinfectar.
    F. Agua caliente con una solución química utilizada para lavar.

Professional Screening Test

BEVERAGE STAFF

Pick the *MOST CORRECT* answer and mark your choice on the answer sheet. Please do not write on this test.

TRUE OR FALSE

1. It is OK to place fingers in glasses when clearing a table provided the guests have already left.
2. When filling a glass with ice, it is OK to use the glass as a scoop because it speeds up service.
3. Glasses should be handled by the rims so you can easily check to be sure they are clean.
4. It is nearly impossible to give good service during the rush.
5. It is OK to drink behind the bar as long as you are not drinking alcohol.
6. People always have good reasons for the requests they make.
7. A state driver's license is the only acceptable form of ID.
8. Clean cans of tomato juice may be chilled in the ice used for drinks.
9. It is not OK to use the same cloth to wipe tabletops and the seats of booths or chairs.
10. Giving regular guests a heavier pour is a good way to show you appreciate their business.
11. Cocktail napkins should only be given to female customers.
12. The best way to keep your cool is not to take things personally.
13. Kegs of beer may be stored on the floor of walk-in coolers.
14. It is OK to have a drink after state closing hours as long as the door is locked.
15. As an hourly worker, there is little you can do to make a restaurant profitable.
16. All wines should be served in chilled glasses.

17. What is the correct way to carry a drink to the table?
 A. In your hand.
 B. On a tray.
 C. Either method is correct.

18. To which side of the guest are glasses typically placed?
 A. Left.
 B. Right.
 C. Either side is OK.

19. What do you do when a guest returns a drink?
 A. Make a fresh drink and charge half price.
 B. Pour the drink into a fresh glass, add mix, and send it back.
 C. Replace the drink, no questions asked.
 D. Buy a round of drinks for the guest's table.

20. What is the correct procedure for clearing a table?
 A. Move around the table to clear it.
 B. Stay in one spot to save time and avoid unnecessary movement in the dining room.
 C. Both procedures are correct.
 D. Neither procedure is correct.

Examen Profesional

EQUIPO TÉCNICO DE BEBIDAS

Escoja la respuesta *MÁS CORRECTA* y márquela en la hoja de respuestas. Por favor no escriba en este examen.

FALSO O VERDADERO

1. Está bien colocar los dedos en los vasos al despejar una mesa proveyendo que los clientes se hayan ido.
2. Al llenar un vaso con hielo, está bien utilizar el vaso como una cuchara porque acelera el servicio.
3. Los vasos deben ser manejados por los aros de modo que usted puede asegurarse fácilmente si están limpios.
4. Es casi imposible dar buen servicio durante la hora cumbre.
5. Está bien beber detrás de la barra con tal que no se esté bebiendo alcohol.
6. La gente siempre tiene buenas razones para hacer las solicitudes que hacen.
7. Una licencia de conducir del estado es la única forma aceptable de ID.
8. Las latas de jugo de tomate limpias pueden ser enfriadas en el hielo y utilizadas para las bebidas.
9. No es correcto utilizar el mismo paño para limpiar las mesas y las sillas.
10. Darles a los clientes regulares un trago más fuerte es una buena forma de mostrarles que usted aprecia sus visitas.
11. Las servilletas de coctel solamente deben ser dadas con las clientes femeninas.
12. La mejor manera de mantenerse tranquilo es no tomar las cosas personalmente.
13. Los barriles de cerveza pueden ser almacenados en el piso del cuarto de refrigeración.
14. Es correcto tomarse una bebida después de la hora de cierre dictada por el estado con tal que la puerta esté cerrada con llave.
15. Como trabajador por hora, es poco lo que usted puede hacer para que el restaurante sea lucrativo.
16. Todos los vinos deben ser servidos en vasos enfriados.

17. **¿Cuál es la forma correcta de llevar una bebida a la mesa?**
    A. Llevarla en su mano.
    B. Llevarla en una bandeja.
    C. Cualquier método es correcto.

18. **¿A qué lado del cliente se colocan típicamente los vasos?**
    A. Izquierdo.
    B. Derecho.
    C. Cualquier lado está bien.

19. **¿Qué hace usted cuando un cliente devuelve una bebida?**
    A. Prepara una nueva y la cobra a mitad de precio.
    B. Sirve la bebida en otro vaso, le agrega más mezcla y la devuelve a la mesa.
    C. Reemplaza la bebida sin hacer preguntas.
    D. Regala una ronda de bebidas a la mesa del cliente.

20. **¿Cuál es el procedimiento correcto de limpiar una mesa?**
    A. Moverse alrededor la mesa para despejarla.
    B. Quedarse en un solo lugar para limpiar los platos y ahorrar tiempo evitando movimientos innecesarios en el comedor.
    C. Ambos procedimientos son correctos.
    D. Ningún procedimiento es correcto.

Professional Screening Test
COACHING STAFF

Instructions: Answer each question by marking the response that most closely describes how you manage people and your beliefs about the people who work for you. Determine how strongly you agree or disagree with each statement and mark your selections on the answer sheet. Please do not write on this test.

1 Strongly Disagree   2 Disagree   3 Neither Agree nor Disagree   4 Agree   5 Strongly Agree

1. Generally speaking, I feel that most of my staff must be closely supervised to ensure that they are really productive.
2. I believe that most of my staff want to do their best while at work.
3. In general, people can be trusted.
4. Most people will tend to goof off unless someone supervises them.
5. To get things done properly, I make it a practice to focus on things that are *not* done right.
6. I believe I have a better idea of what is required to do a particular job than my staff does.
7. I make it a practice to ask myself how I would feel about a certain action before I use it on one of my staff.
8. When staff members are late, I assume they have a valid reason, at least until they have a chance to tell their story.
9. I tend to counsel my staff while the event is fresh and I'm good and mad, so that I'm sure not to omit any of the important details.
10. While counseling, I generally focus on what the person *did*, instead of on the person.
11. At least half of my counseling sessions are dedicated to disciplining my staff.
12. I believe that my staff is always doing the best they can at any particular moment.
13. My best staff members do their work exactly as I tell them to.
14. I feel that work is a place where the staff should have fun.
15. Generally speaking, workers who feel great are more likely to have low rates of absenteeism.
16. I usually find something to compliment my staff about whenever I walk through their work areas.
17. I tend to make sure that rewards are tied to performance.
18. A formal recognition program should be designed to recognize about 15 percent of the top achievers.
19. I make it a practice to punish in private.
20. I make it a practice to reward in private.

Source: From *The Winning Foodservice Manager: Strategies for Doing More with Less* by Wolf J. Rinke, © 1990, pp. 199–201. Adapted by permission of Achievement Publishers, Rockville, Maryland.

EQUIPO TÉCNICO DE ENTRENAMIENTO

INSTRUCCIONES: Responda a cada pregunta marcando la respuesta que describa mejor la forma en que usted maneja a la gente y sus creencias acerca de la gente que trabaja para usted. Determine si está de acuerdo o desacuerdo con cada declaración y marque sus selecciones en la hoja de respuestas. Por favor no escriba en este examen.

1 Fuerte desacuerdo	2 Desacuerdo	3 No está de acuerdo ni de desacuerdo	4 De acuerdo	5 Fuerte acuerdo

1. En general, considero que la mayoría de mi equipo técnico tiene que estar supervisado de cerca para garantizar que sea realmente productivo.
2. Creo que la mayoría de mi equipo técnico quiere hacer lo mejor mientras está en el trabajo.
3. En general, se puede confiar en la gente.
4. La mayoría de la gente tiende a perder el tiempo a menos que alguien la supervise.
5. Para obtener que las cosas se hagan adecuadamente, lo he hecho una práctica el concentrarme en las cosas que no están bien hechas.
6. Creo que tengo una mejor idea que mi equipo técnico de lo que se requiere para hacer el trabajo bien hecho.
7. Lo he hecho una práctica el preguntarme a mi mismo como me sentiría acerca de una acción antes de que yo la utilice con alguien de mi equipo técnico.
8. Cuando un miembro del equipo técnico llega tarde supongo que tiene una razón válida por lo menos hasta que tenga la oportunidad de contarme la razón.
9. Tiendo a aconsejar a mi equipo técnico mientras la situación está fresca y estoy enojado, para no omitir ningún detalle importante.
10. Cuando aconsejo, generalmente me concentro en lo que hizo la persona, en lugar de la persona en sí.
11. Por lo menos la mitad de mis sesiones consejeras están dedicadas a disciplinar a mi equipo técnico.
12. Creo que mi equipo técnico siempre hace lo mejor que se puede en cualquier momento.
13. Mi mejor equipo técnico hace su trabajo exactamente como se lo digo.
14. Siento que el lugar de trabajo debe ser un lugar para divertirse.
15. Hablando en general, el equipo técnico que se siente bien tiene menos probabilidades de ausentarse.
16. Generalmente busco algo para felicitar a mi equipo técnico cuando paso por sus zonas de trabajo.
17. Tiendo a asegurarme que las recompensas estén asociadas con el desempeño del trabajo.
18. Un programa formal de reconocimiento debe ser diseñado para reconocer al 15% de los empleados con grandes logros.
19. Me aseguro de llamar la atención a los empleados en privado.
20. Me aseguro de felicitar a los empleados en privado.

Source: From *The Winning Foodservice Manager: Strategies for Doing More with Less* by Wolf J. Rinke, © 1990, pp. 199–201, Adapted by permission of Achievement Publishers, Rockville, Maryland.

Sanitation Screening Test

Answer Sheet

1. **F**   Bacteria will not grow at temperatures below freezing, but they are only killed by heat above 165°F.

2. **T**   Hands pick up harmful bacteria from the steering wheel in your car, the door knob, etc.

3. **F**   If this were true, undiluted detergent would be the best cleaner.

4. **T**

5. **F**

6. **T**

7. **F**

8. **T**   Hands become contaminated through contact with food. Washing prevents cross-contamination.

9. **F**   Eating or drinking at workstations is a health department violation.

10. **F**   Silverware containers would be filled with clean silverware and so would not soil the hands. Hands should be washed *before* the silverware containers are filled, however.

11. **T**   This is to prevent the possibility of chemical contamination.

12. **T**   Money is one of the dirtiest things you can handle in a restaurant.

13. **T**

14. **F**

15. **F**   All food in the refrigerator must be covered to prevent contamination.

16. **F**   The closest sink could be a food preparation sink. Hands must be washed only in designated hand sinks, never in prep sinks.

17. **D**   **People.** All sources could contaminate food, but people are by far the most common culprit.

18. **B**   **A mixture of bleach and water that cleaning cloths are stored in to kill germs.**

19. **C**   **Between 45°F and 140°F.**

20. **C**   **Report to work but do a job that does not involve handling food.**

Professional Screening Test

SERVICE STAFF
Answer Sheet

1. **F** This practice contaminates your hands and makes your guests uncomfortable.

2. **F** This is a health department violation. Also, if the glass should break in the ice, you will have to empty the ice bin, wipe it dry, and refill it. Broken glass can cause serious injury if swallowed.

3. **F** Never handle glasses where the guest's lips will touch. Handle by the lower third only.

4. **F** A legendary restaurant *must* be able to deliver good service under any circumstances.

5. **F** Food returned from the dining room cannot be re-served. Besides, how do you *know* something hasn't been touched?

6. **T** The reasons make sense to them even if you don't understand or agree.

7. **F** Garbage must be stored in covered containers.

8. **F** Nothing may be stored in ice used for consumption.

9. **T** It is not a health department violation, but it will disgust your guests.

10. **F** Sanitizing solution takes about 30 seconds to 1 minute to kill bacteria.

11. **F**

12. **T**

13. **F** Nothing may be stored on the floor of walk-ins because it makes cleaning impossible.

14. **T**

15. **F**

16. **F** Knives are typically set to the guest's right.

17. **B** **On a tray.**

18. **B** **Right.**

19. **D** **No first aid is necessary.** The coughing indicates that the airway is not obstructed. If the guest were unable to speak, the Heimlich maneuver would be needed to clear the obstruction.

20. **A** **Move around the table to clear it.**

Professional Screening Test

PRODUCTION STAFF
Answer Sheet

1. **T** This prevents airborne particles from contaminating the serviceware.

2. **F** Sanitizing solution takes 30 seconds to 1 minute to kill bacteria.

3. **F** Mops should be washed after each use, but never in a sink where food is prepared.

4. **F** While the center may stay below 45°F, the exterior will be out of temperature.

5. **T**

6. **T** Because they cut more predictably and with less effort, sharp knives are safer than dull knives.

7. **F** Garbage must be stored in covered containers.

8. **T** Hair will contaminate food and drive away guests.

9. **T**

10. **T** This practice prevents cross-contamination.

11. **F** Steam tables do not have the heat output to reheat food. Reheat food on the range and transfer it to the steam table once it reaches 165°F.

12. **T**

13. **T**

14. **T** Chemicals must be stored on shelves below food products or on separate shelves.

15. **F** Eating or drinking is not permitted because it places your hands around your mouth, contaminating them.

16. **F** Damp cleaning cloths should be stored in buckets of sanitizing solution between uses.

17. **E** **All of the above are incorrect storage procedures.**

18. **B** **Clean hot water used for rinsing.**

19. **E** **Lukewarm water with a chemical solution used for sanitizing.** Hot water will cause the sanitizer to evaporate, reducing the sanitizing power.

20. **D** **Hot detergent solution used for washing.**

Professional Screening Test

BEVERAGE STAFF
Answer Sheet

1. **F** This practice contaminates your hands and makes your guests uncomfortable.

2. **F** This is a health department violation. Also, if the glass should break in the ice, you will have to empty the ice bin, wipe it dry, and refill it. Broken glass can cause serious injury if swallowed.

3. **F** Never handle glasses where the guest's lips will touch. Handle by the lower third only.

4. **F** A legendary restaurant *must* be able to deliver good service under any circumstances.

5. **F** Food returned from the dining room cannot be re-served. Besides, how do you *know* something hasn't been touched?

6. **T** The reasons make sense to them even if you don't understand or agree.

7. **F** Any photo ID issued by a government agency, such as a military ID card, is a valid form of identification.

8. **F** Nothing may be stored in ice used for consumption.

9. **T** It is not a health department violation, but it will disgust your guests.

10. **F** People drink to be sociable, not to get numb.

11. **F** Cocktail napkins should be placed under every glass and bottle, no matter who the guest is.

12. **T**

13. **F** Nothing may be stored on the floor of walk-ins because it makes cleaning impossible.

14. **F**

15. **F**

16. **F** Only bulk white or blush wines should be served in chilled glasses.

17. **B** On a tray.

18. **B** Right.

19. **C** Replace the drink, no questions asked.

20. **A** Move around the table to clear it.

Professional Screening Test
COACHING STAFF SCORING SHEET

Score each answer with the following number of points:

1.	1 = 5 pt.	2 = 4 pt.	3 = 3 pt.	4 = 2 pt.	5 = 1 pt.
2.	1 = 1 pt.	2 = 2 pt.	3 = 3 pt.	4 = 4 pt.	5 = 5 pt.
3.	1 = 1 pt.	2 = 2 pt.	3 = 3 pt.	4 = 4 pt.	5 = 5 pt.
4.	1 = 5 pt.	2 = 4 pt.	3 = 3 pt.	4 = 2 pt.	5 = 1 pt.
5.	1 = 5 pt.	2 = 4 pt.	3 = 3 pt.	4 = 2 pt.	5 = 1 pt.
6.	1 = 5 pt.	2 = 4 pt.	3 = 3 pt.	4 = 2 pt.	5 = 1 pt.
7.	1 = 1 pt.	2 = 2 pt.	3 = 3 pt.	4 = 4 pt.	5 = 5 pt.
8.	1 = 1 pt.	2 = 2 pt.	3 = 3 pt.	4 = 4 pt.	5 = 5 pt.
9.	1 = 5 pt.	2 = 4 pt.	3 = 3 pt.	4 = 2 pt.	5 = 1 pt.
10.	1 = 1 pt.	2 = 2 pt.	3 = 3 pt.	4 = 4 pt.	5 = 5 pt.
11.	1 = 5 pt.	2 = 4 pt.	3 = 3 pt.	4 = 2 pt.	5 = 1 pt.
12.	1 = 1 pt.	2 = 2 pt.	3 = 3 pt.	4 = 4 pt.	5 = 5 pt.
13.	1 = 5 pt.	2 = 4 pt.	3 = 3 pt.	4 = 2 pt.	5 = 1 pt.
14.	1 = 1 pt.	2 = 2 pt.	3 = 3 pt.	4 = 4 pt.	5 = 5 pt.
15.	1 = 1 pt.	2 = 2 pt.	3 = 3 pt.	4 = 4 pt.	5 = 5 pt.
16.	1 = 1 pt.	2 = 2 pt.	3 = 3 pt.	4 = 4 pt.	5 = 5 pt.
17.	1 = 1 pt.	2 = 2 pt.	3 = 3 pt.	4 = 4 pt.	5 = 5 pt.
18.	1 = 5 pt.	2 = 4 pt.	3 = 3 pt.	4 = 2 pt.	5 = 1 pt.
19.	1 = 1 pt.	2 = 2 pt.	3 = 3 pt.	4 = 4 pt.	5 = 5 pt.
20.	1 = 5 pt.	2 = 4 pt.	3 = 3 pt.	4 = 2 pt.	5 = 1 pt.

APPENDIX D

Interview Guides

First Interview Guide (English)   **D-1**

Second Interview Guide—Hourly Staff (English)   **D-4**

Third Interview Guide—Hourly Staff (English)   **D-6**

Second Interview Guide—Coaching Staff (English)   **D-8**

Third Interview Guide—Coaching Staff (English)   **D-10**

First Interview Guide

Name: _____ Position: _____

Greeting. Small talk. "How did you hear of this job opening?" (Applicant response) "Before we get started, let me give you some idea of what I'd like to cover today. I want to review your background and experience so that we can decide whether we have opportunities in our organization that are suited to your talents and interests. So I'd like to hear about your jobs, education, interests, outside activities and anything else you'd like to tell me. After we have covered your background, I want to give you more information about our company and answer any questions you might have. OK?"

Y N ?

		Yes Response	No Response
Let's start with a few general questions.			
☐ ☐ ☐	**Did you complete this application by yourself or did someone help with it?**	Did it entirely by myself	Had help
☐ ☐ ☐	**If someone helped, with what areas? Why?**	Nobody helped, wanted a second opinion	Can't read or write well enough

We maintain a drug-free workplace. This means we do not permit our staff to use drugs, alcohol, or tobacco on the job.

☐ ☐ ☐	**How do you feel about that?**	Like the idea, agree with the idea	Argumentative or defensive reply

If you are offered this position, we may ask you take a physical examination at our expense.

☐ ☐ ☐	**How do you feel about that possibility?**	No problem	Argumentative or defensive reply

Thank you for that information. Now I'd like to shift gears. I'm interested in the jobs you've held and what you feel you may have gained from them. Let's start with a brief review of your early work experiences and then we'll look at your more recent jobs in more detail. What do you remember about your very first job?

☐ ☐ ☐	**What attracted you to this job in the first place?**	Work interested me, saw a future, opportunity to learn	Needed a job
☐ ☐ ☐	**In actuality, how did it turn out? What did you learn from it?**	Positive lesson learned, especially one that will help the company	No lesson learned

Where did you go from there? (Continue through all jobs up to the present. Look for recurring patterns. Vary the wording.)

☐ ☐ ☐	**In what ways did this job differ from the last one? In what ways was it the same?**	Answer that shows application of lesson learned in first job	Same situation as first job (if negative)
☐ ☐ ☐	**What was the best part of this job?**	Contribution, challenge, growth	It was easy, lots of time off
☐ ☐ ☐	**What did this job teach you?**	Positive lesson learned	No or negative lesson learned
☐ ☐ ☐	**What factors contributed to your decision to leave?**	Answer showing grasp of personal responsibility and professional curiosity	Answer that blames others or avoids personal responsibility

Y N ?		Yes Response	No Response

Now let's take a closer look at your last position.

Y N ?	Question	Yes Response	No Response
☐ ☐ ☐	**What attracted you to this job?**	Contribution, challenge, growth	Needed a job
☐ ☐ ☐	**What was the most difficult problem you faced on this job? How did you handle it? How did it work out?**	Answer that shows lessons learned and applied from past experience, compatible approach for your company	Answer that indicates past lessons were not learned or style inappropriate for your company
☐ ☐ ☐	**In this job, what types of decisions were beyond your authority?**	Decisions beyond those required by the position under consideration	Decisions similar to those required by the position under consideration
☐ ☐ ☐	**What event triggered your decision to start looking for another position?**	Nothing particular, company did not meet standards of professional excellence	Answer that shows anger or a repeat of previously noted patterns
☐ ☐ ☐	**Do you have a job now? If so, are you planning to keep it? Why?**	Have job, not planning to keep it, moving toward more responsibility	No job, planning to keep present job, moving away from problems
☐ ☐ ☐	**How will you establish priorities if there is a conflict between jobs?**	This job will take priority, no job conflicts to worry about	Depends on the situation, no idea of how priorities will be set
☐ ☐ ☐	**Which past job did you enjoy most? What made it the most enjoyable?**	Money, recognition, participation, chance to contribute, growth	Easiest work, no pressure, didn't enjoy past jobs at all
☐ ☐ ☐	**Of all your supervisors, who did you enjoy working for the most? Why?**	Good teacher, demanded my best, made work fun	No ideas, did my thinking for me, I didn't like any past supervisors

You have given me a good review of your work experience—now let's talk about your education. Why don't we start with high school briefly and then cover more recent schooling and any special training you may have had.

Y N ?	Question	Yes Response	No Response
☐ ☐ ☐	**What school subjects did you enjoy most? What made them enjoyable?**	Challenging, people-oriented	Easy
☐ ☐ ☐	**What part of your academic career was most difficult? Why?**	Teacher didn't care, I wasn't interested in the subject	Had other priorities, took too much work, other people got on my case
☐ ☐ ☐	**What was the best training you ever received? What made it the best?**	Animated, emotional response, specific programs	Intellectual response, vague or no details

Turning to the present, I'd like to give you the opportunity to mention some of your interests and activities outside of work—hobbies, what you do for fun and relaxation, and any community activities.

Y N ?	Question	Yes Response	No Response
☐ ☐ ☐	**How do you spend your spare time?**	Community activities, team sports	Vague or no answer
☐ ☐ ☐	**What have you learned from these spare-time activities?**	Teamwork, organization, attention to detail, any helpful lesson at all	Nothing, never thought about it, just do it to have fun

Y N ?		Yes Response	No Response
☐ ☐ ☐	**Given these commitments, how will you meet the job requirements?**	Reasonable solution that will work for the company	Vague answer, don't know

Now let's try to summarize our conversation. Thinking of all we've covered today, what would you say are some of your strengths—qualities both personal and professional that make you a good prospect for any employer?

☐ ☐ ☐	**Why would you be a good choice for this position?**	Positive sales pitch, specific reasons	Response that disparages others, no particular reason, vague reasons
☐ ☐ ☐	**What contribution do you most want to make to this organization?**	Specific, measurable answer	Generic answer, e.g., be a good employee
☐ ☐ ☐	**How long do you think it will take you to make this contribution?**	Specific time frame, will start immediately	

You've given me some real assets, and now I'd like to hear about areas you'd like to develop further—all of us have qualities that we'd like to change or improve.

☐ ☐ ☐	**What are some of your personal improvement goals?**	Answer that shows a contribution made and recognized	Vague or no answer
☐ ☐ ☐	**What do you see as some of your most pressing training needs?**	Specific answer that shows prior thought	Vague or off-the-cuff response, I don't need any more training

I appreciate your candor, and it has been very helpful in giving me an insight into what makes you tick. At this point, there is just one other question I'm curious about. (ASK WITH A STRAIGHT FACE)

☐ ☐ ☐	**What's the funniest thing that ever happened to you?**	Spontaneous smile, laugh, animated response, ability to laugh at self	Serious answer, no smile, no suggestion

You have given me a good review of your background, and I have enjoyed talking with you. Before we turn to my review of our organization, is there anything else about your background you would like to cover? (Get answer before continuing.) Do you have any *specific* questions or concerns before I tell you more about the company and the way we do things?

INTERVIEWER'S NOTES:

Source: *Swan's How to Pick the Right People Program* by William S. Swan, © 1989, pp. 117–118, by permission of John Wiley & Sons, NY, NY.

Second Interview Guide

HOURLY STAFF

Name: _____   Position: _____

Greeting. Small talk. "How did you happen to become interested in our company?" (Applicant response) "Before we start, I want you to know that this interview will be structured in a similar way to your last one. I want to look at your background and experience in a way that will help us determine how you see your role in the work force and whether a position with our company would be a good fit for both of us. After we have covered your background, I want to give you more specific information about the job and answer any questions you might have."

WILLINGNESS	Yes Response	No Response
Y N ?		
☐ ☐ ☐ This job starts at $____ per ____. How do you feel about the starting salary?	Answer that shows willingness to work their way up	Argumentative reply
☐ ☐ ☐ When the pressure of work is high, where does your energy come from?	Positive feedback from staff and guests, pride in doing a good job	Nervous energy, force of habit, I don't know
☐ ☐ ☐ Was there a time when unexpected events on the job demanded that you change your plans? Tell me about it.	Answer that reflects acceptance of occasional necessity to change plans	Answer that reflects resentment of imposition on personal time

APPROACH		
☐ ☐ ☐ How would you define a good work atmosphere?	Open, participative, respectful, friendly, fun, professional	Controlled, predictable, structured, I don't know
☐ ☐ ☐ How can you help establish and maintain it?	Set a good personal example, clear communication, help co-workers	Follow the rules, stay out of trouble
☐ ☐ ☐ It's not unusual to get really angry at a guest or co-worker. Everybody does it one time or another. Still, there is a big difference between something overt, like getting physical, and something like gently putting people in their place. How many times in the last six months have you felt it was necessary to get tough with a guest or co-worker? Tell me about the worst incident.	Getting rough or angry with someone is never an acceptable solution. Appropriate response given the circumstances of the incident	Answer that indicates that getting angry is a common occurrence or that the applicant really enjoyed putting people in their place

COACHABILITY		
☐ ☐ ☐ For what have you been most frequently criticized?	Answer that provides a personal insight into the person	Things that weren't my fault, answer that blames others
☐ ☐ ☐ What motivates you to do well?	Money, recognition, pride in work	Vague or no answer
☐ ☐ ☐ What can you teach your co-workers?	Specific, reasonable suggestions	Nothing, I don't know

PROFESSIONAL CURIOSITY		
☐ ☐ ☐ What is the most important job in the restaurant?	Pleasing the guest, my job	Intellectual response, I don't know

PROFESSIONAL CURIOSITY

Y N ?		**Yes Response**	**No Response**
☐ ☐ ☐	**Why do you feel that way?**	Restaurant fails if guests aren't happy, company suffers if I mess up	Intellectual response, vague answer, I don't know
☐ ☐ ☐	**What makes you think you have what it takes to succeed in this business?**	Hard worker, high standards, pride in work, enjoy doing a good job	I don't know, I'm always successful at what I do

STATUS

Y N ?		Yes Response	No Response
☐ ☐ ☐	**If you get several offers, how will you decide which company to work for?**	Opportunity to contribute, grow and participate, most financial potential	First offer I get, money (as an overriding concern)
☐ ☐ ☐	**What other types of positions have you applied for?**	Similar positions to the one applied for here	Anything I can find
☐ ☐ ☐	**What will cause you to accept one job over another?**	Responsibility, challenge, style of operation, opportunity to grow	First offer, money, benefits

INTERVIEWER'S NOTES:

Third Interview Guide

HOURLY STAFF

Name: _____ Position: _____

Greeting. Small talk. "What is your understanding of the position you're applying for?" (Applicant response) "Before we get started, I want you to know that this interview will be structured about the same as your first two. I want to look at your background and experience in a way that will help us determine your perspective on the industry and whether a position in our company would be a good fit for both of us. After we cover my questions, I want to give you more information on how we will go about filling the job and then I'd be happy to answer any questions you might have."

WILLINGNESS Y N ?	Yes Response	No Response
☐ ☐ ☐ If you were hiring a person for this job, what would you be looking for?	People-oriented, professionalism, hard worker	Generic answers, e.g., good worker
☐ ☐ ☐ How can I tell that you possess these qualities yourself?	Specific examples, ask my former employers or co-workers	I don't know
☐ ☐ ☐ Tell me about a time when you had to go beyond routine job requirements. How did you feel about it at the time? How do you feel about it now?	Specific example, animated response. Answer that shows acceptance of occasional necessity for extra work.	Can't think of anything. Answer that shows resentment of imposition on personal time.

APPROACH

☐ ☐ ☐ Tell me about a time when you and your boss disagreed on an approach to a problem and how you handled it.	Explained my reasoning, listened to other points of view, came to consensus on how to proceed	Shut up and said nothing, did it my way anyway, did it his or her way and it didn't work
☐ ☐ ☐ What most appeals to you about the restaurant business?	Animated response, interaction with people, lack of routine	Intellectual response, never thought about it, always worked in it
☐ ☐ ☐ What do you do when you get "in the weeds"? Give me an example.	Ask for help, stop and take a deep breath	Tough it out, work harder to catch up, get quiet, jump on co-workers

COACHABILITY

☐ ☐ ☐ Describe the ideal relationship between the supervisor and the staff.	Answer that shows mutual respect and support	One-sided answer
☐ ☐ ☐ Tell me about a policy at your last job that particularly annoyed you. Why?	Policy that interfered with guest service or professional performance	Policy that interfered with personal control
☐ ☐ ☐ What is the best way to "get through" to you?	Simple, direct, honest communication	I always listen, or complicated response

PROFESSIONAL CURIOSITY

☐ ☐ ☐ What are your two favorite restaurants? What makes them your favorites?	Clear answer, good operations, specific reasons, signature items	Mediocre operations, no favorites, vague answers

PROFESSIONAL CURIOSITY

Y N ?		**Yes Response**	**No Response**
☐ ☐ ☐	**What suggestions could you give them on how to do a better job?**	Specific, reasonable suggestions	None or vague suggestions
☐ ☐ ☐	**What have you done to become more effective in your position?**	Active pursuit, e.g., read trade magazines, take seminars, go to shows	Nothing. Passive pursuit, e.g., training imposed by others

STATUS

☐ ☐ ☐	**How does our company compare with the others you are talking with?**	Animated, emotional response that favors the company	As good as any, no opinion
☐ ☐ ☐	**Should you be offered this job, how long will it take you to decide?**	Specific time frame that fits with the organization's needs	Time frame that doesn't fit with the organization's needs

INTERVIEWER'S NOTES:

Second Interview Guide

COACHING STAFF

Name: _____   Position: _____

Greeting. Small talk. "How did you happen to become interested in our company?" (Applicant response) "Before we start, I want you to know that this interview will be structured in a similar way to your last one. I want to look at your background and experience in a way that will help us determine how you see your role in the work force and whether a position with our company would be a good fit for both of us. After we have covered your background, I want to give you more specific information about the job and answer any questions you might have."

WILLINGNESS Y N ?		Yes Response	No Response
☐ ☐ ☐	By what standards do you measure the results of your job?	Specific answers, repeat business, staff advancement	I just feel it
☐ ☐ ☐	How do you want to be remembered after you have left the company?	Specific contribution to growth of business and/or staff	Nice person, good worker
☐ ☐ ☐	Why do you think you will be remembered that way?	Specific examples	Vague answer
☐ ☐ ☐	Tell me about a time when unexpected events on the job demanded that you change plans or reschedule your time.	Answer that reflects acceptance of occasional necessity to change plans	Answer that reflects resentment of imposition on personal time
APPROACH			
☐ ☐ ☐	Tell me about one of your real successes as a manager.	People-related answer	Activity-related answer
☐ ☐ ☐	How would you define a good work atmosphere?	Open, participative, respectful, friendly, fun, professional	Controlled, predictable, structured
☐ ☐ ☐	How would you go about establishing and maintaining it?	Set good personal example, clear communication, involve staff	Define and enforce rules, cut no slack
☐ ☐ ☐	It's not unusual to get really angry at a guest or staff member. Everybody does at one time or another. Still, there is a big difference between something overt, like getting physical, and something like gently putting people in their place. How many times in the last six months have you felt it was necessary to get tough with a guest or staff member? Tell me about the worst incident.	Getting rough or angry with someone is never an acceptable solution; appropriate response given the circumstances of the incident	Answer that indicates that getting angry is a common occurrence or that the applicant really enjoyed putting people in their place
COACHABILITY			
☐ ☐ ☐	Tell me about a recent crisis. What caused it and how did you handle it?	Accept responsibility for problem and solution, no blame, no guilt	Blame others, take credit for fix
☐ ☐ ☐	What did you learn from it?	Positive lesson for the future, insight into personal effectiveness	Never do it again, no apparent lesson learned

COACHABILITY

Y N ?		**Yes Response**	**No Response**
☐ ☐ ☐	**How are you at taking direction?**	Other inputs help me stay on track	Don't like being told what to do
☐ ☐ ☐	**What motivates you to do well?**	Money, recognition, pride in my work	Making people happy, giving good service
☐ ☐ ☐	**What is the biggest single financial mistake you have made in your career? What did you learn from it?**	Answer that shows ability to accept mistakes, learn a positive lesson, and move on without guilt	Don't make mistakes, answer that shows fear of failure or guilt over past events

PROFESSIONAL CURIOSITY

☐ ☐ ☐	**What would you say is the most important job in the restaurant?**	Pleasing the guest, my job	Intellectual response
☐ ☐ ☐	**Why do you feel that way?**	Restaurant fails if guests aren't happy, company suffers if I mess up	Intellectual response, I don't know
☐ ☐ ☐	**What makes you think you have what it takes to be successful in this business?**	Hard worker, high standards, pride in work, enjoy doing a good job	I don't know, I'm always successful at what I do

STATUS

☐ ☐ ☐	**What other types of positions have you been considering?**	Similar positions to the one applied for here	Anything I can find
☐ ☐ ☐	**When do you expect to decide which job to take?**	Specific time frame that fits with the organization's needs	Short time frame
☐ ☐ ☐	**What will cause you to accept one job over another?**	Responsibility, challenge, style of operation, opportunity to grow	First offer, money, benefits

INTERVIEWER'S NOTES:

Third Interview Guide

COACHING STAFF

Name: _____   **Position:** _____

Greeting. Small talk. "What is your understanding of the position you're applying for?" (Applicant response) "Before we get started, I want you to know that this interview will be structured about the same as your first two. I want to look at your background and experience in a way that will help us determine your perspective on the industry and whether a position in our company would be a good fit for both of us. After we cover my questions, I want to give you more information on how we will go about filling the job and then I'd be happy to answer any questions you might have."

WILLINGNESS

Y N ?		Yes Response	No Response
☐ ☐ ☐	What do you see as the most important responsibilities of this job?	Results-oriented answers, serve the staff and guests	Procedure-related answers, serve food, cook food, etc.
☐ ☐ ☐	Why do you want to work here?	Learn something, do it right, make a contribution	Good pay, have fun, no particular reason, friends work here
☐ ☐ ☐	Tell me about a time when you showed initiative and willingness to go beyond routine job requirements.	Specific example, animated response	Can't think of anything
☐ ☐ ☐	How did you feel about it at the time? How do you feel about it now?	Answer that shows acceptance of occasional necessity for extra work	Answer that shows resentment of impositions on personal time

APPROACH

☐ ☐ ☐	To what do you attribute your professional success?	Good staff, focus on guest service, hard work, my own efforts	Ego-centered response, just lucky
☐ ☐ ☐	What do you do when your staff gets "in the weeds"? Give me an example.	Take the pressure off, direct traffic, calm them down	Push harder, kick butt
☐ ☐ ☐	Tell me about a time when you successfully motivated your staff to achieve a difficult goal.	Animated, emotional response that shows appreciation of the staff's efforts, reflects personal humility	Intellectual response that shows manipulation of others or self-importance
☐ ☐ ☐	What should the relationship be between the manager and the staff?	Partners, team-oriented answer	Structured relationship
☐ ☐ ☐	How would you go about establishing and maintaining that relationship?	Set a good example, ask and listen, involve staff in decisions	Be nice, enforce rules, be a good manager
☐ ☐ ☐	Describe the fiscal responsibility you held in your last job.	Clear, specific answers that show similar responsibility to this job	Vague response, responsibility for less than in this job
☐ ☐ ☐	What do you see as the differences between management and leadership?	Directing, manipulating vs. coaching, serving staff	They are the same, no thoughts

Y N ?		Yes Response	No Response

COACHABILITY

☐ ☐ ☐	If you were hiring a person for this job, what would you be looking for?	People-oriented, professionalism, good teacher	Generic answers, e.g., good manager
☐ ☐ ☐	How can I tell that you possess these qualities yourself?	Specific examples, ask my staff or former employers	I don't know
☐ ☐ ☐	What was the best training you ever received? What made it the best?	Animated, emotional response, specific programs	Intellectual response, vague or no details, I don't know
☐ ☐ ☐	What is the best way to "get through" to you?	Simple, direct, honest communication	I always listen or complicated response

PROFESSIONAL CURIOSITY

Y N ?			
☐ ☐ ☐	What appeals to you most about the restaurant business?	Animated, emotional response	Intellectual response
☐ ☐ ☐	What are your two favorite restaurants? What makes them favorites?	Clear, specific answers, names signature items	Slow response, good food, good service
☐ ☐ ☐	What suggestions could you give them on how to do a better job?	Clear, specific answers	No suggestions
☐ ☐ ☐	What have you done most recently to become more effective in your position?	Active pursuit, e.g., read trade magazines, take seminars, go to shows	Passive pursuit, e.g., training imposed by others

STATUS

☐ ☐ ☐	If you get several job offers, how will you decide which company to work for?	Opportunity to contribute, grow, and participate	First offer I get, money (as an overriding concern)
☐ ☐ ☐	How does our company compare with the others you are talking with?	Enthusiastic, emotional response that favors the company	As good as any, no opinion
☐ ☐ ☐	Should you be offered this job, how long will it take you to make a decision?	Specific time frame that fits with the organization's needs	Time frame that doesn't fit with the organization's needs

INTERVIEWER'S NOTES:

APPENDIX E

Coaching Staff Tests

Lifting Test (English)   E-1

Demonstration Test 1 (English)   E-2

Professional Test Answer Sheet (English)   E-7

Professional Test Answer Sheet (Spanish)   E-8

Professional Test Answer Sheet Overlay (English)   E-9

Professional Test (English)   E-10

Professional Test (Spanish)   E-27

Professional Test Answers (English)   E-44

Management Situations (English)   E-52

Management Situations (Spanish)   E-53

Situation Test Evaluation (English)   E-54

Demonstration Test 2 (English)   E-55

Demonstration Test 2 (Spanish)   E-56

Demonstration Test 2 Evaluation (English)   E-58

Lifting Test

COACHING STAFF

Name: _____ **Evaluated By:** _____

Procedure:

The candidate lifts the heaviest object likely to be encountered on the job from where it would normally be found to the most difficult location at which it could logically be placed. This is *not* a timed test.

Materials:

Select an item that has figured in on-the-job lifting injuries. Consider what tasks the person will typically perform in the position as well as situations likely to be encountered in the normal course of business while assisting co-workers.

Demonstration Specification:

Item to be lifted: _____ Weight: _____

Lift from: _____

Lift to: _____

Evaluation Criteria:

Y N ?

- ☐ ☐ ☐ 1. Could the candidate lift the object?
- ☐ ☐ ☐ 2. Did the lift show lack of strain?
- ☐ ☐ ☐ 3. Did the candidate lift with a straight back?
- ☐ ☐ ☐ 4. Did the candidate lift with the legs?
- ☐ ☐ ☐ 5. Did the candidate keep the load close to the body?
- ☐ ☐ ☐ 6. Did the candidate use a proper ladder or stool (if appropriate)?
- ☐ ☐ ☐ 7. Was the object safely under control at all times?
- ☐ ☐ ☐ 8. Was the candidate alert to the physical surroundings during the lift?
- ☐ ☐ ☐ 9. Did the final placement of the object allow for proper air circulation?
- ☐ ☐ ☐ 10. Did the candidate handle the object with care and respect?

Scoring:

Grade each evaluation criterion as it is observed (Y—Yes, N—No, ?—Maybe).
Give two points for each Y, one point for each ?, and no points for N.
If use of a ladder or stool was not appropriate, score Item 6 as Y.
If Item 1 is marked N, the overall evaluation must be No.
If Item 1 is marked ?, the overall evaluation must be Maybe.
If Item 2 is marked N or ?, the overall evaluation must be Maybe.
A score of 16 or better means an overall evaluation of Yes.
A score of 10 to 15 means an overall evaluation of Maybe.
A score of 9 or below means an overall evaluation of No.

Total Score:

_____

OVERALL EVALUATION:

☐ Yes
☐ No
☐ Maybe

Demonstration Test 1

COACHING STAFF

Name: **Evaluated By:**

INVOICE TEST

Procedure:

The candidate is put in the position of a restaurant General Manager and receives four invoices to review and approve for payment. The math on this test is fairly basic, and you may or may not want the candidate to use a calculator. **If you allow one candidate to use a calculator, you must allow all of them to use one.** This is a timed test.

Materials:

Sample invoices.

Evaluation Criteria:

Y N ?

☐ ☐ ☐   1. Did the candidate note that the vodka was listed as three bottles and charged as three cases on Invoice 1?

☐ ☐ ☐   2. Did the candidate correct the total on Invoice 1 to $571.35?

☐ ☐ ☐   3. Did the candidate correct the extension of the tomato paste to $77.72 on Invoice 2?

☐ ☐ ☐   4. Did the candidate correct the extension of the butter to $35.28 on Invoice 2?

☐ ☐ ☐   5. Did the candidate correct the total on Invoice 2 to 314.63?

☐ ☐ ☐   6. Did the candidate note that Invoice 3 belongs to another restaurant?

☐ ☐ ☐   7. Did the candidate note that the top round order was received at $2.57 per pound (Invoice 2) and credited at $2.75 per pound?

☐ ☐ ☐   8. Did the candidate correct the total on Invoice 4 to $52.14?

☐ ☐ ☐   9. Was the test completed efficiently?

☐ ☐ ☐ 10. Were the corrections legible?

Scoring:

Grade each evaluation criterion as it is observed (Y—Yes, N—No, ?—Maybe).
Give two points for each Y, one point for each ?, and no points for N.
A score of 16 or better means an overall evaluation of Yes.
A score of 10 to 15 means an overall evaluation of Maybe.
A score of 9 or below means an overall evaluation of No.

Total Score:

_____

Elapsed Time:

_____

OVERALL EVALUATION:

☐ Yes
☐ No
☐ Maybe

INVOICE #1

M&M DISTRIBUTING
WHOLESALE LIQUOR DISTRIBUTION
PO Box 332 · Lake Edna, CO 80333 · (719) 555-7667

INVOICE NO. **003717**

SOLD TO:

La Maison de Casa House

1776 Independence Highway

Lake Edna, CO 80333

| ACCOUNT NO: 0233 | DATE: February 12, 1993 |

	NO.	UNIT	SIZE	ITEM	PRICE	TOTAL
✓	2	cs	750ml	Jim Beam	81.10	$162.20
✓	3	ea	750ml	Gordon's Vodka	58.20	176.40
✓	2	cs	1L	Bombay Gin	139.90	279.80
✓	4	ea	1L	Remy Martin VSOP	28.70	114.80
RECEIVED BY: A. Packer				PLEASE PAY THIS AMOUNT ☞		$735.20

INVOICE #2

ROCKY MOUNTAIN WAREHOUSE
INSTITUTIONAL GROCERY & SUPPLY
PO Box 1212 · Mt. Cayuga, CO 80341 · (719) 555-1439

INVOICE NO. **N-3003**

SOLD TO:

La Maison de Casa House

1776 Independence Highway

Lake Edna, CO 80333

ACCOUNT NO: 13-447   DATE: February 12, 1993

	NO.	UNIT	SIZE/PACK	ITEM	PRICE	TOTAL
✓	4	cs	6/10	Tomato Paste, Mama Mia	19.43	$ 76.72
✓	2	cs	12/49	Beef Stock, Brown Cow	30.14	60.28
✓	24		lb.	Butter, Block, Clancy's	1.47	33.08
✓	55		lb.	Top Round, USDA Choice, fresh	2.57	141.35
					PLEASE PAY THIS AMOUNT ☞	$311.43

RECEIVED BY: A. Packer

INVOICE #3

FRONT RANGE RESTAURANT SUPPLY
Serving the Hospitality Industry since 1966
44736 Arapahoe Road · Sitzmark Springs, CO 80347 · (719) 555-4594

INVOICE NO. **43843**

SOLD TO:

Harry's House of Hash

1786 Independence Highway

Lake Edna, CO 80333

ACCOUNT NO: 0404   DATE: February 12, 1993

	NO.	UNIT	SIZE/PACK	ITEM	PRICE	TOTAL
✓	3	ea	14"	Wire Whip, French, SS, #115-427	4.69	$ 14.07
✓	2	cs	10½"	Dinner Plate, white, #823-028	67.40	124.80
✓	2	cs	2½ oz.	Ramekin, brown, #110-042	19.33	38.66
✓	5	ea		Thermometer, Pocket Dial, #830-003	4.88	24.40

RECEIVED BY: A. Pickard

PLEASE PAY THIS AMOUNT ☞ | $201.93

Name: _____

INVOICE #4

ROCKY MOUNTAIN WAREHOUSE
INSTITUTIONAL GROCERY & SUPPLY
PO Box 1212 · Mt. Cayuga, CO 80341 · (719) 555-1439

INVOICE NO. **C-0213**

SOLD TO:
La Maison de Casa House
1776 Independence Highway
Lake Edna, CO 80333

ACCOUNT NO: 13-447	DATE: February 12, 1993
ORIGINAL INVOICE NO: N-3003	

CREDIT MEMO

	NO.	UNIT	SIZE/PACK	ITEM	PRICE	TOTAL
✓	18		lb.	Top Round, USDA Choice, fresh	2.75	$49.50
✓	4	ea	lb.	Butter, Block, Clancy's	1.47	5.88
ISSUED BY: James Brown #312					**PLEASE PAY THIS AMOUNT** ☞	$55.38

Professional Test

COACHING STAFF
Answer Sheet

NAME: _____   SSN: _____

This test is designed to indicate how you view the restaurant industry. As a result, you will find that several questions may have more than one correct answer. Check the single answer you think is *MOST CORRECT* based on your point of view. Time is of the essence. The faster you complete the test, the better your index score.

HUMAN REL	OPERATIONS	OPERATIONS	FINANCIAL	MARKETING
A B C D E	A B C D E	A B C D E	A B C D E	A B C D E
1. ☐ ☐ ☐ ☐ ☐	31. ☐ ☐ ☐ ☐ ☐	61. ☐ ☐ ☐ ☐ ☐	91. ☐ ☐ ☐ ☐ ☐	121. ☐ ☐ ☐ ☐ ☐
2. ☐ ☐ ☐ ☐ ☐	32. ☐ ☐ ☐ ☐ ☐	62. ☐ ☐ ☐ ☐ ☐	92. ☐ ☐ ☐ ☐ ☐	122. ☐ ☐ ☐ ☐ ☐
3. ☐ ☐ ☐ ☐ ☐	33. ☐ ☐ ☐ ☐ ☐	63. ☐ ☐ ☐ ☐ ☐	93. ☐ ☐ ☐ ☐ ☐	123. ☐ ☐ ☐ ☐ ☐
4. ☐ ☐ ☐ ☐ ☐	34. ☐ ☐ ☐ ☐ ☐	64. ☐ ☐ ☐ ☐ ☐	94. ☐ ☐ ☐ ☐ ☐	124. ☐ ☐ ☐ ☐ ☐
5. ☐ ☐ ☐ ☐ ☐	35. ☐ ☐ ☐ ☐ ☐	65. ☐ ☐ ☐ ☐ ☐	95. ☐ ☐ ☐ ☐ ☐	125. ☐ ☐ ☐ ☐ ☐
6. ☐ ☐ ☐ ☐ ☐	36. ☐ ☐ ☐ ☐ ☐	66. ☐ ☐ ☐ ☐ ☐	96. ☐ ☐ ☐ ☐ ☐	126. ☐ ☐ ☐ ☐ ☐
7. ☐ ☐ ☐ ☐ ☐	37. ☐ ☐ ☐ ☐ ☐	67. ☐ ☐ ☐ ☐ ☐	97. ☐ ☐ ☐ ☐ ☐	127. ☐ ☐ ☐ ☐ ☐
8. ☐ ☐ ☐ ☐ ☐	38. ☐ ☐ ☐ ☐ ☐	68. ☐ ☐ ☐ ☐ ☐	98. ☐ ☐ ☐ ☐ ☐	128. ☐ ☐ ☐ ☐ ☐
9. ☐ ☐ ☐ ☐ ☐	39. ☐ ☐ ☐ ☐ ☐	69. ☐ ☐ ☐ ☐ ☐	99. ☐ ☐ ☐ ☐ ☐	129. ☐ ☐ ☐ ☐ ☐
10. ☐ ☐ ☐ ☐ ☐	40. ☐ ☐ ☐ ☐ ☐	70. ☐ ☐ ☐ ☐ ☐	100. ☐ ☐ ☐ ☐ ☐	130. ☐ ☐ ☐ ☐ ☐
11. ☐ ☐ ☐ ☐ ☐	41. ☐ ☐ ☐ ☐ ☐		101. ☐ ☐ ☐ ☐ ☐	
12. ☐ ☐ ☐ ☐ ☐	42. ☐ ☐ ☐ ☐ ☐	**APPROACH**	102. ☐ ☐ ☐ ☐ ☐	**ALCOHOL**
13. ☐ ☐ ☐ ☐ ☐	43. ☐ ☐ ☐ ☐ ☐	A B C D E	103. ☐ ☐ ☐ ☐ ☐	131. ☐ ☐ ☐ ☐ ☐
14. ☐ ☐ ☐ ☐ ☐	44. ☐ ☐ ☐ ☐ ☐	71. ☐ ☐ ☐ ☐ ☐	104. ☐ ☐ ☐ ☐ ☐	132. ☐ ☐ ☐ ☐ ☐
15. ☐ ☐ ☐ ☐ ☐	45. ☐ ☐ ☐ ☐ ☐	72. ☐ ☐ ☐ ☐ ☐	105. ☐ ☐ ☐ ☐ ☐	133. ☐ ☐ ☐ ☐ ☐
16. ☐ ☐ ☐ ☐ ☐	46. ☐ ☐ ☐ ☐ ☐	73. ☐ ☐ ☐ ☐ ☐	106. ☐ ☐ ☐ ☐ ☐	134. ☐ ☐ ☐ ☐ ☐
17. ☐ ☐ ☐ ☐ ☐	47. ☐ ☐ ☐ ☐ ☐	74. ☐ ☐ ☐ ☐ ☐	107. ☐ ☐ ☐ ☐ ☐	135. ☐ ☐ ☐ ☐ ☐
18. ☐ ☐ ☐ ☐ ☐	48. ☐ ☐ ☐ ☐ ☐	75. ☐ ☐ ☐ ☐ ☐	108. ☐ ☐ ☐ ☐ ☐	136. ☐ ☐ ☐ ☐ ☐
19. ☐ ☐ ☐ ☐ ☐	49. ☐ ☐ ☐ ☐ ☐	76. ☐ ☐ ☐ ☐ ☐	109. ☐ ☐ ☐ ☐ ☐	137. ☐ ☐ ☐ ☐ ☐
20. ☐ ☐ ☐ ☐ ☐	50. ☐ ☐ ☐ ☐ ☐	77. ☐ ☐ ☐ ☐ ☐	110. ☐ ☐ ☐ ☐ ☐	138. ☐ ☐ ☐ ☐ ☐
21. ☐ ☐ ☐ ☐ ☐	51. ☐ ☐ ☐ ☐ ☐	78. ☐ ☐ ☐ ☐ ☐	111. ☐ ☐ ☐ ☐ ☐	139. ☐ ☐ ☐ ☐ ☐
22. ☐ ☐ ☐ ☐ ☐	52. ☐ ☐ ☐ ☐ ☐	79. ☐ ☐ ☐ ☐ ☐	112. ☐ ☐ ☐ ☐ ☐	140. ☐ ☐ ☐ ☐ ☐
23. ☐ ☐ ☐ ☐ ☐	53. ☐ ☐ ☐ ☐ ☐	80. ☐ ☐ ☐ ☐ ☐	113. ☐ ☐ ☐ ☐ ☐	T F
24. ☐ ☐ ☐ ☐ ☐	54. ☐ ☐ ☐ ☐ ☐	81. ☐ ☐ ☐ ☐ ☐	114. ☐ ☐ ☐ ☐ ☐	141. ☐ ☐
25. ☐ ☐ ☐ ☐ ☐	55. ☐ ☐ ☐ ☐ ☐	82. ☐ ☐ ☐ ☐ ☐	115. ☐ ☐ ☐ ☐ ☐	142. ☐ ☐
26. ☐ ☐ ☐ ☐ ☐	56. ☐ ☐ ☐ ☐ ☐	83. ☐ ☐ ☐ ☐ ☐	116. ☐ ☐ ☐ ☐ ☐	143. ☐ ☐
27. ☐ ☐ ☐ ☐ ☐	57. ☐ ☐ ☐ ☐ ☐	84. ☐ ☐ ☐ ☐ ☐	117. ☐ ☐ ☐ ☐ ☐	144. ☐ ☐
28. ☐ ☐ ☐ ☐ ☐	58. ☐ ☐ ☐ ☐ ☐	85. ☐ ☐ ☐ ☐ ☐	118. ☐ ☐ ☐ ☐ ☐	145. ☐ ☐
29. ☐ ☐ ☐ ☐ ☐	59. ☐ ☐ ☐ ☐ ☐	86. ☐ ☐ ☐ ☐ ☐	119. ☐ ☐ ☐ ☐ ☐	146. ☐ ☐
30. ☐ ☐ ☐ ☐ ☐	60. ☐ ☐ ☐ ☐ ☐	87. ☐ ☐ ☐ ☐ ☐	120. ☐ ☐ ☐ ☐ ☐	147. ☐ ☐
		88. ☐ ☐ ☐ ☐ ☐		148. ☐ ☐
		89. ☐ ☐ ☐ ☐ ☐		149. ☐ ☐
		90. ☐ ☐ ☐ ☐ ☐		150. ☐ ☐

FOR OFFICE USE:

HR:_____ OPS:_____ APP:_____ FIN:_____ MKT:_____ ALC:_____ TOT:_____ TIME:_____ INDEX:_____

Examen Profesional

ENTRENAMIENTO DEL EQUIPO TÉCNICO
Hoja de Respuestas

NOMBRE: **NÚMERO DE SEGURIDAD SOCIAL:**

Esta prueba está diseñada para formar una opinión de cómo usted ve a la industria de los restaurantes. Por lo tanto, usted encontrará que varias preguntas pueden tener más de una respuesta correcta. Marque solamente la respuesta que usted crea sea más correcta basándolo en su punto de vista personal. El tiempo es esencial. Entre más rápido complete usted la prueba, mejor será su puntuación.

REL HUMANAS	OPERACIONES	OPERACIONES	FINANZAS	MERCADEO
A B C D E	A B C D E	A B C D E	A B C D E	A B C D E
1. ☐ ☐ ☐ ☐ ☐	31. ☐ ☐ ☐ ☐ ☐	61. ☐ ☐ ☐ ☐ ☐	91. ☐ ☐ ☐ ☐ ☐	121. ☐ ☐ ☐ ☐ ☐
2. ☐ ☐ ☐ ☐ ☐	32. ☐ ☐ ☐ ☐ ☐	62. ☐ ☐ ☐ ☐ ☐	92. ☐ ☐ ☐ ☐ ☐	122. ☐ ☐ ☐ ☐ ☐
3. ☐ ☐ ☐ ☐ ☐	33. ☐ ☐ ☐ ☐ ☐	63. ☐ ☐ ☐ ☐ ☐	93. ☐ ☐ ☐ ☐ ☐	123. ☐ ☐ ☐ ☐ ☐
4. ☐ ☐ ☐ ☐ ☐	34. ☐ ☐ ☐ ☐ ☐	64. ☐ ☐ ☐ ☐ ☐	94. ☐ ☐ ☐ ☐ ☐	124. ☐ ☐ ☐ ☐ ☐
5. ☐ ☐ ☐ ☐ ☐	35. ☐ ☐ ☐ ☐ ☐	65. ☐ ☐ ☐ ☐ ☐	95. ☐ ☐ ☐ ☐ ☐	125. ☐ ☐ ☐ ☐ ☐
6. ☐ ☐ ☐ ☐ ☐	36. ☐ ☐ ☐ ☐ ☐	66. ☐ ☐ ☐ ☐ ☐	96. ☐ ☐ ☐ ☐ ☐	126. ☐ ☐ ☐ ☐ ☐
7. ☐ ☐ ☐ ☐ ☐	37. ☐ ☐ ☐ ☐ ☐	67. ☐ ☐ ☐ ☐ ☐	97. ☐ ☐ ☐ ☐ ☐	127. ☐ ☐ ☐ ☐ ☐
8. ☐ ☐ ☐ ☐ ☐	38. ☐ ☐ ☐ ☐ ☐	68. ☐ ☐ ☐ ☐ ☐	98. ☐ ☐ ☐ ☐ ☐	128. ☐ ☐ ☐ ☐ ☐
9. ☐ ☐ ☐ ☐ ☐	39. ☐ ☐ ☐ ☐ ☐	69. ☐ ☐ ☐ ☐ ☐	99. ☐ ☐ ☐ ☐ ☐	129. ☐ ☐ ☐ ☐ ☐
10. ☐ ☐ ☐ ☐ ☐	40. ☐ ☐ ☐ ☐ ☐	70. ☐ ☐ ☐ ☐ ☐	100. ☐ ☐ ☐ ☐ ☐	130. ☐ ☐ ☐ ☐ ☐
11. ☐ ☐ ☐ ☐ ☐	41. ☐ ☐ ☐ ☐ ☐		101. ☐ ☐ ☐ ☐ ☐	
12. ☐ ☐ ☐ ☐ ☐	42. ☐ ☐ ☐ ☐ ☐	**MÉTODO**	102. ☐ ☐ ☐ ☐ ☐	**ALCOHOL**
13. ☐ ☐ ☐ ☐ ☐	43. ☐ ☐ ☐ ☐ ☐	A B C D E	103. ☐ ☐ ☐ ☐ ☐	131. ☐ ☐ ☐ ☐ ☐
14. ☐ ☐ ☐ ☐ ☐	44. ☐ ☐ ☐ ☐ ☐	71. ☐ ☐ ☐ ☐ ☐	104. ☐ ☐ ☐ ☐ ☐	132. ☐ ☐ ☐ ☐ ☐
15. ☐ ☐ ☐ ☐ ☐	45. ☐ ☐ ☐ ☐ ☐	72. ☐ ☐ ☐ ☐ ☐	105. ☐ ☐ ☐ ☐ ☐	133. ☐ ☐ ☐ ☐ ☐
16. ☐ ☐ ☐ ☐ ☐	46. ☐ ☐ ☐ ☐ ☐	73. ☐ ☐ ☐ ☐ ☐	106. ☐ ☐ ☐ ☐ ☐	134. ☐ ☐ ☐ ☐ ☐
17. ☐ ☐ ☐ ☐ ☐	47. ☐ ☐ ☐ ☐ ☐	74. ☐ ☐ ☐ ☐ ☐	107. ☐ ☐ ☐ ☐ ☐	135. ☐ ☐ ☐ ☐ ☐
18. ☐ ☐ ☐ ☐ ☐	48. ☐ ☐ ☐ ☐ ☐	75. ☐ ☐ ☐ ☐ ☐	108. ☐ ☐ ☐ ☐ ☐	136. ☐ ☐ ☐ ☐ ☐
19. ☐ ☐ ☐ ☐ ☐	49. ☐ ☐ ☐ ☐ ☐	76. ☐ ☐ ☐ ☐ ☐	109. ☐ ☐ ☐ ☐ ☐	137. ☐ ☐ ☐ ☐ ☐
20. ☐ ☐ ☐ ☐ ☐	50. ☐ ☐ ☐ ☐ ☐	77. ☐ ☐ ☐ ☐ ☐	110. ☐ ☐ ☐ ☐ ☐	138. ☐ ☐ ☐ ☐ ☐
21. ☐ ☐ ☐ ☐ ☐	51. ☐ ☐ ☐ ☐ ☐	78. ☐ ☐ ☐ ☐ ☐	111. ☐ ☐ ☐ ☐ ☐	139. ☐ ☐ ☐ ☐ ☐
22. ☐ ☐ ☐ ☐ ☐	52. ☐ ☐ ☐ ☐ ☐	79. ☐ ☐ ☐ ☐ ☐	112. ☐ ☐ ☐ ☐ ☐	140. ☐ ☐ ☐ ☐ ☐
23. ☐ ☐ ☐ ☐ ☐	53. ☐ ☐ ☐ ☐ ☐	80. ☐ ☐ ☐ ☐ ☐	113. ☐ ☐ ☐ ☐ ☐	V F
24. ☐ ☐ ☐ ☐ ☐	54. ☐ ☐ ☐ ☐ ☐	81. ☐ ☐ ☐ ☐ ☐	114. ☐ ☐ ☐ ☐ ☐	141. ☐ ☐
25. ☐ ☐ ☐ ☐ ☐	55. ☐ ☐ ☐ ☐ ☐	82. ☐ ☐ ☐ ☐ ☐	115. ☐ ☐ ☐ ☐ ☐	142. ☐ ☐
26. ☐ ☐ ☐ ☐ ☐	56. ☐ ☐ ☐ ☐ ☐	83. ☐ ☐ ☐ ☐ ☐	116. ☐ ☐ ☐ ☐ ☐	143. ☐ ☐
27. ☐ ☐ ☐ ☐ ☐	57. ☐ ☐ ☐ ☐ ☐	84. ☐ ☐ ☐ ☐ ☐	117. ☐ ☐ ☐ ☐ ☐	144. ☐ ☐
28. ☐ ☐ ☐ ☐ ☐	58. ☐ ☐ ☐ ☐ ☐	85. ☐ ☐ ☐ ☐ ☐	118. ☐ ☐ ☐ ☐ ☐	145. ☐ ☐
29. ☐ ☐ ☐ ☐ ☐	59. ☐ ☐ ☐ ☐ ☐	86. ☐ ☐ ☐ ☐ ☐	119. ☐ ☐ ☐ ☐ ☐	146. ☐ ☐
30. ☐ ☐ ☐ ☐ ☐	60. ☐ ☐ ☐ ☐ ☐	87. ☐ ☐ ☐ ☐ ☐	120. ☐ ☐ ☐ ☐ ☐	147. ☐ ☐
		88. ☐ ☐ ☐ ☐ ☐		148. ☐ ☐
		89. ☐ ☐ ☐ ☐ ☐		149. ☐ ☐
		90. ☐ ☐ ☐ ☐ ☐		150. ☐ ☐

FOR OFFICE USE:

HR:_____ OPS:_____ APP:_____ FIN:_____ MKT:_____ ALC:_____ TOT:_____ TIME:_____ INDEX:_____

Professional Test

COACHING STAFF
Answer Sheet Overlay

NOTE: To save time when grading the Professional Test, make a copy of this sheet on clear transparency film and lay it over the candidate's completed test. This should enable you to easily note the number of questions marked correctly and incorrectly. You can then simply transfer the score to the blocks at the bottom of the answer sheet. The answer sheet and test are not returned to the applicant, so it is your choice whether to physically mark the answer to a specific question as correct or incorrect.

HUMAN REL

#	Answer
1	D
2	A
3	E
4	E
5	C
6	C
7	D
8	B
9	D
10	A
11	E
12	B
13	A
14	C
15	D
16	C
17	A
18	C
19	B
20	A
21	B
22	C
23	D
24	A
25	E
26	B
27	B
28	A
29	D
30	D

OPERATIONS

#	Answer
31	E
32	D
33	C
34	A
35	D
36	A
37	C
38	A
39	B
40	C
41	B
42	E
43	C
44	E
45	E
46	A
47	D
48	C
49	A
50	D
51	C
52	B
53	C
54	A
55	B
56	C
57	D
58	C
59	B
60	E

OPERATIONS

#	Answer
61	D
62	B
63	C
64	B
65	E
66	B
67	D
68	B
69	C
70	E

APPROACH

#	Answer
71	B
72	E
73	C
74	C
75	D
76	E
77	A
78	E
79	E
80	B
81	B
82	D
83	A
84	C
85	E
86	D
87	D
88	D
89	B
90	C

FINANCIAL

#	Answer
91	A
92	C
93	A
94	C
95	B
96	D
97	E
98	C
99	A
100	D
101	E
102	B
103	A
104	C
105	D
106	A
107	A
108	B
109	D
110	C
111	E
112	C
113	C
114	B
115	D
116	B
117	E
118	B
119	B
120	C

MARKETING

#	Answer
121	D
122	B
123	A
124	E
125	A
126	C
127	A
128	C
129	C
130	B

ALCOHOL

#	Answer
131	C
132	B
133	C
134	A
135	A
136	A
137	A
138	E
139	E
140	B

#	T/F
141	T
142	T
143	F
144	F
145	F
146	F
147	T
148	T
149	F
150	F

Professional Test

COACHING STAFF

Pick the *MOST CORRECT* answer and mark your choice on the answer sheet. Please do not write on this test.

HUMAN RELATIONS

1. **Where would you start looking when you need to fill a vacancy?**
   A. Newspaper want-ad respondents.
   B. Staff of competing restaurants.
   C. Walk-in applicants.
   D. Existing staff.
   E. Employment agencies.

2. **Which of the following would you say is the most important step in developing a quality staff?**
   A. Hiring.
   B. Orientation.
   C. Training.
   D. Coaching.
   E. Discipline.

3. **Under equal employment opportunity laws, what can you require of servers?**
   A. That they have never been in trouble with the law.
   B. That they be female.
   C. That they be under 26 years old.
   D. That they be citizens of the United States.
   E. That they be efficient and friendly.

4. **When is the best time to look for potential staff members?**
   A. Around school holidays.
   B. Just before peak business periods.
   C. When vacancies are about to open up.
   D. On a regular schedule throughout the year.
   E. All the time.

5. **What is the main goal of a staff orientation program?**
   A. To establish a system of discipline and rewards for the staff.
   B. To establish a training plan and method for evaluating progress.
   C. To communicate information and create a positive response to the company and the job.
   D. To assess the reaction of other workers to the new worker and finish job testing.
   E. To let new workers know who is the boss.

6. **Which method of training would you use when teaching servers suggestive selling?**
   A. Written instructions.
   B. Classroom training.
   C. Role-playing.
   D. On-the-job instruction.
   E. None of the above.

7. **Which method of training would you use when showing someone how to clean a piece of equipment?**
   A. Written instructions.
   B. Classroom training
   C. Role-playing.
   D. On-the-job instruction.
   E. None of the above.

8. **Which method of training would you use when trying to pass along new ideas to a group?**
   A. Written instructions.
   B. Classroom training.
   C. Role-playing.
   D. On-the-job instruction.
   E. None of the above.

9. **Who do you think makes the most effective trainer for operational subjects?**
    A. An outside consultant.
    B. The General Manager.
    C. The department supervisor.
    D. A skilled co-worker.
    E. A company training director.

10. **What do you think your staff wants most from their jobs?**
    A. Appreciation for the work they do.
    B. Higher wages.
    C. Being "in" on things.
    D. Health insurance and benefits.
    E. Job security.

11. **In your experience, which statement is true about working with minorities?**
    A. They must be treated a little differently from other workers.
    B. They can be more difficult to motivate than other workers.
    C. It is more difficult to know what they really want from you.
    D. They tend to be less productive than other workers.
    E. They are no different from anyone else.

12. **Where does the primary responsibility lie for high staff turnover in restaurants?**
    A. With the individual workers involved.
    B. With the management of the restaurant.
    C. With the rate of pay in restaurants.
    D. With prevailing values in our society.
    E. With increased competition from other industries.

13. **How do you bring out the best in your crew?**
    A. Set a personal example that reflects everything you expect of your staff.
    B. Set high standards and manage your crew's activities.
    C. Develop standard procedures in all major areas.
    D. Conduct extensive and consistent skill training for all positions.

14. **As a restaurant manager, what is the fastest way to advance your career?**
    A. Do personal favors for the owners.
    B. Stand out from the competition.
    C. Take classes and attend seminars.
    D. Teach your subordinates how to do your job.
    E. Make sure you get the credit when things go well.

15. **It is going to be a busy Saturday night. One of your service staff reports for work at 4:00 P.M. in a clean but wrinkled uniform. How would you handle it?**
    A. Assign him to his regular station.
    B. Assign him to a station in the back of the dining room.
    C. Send him home to press the uniform before allowing him to go on the clock.
    D. Have him work in the kitchen, out of sight of the guests.
    E. Send him home without pay.

16. **It is going to be a busy Saturday night. One of your service staff reports for work at 5:30 P.M. in a clean but wrinkled uniform. How would you handle it?**
    A. Assign her to her regular station.
    B. Assign her to a station in the back of the dining room.
    C. Send her home to press the uniform before allowing her to go on the clock.
    D. Have her work in the kitchen, out of sight of the guests.
    E. Send her home without pay.

17. **What would you consider to be a mistake when giving a performance appraisal review?**
    A. Focusing on the mistakes a worker has made.
    B. Having workers set their own improvement goals.
    C. Encouraging staff to rate themselves.
    D. Allowing staff to comment on their evaluation.
    E. Changing a grade after discussion with the worker.

18. **When there are several candidates for a vacancy, whom do you hire?**
    A. The one with the best looks.
    B. The one who most needs the job.
    C. The most qualified person.
    D. The one likely to stay the longest.
    E. The one with the most experience.

You have noticed an operational problem that must be addressed immediately. The answer is not immediately obvious to you. Whatever the solution, it promises to be a major change that will affect most of your staff.

19. **How would you determine the most appropriate response to the problem?**
    A. Study the situation and develop your own plan.
    B. Hold a general staff meeting to reach consensus on what to do.
    C. Call in a consultant.
    D. Talk it over with your supervisors.
    E. Do nothing and see if the problem goes away.

20. **How would you proceed?**
    A. Be sure that everyone is trained to deal with the change before implementation.
    B. Select two or three peer leaders and train them to deal with the change.
    C. Implement the change, see what problems come up, and then deal with them promptly.
    D. Instruct each staff member on the principles of adapting to change.
    E. Implement the change as quickly as possible.

21. **How do you minimize resistance from your staff?**
    A. Dismiss those workers who do not cooperate.
    B. Involve the staff in the planning and implementation process.
    C. Be firm about it and don't give dissention a chance to start.
    D. Allow your staff to get used to the change before asking for their comments.
    E. Hold a staff meeting and explain why the change needed to be made.

22. **Which of the following is an example of proper delegation of responsibility?**
    A. The bartender tells the cook to prepare more food for the happy hour buffet.
    B. The kitchen manager tells an assistant cook to fire the dishwasher.
    C. The dining room manager tells a server to rearrange the table settings.
    D. The cook tells the manager that the refrigeration is not working properly.
    E. The greeter takes a drink order when the server is busy.

23. **What is the best thing to do when you have to give an unfavorable performance review?**
    A. Apologize and be sympathetic.
    B. Terminate the person immediately.
    C. Offer the person a different position.
    D. Set specific improvement goals with the person.
    E. Make sure the person understands his personal failings.

24. **What would you do when you are forced to terminate a member of your staff?**
    A. Be sure you have counseled the individual and documented your warnings in writing.
    B. Work your way around to the subject gradually.
    C. Offer to provide a good recommendation and help the person find another job.
    D. Call your attorney.
    E. All of the above.

25. **What is the best measure of a supervisor's effectiveness?**
    A. Work skills.
    B. Health department scores.
    C. Profitability.
    D. Average check.
    E. Staff development.

26. **What is your goal when creating a staff schedule?**
    A. To minimize labor cost.
    B. To ensure a high level of guest service.
    C. To match the labor schedule to the budget.

D. To distribute the available hours equitably among the staff.

E. To accommodate the special requests of the workers.

27. What would you do with a newly completed staff schedule?

A. Circulate it on the first day of the new work period.

B. Post it a week prior to the new work period.

C. Finalize it so no further revisions are necessary.

D. Place it in your files for future reference.

E. Bring it up for approval at a staff meeting.

28. It is mid-March and one of your staff asks you for the Mother's Day weekend off. It seems his twin sister is getting married on that May weekend and has asked him to be part of the wedding party. Mother's Day is traditionally one of the busiest and most hectic days of the year in your restaurant. What do you do?

A. Give him the weekend off and rework the schedule.

B. Explain that Mother's Day is too busy and you cannot allow him to go.

C. Tell him you will do the best you can to accommodate his request.

D. Tell him he must find a replacement to work for him that weekend.

E. It depends on how good a worker he is.

29. It is mid-November and one of your staff asks you for Thanksgiving Day off. Thanksgiving is usually a busy day in the restaurant. What do you do?

A. Give her the day off and rework the schedule.

B. Explain that Thanksgiving Day is too busy and you cannot allow her to go.

C. Tell her you will do the best you can to accommodate her request.

D. Tell her she must find a replacement to work for her that day.

E. It depends on how good a worker she is.

30. It is July 3 and one of your staff asks you for the day off tomorrow. Independence Day is not usually a very busy day in the restaurant. What do you do?

A. Give him the day off and rework the schedule.

B. Explain that because of the late request, you cannot allow him to go.

C. Tell him you'll do the best you can to accommodate his request.

D. Tell him he must find a replacement to work for him tomorrow.

E. It depends on how good a worker he is.

OPERATIONS

31. Generally, what is the most cost-effective way to maintain equipment?

A. Replace it as soon as it breaks.

B. Employ a full-time equipment troubleshooter.

C. Maintain all equipment yourself.

D. Hire an outside maintenance firm.

E. Practice preventive maintenance.

32. Which factor is most influential in determining the type of cooking equipment a restaurant uses?

A. The size of the kitchen.

B. Local ordinances.

C. Utility rates.

D. The restaurant's menu.

E. The capital improvements budget.

33. What would be your first question to consider in the purchase of a new piece of equipment?

A. How much will it cost to buy?

B. What is its rate of energy consumption?

C. How will it improve guest satisfaction?

D. How much labor will it save?

E. What is the experience of others using the machine?

34. Which of the following practices would you correct *immediately*?

A. A fry cook juggling ice cubes at his workstation, out of guests' sight.

B. Cutting vegetables with a very sharp French knife.

C. Placing a bus tub on a chair in the dining room.
D. Standing on a folding ladder to reach a high shelf.
E. Using an aluminum tray to carry drinks.

35. What is the proper first aid for a minor burn in the kitchen?
A. Calling 911.
B. Putting ice on the burned area.
C. Putting butter on the burned area.
D. Holding the burned area under cool water.
E. Holding the burned area under warm water.

36. If the criterion is the most frequent cause of accidents, what is the most dangerous item in the kitchen?
A. The floor.
B. The deep fat fryer.
C. The French knife.
D. The slicing machine.
E. The dish machine.

37. What does "first in, first out" refer to?
A. Changing suppliers regularly to keep them honest.
B. Traffic control for trucks in the loading area.
C. Using food supplies in the order they were received.
D. Determining who gets laid off based on seniority.
E. None of the above.

38. What is the best document to use when receiving the grocery order?
A. The purchase order.
B. The supplies requisition.
C. The purveyor's invoice.
D. The standardized recipe.
E. The DICE System book.

39. What information do USDA grades on meat provide?
A. The plant where the meat was processed.
B. The quality of the meat.
C. The date the meat was processed.
D. The sanitary or wholesome condition of the meat.
E. The cut of meat.

40. Where would you expect to find a description of the characteristics of a desired food product?
A. The vendors cost-plus sheet.
B. The tying agreement.
C. The specification sheet.
D. The rebate certificate.
E. The DICE System book.

41. How does forecasting help to control production?
A. It ensures that food will be produced according to standard procedures.
B. It helps avoid under- or overproduction.
C. It guarantees sufficient inventories to meet production needs.
D. It helps determine job assignments.
E. Forecasting relates to sales — it has nothing to do with production.

42. What can you assume when an item is returned to the kitchen by the guest?
A. Someone in the kitchen screwed the order up.
B. The server didn't explain the item properly to the guest.
C. Something is wrong with the food.
D. The guest is in a bad mood.
E. You can't assume anything when an item is returned.

43. Which item is *not* part of portion control?
A. Purchasing specifications.
B. Standardized recipes.

C. Properly adjusted cooking equipment.
D. Waste control.
E. Putting the proper amount on the plate.

44. What is your best course of action when a government official arrives to inspect the restaurant?
A. Ask the official to communicate only with you and not to talk to your staff.
B. Insist on your right to advance notice and reschedule the inspection.
C. Allow the official to conduct the inspection alone.
D. Follow the official at a distance and make notes on how the inspection is conducted.
E. Accompany the official on the inspection.

45. What does a yield analysis determine?
A. The price of a menu item.
B. The tasks involved in preparing a menu item.
C. The raw cost of a menu item.
D. How long a menu item can be safely held before service.
E. How much usable food is contained in a purchased quantity.

46. How do you control theft in the restaurant?
A. Expect the best from your staff and create an environment where they won't want to steal.
B. Watch everyone like a hawk.
C. Have very tight control systems and monitor them continually.
D. Double-check every transaction.
E. Conduct unannounced locker and bag inspections.

47. Which of the following actions is most likely to decrease energy consumption?
A. Not tampering with the heat settings on kitchen equipment once they have been turned on.
B. Cooking foods rapidly at high heat.
C. Using cold water for cooking.
D. Cooking foods in large quantities.
E. Cooking foods in small batches.

Match the following terms with their proper definitions:

48. **American service**	A. Food is brought on platters and served at the table.
49. **Russian service**	B. Guests help themselves from a long table or tables filled with food.
50. **Banquet service**	C. Food is brought in bowls and on platters, and guests help themselves at the table.
51. **Family service**	D. Food is portioned in the kitchen and brought out to guests on plates.
52. **Buffet service**	E. There is no such term.

53. Which of the following procedures has the most potential to cause foodborne illness?
A. Reheating a previously cooked food product on the range.
B. Initial cooking of a food product.
C. Cooling a cooked food product in the walk-in.
D. Preparation activities (cutting, mixing, etc.) of a food product.

54. You notice that one of your staff has an open cut on her hand. What is the best way to handle it?
A. Exclude her from food-handling until the cut heals.
B. Send her home, without pay, until the cut heals.
C. Send her home, with pay, until the cut heals.
D. To avoid upsetting the guests, assign her to a workstation out of sight of the dining room.
E. File a Workers' Compensation claim.

53. Which of the following is proper salad bar procedure?
A. Keeping food containers topped off with fresh, refrigerated product.
B. Replacing nearly empty food containers with full ones.
C. Reusing serving utensils when food containers are filled.
D. Allowing guests to refill their salad bowls.
E. Placing ice on salad greens to keep them cold and crisp.

56. What would you do when you notice a guest asking for more silverware because hers is dirty?
A. Polish the replacement silverware with a clean towel to be sure there is not another problem.
B. Explain to her that the silverware has been sanitized even though some pieces may have water spots.
C. Check the ware-washing procedure to ensure that everything is being done properly.

D. See that the offending silverware is thrown away.

E. Reprimand the dishwasher along with the person who set the table.

57. Where would you expect to find reservations for banquet rooms and large parties?

A. The daily communication log.

B. The DICE System book.

C. The sales analysis book.

D. The function book.

E. The staff bulletin board.

58. When should you check the restrooms?

A. Immediately before the rush.

B. Immediately after the rush.

C. Every half hour throughout the day.

D. At least four times a day.

E. Whenever you get a complaint.

59. What would you do when the electronic POS system stops working?

A. Close the restaurant until the system is fixed.

B. Switch to a manual ordering system.

C. Offer a discount to diners in the restaurant.

D. Hire an outside bookkeeper until it is fixed.

60. Which of the following is *not* a consideration in choosing a china pattern?

A. The price.

B. The color and pattern.

C. Whether it is a stocked item.

D. Its durability.

E. The manufacturer.

61. What is the first thing to do when there has been an injury on the job?

A. Try to have the injured worker use his own health insurance for treatment.

B. Unless you witnessed the accident, be suspicious that it happened at work.

C. File a Workers' Compensation claim.

D. Arrange for immediate treatment under your Workers' Compensation policy.

E. If the injury is minor, have the restaurant pay the costs and don't file a Workers' Comp claim.

62. Which of the following statements is true with regard to tips and tip reporting?

A. Tips are strictly a transaction between the server and the guest.

B. Employers must file an annual report of tip income for each tipped employee.

C. Tipped workers must make a monthly report to the IRS of all tip income received.

D. Only tip income in excess of $30 per month needs to be reported.

E. Management can require tipped employees to share a portion of their tips with the kitchen staff.

63. What is HACCP?

A. A federal agency concerned with the control of hazardous chemicals.

B. An agency that licenses the music played in restaurants.

C. A system to prevent foodborne illness.

D. An enzyme compound that dissolves grease in drain lines.

E. None of the above.

64. If a business insurance claim is approved for payment, how much will the carrier generally pay?

A. The full amount of the insurance coverage.

B. The amount of the loss.

C. An amount equal to the premium.

D. 80% of the amount of the claim.

E. The amount of the deductible.

65. Which of the following statements is *not* true regarding INS documentation?

A. You do not have to complete an I-9 form for everyone who applies for employment.

B. You must complete an I-9 form within three business days of the start of employment.

C. You can fire any worker who fails to produce the required documentation within three business days.

D. You are not responsible if the worker presents a false document as long as it looks good.

E. All of the above statements are true.

66. **What is a product thermometer?**
    A. The pop-up indicator in a turkey that tells when it is done.
    B. A small pocket thermometer used to check food temperatures.
    C. The wall-mounted thermometer that monitors refrigeration temperatures.
    D. The thermostat that controls the temperature in the kitchen.
    E. None of the above.

67. **How can you get detailed information about what happens in the restaurant on your days off?**
    A. Ask the owner.
    B. Ask your supervisors.
    C. Check the DICE System book.
    D. Check the daily communication log.
    E. Hold a staff meeting.

68. **What does the Occupational Safety and Health Act require of foodservice operators?**
    A. That they provide insurance for work-related accidents.
    B. That they take steps to reduce job hazards.
    C. That they prevent work-related accidents.
    D. That they compensate workers for loss of pay due to accidents on the job.
    E. That they report all on-the-job accidents.

69. **What age does a worker have to be in order to operate a slicing machine?**
    A. 14 years old.
    B. 16 years old.
    C. 18 years old.
    D. 21 years old.
    E. Age is not an issue in this case.

70. **Which of the following records are you *not* required to retain?**
    A. Time cards.
    B. Employment applications.
    C. INS documentation.
    D. Guest checks.
    E. Vendor invoices.

APPROACH

71. **When it comes to guest complaints, which statement do you most agree with?**
    A. No news is good news.
    B. Complaints are special gifts.
    C. A satisfaction level of about 90% is realistic for a full-service restaurant.
    D. You can't expect to please all the people all the time.
    E. Some people complain just to get attention.

72. **Where would you concentrate your attention to maximize profitability?**
    A. Advertising and promotion.
    B. The average check.
    C. Food cost.
    D. Labor cost.
    E. Guest service.

73. **Who should be authorized to comp a guest's meal?**
    A. The manager.
    B. The dining room supervisor.
    C. The server.
    D. All of the above.
    E. It depends on the reason for the comp.

74. **Your food cost last month was 32.4%. This month it will be 33.1%. What should you do?**
    A. Check portion control procedures.

    B. Substitute less expensive ingredients.
    C. Check the sales mix.
    D. Raise the menu prices.
    E. Look for evidence of theft.

75. What would you do first if you thought your labor cost was too high?
    A. Reduce hours equally across the board.
    B. Cut back the hours for part-time workers.
    C. Lay off marginal workers.
    D. Raise menu prices.
    E. Concentrate on sales training.

76. If food was coming out of the kitchen too slowly, what would be the likely cause of the problem?
    A. The cooks are incompetent.
    B. The orders are not being placed properly.
    C. The kitchen equipment is inadequate.
    D. The kitchen manager is not paying attention.
    E. None of the above.

77. How would you deal with a complaint from an irate guest?
    A. Apologize and immediately resolve the problem in favor of the guest.
    B. Try to keep the guest from disturbing the dining room.
    C. Analyze market share data to determine if the problem is worth worrying about.
    D. Listen to the problem, explain what caused it, and negotiate a mutually acceptable solution.
    E. Help the guest understand your side of the situation.

78. When would you *not* think it appropriate to comp all (or part) of a guest's meal?
    A. The guest had a longer wait than you led him to expect.
    B. The server was late bringing the salad.
    C. The guest did not care for the entree.
    D. The guests had an argument and decided to leave before finishing their meals.
    E. All of these situations could call for a comp.

79. When is attention to guest service most important?
    A. At lunch, because luncheon guests tend to eat with you more frequently.
    B. At dinner, because the average check is higher.
    C. On special occasions, because these are more important events to diners.
    D. At banquets, because they are larger accounts.
    E. All the time, whether or not the restaurant's doors are open for business.

80. What would you do first if you notice your sales declining?
    A. Check the state of the local economy.
    B. Talk to your guests.
    C. Start an aggressive advertising campaign.
    D. Raise menu prices.
    E. Hold a staff meeting focused on sales training.

81. As a restaurant manager, for whom do you work?
    A. Your owners.
    B. Your staff.
    C. Your guests.
    D. Yourself.
    E. Your state health department.

82. You want to replace some pieces of kitchen equipment with new items that use more current technology. Neither you nor anyone else on your staff has any experience with the new equipment. How would you make the decision?
    A. Think it over and make the decision yourself.
    B. Hire a consultant.
    C. Form a committee from those who will use the equipment to do the research.
    D. Put it to a vote of the staff.
    E. Hold a staff meeting for as long as it takes to reach consensus.

83. **You need to buy a new television set for the bar. How do you make the decision?**
    A. Think it over and make the decision yourself.
    B. Hire a consultant.
    C. Form a committee to make the decision.
    D. Put it to a vote of the staff.
    E. Hold a staff meeting for as long as it takes to reach consensus.

84. **It is a busy night and the wait is running long. You have a table that has just been cleared but has not yet been reset. An irate guest comes up and demands that you seat his party at that table immediately. He is the next party on your waiting list. What do you do?**
    A. Seat his party at that table immediately.
    B. Tell him to sit down and wait his turn.
    C. Seat his party as soon as the table has been reset.
    D. Buy his party a drink and ask them to wait until the table is ready.

85. **What is your most important responsibility as a restaurant manager?**
    A. To make a profit.
    B. To manage the activities of the staff.
    C. To increase sales volume.
    D. To protect the assets of the restaurant.
    E. To make sure the guests are happy.

86. **What is the best way to identify the operating problems of your restaurant?**
    A. Call in a consultant.
    B. Talk to your guests.
    C. Talk with the supervisors.
    D. Talk to your staff.
    E. Attend a restaurant management seminar.

87. **Which of the following is most likely to improve the productivity of your staff?**
    A. Developing detailed job descriptions that spell out all activities to be performed.
    B. Establishing a comprehensive policies and procedures manual.
    C. Letting the staff set their own work rules.
    D. Defining jobs in terms of the results to be achieved.

88. **Which of the following gives the most valid indication of a manager's effectiveness?**
    A. The restaurant's financial performance in comparison with national averages.
    B. The rate of staff turnover.
    C. Increased profitability over the preceding period.
    D. The rate of repeat business.
    E. The number of internal job promotions.

89. **Which of the following statistics is most valuable in determining dining room staffing requirements in a *table service* restaurant?**
    A. Analysis of entree sales.
    B. Guests seated per hour.
    C. Projected daily sales.
    D. Sales per hour.
    E. Number of meals served daily.

90. **Which of the following statistics is most valuable in determining staffing requirements in a *fast food* restaurant?**
    A. Projected daily sales.
    B. Analysis of entree sales.
    C. Sales per hour.
    D. Number of meals served daily.
    E. Promotional coupons redeemed.

FINANCIAL

91. **Simply stated, what is an invoice?**
    A. A bill.
    B. A purchase order.
    C. A sales history.

D. A statement of account.

E. A production forecast.

92. **What does cash flow represent?**

    A. The restaurant's sales volume.

    B. The restaurant's profitability.

    C. The difference between receipts and expenditures.

    D. All of the above.

    E. None of the above.

93. **Your liquor salesperson has just offered you a deal: 20% off on orders of over three cases of Kahlua if you place the order immediately. You normally go through three to four bottles of Kahlua in a month. What do you do?**

    A. Pass.

    B. Buy more than three cases and save the restaurant some money.

    C. Buy more than three cases and invent a new specialty drink.

    D. Buy more than three cases and resell part of the stock at a profit.

94. **Where do you find the financial position of a restaurant at a particular time?**

    A. The income statement.

    B. The cost-of-goods-sold statement.

    C. The balance sheet.

    D. The cash flow statement.

    E. The capital inventory schedule.

95. **This past month, a restaurant had cash receipts totaling $94,400 and disbursements of $73,900. It closed with a bank balance of $38,280. What was the bank balance at the beginning of the month?**

    A. $12,780.

    B. $17,780.

    C. $20,500.

    D. $25,500.

    E. $38,280.

96. **Which of the following is most useful to the manager in the daily management of a restaurant?**

    A. The balance sheet.

    B. The income statement.

    C. The cash flow statement.

    D. The food cost from purchases.

    E. The daily bank balance.

97. **What portion of a typical restaurant's sales is pretax income?**

    A. 40% to 45%.

    B. 30% to 35%.

    C. 20% to 25%.

    D. 10% to 15%.

    E. Under 5%.

98. **A bottle of your well gin contains 38 ounces and costs $93 per case. Your standard shot is 1½ ounces. A drink sells for $2.75. What is a bottle of gin worth?**

    A. $7.75.

    B. $33.80.

    C. $69.50.

    D. $93.00.

    E. None of the above.

99. **Your well Scotch costs 26¢ per ounce, club soda costs 4¢ per ounce, ice costs 1¢ per ounce, and stir sticks are a penny a piece. Your restaurant's recipe for a Scotch and soda calls for 1½ ounces of Scotch, 5 ounces of soda, and 4 ounces of ice. The drink sells for $2.75. What is the pouring cost percentage of a Scotch and soda?**

    A. 14.2%.

    B. 21.5%.

    C. 22.9%.

    D. 23.3%.

    E. None of the above.

100. All other things being equal, which one of the following items would you encourage your staff to sell?
   A. An enchilada plate selling for $6.95 with a 20% food cost.
   B. A chicken sandwich selling for $4.95 with a 32% food cost.
   C. A fried catfish platter selling for $8.95 with a 38% food cost.
   D. A steak dinner selling for $12.95 with a 50% food cost.

101. Let's say your target food cost is 34%. You are evaluating a new menu item with a portion cost of 82¢. How would you price it on the menu?
   A. $1.95.
   B. $2.25.
   C. $2.41.
   D. $2.50.
   E. There is not enough information to answer the question.

102. The average check is the restaurant's total food sales divided by what number?
   A. The average value of a typical guest check.
   B. The number of guests served.
   C. The number of entrees sold.
   D. The average number of people in the party.
   F. The number of seats in the restaurant.

103. If you wish to allow for labor costs in establishing menu prices, which of these items probably has the highest cost percentage?
   A. A chef's salad.
   B. Scrambled eggs with bacon and toast.
   C. A cheeseburger with french fries.
   D. A pork chop with apple sauce.

Assume your restaurant serves an average of 200 meals a day. Lunch accounts for 40% of your business, and 60% is accounted for in the evening. Your average lunch check is $5 and your average dinner check is $10.

104. What is your average daily sales figure?
   A. $800.
   B. $1,200.
   C. $1,600.
   D. $2,400.
   E. There is not enough information to calculate the answer.

105. To increase sales by $200 per day, by what percent do you have to increase the average dinner check?
   A. 10.0%.
   B. 13.2%.
   C. 16.7%.
   D. 19.5%.
   E. There is not enough information to calculate the answer.

106. What will happen to variable costs as sales volume increases?
   A. They will increase.
   B. They will stay the same.
   C. They will decrease.
   D. Variable costs are not related to sales volume.

107. What happens when a restaurant's costs equal its sales?
   A. It earns a profit.
   B. It breaks even.
   C. It loses money.
   D. It has a positive cash flow.

108. Which of the following is normally used to prepare an operating budget?
   A. Historical data and financial records.
   B. Sales records and receipts.
   C. Quality and quantity standards.
   D. Records of food purchases.
   E. The DICE System book.

109. Last month, your restaurant's total receipts were $66,500, of which $4,100 was sales tax, $15,600 was beverage sales, and the rest was food sales. Your food purchases were $16,800 and your kitchen payroll was $9,900. You spent $550 on paper supplies. Opening food inventory was $5,400 and closing inventory was $4,000. What was your food cost percentage for the month?
  A. 27.3%.
  B. 32.9%.
  C. 35.9%.
  D. 38.9%.
  E. There is not enough information to answer the question.

You want to find a daily special for next week and have been searching through your cookbook collection looking for a likely menu item. You come upon the following recipe for Hungarian Goulash that looks interesting:

2½ lb. top round	2 T. paprika
3 T. flour	4 t. butter
1 t. salt	1 c. tomato puree
1 t. pepper	1 c. beef stock

You call your suppliers and receive the following cost information:

Top round	$2.75/1 lb.	Paprika	$3.00/1 lb.
Flour	$7.50/50 lb.	Butter	$1.50/1 lb.
Salt	$0.40/1 lb.	Tomato puree	$19.50/6/10
Pepper	$9.00/1 lb.	Beef stock	$30.50/12/49 oz.

110. The recipe as written makes 5 servings. You plan to produce 55 servings if you offer it as a special. Approximately how much flour will you need for the larger quantity?
  A. 1 c.
  B. 30 t.
  C. 2 c.
  D. 1 lb.
  E. None of the above.

111. How much salt will you use for 55 servings?
  A. 11 t.
  B. 11 T.
  C. ¼ c.
  D. ½ c.
  E. None of the above.

112. What will be the approximate meat portion per serving at 55 servings?
  A. 4 ounces.
  B. 6 ounces.
  C. 8 ounces.
  D. 12 ounces.
  E. None of the above.

113. What is the portion cost on Hungarian Goulash?
  A. $1.23.
  B. $1.53.
  C. $1.82.
  D. $2.10.

114. You have a product that you sell as a takeout item for $6.95. The food on the plate costs $2.50, the packaging costs 25¢, and it takes about $2 in labor to prepare the item. What is your food cost percentage on this product?
  A. 34.4%.
  B. 36.0%.
  C. 38.8%.
  D. 68.3%.
  E. None of the above.

115. **You have a product that you sell for $8.50 with a portion cost of $3. What is its gross margin?**
    A. 35.3%.
    B. 64.7%.
    C. $3.00.
    D. $5.50.
    E. None of the above.

116. **You are planning a smoked salmon appetizer for the menu. You expect a 75% EP yield from a whole 12-pound smoked salmon that you can purchase for $100. You can also purchase sliced smoked salmon for $11.55 a pound. You have been told (in no uncertain terms!) to keep your operating costs as low as possible. You expect to use about 50 pounds of salmon a week. Based on your experience, which product do you buy?**
    A. Whole salmon.
    B. Sliced salmon.
    C. There is not enough information to answer the question.

117. **Let's say that you *really* blow it with a party of four. Let's also say that the typical guest normally dines with you three times a month and that your average check is $20. What is this error likely to cost the company in lost busines over the next five years?**
    A. Under $4,000.
    B. $10,000 to $15,000.
    C. $25,000 to $30,000.
    D. $50,000 to $60,000.
    E. Over $85,000.

118. **Your bookkeeper asks you where to post the invoice for charcoal used for cooking. What do you tell him?**
    A. Put it under utilities expense.
    B. Consult the Uniform System of Accounts for Restaurants.
    C. Create a separate category if it is over $100.
    D. Put it under cost of goods sold.
    E. Call the accountant.

119. **Cumulative purchases will give a reasonably accurate indication of food cost after how many days?**
    A. 5 days.
    B. 10 days.
    C. 30 days.
    D. It cannot be done.

120. **Which of the following prices should you use when calculating the value of the food inventory?**
    A. The lowest receipt price of each item.
    B. The highest receipt price of each item.
    C. The last receipt price of each item.
    D. The average receipt price of each item.

MARKETING

121. **Which of the following is a valid source of internal marketing information?**
    A. Chamber of Commerce statistics.
    B. Articles in restaurant trade magazines.
    C. Interviews with salaried staff.
    D. Guest questionnaires.
    E. Results of media restaurant polls.

122. **Which of the following differentiates a foodservice operation from its competition?**
    A. Lunch and dinner menus.
    B. Valet parking.
    C. Friendly, courteous service.
    D. Fresh foods.
    E. Television advertising.

123. **What is the main advantage of point-of-purchase advertising?**
    A. It influences people who are already interested in spending their money.
    B. It cannot be easily ignored by guests.

C. It appeals to every market segment.

D. It costs no money.

E. Guests are not consciously aware of the sales message.

124. **You are managing an upscale restaurant noted for contemporary cuisine. The restaurant is located in a wealthy area of a large city. What do you consider to be the most effective place to advertise?**

A. The local penny-saver classified newspaper.

B. The restaurant section of the local newspaper.

C. A local newspaper catering to senior citizens.

D. The local Top-40 radio station.

E. A monthly magazine catering to the upper middle class.

125. **For which group are afternoon menus best designed?**

A. Retirees.

B. Executives.

C. Families.

D. Working parents.

E. All of the above.

126. **Which of the following best characterizes suggestive selling?**

A. Donating food to a church.

B. Sponsoring a local fund-raising event.

C. Recommending a dessert on the menu.

D. Putting an advertisement in a city magazine.

E. A table tent.

127. **If your restaurant donates leftover food to a soup kitchen or sponsors a Little League team, which of the following are you doing?**

A. Public relations.

B. Marketing.

C. Merchandising.

D. Advertising.

E. Promotion.

128. **Which of the following is an example of point-of-purchase advertising?**

A. A billboard.

B. A radio advertisement.

C. A table tent.

D. A magazine display ad.

E. Promotional copy on the back of the guest check.

129. **Which of the following is *not* an objective of foodservice promotion?**

A. To make a profit.

B. To create staff appreciation.

C. To increase customer counts.

D. To break the routine for the restaurant's guests.

E. To break the routine for the restaurant's staff.

130. **Establishing signature items in your restaurant is making good use of which of the following?**

A. Competitive price points.

B. Product differentiation.

C. Pricing psychology.

D. Market research.

E. Market segmentation.

ALCOHOL SERVICE

131. **Which of the following foods is most effective for *slowing* the rate of alcohol absorption?**

A. Popcorn.

B. Candy.

    C. Cheese.
    D. Black coffee.
    E. All are equally effective.

132. **Which of the following *increases* the rate of alcohol absorption in the body?**
    A. Water.
    B. Carbonated beverages.
    C. Protein foods.
    D. Sweets.
    E. None of the above.

133. **Which of the following is typically *not* considered a valid form of ID?**
    A. A birth certificate.
    B. A driver's license.
    C. An alien registration card.
    D. A Social Security card.
    E. All are valid for identification.

134. **Which of the following statements accurately describes the law?**
    A. It is legal to serve alcohol to intoxicated persons if they are not going to be driving.
    B. It is illegal to serve alcohol to intoxicated persons.
    C. It is illegal to serve more than three drinks per hour to a person.
    D. It is legal for a minor to drink if his parents purchase the alcoholic beverage.
    E. All of the above are accurate statements.

135. **You should stop alcohol service to a person doing which of the following?**
    A. Flirting.
    B. Losing inhibitions.
    C. Being a nuisance.
    D. Spilling drinks.
    E. Being unusually quiet.

136. **Which of the following is *not* an equivalent drink to the others when considering alcohol content?**
    A. 12 ounces of beer.
    B. 8 ounces of wine.
    C. 1¼ ounces of 80 proof liquor.
    D. All are equal in alcohol content.

137. **A guest has definitely had too much to drink and he is about to leave the restaurant. You approach him to offer a taxi home. He declines your offer and insists he is going to drive home. What do you do?**
    A. Ask him to be careful and allow him to drive.
    B. If he gets into his car, call the police.
    C. Grab his keys and keep them.
    D. Continue to press your case.
    E. Call the owner.

138. **A woman has definitely had too much to drink and wants another glass of wine. She swears she is not driving, a statement that is confirmed by her boyfriend. He is not drunk and assures you that he is driving her home and will see that she gets there safely. He asks you to bring the wine. What do you do?**
    A. Bring the drink as requested.
    B. Call the police.
    C. Call the owner.
    D. Refuse to serve the drink.
    E. Suggest nonalcoholic alternatives.

139. **A group of young people come into the restaurant and orders alcoholic beverages. They have no proof of age with them. They assure you they are over 21 years old. This is verified by an older guest who overheard the conversation and whom you recognize as an off-duty police officer. What do you do?**
    A. Bring the drinks.
    B. Call the police department to confirm the identity of the older guest.
    C. Call the owner.
    D. Refuse to serve the drinks.
    E. Suggest nonalcoholic alternatives.

140. Which of the following practices will *not* help to avoid overconsumption?
    A. Serving one drink at a time.
    B. Making guests come to the bar to order.
    C. Serving rounds when most glasses are empty.
    D. Removing empty glasses from the table before serving a new round.
    E. Putting water on the table.

Please answer the following questions TRUE or FALSE.

141. You may be held personally liable for the actions of intoxicated guests.
142. The use of cocaine or marijuana in conjunction with alcohol will intensify the alcohol's effect.
143. A driver registering a .8% BAC is considered to have been driving while impaired.
144. If an out-of-state person is of legal age to drink in his home state, he can drink in your restaurant.
145. High altitude lessens the effect of alcohol.
146. Alcohol is a depressant that decreases appetite.
147. A person with a higher percentage of fat will absorb alcohol faster than a more muscular person.
148. The body processes alcohol at the rate of one drink per hour, regardless of size.
149. When discontinuing service to intoxicated guests, a hand on their shoulder will help keep them calm.
150. A breathalizer measures the amount of alcohol in the blood.

Examen Profesional

ENTRENAMIENTO DEL EQUIPO TÉCNICO

Escoja la respuesta *MÁS CORRECTA* y marque su opción en la hoja de respuestas. Por favor no escriba en el examen.

RELACIONES HUMANAS

1. **¿Dónde comenzaría a buscar cuando usted necesite llenar una vacante?**
   A. En los anuncios del periódico.
   B. El equipo técnico de restaurantes competidores.
   C. Solicitantes de empleo que entren al restaurante.
   D. Equipo técnico existente.
   E. Agencias de colocación.

2. **¿Cuál de las siguientes diría usted que es el paso más importante para formar un equipo técnico de calidad?**
   A. Contratar.
   B. Orientar.
   C. Entrenar.
   D. Dirigir.
   E. Disciplinar.

3. **Bajo las leyes de igualdad de oportunidad de empleo, ¿qué puede usted requerir de los servidores?**
   A. Que nunca hayan tenido problemas con la ley.
   B. Que sean mujeres.
   C. Que sean menores de 26 años de edad.
   D. Que sean ciudadanos de los Estados Unidos.
   E. Que sean eficientes y amistosos.

4. **¿Cuándo es mejor buscar miembros del equipo técnico potenciales?**
   A. Alrededor de los días festivos de los colegios.
   B. Justamente antes de los períodos más ocupados en los negocios.
   C. Cuando las vacantes estén a punto de abrir.
   D. En un horario regular durante el año.
   E. Siempre.

5. **¿Cuál es el objetivo principal de un programa de orientación para el equipo técnico?**
   A. Establecer un sistema de disciplina y recompensas para el equipo técnico.
   B. Establecer un plan y método de evaluación de progreso.
   C. Comunicar información y crear una respuesta positiva de la compañía y del trabajo.
   D. Evaluar la reacción de otros trabajadores hacia el nuevo trabajador y terminar las pruebas del trabajo.
   E. Permitir a los nuevos trabajadores saber quien está encargado.

6. **¿Cuál método de entrenamiento utilizaría al enseñarle a un mesero como vender sugestivamente?**
   A. Instrucciones escritas.
   B. Entrenamiento en la clase.
   C. Demostración.
   D. Instrucción en el trabajo.
   E. Ninguno de los anteriores.

7. **¿Cuál método de entrenamiento utilizaría usted al mostrarle a alguien como limpiar una parte del equipo?**
   A. Instrucciones escritas.
   B. Entrenamiento en la clase.
   C. Demostración.
   D. Instrucción en el trabajo.
   E. Ninguno de los anteriores.

8. **¿Cuál método de entrenamiento utilizaría usted al intentar comunicar nuevas ideas a un grupo?**
   A. Instrucciones escritas.
   B. Entrenamiento en la clase.
   C. Demostración.
   D. Instrucción en el trabajo.
   E. Ninguno de los anteriores.

9. **¿Quién cree ud. que es el entrenador más efectivo de temas operacionales?**
   A. Un asesor.
   B. El administrador general.
   C. El supervisor de departamento.
   D. Un colega calificado.
   E. El director de entrenamiento de la compañía.

10. **¿Qué cree ud. que su equipo técnico espera de sus trabajos?**
    A. Aprecio por el trabajo que hacen.
    B. Mejores sueldos.
    C. Estar enterado de las cosas.
    D. Beneficios de seguro y salud.
    E. La seguridad de tener trabajo.

11. **En su experiencia, ¿cuál de las declaraciónes es verdadera acerca de trabajar con minorías?**
    A. Deben ser tratados de forma diferente a los otros trabajadores.
    B. Pueden ser más difíciles de motivar que otros trabajadores.
    C. Es más difícil saber lo que ellos esperan realmente de usted.
    D. Tienden a ser menos productivos que otros trabajadores.
    E. No son diferentes de los otros.

12. **¿Dónde cae la responsabilidad principal para el alto uso de equipo técnico de los restaurantes?**
    A. En los trabajadores individuales involucrados.
    B. En la administración del restaurante.
    C. En la nómina de pago de los restaurantes.
    D. En los valores que prevalecen en nuestra sociedad.
    E. En la competencia aumentada por otras industrias.

13. **¿Qué haría usted para que sus empleados dieran lo mejor de sí?**
    A. Establecer ejemplo personal que refleje todo lo que usted espera de su equipo técnico.
    B. Establecer normas altas y administrar las actividades de su equipo.
    C. Desarrollar procedimientos en todas las áreas mayores.
    D. Conducir extensiva y consistentemente el entrenamiento para todas las posiciones.

14. **Como un administrador de restaurante, ¿cuál es la forma más rápida de avanzar en su carrera?**
    A. Hacerle favores personales a los propietarios.
    B. Resaltar en la competencia.
    C. Tomar clases y asistir a seminarios.
    D. Enseñarle a sus subalternos como hacer su trabajo.
    E. Asegurarse que usted reciba crédito cuando las cosas vayan bien.

15. **Va a ser una noche del sábado muy ocupada. Un miembro del equipo técnico de servicio se presenta a trabajar a las 4:00 PM con un uniforme limpio pero muy arrugado. ¿Cómo manejaría usted esto?**
    A. Lo asigna a su estación regular.
    B. Lo asigna a una estación en la parte trasera del restaurante.
    C. Lo envía a planchar su uniforme antes de permitirle que continúe.
    D. Lo envía a trabajar en la cocina, fuera de la vista de los clientes.
    E. Le envía a su casa sin pago.

16. **Va a ser una noche del sábado muy ocupada. Un miembro del equipo técnico de servicio se reporta a su trabajo a las 5:30 PM en un uniforme limpio pero muy arrugado. ¿Cómo lo manejaría usted?**
    A. Lo asigna a su estación regular.
    B. Le asigna a una estación en la parte trasera del comedor.
    C. Le envía a planchar el uniforme antes de permitirle que continúe.
    D. Lo envía a trabajar en la cocina, fuera de la vista de los clientes.
    E. Lo envía a su casa sin pago.

17. **¿Qué consideraría usted como un error al dar una evaluación de desempeño de trabajo?**
    A. Concentrarse en los errores que el trabajador ha hecho.
    B. Hacer que el trabajador establezca sus propios objetivos de mejoramiento.
    C. Animar al equipo técnico a calificarse ellos mismos.
    D. Dejar que el equipo técnico comente en su evaluación.
    E. Cambiar la calificación después de discutir con el trabajador.

18. **Cuando hay varios candidatos para una vacante, ¿a quién contrata usted?**
    A. Al que tenga mejor apariencia.
    B. Al que más necesite el trabajo.
    C. A la persona más calificada.
    D. Al que tenga más interés de quedarse en el trabajo.
    E. La persona con más experiencia.

Usted ha notado un problema operacional que debe ser discutido inmediatamente. La respuesta no es inmediatamente obvia para usted. Cualquier solución promete un cambio que afectará a la mayoría del equipo técnico.

19. **¿Cómo determinará la respuesta más apropiada al problema?**
    A. Estudia la situación y desarrolla su propio plan.
    B. Tiene una reunión del equipo técnico general para llegar a un concenso de lo que se va a hacer.
    C. Llama a un asesor.
    D. Lo discute con sus supervisores.
    E. Ignorarlo y esperar a que se olvide.

20. **¿Cómo procedería usted?**
    A. Asegúrese que cada uno sea entrenado para tratar con el cambio antes de que se implemente.
    B. Seleccione dos o tres dirigentes y entrénelos para que traten con el cambio.
    C. Implemente el cambio, vea qué problemas trae y trátelos con prontitud.
    D. Instruya a cada miembro del equipo técnico en los principios de cómo adaptarse al cambio.
    E. Implemente el cambio tan rápido como sea posible.

21. **¿Cómo podría minimizar la resistencia de su equipo técnico?**
    A. Despida a aquellos trabajadores que no cooperen.
    B. Involucre al equipo técnico en la planificación y el proceso de implementación.
    C. Sea firme y no dé oportunidad de que comience una discusión.
    D. Permita a su equipo técnico que se acostumbre al cambio antes de pedir comentarios.
    E. Llame a una reunión al equipo técnico y explique por qué el cambio era necesario.

22. **¿Cuál de los siguientes es un ejemplo de delegación de responsabilidad adecuada?**
    A. El cantinero le dice al cocinero que preparare más comida para el buffet del "Happy Hour."
    B. El administrador de cocina le dice a un cocinero auxiliar que despida al lavador de platos.
    C. El administrador del comedor le dice a un mesero que reorganize la posición de las mesas.
    D. El cocinero le dice al administrador que la refrigeración no está funcionando adecuadamente.
    E. El anfitrión toma una orden de bebidas cuando el mesero está ocupado.

23. **¿Qué es lo mejor que se puede hacer cuando tiene que dar una evaluación de desempeño de trabajo desfavorable?**
    A. Se excusa y es compasivo.
    B. Despide a la persona inmediatamente.
    C. Le ofrece a la persona una posición diferente.
    D. Establece objetivos específicos de mejora con los miembros del equipo técnico.
    E. Se asegura que el trabajador entienda sus defectos personales.

24. **¿Qué haría usted cuando es forzado a despedir a un miembro de su equipo técnico?**
    A. Se asegura de haber aconsejado al individuo y de haber documentado las advertencias por escrito.
    B. Se acerca al tema gradualmente.
    C. Ofrece darle buenas recomendaciones y le ayuda a buscar otro trabajo.
    D. Llama su abogado.
    E. Todo lo anterior.

25. **¿Cuál es la mejor medida de la efectividad de un supervisor?**
    A. Habilidades de trabajo.
    B. Puntaje del Departamento de Salud.
    C. Ganancias.
    D. Una nota promedio.
    E. El desarrollo del equipo técnico.

26. **¿Cuál es su objetivo al crear un horario para el equipo técnico?**
    A. Minimizar el costo de trabajo.
    B. Asegurarse de un nivel alto de servicio a los clientes.
    C. Concordar el horario de trabajo con el presupuesto.
    D. Distribuir las horas disponibles equitativamente entre el equipo técnico.
    E. Acomodar las solicitudes especiales de los trabajadores.

27. **¿Qué hace usted con un horario de trabajo del equipo técnico recién completado?**
    A. Circularlo el primer día del nuevo período de trabajo.
    B. Poner un aviso con una semana de anticipación del nuevo período de trabajo.
    C. Terminarlo para que nuevas revisiones no sean necesarias.
    D. Colocarlo en su archivos para uso en el futuro.
    E. Mencionarlo para obtener la aprobación en una reunión con el equipo técnico.

28. **Es mediados de marzo y un miembro del equipo técnico le pide libre el fin de semana que corresponde con el día de la madre. Al parecer su hermana gemela se va a casar ese fin de semana de mayo y le ha pedido ser parte de la corte nupcial. El día de la madre es tradicionalmente uno de los días más llenos y ocupados del restaurante de todo el año. ¿Qué hace usted?**
    A. Le da el fin de semana libre y reorganiza el horario usted mismo.
    B. Le explica que el día de la madre es demasiado ocupado y no le puede permitir que vaya.
    C. Le dice que usted hará lo mejor que pueda para acomodar la solicitud.
    D. Le dice que tiene que buscar un reemplazo para que trabaje ese fin de semana.
    E. Depende de que tan buen trabajador sea.

29. **Es mediados de noviembre y un miembro del equipo técnico le pide el día de acción de gracias libre. El día de acción de gracias es generalmente un día muy ocupado en el restaurante. ¿Qué hace usted?**
    A. Le da el día libre y reorganiza el horario usted mismo.
    B. Le explica quel el día de acción de gracias es demasiado ocupado y no le puede permitir que se vaya.
    C. Le dice que usted hará la mejor que pueda para acomodarle la solicitud.
    D. Le dice que tiene que buscar un reemplazo para que trabaje ese día.
    E. Depende de qué tan buen trabajador sea.

30. **Es el 3 de julio y un miembro del equipo técnico le pide mañana libre. El día de la independencia no es generalmente un a día muy ocupado en el restaurante. ¿Qué hace usted?**
    A. Le da el día libre y reorganiza el horario usted mismo.
    B. Le explica que por la tardanza en la solicitud usted no le puede dar el día libre.
    C. Le dice que usted hará lo mejor que pueda para acomodarle la solicitud.
    D. Le dice que tiene que buscar un reemplazo para trabajar mañana.
    E. Depende de qué tan buen trabajador sea.

OPERACIONES

31. **Generalmente, ¿cuál es la forma más costo–eficiente de mantener el equipo?**
    A. Reemplaza el equipo tan pronto como se rompa.
    B. Emplea un equipo encargado de mantenimiento a jornada completa.
    C. Mantiene todo el equipo usted mismo.
    D. Contrata una firma de mantenimiento.
    E. Practica mantenimiento preventivo.

32. **¿Cuál es el factor que influye más para determinar el tipo de equipo para la cocina que el restaurante necesita?**
    A. El tamaño de la cocina.
    B. Las ordenanzas locales.
    C. La tasa de utilidad.
    D. El menú del restaurante.
    E. El presupuesto de mejoramiento de capital.

33. **¿Cuál sería su primer pregunta al considerar la compra de una pieza de equipo nueva?**
    A. ¿Cuánto costaría comprarlo?
    B. ¿Cuál es la tasa de consumo de energía?

C. ¿Cómo mejoraría la satisfacción del cliente?

D. ¿Cuánto trabajo ahorraría?

E. ¿Cuál es la experiencia de otros al utilizar la máquina?

34. ¿Cuál de las siguientes prácticas corregiría usted inmediatamente?

A. El que los cocineros jueguen con cubos de hielo en el área de trabajar fuera de la vista del cliente.

B. El que corten verduras con un cuchillo francés muy afilado.

C. El que coloquen un balde en una silla del comedor.

D. El que usen una escalera desplegable para alcanzar un estante alto.

E. El que utilizen una bandeja de aluminio para llevar bebidas.

35. ¿Cuáles son los primeros auxilios adecuados para una quemada de primer grado en la cocina?

A. Llamar al 911.

B. Poner hielo en el área quemada.

C. Poner mantequilla en el área quemada.

D. Poner el área de la quemadura bajo agua fría.

E. Poner el área de la quemadura bajo agua caliente.

36. Si el criterio fuera la causa más frecuente de accidentes, ¿cuál es el instrumento más peligroso en la cocina?

A. El piso.

B. El freidor de grasa.

C. El cuchillo francés.

D. La máquina de rebanar.

E. La lavadora de platos.

37. ¿A qué se refiere el dicho "lo que entra primero, sale primero"?

A. Al cambio regular de suministradores para mantenerlos honestos.

B. Al control de tráfico de los camiones en el área de cargamento.

C. Utilizar los víveres en el orden que fueron recibidos.

D. Determinar a quien se despide basado en la antigüedad del empleado.

E. Ninguno de los anteriores.

38. ¿Cuál sería el mejor documento que se debe utilizar al recibir la orden del mercado?

A. La orden de compra.

B. La orden de las provisiones.

C. La factura del proveedor.

D. La receta normal

E. El libro del Sistema DICE.

39. ¿Qué información provee el puntaje del USDA en la carne?

A. La planta donde la carne fue procesada.

B. La calidad de la carne.

C. La fecha que la carne fue procesada.

D. La condición sanitaria de la carne.

E. El corte de la carne.

40. ¿Dónde esperaría usted encontrar una descripción de las características de un producto alimenticio deseado?

A. Hoja de costo de los vendedores.

B. El acuerdo del sindicato.

C. La hoja de especificación.

D. El certificado de descuento.

E. El libro de sistema DICE.

41. ¿Cómo ayuda la pronosticación a controlar la producción?

A. Asegura que el alimento sea producido de acuerdo con los procedimientos establecidos.

B. Ayuda a evitar la baja o sobreproducción.

C. Garantiza que habrá suficientes inventarios para reunir las necesidades de producción.

D. Ayuda a determinar asignaciones de trabajo.

E. La pronosticación se relaciona con las ventas; no tiene nada que ver con la producción.

42. ¿Qué puede usted suponer cuando un plato es regresado a la cocina por el cliente?

A. Alguien en la cocina se equivocó con la orden.

B. El mesero no explicó el plato adecuadamente al cliente.

C. Hay algo malo con la comida.

D. El cliente está de mal humor.

E. Usted no puede suponer nada cuando un plato es regresado.

43. ¿Cuál detalle *no* es parte del control de porciones?

A. Especificaciones de compra.

B. Recetas normalizadas.

C. Equipo de cocina ajustado adecuadamente.

D. Control de desperdicio.

E. Poner la cantidad adecuada en el plato.

44. ¿Cuál es su mejor plan de acción cuando un oficial del gobierno llega a inspeccionar el restaurante?

A. Pedirle al oficial que se comunique solamente con usted y que no hable con su equipo técnico.

B. Insistir en el derecho de aviso previo y cambiar la fecha de la inspección.

C. Permitir al oficial que conduzca su inspección sólo.

D. Seguir al oficial de lejos y tomar notas de cómo conduce la inspección.

E. Acompañar al oficial durante la inspección.

45. ¿Qué determina un análisis de rendimiento?

A. El precio de un artículo en el menú.

B. Las tareas involucradas en preparar un artículo del menú.

C. El costo bruto de un artículo del menú.

D. Cuanto tiempo se puede mantener un artículo del menú en buenas condiciones antes de servirlo.

E. Cuanta cantidad de alimento es utilizable en el contenido de una cantidad comprada.

46. ¿Cómo controlaría el robo en el restaurante?

A. Esperando lo mejor de su equipo técnico y creando un ambiente donde no quieran robar.

B. Observar a todos como un halcón.

C. Tener un sistema de control minusioso y vigilarlos continuamente.

D. Volver a revisar cada transacción.

E. Conducir inspecciones sin ser anunciadas de los casilleros y las bolsas.

47. ¿Cuál de las siguientes acciones es más probable que disminuya el consumo de energía?

A. Evite el juego con las temperaturas del equipo de cocina una vez que hayan sido encendidos.

B. Cocine alimentos rápidamente a fuego alto.

C. Utilice agua fría para cocinar.

D. Cocine alimentos en grandes cantidades.

E. Cocine alimentos en pequeñas cantidades.

Concuerde los siguientes términos con las definiciones adecuadas:

48. **Servicio americano**   A. El alimento es traído en bandejas y servido en la mesa.

49. **Servicio ruso**   B. Los clientes se sirven de una mesa larga o de mesas con comida.

50. **Servicio de banquete**   C. La comida es servida en moldes y bandejas y los clientes se sirven en las mesas.

51. **Servicio familiar**   D. Las porciones de comida son servidas en la cocina y llevadas a los clientes en las mesas.

52. **Servicio buffet**   E. No hay tal término.

53. ¿Cuál de los siguientes procedimientos tienen el potencial más alto de provocar enfermedades transmitidas por la comida?

A. Recalentando un producto alimenticio previamente cocinado en la estufa.

B. La primera etapa en la que se cocina al producto alimenticio.

C. Enfriar una comida en el corredor.

D. Las actividades de preparación (corte, mezcla, etc.) de un producto alimenticio.

54. Usted nota que un miembro de su equipo técnico tiene una cortada abierta en su mano. ¿Cuál es la mejor forma de manejar esto?

A. Excluirlo de toda responsabilidad de manejo de comida hasta que la cortada esté curada.

B. Lo envía a su casa sin pago hasta que la cortada esté curada.

C. Lo envía a su casa con pago hasta que la cortada esté curada.

D. Para evitar molestar a los clientes, le asigna a una estación de trabajo fuera de la vista del comedor.

E. Archiva una reclamo al compensador de trabajadores.

55. ¿Cuál de los siguientes es un procedimiento adecuado en el bar de ensaladas?

   A. Mantener los contenedores de alimentos llenos de productos frescos.
   B. Reemplazar contenedores de alimentos casi vacíos con otros llenos.
   C. Utilizar de nuevo los utensilios para servir cuando los contenedores son rellenados.
   D. Permitir que los clientes llenen sus platos de la ensalada.
   E. Colocar hielo en la ensalada para mentenerla fresca y crocante.

56. ¿Qué hace usted cuando un cliente le pide cubiertos nuevos porque los suyos están sucios?

   A. Pulir los cubiertos de reemplazo con una toalla limpia para asegurarse que no haya otro problema.
   B. Explicarle que los cubiertos han sido lavados aunque algunas piezas tengan manchas del agua.
   C. Revisa el procedimiento de lavado de los cubiertos para asegurarse que todo esté hecho adecuadamente.
   D. Ver que los cubiertos sucios sean botados.
   E. Regañar a lavador de cubiertos junto con la persona que organizó la mesa.

57. ¿Dónde esperaría encontrar usted reservaciones para banquetes y fiestas grandes?

   A. El libro de comunicación diaria.
   B. El libro de Sistema de DICE.
   C. El libro de análisis de ventas.
   D. El libro de función.
   E. El mural del equipo técnico.

58. ¿Cuándo deberá revisar usted los baños?

   A. Inmediatamente antes de la hora de más uso.
   B. Inmediatamente después de la hora de más uso.
   C. Cada media hora durante el día.
   D. Al menos cuatro veces al día.
   E. Cada vez que le den una queja.

59. ¿Qué haría usted cuando el sistema electrónico POS deja de trabajar?

   A. Cierra el restaurante hasta que el sistema sea arreglado.
   B. Cambia a un sistema de ordenanza manual.
   C. Ofrece un descuento a los clientes en el restaurante.
   D. Contrata a un contador hasta que el sistema sea arreglado.

60. ¿Cuál de las siguientes no sería una consideración al elegir un diseño para las vajillas?

   A. El precio.
   B. El color y diseño.
   C. Si lo tienen en almacenamiento.
   D. Durabilidad.
   E. El fabricante.

61. ¿Cuál es la primera cosa que debe hacer cuando hay una lesión en el trabajo?

   A. Intentar que el trabajador perjudicado utilice su propio seguro de salud.
   B. A menos que usted haya visto el accidente, tenga desconfianza de que ocurrió en el trabajo.
   C. Archivar una reclamo para el compensador de trabajadores.
   D. Arreglar para que haya tratamiento inmediato bajo su póliza de compensación de trabajadores.
   E. Si la lesión es menor, el restaurante paga el costo y no archiva un reclamo de compesación de trabajadores.

62. ¿Cuál de las siguientes declaraciones es verdadera con respecto a propinas y declaración de propinas?

   A. Las propinas son estrictamente una transacción entre el servidor y el cliente.
   B. Las compañías tienen que archivar un informe de ingreso anual de propinas por cada empleado.
   C. Los empleados con propinas tienen que presentar un informe mensual de ingreso de propinas recibidas con el IRS.
   D. Solamente ingreso de propinas en exceso de $30.00 mensuales debe ser reportado.
   E. La administración puede requerir que los empleados con propinas compartan una porción con el equipo técnico de cocina.

63. ¿Qué es HACCP?

   A. Una agencia federal interesada en el control de productos químicos peligrosos.
   B. Una agencia que autoriza la música tocada en los restaurantes.
   C. Un sistema para evitar a lo transmisión de enfermedades a causa de la comida.
   D. Una mezcla de enzimas que disuelve grasa en las líneas de desagüe.
   E. Ninguno de los anteriores.

64. **Si un reclamo de seguro del negocio es aprobado para que sea pagado, ¿cuánto pagará el portador generalmente?**
   A. La cantidad completa de la cobertura del seguro.
   B. La cantidad de la pérdida.
   C. Una cantidad igual a la prima.
   D. 80% de la cantidad del reclamo.
   E. La cantidad deducible.

65. **¿Cuál de las siguientes declaraciones *no* es considerada verdadera con respecto a la documentación del INS?**
   A. Usted no tiene que completar un formulario I-9 por cada empleado que solicite empleo.
   B. Usted debe completar un formulario I-9 en un plazo de 3 días hábiles del comienzo del empleo.
   C. Usted puede despedir a cualquier trabajador que falle en producir la documentación requerida en el plazo de 3 días hábiles.
   D. Usted no es responsable si el trabajador presenta un documento falso con tal que se vea bien.
   E. Todas las declaraciones anteriores son verdaderas.

66. **¿Qué es un termómetro de producto?**
   A. El indicador que se levanta en un pavo y que le dice a usted cuando está listo.
   B. Un termómetro pequeño de bolsillo utilizado para medir las temperaturas en las comidas.
   C. El termómetro montado en la pared que regula las temperaturas de refrigeración.
   D. El termostato que controla la temperatura en la cocina.
   E. Ninguno de los anteriores.

67. **¿Dónde puede obtener información detallada acerca de lo que pasó en el restaurante en los días que usted no estuvo?**
   A. Le pregunta al dueño.
   B. Le pregunta a sus supervisores.
   C. En el libro de sistema DICE.
   D. Revisa el registro de comunicación diaria.
   E. Tiene una reunión con el equipo técnico.

68. **¿Qué requiere el Acto Ocupacional de Seguridad y Salud a los operadores de servicio de comida?**
   A. Que provean seguro para los accidentes relacionados con el trabajo.
   B. Que tomen medidas para reducir peligros en el trabajo.
   C. Que eviten accidentes relacionados con el trabajo.
   D. Que compensen a los trabajadores por la pérdida de pago debido a accidentes en el trabajo.
   E. Que reporten todos los accidentes en el trabajo.

69. **¿A qué edad puede un trabajador operar una máquina rebanadora?**
   A. 14 años de edad.
   B. 16 años de edad.
   C. 18 años de edad.
   D. 21 años de edad.
   E. La edad no es un problema en este caso.

70. **¿Cuál de los siguientes registros *no* le es requerido a usted retener?**
   A. Las tarjetas de horas trabajadas.
   B. Las aplicaciones de empleo.
   C. La documentación del INS.
   D. Cuentas de los clientes.
   E. Las facturas del proveedor.

EL MÉTODO

71. **Con respecto a quejas de los clientes, ¿con cuál declaración está usted más de acuerdo?**
   A. El no tener noticias indica buenas noticias.
   B. Las quejas son regalos especiales.
   C. Un nivel de satisfacción cerca del 90% es realista para un restaurante con servicio completo.
   D. Usted no puede esperar satisfacer a toda la gente todo el tiempo.
   E. Alguna gente se queja sólo para obtener atención.

72. ¿Dónde concentraría su atención para maximizar las ganancias?
A. Publicidad y promoción.
B. La cuenta promedio.
C. Costo de la comida.
D. Costo de trabajo.
E. Servicio de los clientes.

73. ¿Quién debe ser autorizado para compensar una comida a un cliente?
A. El administrador.
B. El supervisor del comedor.
C. El mesero.
D. Todos los anteriores.
E. Depende de la razón para la compensación.

74. El costo del alimento el mes pasado fue de un 32.4%. Este mes será de un 33.1%. ¿Qué hace usted?
A. Revisa los procedimientos de control de porción.
B. Sustituye los ingredientes menos caros.
C. Revisa la mezcla de ventas.
D. Sube los precios en el menú.
E. Busca evidencia de robo.

75. ¿Cuál es la primer acción que usted tomaría si pensara que el costo de su trabajo es muy alto?
A. Reduce las horas por igual.
B. Disminuye las horas para trabajadores de medio tiempo.
C. Despide a trabajadores marginales.
D. Sube los precios del menú.
E. Se concentra en entrenamiento de ventas.

76. Si la comida estuviera saliendo de la cocina demasiado lentamente, ¿cuál sería probablemente la causa del problema?
A. Los cocineros son incompetentes.
B. Las órdenes no están siendo situadas adecuadamente.
C. El equipo de cocina es inadecuado.
D. El administrador de cocina no está prestando atención.
E. Ninguno de los anteriores.

77. ¿Cómo manejaría usted una queja de un cliente irritado?
A. Se excusa e inmediatamente resuelva el problema a favor del cliente.
B. Intenta mantenerlo sin que moleste el resto del comedor.
C. Analiza la información de participación en el mercado para determinar si vale la pena preocuparse por el problema.
D. Escucha el problema, explica qué lo provocó y negocia una solución mutua aceptable.
E. Ayuda a que el cliente entienda su punto de vista en esta situación.

78. ¿Cuándo no consideraría usted apropiado dar gratis toda o parte de una comida al cliente?
A. Tuvieron una espera más larga de lo que usted les indicó que era la espera.
B. El mesero trajo la ensalada tarde.
C. El cliente no quizo su plato principal.
D. Los clientes tuvieron una discusión y decidieron irse antes de acabar sus comidas.
E. Todas estas situaciones pueden son propicias como para dar comida gratis.

79. ¿Cuándo es darle atención al servicio de los clientes más importante?
A. En el almuerzo, porque los clientes que almuerzan tienden a comer con usted con más frecuencia.
B. En la cena, debido a que la cuenta promedio es más alta.
C. En ocasiones especiales, debido a que son eventos más importantes para los clientes.
D. En banquetes, debido a que son cuentas mayores.
E. Siempre, ya sea que las puertas del restaurante estén abiertas para hacer negocio o no.

80. ¿Qué acción tomaría usted si notara que sus ventas están declinando?
A. Revisa el estado de la economía local.
B. Habla con sus clientes.
C. Comienza una campaña publicitaria agresiva.
D. Sube los precios del menú.
E. Tiene una reunión con el equipo técnico enfocada en entrenamiento de ventas.

81. **Como administrador de restaurante, ¿para quién trabaja usted?**
    A. Sus propietarios.
    B. Su equipo técnico.
    C. Sus clientes.
    D. Usted mismo.
    E. El departamento de salud del estado.

82. **Usted quiere reemplazar algunas piezas del equipo de cocina con partes más modernas que utilizen nueva tecnología. Ni usted ni otra persona en su equipo técnico tiene experiencia con el nuevo equipo. ¿Cómo toma usted la decisión?**
    A. Lo piensa y toma la decisión usted mismo.
    B. Contrata a un asesor.
    C. Forma un comité con aquellos que utilizarán la maquinaria para que hagan la investigación.
    D. Lo pone a voto con su equipo técnico.
    E. Tiene una reunión que tome el tiempo necesario hasta que llegue a un consenso.

83. **Usted necesita comprar un televisor para el bar. ¿Cómo toma la decisión?**
    A. Lo piensa y toma la decisión usted mismo.
    B. Contrata a un asesor.
    C. Forma un comité para tomar la decisión.
    D. Lo pone a voto con su equipo técnico.
    E. Tiene una reunión que tome el tiempo necesario hasta que llegue a un consenso.

84. **Es una noche ocupada y la espera se está alargando. Usted tiene una mesa que se ha despejado pero todavía no ha sido reorganizada. Un cliente irritado demanda que lo siente en ésa mesa inmediatamente. El es la siguiente persona en la lista de espera. ¿Qué hace usted?**
    A. Lo sienta en esa mesa inmediatamente.
    B. Le dice que se siente y espere su turno.
    C. Siente al grupo tan pronto como la mesa haya sido reorganizada.
    D. Compense al grupo con una bebida y pídales que esperen hasta que la mesa esté lista.

85. **¿Cuál es su responsabilidad más importante como administrador del restaurante?**
    A. Hacer ganancias.
    B. Manejar las actividades del equipo técnico.
    C. Aumentar el volumen de ventas.
    D. Proteger los valores del restaurante.
    E. Asegurarse que los clientes sean felices.

86. **¿Cuál es la mejor forma de identificar problemas de operación en su restaurante?**
    A. Llama a un asesor.
    B. Habla con los clientes.
    C. Habla con sus supervisores.
    D. Habla con su equipo técnico.
    E. Asiste a un seminario de administración de restaurantes.

87. **¿Cuál de la siguientes es más probable que mejore la productividad del equipo técnico?**
    A. Desarrollar descripciones detalladas de trabajos que describan todas las actividades por desempeñarse.
    B. Establecer un manual completo de pólizas y procedimientos.
    C. Permitir que el equipo técnico imponga sus propias reglas de trabajo.
    D. Definir trabajos en términos de los resultados que deben ser logrados.

88. **¿Cuál de las siguientes sería la indicación más válida de efectividad de un administrador?**
    A. El desempeño financiero del restaurante en comparación con promedios nacionales.
    B. La tasa de volumen del equipo técnico.
    C. El aumento de las ganacias en comparación con el período anterior.
    D. La tasa de negocio repetido.
    E. La cantidad de promociones de trabajos internos.

89. **¿Cuál de las siguientes estadísticas serían más valiosas para determinar los requisitos para proveer equipo técnico en el comedor de un restaurante con *servicio en la mesa*?**
    A. El análisis de ventas de platos principales.
    B. El número de clientes sentados por hora.
    C. Las ventas diarias proyectadas.

D. Las ventas por hora.

E. El número de comidas servidas diariamente.

90. **¿Cuál de las siguientes estadísticas serían más valiosas para determinar los requisitos para proveer equipo técnico para un restaurante de *comida rápida*?**

A. Ventas diarias proyectadas.

B. Análisis de ventas de platos principales.

C. Ventas por hora.

D. El número de comidas servidas diariamente.

E. Cupones promoción de ventas devueltos.

FINANZAS

91. **Simplemente, ¿qué es una factura?**

A. Un recibo.

B. Una orden de compra.

C. Una historia de ventas.

D. Un estado de cuenta.

E. Un proyecto de producción.

92. **¿Qué representa un flujo de dinero?**

A. El volumen de ventas del restaurante.

B. Las ganancias del restaurante.

C. La diferencia entre recibos y gastos.

D. Todo lo anterior.

E. Ninguno de los anteriores.

93. **Su vendedor de licor le ha ofrecido un trato: 20% de descuento en órdenes de 3 cajas de Kahlua si usted pone la orden inmediatamente. Usted normalmente utiliza de 3 a 4 botellas de Kahlua en un mes. ¿Qué hace usted?**

A. Pasa.

B. Comprar 3+ cajas y le ahorra al restaurante dinero.

C. Comprar 3+ cajas e inventar una nueva bebida especial.

D. Comprar 3+ cajas y revender parte de las existencias con una ganancia.

94. **¿Donde encontraría la posición financiera de un restaurante en un momento dado?**

A. Un estado de ingresos y gastos.

B. Un estado de costo de bienes vendidos.

C. Una hoja de balance.

D. El estado de cuenta corriente.

E. El plan de inventario capital.

95. **Este mes, un restaurante ha tenido ingresos de ventas con un total $94,400 y desembolso de $73,900. Cerró con un saldo bancario de $38,280. ¿Cuál fue el saldo bancario al comienzo del mes?**

A. $12,780

B. $17,780

C. $20,500

D. $25,500

E. $38,280

96. **¿Cuál de las siguientes es más útil para el administrador en la administración diaria de un restaurante?**

A. La hoja de balance.

B. El estado de ingresos y gastos.

C. El estado de la cuenta corriente.

D. Costo de alimento a la hora de las compras.

E. El saldo bancario diario.

97. **¿Qué porción de ventas típicas de un restaurante son ingresos anteriores a los impuestos?**

A. 40–45%

B. 30–35%

C. 20–25%

D. 10–15%

E. Menos del 5%

98. **Una botella de ginebra de la reserva contiene 38 onzas y cuesta $93.00 por caja. Un trago regular contiene 1½ onzas. Una bebida se vende a $2.75. ¿Cuánto cuesta una botella de ginebra?**

   A. $7.75

   B. $33.80

   C. $69.50

   D. $93.00

   E. Ninguno de los anteriores

99. **Su escocés de la reserva cuesta 26¢ por onza, la gaseosa cuesta 4¢ por onza, el hielo cuesta 1¢ por onza y un palillo de revolver cuesta 1¢ cada uno. La receta de su restaurante para un scotch con gaseosa pide 1 onza de scotch, 5 onzas de gaseosa y 4 onzas de hielo. La bebida se vende a $2.75. ¿Cuál es el porcentaje de costo de trago de un scotch con gaseosa?**

   A. 14.5%

   B. 21.5%

   C. 22.9%

   D. 23.3%

   E. Ninguno delos anteriores

100. **Con todo el resto constante, ¿cuál de los siguientes artículos animaría usted a su equipo técnico a vender?**

   A. Una enchilada que se vende por $6.95 con un 20% de costo de alimento.

   B. Un sandwich de pollo que se vende por $4.95 con un 32% de costo de alimento.

   C. Una bandeja de bagre freído que se vende por $8.95 con un 38% de costo de alimento.

   D. Un filete de carne que se vende por $12.95 con un 50% de costo de alimento.

101. **Vamos a decir que su objetivo de costo de alimento es de 34%. Usted está evaluando un nuevo artículo en el menú con un costo por porción de 82¢. ¿Qué precio le pondría en el menú?**

   A. $1.95

   B. $2.25

   C. $2.41

   D. $2.50

   E. No hay suficiente información para responder la pregunta.

102. **¿La cuenta promedio corresponde a las ventas de alimento totales del restaurante divididas por cuál número?**

   A. El valor promedio de una cuenta de clientes típica.

   B. La cantidad de clientes servidos.

   C. La cantidad de entradas vendidas.

   D. El número de gente promedio en un grupo.

   E. El número de sillas en el restaurante.

103. **Si usted desea permitir que el costo de la mano de obra establezca los precios del menú, ¿cuál de estos artículos tendrán probablemente el costo con porcentaje mas alto?**

   A. La ensalada de chef.

   B. Los huevos revueltos con tocineta y tostadas.

   C. Hamburguesa con queso y papas fritas.

   D. Chuleta de cerdo con salsa de manzana.

Supongamos que su restaurante sirve un promedio de 200 comidas en un día. 40% de su negocio es durante el almuerzo y 60% ocurre por la noche. Su cuenta promedio de almuerzo es de $5.00 y su cuenta promedio de la cena es de $10.00.

104. **¿Cuál su promedio de ventas diarias?**

   A. $000

   B. $1200

   C. $1600

   D. $2400

   E. No hay información suficiente para calcular la respuesta.

105. **Aumentan las ventas $200 por día, ¿qué porcentaje tendrá usted que aumentar el promedio de cuentas de la cena?**

   A. 10.0%

   B. 13.2%

C. 16.7%

D. 19.5%

E. No hay información suficiente para calcular la respuesta.

106. ¿Qué le ocurrirá a los costos variables a medida que el volumen de ventas aumenta?

A. Aumentarán.

B. Permanecerán iguales.

C. Disminuirán.

D. Los costos variables no están relacionados con los volúmenes de ventas.

107. ¿Qué ocurre cuando el costo de un restaurante es igual a sus ventas?

A. Gana una ganancia.

B. Rompe igual.

C. Pierde dinero.

D. Tiene una corriente de fondos positiva.

108. ¿Cuál de las siguientes es normalmente utilizada para preparar un presupuesto operativo?

A. Registros de información históricos y financieros.

B. Los registros de ventas y recibos.

C. Las normas de calidad y cantidad.

D. Registros de compras de alimentos.

E. El libro de sistema de DICE.

109. El mes pasado, los recibos totales del restaurante tuvieron $66,500 de los cuales $4,100 fueron impuesto sobre las ventas, $15,600 fueron ventas de bebidas y el resto fueron ventas de comida. Sus compras de alimento fueron de $16,800 y su nómina de cocina fue de $9,900. Usted gastó $550 en provisiones de papel. La apertura de inventario de los alimentos fue $5,400 y el cierre de inventario fue de $4,000. ¿Cuál fue el costo los alimentos durante el mes?

A. 27.3%

B. 32.9%

C. 35.9%

D. 38.9%

E. No hay suficiente información para responder la pregunta.

Usted quiere encontrar un especial del día para la siguiente semana y sigue buscando a través de su colección de libros de cocina un artículo del menú que sea suceptible. Usted se atraviesa con la siguiente receta para goulash húngaro que se vé muy interesante:

2 lb. de filete de res	2 cucharadas de paprika
3 cucharadas de harina	4 cucharaditas de mantequilla
1 cucharadita de sal	1 taza de puré de tomate
1 cucharadita de pimienta	1 taza de consomé de carne

Usted llama a su proveedor y recibe la siguiente información del costo:

filete	$2.75/1 lb.	paprika	$3.00/1 lb.
harina	$7.50/50 lb.	mantequilla	$1.50/1 lb.
sal	$0.40/1 lb.	puré de tomate	$19.50/6/10
pimienta	$9.00/1 lb.	consomé de carne	$30.50/12/49 oz.

110. La receta tal y como está escrita hace 5 porciones. Usted proyecta producir 55 porciones si usted lo ofreciera como un especial. ¿Aproximadamente cuánta harina necesitará para esta gran cantidad?

A. 1 taza.

B. 30 cucharaditas.

C. 2 tazas.

D. 1 lb.

E. Ninguno de los anteriores.

111. ¿Cuánta sal utilizaría para 55 porciones?

A. 11 cucharaditas.

B. 11 cucharadas.

C. ¼ taza.

D. ½ taza.

E. Ninguno de los anteriores.

112. **¿Cuál será la porción apróximada de carne para 55 porciones?**
    A. 4 onzas.
    B. 6 onzas.
    C. 8 onzas.
    D. 12 onzas.
    E. Ninguno del anterior.

113. **¿Cuál es el costo de la porción de goulash húngaro?**
    A. $1.23
    B. $1.53
    C. $1.82
    D. $2.10
    E. Ninguno de los anteriores.

114. **Usted tiene un producto que se vende como un artículo de servicio a domicilio por $6.95. La comida en el plato cuesta $2.50 y los costos de empaque cuestan 25¢. Se gasta por lo menos $2.00 en la preparación. ¿Cuál es el porcentaje de costo de alimento en este producto?**
    A. 34.4%
    B. 36.0%
    C. 38.8%
    D. 68.3%
    E. Ninguno de los anteriores.

115. **Usted tiene un producto que se vende a $8.50 con un costo por porción de $3.00. ¿Cuál es su margen de ganancias totales?**
    A. 35.3%
    B. 64.7%
    C. $3.00
    D. $5.50
    E. Ninguno de los anteriores.

116. **Usted está planificando un aperitivo de salmón ahumado para el menú. Usted espera que un 75% del producto sea comestible con un rendimiento de un salmón ahumado de 12 lbs. que puede comprar a $100.00. También puede comprar salmón ahumado rebanado por $11.55 la libra. A usted le han dicho (¡en términos exactos!) de mantener sus costos operativos tan bajos como le sea posible. Usted espera utilizar cerca de 50 lb. de salmón por semana. Basado en su experiencia, ¿qué producto compra usted?**
    A. Salmón entero.
    B. Salmón rebanado.
    C. No hay suficiente información para responder la pregunta.

117. **Digamos que el restaurante realmente se ha equivocado con un grupo típico de cuatro. También vamos a suponer que el típico cliente de su restaurante come normalmente tres veces al mes y su cuenta promedio es de $20.00. Probablemente, ¿cuánto le sale costando este error a la compañía con el negocio perdido de los siguientes cinco años?**
    A. Bajo $4,000
    B. $10,000–$15,000
    C. $25,000–$30,000
    D. $50,000–$60,000
    E. Más de $85,000

118. **Su contador le pregunta en dónde debe poner la factura del carbón utilizado para cocinar. ¿Qué le dice usted?**
    A. Ponerlo bajo el gasto de utilidades.
    B. Consulte al sistema uniforme de cuentas de restaurantes.
    C. Crea una categoría separada si es mayor de $100.00.
    D. Lo pone bajo el costo de bienes vendidos.
    E. Llama al contador.

119. **Las compras acumuladas le darán una indicación razonable y exacta del costo de la comida después de cuántos días?**
    A. 5 días.
    B. 10 días.

C. 30 días.

D. No puede ser hecho.

120. **¿Cuál de los siguientes precios utilizaría usted al calcular el valor del inventario de los alimentos?**

    A. El recibo más bajo de precio de cada artículo.

    B. El recibo más alto de precio de cada artículo.

    C. El último precio en el recibo de cada artículo.

    D. El recibo promedio de cada artículo.

COMERCIO

121. **¿Cuál de las siguientes sería la fuente mas válida de información de mercadotecnia interna?**

    A. Las estadísticas de la cámara de comercio.

    B. Los artículos en las revistas comerciales de restaurantes.

    C. Entrevistas con equipo técnico asalariado.

    D. Cuestionarios para los clientes.

    E. Resultados de encuestas de los medios en restaurantes.

122. **¿Cuál de las siguientes diferenciaría una operación de servicio de comidas de sus competidores?**

    A. Los menúes de almuerzos y cenas.

    B. Estacionamiento con valet.

    C. Servicio amistoso y cortés.

    D. Comida fresca.

    E. Publicidad en la televisión.

123. **¿Cuál es la ventaja principal de la publicidad de punto de compra?**

    A. Influye a la gente que ya está interesada en gastar dinero.

    B. No puede ser facilmente ignorado por los clientes.

    C. Atrae a todos los segmentos del mercado.

    D. No cuesta dinero.

    E. Los clientes no están conscientes del mensaje de ventas.

124. **Usted está manejando un restaurante de alta calidad notado por su cocina contemporánea. El restaurante está localizado en un área muy rica de una ciudad grande. ¿Cuál consideraría usted el lugar más efectivo para publicar?**

    A. El periódico de baratillos locales.

    B. En la sección de restaurantes del periódico local.

    C. El periódico local que se ofrece a los ciudadanos de edad.

    D. La estación de radio local que toca música pop.

    E. En la revista mensual que ofrece a la clase media alta.

125. **¿A cuáles grupos les va mejor los menúes de las tardes?**

    A. Jubilados.

    B. Ejecutivos.

    C. Familias.

    D. Padres de trabajadores.

    E. Todos los anteriores.

126. **¿Cuál de los siguientes caracterizan mejor a las ventas sugestivas?**

    A. Donarle comida a una iglesia.

    B. Patrocinar eventos locales para recaudar fondos.

    C. Recomendando un postre en el menú.

    D. Poniendo un anuncio en una revista urbana.

    E. Una mesa carpada.

127. **Si su restaurante dona comida sobrante a una campaña de comida para los pobres o patrocina un equipo de liga menor, ¿cuál de las siguientes haría usted?**

    A. Relaciones públicas.

    B. Publicidad.

    C. Comercializar.

D. Anunciar.

E. Promover.

128. ¿Cuál de las siguientes es un ejemplo de publicidad en el punto de compra?

A. Carteleras.

B. Anuncios en la radio.

C. Mesas carpadas.

D. Propaganda en revistas.

E. Promoción de ventas detrás de las cuentas de los clientes.

129. ¿Cuál de las siguientes *no* es un objetivo de promoción para el servicio de comidas?

A. Hacer ganancias.

B. Crear apreciación por el equipo técnico.

C. Aumentar el número de clientes.

D. Romper la rutina para los clientes del restaurante.

E. Romper la rutina para el equipo técnico del restaurante.

130. Establecer comidas especiales de la casa en su restaurante es hacer buen uso de lo siguiente:

A. Puntos de precios competitivos.

B. La diferenciación del producto.

C. Psicología de apreciación.

D. Estudio del mercado.

E. Segmentación del mercado.

SERVICIO DE ALCOHOL

131. ¿Cuál de los siguientes alimentos serían más efectivos por disminuir la tasa de absorción de alcohol?

A. Palomitas de maíz.

B. Barra de caramelo.

C. Queso.

D. Café negro.

E. Todo sería igualmente efectivo.

132. ¿Cuál de los siguientes aumentaría la tasa de absorción de alcohol en el cuerpo?

A. Agua.

B. Bebidas carbonatadas.

C. Alimentos proteínicos.

D. Dulces.

E. Ninguno de los anteriores.

133. ¿Cuál de los siguientes tipicamente *no* sería considerado una forma válida de identificación?

A. Partida de nacimiento.

B. Licencia de conducir.

C. Tarjeta de registro extranjero.

D. Tarjeta de seguro social.

E. Todas son formas válidas de identificación.

134. ¿Cuál de las siguientes declaraciones describen exactamente la ley?

A. Es legal servir alcohol a personas intoxicadas si van a conducir.

B. Es ilegal servirle alcohol a personas intóxicadas.

C. Es ilegal servirle más de tres bebidas por hora a una persona.

D. Es legal que un menor beba si sus padres le compran la bebida alcohólica.

E. Todas las anteriores son declaraciones exactas.

135. ¿Usted deberá parar el servicio de alcohol a una persona que está demostrando cuáles de los siguientes comportamientos?

A. Coqueteando.

B. Perdiendo las inhibiciones.

C. Siendo una molestia.

D. Regando bebidas.

E. Esta muy callado.

136. **¿Cuál de las siguiente *no* es una bebida equivalente con otras cuando se considera el contenido de alcohol?**

A. 12 onzas de cerveza.

B. 8 onzas de vino.

C. 1 onza de licor de 80 de prueba.

D. Todo son iguales en contenido de alcohol.

137. **Un cliente definitavemente ha bebido demasiado y está listo para irse del restaurante. Usted se acerca para ofrecerle un taxi que lo lleve a casa. Rechaza su oferta e insiste que va a conducir a casa. ¿Qué haría usted?**

A. Le pide que sea cuidadoso y le permite conducir.

B. Si la persona entra en su carro, llama a la policía.

C. Agarra sus llaves y las guarda.

D. Continúa presionando su caso.

E. Llama al dueño.

138. **Una mujer definitivamente ha bebido demasiado y quiere otra copa de vino. Jura que no va a conducir, declaración que es confirmada por su novio. Él no está bebido y le garantiza que él la va a llevar a casa y asegurarse que llegue bien. Él le pide que traiga el vino. ¿Qué hace usted?**

A. Trac la bebida como fue solicitada.

B. Llama a la policía.

C. Llama al dueño.

D. Rehusa servirle la bebida.

E. Sugiere una bebida sin alcohol como alternativa.

139. **Un grupo de seis jóvenes llega al restaurante y ordena bebidas alcohólicas. Usted les pide prueba de mayoría de edad y ellos le dicen que no tienen identificación. Le aseguran que son mayores de 21 años de edad. Esto es verificado por un cliente mayor a quien usted reconoce como un oficial de la policía en civil. ¿Qué hace usted?**

A. Trae las bebidas.

B. Llama al departamento de policía para confirmar la edad del cliente mayor.

C. Llama al dueño.

D. Les rehusa servirles las bebidas.

E. Les sugiere las bebidas sin alcohol como alternativa.

140. **¿Cuál de las siguientes prácticas *no* ayudarán a evitar el sobreconsumo?**

A. Servir una bebida a la vez.

B. Hacer que los clientes vayan al bar a ordenar.

C. Servir las rondas cuando la mayoría de los vasos estén vacíos.

D. Retirar los vasos vacíos de las mesas antes de servir una ronda nueva.

E. Poner agua en la mesa.

Por favor responda a las siguientes preguntas VERDADERO O FALSO.

141. A usted se le puede hacer responsable por las acciones de clientes intoxicados.

142. El uso de cocaína o marihuana conjuntamente con alcohol intensifica el efecto.

143. Un conductor que registre .8% de BAC es considerado como si estuviera conduciendo bajo el efecto del alcohol.

144. Si una persona de fuera del estado es de edad legal para beber en su estado, puede beber en su restaurante.

145. La altitud disminuye el efecto del alcohol.

146. El alcohol es un deprimente que disminuye el apetito.

147. Una persona con un porcentaje alto de grasa absorbe alcohol más rápido que una persona musculosa.

148. El cuerpo procesa alcohol en un ritmo de una bebida por hora, sin importar el tamaño.

149. Al descontinuar el servicio a un cliente intoxicado, una mano en el hombro les ayudará a calmarse.

150. Un medidor de aliento (breathalizer) mide la cantidad de alcohol en la sangre.

Coaching Staff

PROFESSIONAL TEST
Answers

HUMAN RELATIONS

1. **D** **Existing staff.** There are two ways to look at this question, and either gives the same answer. In one sense, if you want to fill a vacancy, starting the search with existing staff shows a desire to promote from within, a situation that normally has a positive impact on morale. If the position is entry level, where internal promotions might not be possible, starting with existing staff indicates the individual is used to an atmosphere where workers are eager to recommend the operation to their friends.

2. **A** **Hiring.** You can't make quality menu items with substandard ingredients, and the same is true with staff. Orientation, training, coaching, and discipline can help good people get better, but they won't make bad people into good people. Take the time to start with the right people.

3. **E** **That they be efficient and friendly.** All the other choices are discriminatory practices that must be avoided in hiring.

4. **E** **All the time.** You must always be in a position to hire those "natural stars" whenever they come along because they won't be looking for work for very long.

5. **C** **To communicate information and create a positive response to the company and the job.**

6. **C** **Role-playing.** The best way to learn is by doing. Role-playing will give people a chance to experiment with new skills and become comfortable with them before going "on stage."

7. **D** **On-the-job instruction.** Anything that involves developing physical skills can only be effectively learned by doing.

8. **B** **Classroom training.** When no physical skills are involved and there are a number of people to train, classroom sessions are usually the most effective.

9. **D** **A skilled co-worker.** The worker is always closer to the job and therefore knows more about its current intricacies than even the most experienced supervisor. Involving the staff in training is also an excellent way to eliminate the "them against us" mentality in a foodservice operation.

10. **A** **Appreciation for the work they do.** When you ask most managers this question, the majority usually think their crew is looking for the money. When you ask hourly staff, money takes fifth place. If you want to lower turnover, it helps to know what your staff wants.

11. **E** **They are no different from anyone else.** Beware of generalizations about any group of people. Remember that somewhere in the world, *you* are a minority!

12. **B** **With the management of the restaurant.** Remember that people stay or go because they want to. The more unpleasant the working environment, the less time people will want to spend in your organization, and the climate of a restaurant always reflects the person at the top.

13. **A** **Set a personal example that reflects everything you expect of your staff.** What they see is what you will get. Anything else is wasted effort.

14. **D** **Teach your subordinates how to do your job.** When you teach your crew to do your job, they get excited by the opportunity to improve their skills. As you eliminate tasks from your workload, it leaves you open to develop new skills yourself.

15. **C** **Send him home to press the uniform before allowing him to go on the clock.** A legendary restaurant has clear standards that are never compromised. Failure to enforce your standards is the same as having no standards at all.

16. **C** **Send her home to press the uniform before allowing her to go on the clock.** The situation is no different from that in question 15. It will certainly make everyone's job a little harder for a while, but it will deliver a clear message to all that you mean what you say. In my experience, people do not resent tough standards as much as they dislike inconsistent enforcement.

17. **A** **Focusing on the mistakes a worker has made.** The purpose of a performance appraisal is to improve a person's effectiveness on the job, a goal that is not served by this sort of power trip. Dwelling on past errors will only create an environment where communication will be difficult and resentment will replace respect.

18. **C** **The most qualified person.** To build a legendary restaurant, you must always hire the most qualified people you can find when a vacancy occurs. This means finding people more qualified than you are. The person with the most experience is not necessarily the most qualified person.

E-44

19. **B** **Hold a general staff meeting to reach consensus on what to do.** You have already determined that you don't know what to do, so involving the collective perspectives of the staff will give you the best possible solution. More important, because everyone was involved in reaching the action plan, your staff will *make* the solution work. With consensus, it takes longer to come up with an answer, but the implementation time is very short.

20. **A** **Be sure that everyone is trained to deal with the change before implementation.** Any change, even positive change, is traumatic. Familiarizing everyone with impending change before they have to deal with it will help keep their insecurities down and their enthusiasm up.

21. **B** **Involve the staff in the planning and implementation process.** This is really a similar answer to the previous one. The more people are part of something, the more they will support it. The more it is someone else's idea being forced on them, the less support it will receive.

22. **C** **The dining room manager tells a server to rearrange the table settings.** Delegation is different from ordering people around. Proper delegation happens when you pass along a task that is your responsibility to someone else who can properly do it. Tasks like termination cannot be delegated.

23. **D** **Set specific improvement goals with the person.** It is always best to focus on the positive rather than dwell on the negative. Remember, the goal of performance appraisal is to improve performance, not to tear someone down.

24. **A** **Be sure you have counseled the individual and documented your warnings in writing.** Unless these steps have been taken, you are not in a defensible position in a labor board hearing. Failure to provide documented counseling can also indicate lack of commitment to the success of your staff.

25. **E** **Staff development.** All of the possible answers are elements that an effective supervisor would do better on than an unskilled one. Still, the distinguishing factor of great supervisors is their ability to teach and bring out the best in those who work with and for them.

26. **B** **To ensure a high level of guest service.** Guest service is the reason the operation exists and the only reason you have staff in the first place! If you want to minimize hours, fire everybody!

27. **B** **Post it a week prior to the new work period.** Your staff has a life, too. Common courtesy dictates that they have enough advance notice of their work schedules to be able to make personal plans.

28. **A** **Give him the weekend off and rework the schedule.** This is sufficient notice and obviously a special occasion. Since Mother's Day is not until May, the work schedule is not even written yet!

29. **D** **Tell her she must find a replacement to work for her that day.** It is always better to find a way to say yes than to say no. In this case, the schedule is probably posted.

30. **D** **Tell him he must find a replacement to work for him tomorrow.** A good manager would not have people scheduled if they were not needed, and arranging coverage for schedule changes on such short notice is the responsibility of the staff members involved.

OPERATIONS

31. **E** **Practice preventive maintenance.** The best way to maintain equipment is to not have it break down at all. This means keeping it clean and lubricated. It also means staying ahead of problems by replacing seals, keeping screws tight, etc. In other words, preventive maintenance.

32. **D** **The restaurant's menu.** The menu drives every decision regarding the kitchen equipment. The other choices are all factors in equipment selection, but they only have relevance *after* the question of menu has been answered.

33. **C** **How will it improve guest satisfaction?** While all of the possible answers bear on an equipment decision, the primary consideration has to be its impact on making your guests happy, since that is Job #1 in the restaurant.

34. **A** **A fry cook juggling ice cubes at his workstation, out of guests' sight.** The reason you stop this practice immediately is that should an ice cube fall into the fryer, it will instantly vaporize. Essentially, it explodes, throwing hot oil all over the cook and the kitchen.

35. **D** **Holding the burned area under cool water.** A burn is an overload of heat on body tissue. The logical cure is to remove the excess heat. Neither butter nor warm water can accomplish this. Ice will remove heat but is eliminated as a correct answer because it can permanently damage sensitive tissue.

36. A **The floor.** Primarily because it is taken for granted, the floor causes more lost-time accidents through falls than any of the other choices.

37. C **Using food supplies in the order they were received.** This is an important part of kitchen management because it helps ensure that fresh products will always be served to the guests. If items are not properly rotated, older products can easily deteriorate to a point where they must be discarded.

38. A **The purchase order.** The purchase order tells you what was ordered, while the purveyor's invoice only tells you what the driver has on the truck. Using a purchase order for receiving will alert you if an item you wanted was *not* in the shipment.

39. B **The quality of the meat.** The carcass roll identifies the plant where the meat was processed, but the USDA grade (prime, choice, etc.) deals only with meat quality.

40. C **The specification sheet.** The spec sheet is the purchasing blueprint for the food items used in the restaurant.

41. B **It helps avoid under- or overproduction.** Forecasting is simply an educated guess as to how much of every product you think you will sell on a given day. Forecasting also provides a basis for ordering. While the forecast will seldom exactly equal demand, it will be much closer than just preparing (or ordering) based on the whim of the kitchen manager.

42. E **You can't assume anything when an item is returned.** There are thousands of reasons for an item to be returned. Consider it an opportunity to give an extra level of service, fix it, and discuss the probable causes later. This is not to suggest that patterns of problems should not be identified and solved.

43. C **Properly adjusted cooking equipment.** Keeping cooking equipment properly calibrated is a factor in food quality but not *necessarily* an element of portion control. All of the other choices combine to permit an operator to consistently know (and control) the cost of each portion served.

44. E **Accompany the official on the inspection.** The health department, fire department, and OSHA, among others, all have a need (and the right!) to see what you are doing. Your best approach is to accept official inspections as a fact of life, like gravity. When inspectors arrive unannounced, as they usually will, accompany them on their tour and listen to what they have to say. Ask for their suggestions as to how best to remedy the problems they find. Above all, do not get defensive. They can make your life miserable if you do and can often be among your best allies if you meet them halfway.

45. E **How much usable food is contained in a purchased quantity.** An example of a yield analysis is carving a 20-pound turkey and weighing the amount of servable meat.

46. A **Expect the best from your staff and create an environment where they won't want to steal.** This is the only effective way to control theft because it addresses the cause of the problem from the perspective of a coach rather than that of a cop. This is not to minimize the need for control systems and due diligence—just don't make a career of it or you will stifle creativity and foster the very behavior you are trying to eliminate.

47. D **Cooking foods in large quantities.** Larger quantities take less energy per portion to prepare. While energy conservation is always a worthwhile pursuit, be careful not to prepare larger quantities than you can use in a timely manner.

48. D **Food is portioned in the kitchen and brought out to guests on plates.**

49. A **Food is brought on platters and served at the table.**

50. D **Food is portioned in the kitchen and brought out to guests on plates.**

51. C **Food is brought in bowls and on platters, and guests help themselves at the table.**

52. B **Guests help themselves from a long table or tables filled with food.**

53. C **Cooling a cooked food product in the walk-in.** All of the other choices are activities conducted under close observation by the kitchen staff. Because cooling takes place out of sight, it is more likely to be the place where food can remain out of temperature the longest.

54. A **Exclude her from food-handling until the cut heals.** This is the most correct choice of those offered. In practice, covering the wound with a surgical glove and having the staff member work out of sight of guests is a more likely solution. The important thing is that you never risk the wound or its bandage coming in contact with food.

55. B **Replacing empty food containers with full ones.** Of the choices offered, topping off containers, reusing serving utensils, or allowing salad bowls to be refilled are all forms of cross-contamination. Placing ice on the salad greens may help keep them crisp, but will also make for sloppy salads.

56. C **Check the ware-washing procedure to ensure that everything is being done properly.** Address the causes, not the symptoms. If you have a problem, fix it and move on. Polishing silverware is a health department violation; explaining things to the guest will not make her happy; and throwing the silverware away is unnecessary (and a little dramatic). It is certainly appropriate to be sure that your staff understands the importance of ensuring that only spotless flatware reaches the guest, but a reprimand comes out of the cop mentality and is likely to do more harm than good.

57. D **The function book.** Any operation that does catering or group functions or that accepts reservations for large parties should have a function book where the details of these commitments can be found by anyone on the staff.

58. C **Every half hour throughout the day.** A majority of your guests will make assumptions about the cleanliness of your kitchen based on the cleanliness of your restrooms. Since restrooms can get trashed in an instant, the only way to stay ahead of them is to check them frequently throughout the day.

59. B **Switch to a manual ordering system.** The POS (point of sale) system is an electronic system that allows orders to be placed on a terminal in the dining room and printed out in the kitchen. While this is a great convenience, the industry survived for centuries without it. Management should have a solid manual backup system and train the staff in how to use it. This way, when the POS system breaks down (and at some time it surely will), staff can switch to the manual program and maintain a high level of guest service without panic.

60. E **The manufacturer.** If all of the other criteria are met, the manufacturer is irrelevant.

61. D **Arrange for immediate treatment under your Worker's Compensation policy.** Your first priority is always getting treatment for the injured worker. Paperwork comes later. Generally, personal insurance will not pay for on-the-job injuries.

62. B **Employers must file an annual report of tip income for each tipped employee.** Employees must report their tips to the employer every pay period for income tax purposes.

63. C **A system to prevent foodborne illness.** HACCP stands for Hazard Analysis/Critical Control Points. It is a system for evaluating the way a restaurant handles all the components of its most popular menu items. An HACCP inspection will identify those points in the process that are most likely to contribute to the contamination of the product and design procedures to ensure that the risk is minimized. Many people think (hope!) that HACCP will eventually replace, or at least supplement, the typical 44-point sanitation inspection.

64. B **The amount of the loss.**

65. E **All of the above statements are true.**

66. B **A small pocket thermometer used to check food temperatures.** Every member of the food preparation staff and every attendant on a cafeteria line or salad bar should have a product thermometer to monitor food temperatures.

67. D **Check the daily communication log.** It is essential that the daily activities of the restaurant be recorded so that off-duty staff can stay informed of events. Every restaurant should have some sort of daily log for this purpose.

68. B **That they take steps to reduce job hazards.** While it is impossible to totally eliminate the possibility of accidents, it *is* possible to actively work to eliminate hazards.

69. C **18 years old.** Federal law now requires that workers be at least 18 years old before they can operate a slicer.

70. E **Vendor invoices.**

APPROACH

71. B **Complaints are special gifts.** Only one person in 25 will actually tell you when they have a complaint. The rest will simply go away, never return, and tell their friends to stay away, too. When you get a complaint, it is a rare insight into what may be killing your business. Accept the information with gratitude and fix the problem immediately.

72. E **Guest service.** Profitability comes from increasing the number of happy guests who regularly return to your restaurant. The other choices are factors that have value only if you are providing a high level of guest service. If you do not have happy guests, none of the other choices matter.

73. D   All of the above. Comps are usually given in response to a guest complaint and the faster a complaint is resolved, the better. Authorizing supervisors and servers to handle complaints in this manner is a statement about your commitment to guest gratification and your faith in your staff.

74. C   Check the sales mix. This is the most nonjudgmental response because a change in sales mix triggers a change in food cost without it being anyone's "fault." Here is how it works: Let's say you have two items on your menu—a chicken item with a 30% cost and a steak with a 50% cost. If you sell a higher percentage of steaks this month than last month, you should expect a higher food cost percentage, making the situation presented in this question not a problem at all. The most productive response to a problem is to first determine if there really is a problem.

75. E   Concentrate on sales training. In this case, your labor is not too high, your sales are just too low! Labor cost only has relevance in relationship to sales, and the most positive response to the problem posed in this question is to address the question of how to raise sales.

76. E   None of the above. There is seldom a single cause of a problem and it is dangerous to jump to conclusions.

77. A   Apologize and immediately resolve the situation in favor of the guest. The apology will help keep the guest from becoming more defensive. Resolving a complaint in favor of the guest is the only resolution that will be in the true long-term interests of the restaurant.

78. E   All of these situations could call for a comp. Guests come to the restaurant for a good time. Whenever they don't have that experience, regardless of whose "fault" it is, they will only remember that their last trip to your restaurant was not fun. In the case of the argument, comping the meal shows an unexpected compassion that will be memorable and might salvage what could otherwise be permanently lost patronage.

79. E   All the time, whether or not the restaurant's doors are open for business. Guest service is not what you do, it's a state of mind.

80. B   Talk to your guests. People come to your restaurant because they want to. Declining sales indicate that guests do not want to patronize you. The only way to really find out why is to ask them. In fact, this is a good idea no matter what your sales trend.

81. B   Your staff. In a legendary restaurant, the managers work for the staff and the staff works for the guests.

82. C   Form a committee from those who will use the equipment to do the research. People who will have to live with the results of a decision are the most appropriate ones to make it. In this way, even if the "wrong" equipment is selected, they will *make* it work!

83. A   Think it over and make the decision yourself. This is not a decision that will impact anyone else in the organization, so keep it simple. If you don't have time to handle it yourself, delegate it to someone else on your staff (who will be thrilled by your gesture of trust!).

84. C   Seat his party as soon as the table has been reset. You never seat guests at an unset table or speak to them in a harsh manner. In this case, the party would be seated before their drinks could be made (and alcohol might make the problem worse). If you feel the need to make a gesture, you might comp an appetizer once the party is seated.

85. E   To make sure the guests are happy. If the guests are not happy, nothing else you do has any consequence.

86. D   Talk to your staff. In 25 years of consulting, I have yet to run into an operating problem that couldn't be precisely identified by the staff. They may not know how to fix it, but they always know what is making their jobs difficult.

87. D   Defining jobs in terms of the results to be achieved. When you only specify the results, you leave your staff free to interpret their jobs in a way that works best for them. The results are greater productivity, higher job satisfaction, and improved guest service.

88. D   The rate of repeat business. If the most important job in the restaurant is to make sure the guests are happy, then the rate of repeat business shows how well that job is being done. All of the other choices are measures of management effectiveness, but they must be taken in context. For example, the operation's financial performance could exceed national ratios and still be in a declining sales posture. The importance of the staff turnover rate depends on whether it is increasing or decreasing. Increased profitability could come from an influx of business following a major advertising appeal to first-time diners. A high number of internal job promotions could be the result of high staff turnover.

89. B   Guests seated per hour. Because service must be provided from the time a guest is seated, the number of guests seated per hour is the best indicator of staffing needs. Sales per hour are not recorded until the guests leave. All other indicators do not provide hourly statistics and so are less useful in staffing.

90. C   Sales per hour. In a fast food operation, sales are made within minutes of the guests' arrival, meaning that sales per hour are an accurate indication of when staff are needed.

FINANCIAL

91. **A** **A bill.** The company is obligated to pay the amount of the invoice. Whenever someone on the staff signs an invoice, they are effectively signing a check.

92. **C** **The difference between receipts and expenditures.** Cash flow differs from profitability in that it measures the absolute movement of money. For example, a quarterly insurance premium of $300 impacts profitability in the amount of $100 per month. It affects cash flow to the extent of $300 in the month the payment is made.

93. **A** **Pass.** One of the keys to foodservice profitability is to maintain minimal inventories and turn them frequently. There is no deal good enough (and no storeroom big enough) to warrant tying up excess money and space for products that do not move.

94. **C** **The balance sheet.** The balance sheet lists the balances in all accounting categories. The income statement and capital inventory are reflected on the balance sheet. Cost-of-goods sold is reflected on the income statement. The cash flow statement is an internal management report.

95. **B** **$17,780.** Sales of $94,400 minus expenditures of $73,900 leave a net cash gain of $20,500 for the month. A closing balance of $38,280 minus the cash gained of $20,500 gives an opening balance of $17,780.

96. **D** **The food cost from purchases.** Barring any unusually large acquisitions, food cost from purchases will be accurate to within ½% after ten days.

97. **E** **Under 5%.** According to statistical studies by the National Restaurant Association, the typical full-service restaurant earns a median pretax profit of 3.5% to 4.0% of sales.

98. **C** **$69.50.** This is an interpretation question. A bottle of gin *costs* $7.75, but its *worth* is based on how much revenue it can generate. In this example, $93.00 per case divided by 12 bottles gives a cost per bottle of $7.75. Each bottle contains 25.3 shots (38 ounces divided by 1½ ounces). Multiplying 25.3 by $2.75 per drink equals $69.58. Allowing for the fact that you cannot get every drop of liquor out of the bottle makes $69.50 the most correct answer.

99. **A** **14.2%.** Pouring cost is generally calculated only on the liquor portion of the drink. In this case, 1½ ounces at 26¢ per ounce gives a cost of 39¢. Dividing that by the selling price of $2.75 gives a pouring cost of 14.2%.

100. **D** **A steak dinner selling for $12.95 with a 50% food cost.** This question tests the applicant's understanding of the fact that you don't pay bills with percentages. While the steak has the highest food cost percentage, its gross margin (the amount of money you get to keep every time you sell it) is $6.48. Gross margin on the other choices is as follows: enchiladas, $5.56; chicken sandwich, $3.37; and catfish, $5.55.

101. **E** **There is not enough information to answer the question.** An item with a portion cost of 82¢ would have to sell at $2.41 to have a 34% cost. I doubt that you would price a menu item at $2.41. In the real world, there are a number of factors that will determine selling price, including what the item typically sells for in your market, the price points of the rest of your menu, the presentation, etc. Without knowing the impact of these other factors, there is really not enough information to answer the question.

102. **B** **The number of guests served.**

103. **A** **A chef's salad.** The labor involved in preparing a chef's salad is significantly more than for any of the other choices.

104. **C** **$1,600.** You serve 80 lunches at an average check of $5 or $400 in midday sales. Your dinner business averages 120 meals at $10, or $1,200 in sales.

105. **C** **16.7%.** The $200 increase divided by $1,200 in current dinner sales equals 16.7%.

106. **A** **They will increase.** Variable costs vary with the sales volume.

107. **B** **It breaks even.**

108. **A** **Historical data and financial records.**

109. **D** **38.9%.** Food sales were $46,800 ($66,500 total sales less $4,100 sales tax less $15,600 beverage sales). Cost of food consumed was $16,800 in purchases plus $1,400 worth of food consumed from inventory ($5,400 opening value less $4,000 closing value)—a total of $18,200. Food consumed divided by food sales equals the food cost percentage for this example of 38.9%.

110. **C** **2 cups.** There are 16 tablespoons in a cup. The expanded recipe requires 33 tablespoons of flour, which is approximately 2 cups.

111. E   None of the above. Salt does not increase or decrease proportionately with the recipe. The proper amount of salt has to be determined by taste.

112. C   8 ounces. The meat ingredient of the recipe is 2½ pounds and yields 5 servings. Converting the meat portion to ounces (2½ times 16 ounces per pound) equals 40 ounces. This result, divided by 5 servings, gives a portion size of 8 ounces.

113. C $1.82. Applicants should be able to figure this out without conversion tables. For the recipe as listed, the meat cost is $8.25 (2½ × $2.75), the flour costs a penny, salt and pepper costs are negligible, paprika adds 7.5¢ (1 tablespoon of paprika equals ⅜ ounce), butter cost is about 6¢ (1 pound equals 2 cups). The tomato puree portion is 27¢ (a #10 can contains 12 to 13 cups, 6 cans per case), and the beef stock adds an additional 41.5¢ (12 cans per case at 49 ounces each). The total cost to produce the recipe is approximately $9.08, or $1.82 per portion.

114. B   36.0%. Food cost is only the edible portion of the meal, in this case $2.50. Dividing the cost by the selling price of $6.95 gives a food cost percentage of 36%.

115. D $5.50. Gross margin is the difference between the sales price and the cost.

116. B   Sliced salmon. The whole salmon works out to $11.11 per pound ($100 cost divided by 12 pounds divided by the 75% yield). While this is 44¢ per pound less than the sliced product, the labor involved in slicing whole salmon will offset the lower product cost. If you use 50 pounds of salmon a week, that will mean slicing over 5½ whole salmon. The total cost differential is $22 (50 pounds times 44¢ per pound) or about $4 per salmon. If you can slice salmon accurately for less than $4 per fish, you can work for me anytime!

117. E   Over $85,000. There is a slight trick in this question to prove a point. Each person you lose will cost you $3,600 over 5 years (3 visits per month times $20 per visit times 60 months). For the party of 4, the loss is $14,400. The trick is that the typical dissatisfied guest will tell 8 to 10 other people. One in 5 will tell 20 others. The people who hear the horror story are unlikely to come to your restaurant. If each of the 4 original guests only tells 5 others (and statistically, they will tell 8 to 10), it means 20 more lost guests. At $3,600 each, this represents another $72,000 in lost business. The total cost to you is already $86,400!

118. B   Consult the Uniform System of Accounts for Restaurants. The Uniform System of Accounts for Restaurants is the standardized accounting system for the industry. Its use ensures that your financial results will be in a form that can be meaningfully compared with industry statistics.

119. B   10 days. Within ten days, food cost from purchases will be within ½% of actual food cost, assuming that you have not made abnormal increases or decreases in inventory.

120. C   The last receipt price of each item.

MARKETING

121. D   Guest questionnaires.

122. B   Valet parking.

123. A   It influences people who are already interested in spending their money. Point-of-purchase advertising takes place at the cash register or at the table. You can be sure that everyone who enters a restaurant plans to buy, not browse.

124. E   A monthly magazine catering to the upper middle class. This medium is read by those people most likely to patronize an upscale restaurant.

125. A   Retirees. Of the available choices, retirees are the ones most likely to be able to dine in the afternoon.

126. C   Recommending a dessert on the menu. Suggestive selling is an overt act on the part of the server.

127. A   Public relations.

128. C   A table tent. A table tent makes a suggestion at the place where the sale will be made. Promotional copy on the back of the check can be helpful to promote sales on future visits, but guests don't get the check until the sale is completed.

129. B   To create staff appreciation.

130. B   Product differentiation.

ALCOHOL SERVICE

131. C Cheese. Protein foods slow the absorption rate of alcohol.

132. B Carbonated beverages. The carbonation helps the alcohol get into the bloodstream faster.

133. D A Social Security card. It does not show a birth date and is not a valid ID for the purchase of alcohol.

134. B It is illegal to serve alcohol to intoxicated persons.

135. D Spilling drinks. This is one of the signs of someone in the "red zone."

136. B 8 ounces of wine. The equivalent amount of wine is four ounces.

137. B If he gets into his car, call the police. In many states, this is the law. Good guest relations notwithstanding, I would rather have a guest angry at me than dead.

138. E Suggest nonalcoholic alternatives. This will keep the situation focused on positive factors rather than negative ones. In general, it is always preferable to tell people what you *can* do for them rather than what you *can't!*

139. E Suggest nonalcoholic alternatives. See the answer to question 138.

140. B Making guests come to the bar to order. This will not slow consumption and only provides poor service.

141. T In most states, the person who serves alcohol to an intoxicated person is personally liable.

142. T This can be a dangerous combination both for the individual and the restaurateur.

143. F The legal limit for DWI depends on your state, but anyone with a BAC of .8 is most likely *dead*! Now if the question said *.08*, that would be a different story!

144. F It's your state and your liquor license.

145. F High altitude intensifies the effects of alcohol.

146. F Alcohol is a depressant, but one that initially increases appetite—that's why we serve it in restaurants!

147. T Fat absorbs alcohol more rapidly than muscle.

148. T The rate of alcohol absorption varies with body composition, but the rate at which the liver eliminates alcohol from the system is constant for everyone.

149. F While occasionally a light touch can be calming, it is not a wise idea to touch intoxicated persons because you can never be sure how they will react.

150. F A breathalizer measures the amount of alcohol in the *lungs*, which is then converted to a BAC (blood alcohol content) reading.

Management Situations

1. You are the general manager of a full-service restaurant in Boise, Idaho. You have taken the weekend off and come into the restaurant at about 6:15 P.M. on Saturday night to cash a check on your way to a movie with your family. When you arrive, you find that the manager on duty has gone home sick. No one on the staff has called another manager to come in.

   This is what you find when you get in the door:

   You had planned a special "Maine Lobster Night" and promoted it heavily during the last week. The public seems to be really excited about the idea and your place is packed. The lobster was due this afternoon on a plane that was grounded by snow in Boston this morning. There is no lobster in the restaurant.

   Perhaps because of the lobster confusion, the kitchen is getting backed up. Orders that should be out in 20 minutes are starting to take almost 45 minutes. Your sous-chef and one of the dishwashers are complaining and threatening to walk out. Many of your guests tonight are planning to attend the symphony concert that starts at 8:00 P.M.!

   Perhaps because of the kitchen backup, the turn is slow. Your greeter has told waiting arriving guests their tables will be ready in 20 minutes or so. Most have already been waiting at least that long, and it is starting to look like it might be at least another half hour before you can seat them!

   A. How would you handle things tonight? What would you do—how and in what order? Please note that suicide or resignation is not an option!

   B. What do you see as the factors that created the problem?

   C. How would you handle things over the next few days? What would you do—how and in what order?

2. It is 7:00 on Friday night. You are the manager on duty in a popular 200-seat "special occasion" restaurant noted for its extensive wine list. You have a table for 12 in the middle of the main dining room celebrating a wedding. The host is a prominent businessperson who happens to be one of your best regular patrons. They started at 6:00 with oysters and four bottles of Dom Perignon. They are now into their second round of appetizers and have ordered your most expensive entrees, the server has just opened their fourth bottle of your Chateau Lafite, and the group is getting louder as the evening progresses.

   In the last 20 minutes, other parties in the dining room have made comments to you about the behavior of these people. As you are walking through the dining room, the host rises and, in a voice that echoes through the room, proposes an off-color toast to the bride and groom. Every other guest in the dining room looks at you.

   A. What, if anything, do you do now?

   B. What, if anything, do you do over the next few days?

1. Usted es el administrador general de un restaurante de servicio completo en Boise, Idaho. Usted se tomó el fin de semana libre y llegó al restaurante cerca de las 6:15 PM la noche del sábado a cobrar un cheque cuando iba de camino al cine con su familia. Cuando usted llegó, usted se enteró que el administrador en servicio se había ido a casa enfermo. Nadie en el equipo técnico ha llamado a otro administrador para que venga.

Esto es lo que usted encuentra cuando usted entra por la puerta:

Usted había planificado una "Noche de Langostas de Maine" especial y la promovió mucho durante la semana pasada. El público se ve muy entusiasmado con la idea y el lugar está lleno. La langosta tenía que haber llegado de Boston en un avión que llegaba por la tarde pero que fue retrasado debido a la nieve de esta mañana. No hay langosta en el restaurante.

Quizás debido a la confusión con la langosta, la cocina se está retrasando. Las órdenes que deben estar listas en 20 minutos se están demorando casi 45 minutos. Su chef de sous y uno de los lavadores de platos se están quejando y amenazando con irse. Muchos de los clientes piensan asistir al concierto de la sinfonía que comienza a las 8:00 PM!

Quizás debido al retraso en la cocina, la situación es lenta. Su anfitrión le ha dicho a los clientes que la espera será de 20 minutos aproximadamente. Muchos de los clientes ya han estado esperando por lo menos ese tiempo y está comenzando a parecer que puede ser más o menos otra media hora antes que pueda sentarlos.

A. ¿Cómo manejaría usted la situación esa noche? ¿Qué haría, cómo lo haría y en qué orden lo haría? ¡Por favor note que el suicidio o renunciar no son opciones!

B. ¿Qué cree usted fueron los factores que crearon el problema?

C. ¿Cómo manejaría usted las cosas en los siguientes días? ¿Qué haría usted, cómo lo haría y en qué orden lo haría?

2. Son las 7:00 PM el viernes en la noche. Usted es el administrador en servicio en un restaurante de "ocasiones especiales" de 200 puestos de capacidad famoso por su extensiva selección de vinos. Usted tiene una mesa de 12 en medio del comedor principal celebrando una boda. La anfitriona es una mujer de negocios muy destacada que también frecuenta mucho el restaurante. Comenzaron a las 6:00 con ostras y cuatro botellas de Dom Perignon. Ahora están en su segunda vuelta de aperitivos, y han ordenado sus platos más caros, el mesero acaba de abrir la cuarta botella de su Chateau Lafitte y el grupo se está poniendo más bullicioso al avanzar la noche.

En los últimos 20 minutos, otros clientes en el comedor le han hecho comentarios acerca del comportamiento de los clientes de la boda. Al caminar a través del comedor, la anfitriona se levanta y en una voz que resuena a través del salón, propone una brindis de tonos muy bajos para los novios. Todos los demás clientes en el comedor lo voltean a ver a usted.

A. ¿Qué, si cualquier cosa, haría usted?

B. ¿Qué, si cualquier cosa, hace usted en los siguientes días?

Situation Test Evaluation

COACHING STAFF

Name: **Evaluated By:**

Scoring:

Grade each evaluation criterion as it is observed (Y—Yes, N—No, ?—Maybe).
Give two points for each Y, one point for each ?, and no points for N.
A score of 16 or better means an overall evaluation of Yes.
A score of 10 to 15 means an overall evaluation of Maybe.
A score of 9 or below means an overall evaluation of No.

SITUATION 1:

Y N ?

☐ ☐ ☐   1. Did the candidate come up with a solution without hesitation?
☐ ☐ ☐   2. Was it a guest-oriented solution?
☐ ☐ ☐   3. Would the solution work for the house?
☐ ☐ ☐   4. Did the candidate take control of the situation?
☐ ☐ ☐   5. Were the candidate's priorities appropriate?
☐ ☐ ☐   6. Did the candidate grasp the real causes underlying the situation?
☐ ☐ ☐   7. Did the candidate take a positive (versus negative) approach to the situation?
☐ ☐ ☐   8. Did the candidate accept personal responsibility for the situation?
☐ ☐ ☐   9. Did the candidate take care of their family first?
☐ ☐ ☐ 10. Would the candidate's long-term approach be likely to prevent a similar occurrence in the future?

Total Score:

_____

OVERALL EVALUATION:

☐ Yes
☐ No
☐ Maybe

SITUATION 2:

Y N ?

☐ ☐ ☐   1. Did the candidate come up with a solution without hesitation?
☐ ☐ ☐   2. Would the solution retain the good will of the wedding party?
☐ ☐ ☐   3. Would the solution retain the good will of the other guests?
☐ ☐ ☐   4. Would the solution work for the house?
☐ ☐ ☐   5. Did the candidate take control of the situation?
☐ ☐ ☐   6. Were the candidate's priorities appropriate?
☐ ☐ ☐   7. Did the candidate's solution avoid embarrassment to the host?
☐ ☐ ☐   8. Did the candidate take a positive (versus negative) approach to the situation?
☐ ☐ ☐   9. Did the candidate accept personal responsibility for the situation?
☐ ☐ ☐ 10. Would the candidate's long-term approach be likely to prevent a similar occurrence in the future?

Total Score:

_____

OVERALL EVALUATION:

☐ Yes
☐ No
☐ Maybe

Demonstration Test 2
COACHING STAFF

You are the new manager of The Barn, a small barbecue restaurant. Guests pass along a cafeteria-like line to make their selections and pay at the end of the line. All dining room workers are trained in each position (server, cashier, dining room service, etc.). The restaurant opens at 11:00 A.M. and closes at 10:30 P.M. Monday through Friday. Saturday hours are from 11:00 A.M. to 8:30 P.M. You are closed on Sunday.

This is what you know about your dining room crew:

Bonnie	can work days only.
Susan	can work any shift.
Ray	works afternoons and evenings only, can't start until after 2:00.
Karen	can work days only.
Leon	can work afternoons and evenings anytime.
Laurie	can work any shift.
Chris	can work afternoons and evenings, has class on Tuesday and Thursday.
Kathy	can only work days, three hours maximum, has to leave by 2:30 to pick up her child.
Claire	can work afternoons and evenings; takes the bus so must leave by 10:00 P.M.

You have been keeping hourly register readings for the past week, and here is what you have recorded.

	12	1	2	3	4	5	6	7	8	9	10	11	TOTAL
Monday	$174	$224	$134	$100	$105	$ 89	$ 75	$ 88	$ 72	$ 91	$ 72	$ 4	$1,228
Tuesday	194	224	158	81	88	61	76	94	80	78	27	4	1,165
Wednesday	252	276	153	87	95	74	102	97	112	97	39	6	1,390
Thursday	200	234	148	101	105	84	78	107	106	95	58	2	1,318
Friday	337	390	233	169	154	144	142	149	103	144	83	5	2,053
Saturday	186	158	91	89	109	101	92	99	104	44	—	—	1,073

You expect sales volume to stay the same next week. The current schedule was prepared by a former manager and has not changed in six months. A copy is on the following page. Prepare the dining room staff schedule for Thursday on the form provided.

Assume the following when creating the schedule:

All staff members are equally qualified and productive.

You must provide a minimum 4-hour shift unless the staff member requests otherwise.

There is no requirement that anyone work a full-time shift.

Schedule in increments no smaller than half hours.

Sidework requirements: preopening—1½ hours; midafternoon (2 to 3 P.M.)—1 hour; preclosing—1 hour.

Your staff said that the first hour of business on Thursday is when they felt they were most productive and provided the best service to guests.

You may complete this test at home. Make sure you know when and where you must return your solution to this problem. **Be sure to put your name on the revised schedule before returning it.**

Examen de Demostración 2
EQUIPO TÉCNICO DE ENTRENAMIENTO

Usted es el nuevo administrador de La Granja, un restaurante pequeño de barbacoa. Los clientes pasan por el mostrador al estilo de cafetería a seleccionar su pedido y pagan al final de la fila. Todos los trabajadores del comedor están entrenados en cada posición (servidores, cajeros, servicios del comedor, etc.). El restaurante abre a 11:00 AM y cierra a las 10:30 PM de lunes a viernes. Las horas los sábados son de 11:00 AM a 8:30 PM. Está cerrado el domingo.

Esto es lo que usted sabe acerca de su equipo técnico del comedor:

Bonnie	puede trabajar durante el día solamente
Susan	puede trabajar cualquier turno
Ray	trabaja tardes y noches solamente, puede empezar después de las 2:00 PM
Karen	puede trabajar durante el día solamente
Leon	puede trabajar tardes y noches a cualquier hora
Laurie	puede trabajar cualquier turno
Chris	puede trabajar tardes y noches, tiene clases los martes y jueves
Kathy	puede trabajar durante el día 3 horas max., tiene que irse a las 2:30 PM a recoger a su hijo.
Claire	puede trabajar tardes y noches, toma el autobus así que tiene que salir a las 10:00 PM

Usted ha estado manteniendo un registro de horas durante la semana pasada y aquí está lo que ha recopilado:

	12	1	2	3	4	5	6	7	8	9	10	11	TOTAL
Lunes	$174	$224	$134	$100	$105	$ 89	$ 75	$ 88	$ 72	$ 91	$ 72	$ 4	$1,228
Martes	194	224	158	81	88	61	76	94	80	78	27	4	1,165
Miercoles	252	276	153	87	95	74	102	97	112	97	39	6	1,390
Jueves	200	234	148	101	105	84	78	107	106	95	58	2	1,318
Viernes	337	390	233	169	154	144	142	149	103	144	83	5	2,053
Sábado	186	158	91	89	109	101	92	99	104	44	—	—	1,073

Usted espera que el volúmen de ventas permanezca igual la siguiente semana. El horario actual fue preparado por el administrador anterior y no ha habido cambios en los últimos seis meses. Una copia es incluida en la siguiente página. Prepare el horario del equipo técnico del comedor para el jueves utilizando el formulario adjunto.

Suponga lo siguiente al crear el horario:

Todos los miembros del equipo técnico son igualmente calificados y productivos.
Usted tiene que proveer un turno de 4 horas mínimo a menos que el miembro del equipo técnico lo solicite de otra manera.
No se requiere que alguien trabaje un turno de jornada completa.
Aumentos en los horarios de menos de media hora.
Los requisitos de trabajo aparte: pre-apertura = 1½ horas; a mediados de la tarde (2–3 PM) = 1 hora; pre-cierre = 1 hora.
Su equipo técnico dijo que la primera hora de negocio el jueves es cuando ellos se sienten más productivos y ofrecen el mejor servicio a los clientes.

STAFFING SCHEDULE (Original)

Restaurant ___The Barn___   Department _____   Dining Room _____   Period _____

	10	11	12	1	2	3	4	5	6	7	8	9	10	11		TOTAL
Bonnie	▓	▓	▓	▓												4.0
Karen	▓	▓	▓	▓												4.0
Susan	▓	▓	▓	▓	▓											5.0
Laurie	▓	▓	▓	▓	▓											5.0
Claire					▓	▓	▓	▓	▓	▓	▓	▓				8.0
Ray						▓	▓	▓	▓	▓	▓	▓	▓	▓		8.0
Leon						▓	▓	▓	▓	▓	▓	▓	▓	▓		8.0
TOTAL STAFFING	4.0	4.0	4.0	4.0	3.0	3.0	3.0	3.0	3.0	3.0	3.0	3.0	3.0	2.0		42.0

STAFFING SCHEDULE (Revised)

Restaurant ___The Barn___   Department _____   Dining Room _____   Period _____

Prepared by _____

	10	11	12	1	2	3	4	5	6	7	8	9	10	11		TOTAL
TOTAL STAFFING																

Demonstration Test 2
Evaluation

COACHING STAFF

SCHEDULE TEST

Procedure:

Candidates receive the scheduling problem information and complete the schedule overnight. They are instructed to return the problem by a specified time.

Situation:

The opportunity exists to reduce labor hours by 25 percent while increasing productivity and guest service. See the solution below.

Solution:

The target productivity level is $50 per labor hour ($200 in sales during the first hour of business on Thursday divided by 4 hours scheduled). Divide the hourly sales by $50 to determine the staffing hours required to produce the desired productivity. Add the sidework requirements. Round the total hour requirements to the same increment as that used in scheduling. (If scheduling in half-hour increments, target hours are expressed to the nearest half hour; if scheduling in quarter-hours, target hours are rounded to the nearest 15 minutes, etc.) Develop a schedule where actual hours parallel target hours as closely as possible. See the enclosed sample solution.

Evaluation Criteria:

Y N ?

☐ ☐ ☐ 1. Was the test returned at the agreed-upon time?
☐ ☐ ☐ 2. Were 1 to 2 hours scheduled between 10 A.M. and 11 A.M.?
☐ ☐ ☐ 3. Were 3½ to 4½ hours scheduled between 11 A.M. and noon?
☐ ☐ ☐ 4. Were 4 to 5 hours scheduled between noon and 1 P.M.?
☐ ☐ ☐ 5. Were 3½ to 4½ hours scheduled between 1 P.M. and 2 P.M.?
☐ ☐ ☐ 6. Were 3½ to 4½ hours scheduled between 2 P.M. and 3 P.M.?
☐ ☐ ☐ 7. Were 1½ to 2½ hours scheduled between 3 P.M. and 4 P.M.?
☐ ☐ ☐ 8. Were 2 to 3 hours scheduled between 4 P.M. and 5 P.M.?
☐ ☐ ☐ 9. Were 2 to 3 hours scheduled between 5 P.M. and 6 P.M.?
☐ ☐ ☐ 10. Were 2½ to 3½ hours scheduled between 6 P.M. and 7 P.M.?
☐ ☐ ☐ 11. Were 2½ to 3½ hours scheduled between 7 P.M. and 8 P.M.?
☐ ☐ ☐ 12. Were 2½ to 3½ hours scheduled between 8 P.M. and 9 P.M.?
☐ ☐ ☐ 13. Were 1 to 1½ hours scheduled between 9 P.M. and 10 P.M.?
☐ ☐ ☐ 14. Were 1 to 1½ hours scheduled between 10 P.M. and 11 P.M.?
☐ ☐ ☐ 15. Were 28 to 32 total hours scheduled?
☐ ☐ ☐ 16. Did the schedule avoid having *everybody* work on Thursday?
☐ ☐ ☐ 17. Did the schedule match the work restrictions of the staff?
☐ ☐ ☐ 18. Was the schedule prepared in half-hour increments?
☐ ☐ ☐ 19. Except for Kathy, was the minimum time scheduled at least 4 hours?
☐ ☐ ☐ 20. Was the schedule neat and legible?

Scoring:

Grade each evaluation criterion as Y—Yes, N—No, ?—Maybe.
Give two points for each Y, one point for each ?, and no points for N.
A score of 32 or better means an overall evaluation of Yes.
A score of 20 to 31 means an overall evaluation of Maybe.
A score of 19 or below means an overall evaluation of No.

Total Score:

_____

OVERALL EVALUATION:

☐ Yes
☐ No
☐ Maybe

STAFFING REQUIREMENTS

Restaurant ___ The Barn ___   Department ___ Dining Room ___   Period ___ Thursday ___

	10	11	12	1	2	3	4	5	6	7	8	9	10	11	TOTAL
Estimated Sales			$200	$234	$148	$101	$105	$84	$78	$107	$106	$95	$58	$2	$1318
Service Hours*			4.0	4.7	3.0	2.0	1.7	1.6	2.1	2.1	2.1	1.9	1.2	---	26.7
Sidework	1.5					1.0								1.0	3.5
Target Hours#	1.5		4.0	4.5	3.0	3.0	2.0	1.5	1.5	2.0	2.0	1.0	1.0	1.0	30.0

NOTES: (*)   Hourly sales divided by $50 (target productivity)
           (#)   Service hours plus sidework rounded to the nearest half hour (because scheduling is done in half hour increments)

STAFFING SCHEDULE

Restaurant ___ The Barn ___   Department ___ Dining Room ___   Period ___ Thursday ___

	10	11	12	1	2	3	4	5	6	7	8	9	10	11	TOTAL
Kathy															3.0
Bonnie															4.5
Susan or Karen															5.0
Laurie															6.0
Claire															5.0
Leon or Ray															6.0
TOTAL STAFFING	1.5	4.0	4.0	3.0	3.0	2.0	2.0	2.0	2.0	2.0	2.0	1.0	1.0		29.5
TARGET HOURS	1.5		4.0	4.5	3.0	3.0	2.0	1.5	1.5	2.0	2.0	1.0	1.0	1.0	30.0

A P P E N D I X   F

Beverage Staff Tests

Lifting Test (English)   **F-1**

Demonstration Test 1A (English)   **F-2**

Demonstration Test 1B (English)   **F-3**

Professional Test Answer Sheet (English)   **F-4**

Professional Test Answer Sheet (Spanish)   **F-5**

Professional Test Answer Sheet Overlay (English)   **F-6**

Professional Test (English)   **F-7**

Professional Test (Spanish)   **F-20**

Professional Test Answers (English)   **F-34**

Beverage Situations (English)   **F-40**

Beverage Situations (Spanish)   **F-41**

Situation Test Evaluation (English)   **F-42**

Demonstration Test 2 (English)   **F-43**

Lifting Test

BEVERAGE STAFF

Name: _____   **Evaluated By:** _____

Procedure:

The candidate lifts the heaviest object likely to be encountered on the job from where it is normally found to the most difficult location at which it can logically be placed. This is *not* a timed test.

Materials:

Select an item that has figured in on-the-job lifting injuries. Consider what tasks the candidate will typically perform in the position as well as situations likely to be encountered in the normal course of business while assisting co-workers.

Demonstration Specification:

Item to be lifted: _____ Weight: _____

Lift from: _____

Lift to: _____

Evaluation Criteria:

Y N ?

☐ ☐ ☐   1. Could the candidate lift the object?
☐ ☐ ☐   2. Did the lift show lack of strain?
☐ ☐ ☐   3. Did the candidate lift with a straight back?
☐ ☐ ☐   4. Did the candidate lift with the legs?
☐ ☐ ☐   5. Did the candidate keep the load close to the body?
☐ ☐ ☐   6. Did the candidate use a proper ladder or stool (if appropriate)?
☐ ☐ ☐   7. Was the object safely under control at all times?
☐ ☐ ☐   8. Was the candidate alert to the physical surroundings during the lift?
☐ ☐ ☐   9. Did the final placement of the object allow for proper air circulation?
☐ ☐ ☐ 10. Did the candidate handle the object with care and respect?

Scoring:

Grade each evaluation criterion as it is observed (Y—Yes, N—No, ?—Maybe).
Give two points for each Y, one point for each ?, and no points for N.
If use of a ladder or stool was not appropriate, score Item 6 as Y.
If Item 1 is marked N, the overall evaluation must be No.
If Item 1 is marked ?, the overall evaluation must be Maybe.
If Item 2 is marked N or ?, the overall evaluation must be Maybe.
A score of 16 or better means an overall evaluation of Yes.
A score of 10 to 15 means an overall evaluation of Maybe.
A score of 9 or below means an overall evaluation of No.

Total Score:

_____

OVERALL EVALUATION:

☐ Yes
☐ No
☐ Maybe

Demonstration Test 1A

BEVERAGE STAFF

Name: _____ Evaluated By: _____

NOTE: There are two Demonstration Tests included for the beverage staff. Demonstration Test 1A is the preferred screening for those operations where liquor is dispensed directly from the bottle. Operations that utilize metered pouring may prefer to use Demonstration Test 1B to gain insight into a candidate's job skills.

POURING TEST

Procedure:

The candidate is asked to pour ten of your standard-size shots from a bottle. This is a timed test.

Materials:

Empty liquor bottle, pour spout, and ten glasses.

Setup:

Fill the bottle with just enough water to pour ten of your standard shots. Give the candidate the materials on a tray and have them pour one shot into each glass.

Evaluation Criteria:

Y N ?

☐ ☐ ☐ 1. Did the candidate wash her hands before starting work?
☐ ☐ ☐ 2. Did the candidate use proper handwashing technique?
☐ ☐ ☐ 3. Did the candidate organize the materials provided before starting?
☐ ☐ ☐ 4. Did the candidate run out of liquid before running out of glasses?
☐ ☐ ☐ 5. Were all shots of equal size?
☐ ☐ ☐ 6. Did the candidate demonstrate a smooth pouring technique?
☐ ☐ ☐ 7. Did the candidate have a pleasant expression while working?
☐ ☐ ☐ 8. Did the candidate avoid spills?
☐ ☐ ☐ 9. Did the candidate demonstrate confidence while working?
☐ ☐ ☐ 10. Did the candidate converse with the observer while working?

Scoring:

Grade each evaluation criterion as it is observed (Y—Yes, N—No, ?—Maybe).
Give two points for each Y, one point for each ?, and no points for N.
A score of 16 or better means an overall evaluation of Yes.
A score of 10 to 15 means an overall evaluation of Maybe.
A score of 9 or below means an overall evaluation of No.

Total Score:

_____

Elapsed Time:

_____

OVERALL EVALUATION:

☐ Yes
☐ No
☐ Maybe

Demonstration Test 1B

BEVERAGE STAFF

Name: _____ **Evaluated By:** _____

NOTE: There are two Demonstration Tests included for the beverage staff. Demonstration Test 1A is the preferred screening for operations where liquor is dispensed directly from the bottle. Operations that utilize metered pouring may prefer to use Demonstration Test 1B to gain insight into a candidate's job skills.

FRUIT TEST

Procedure:

The candidate is asked to cut bar fruit (orange slices, lemon twists, and lime wedges) and place the finished products in the refrigerator.

Materials:

Selection of fruit (some with blemishes), knives, cutting board, containers, clear wrap, marking pen.

Setup:

The fruit, knives, cutting board, and container are placed in obvious positions. The clear wrap and marking pen are on the periphery of the work area in a position that makes them less obvious as being part of the test.

Evaluation Criteria:

Y N ?

☐ ☐ ☐   1. Did the candidate wash his hands before starting work?
☐ ☐ ☐   2. Did the candidate use proper handwashing technique?
☐ ☐ ☐   3. Was the fruit cut uniformly?
☐ ☐ ☐   4. Was the finished product free of any blemished fruit?
☐ ☐ ☐   5. Was a safe cutting technique used? (fingertips protected)
☐ ☐ ☐   6. Did the candidate demonstrate a smooth cutting technique?
☐ ☐ ☐   7. Was the fruit placed in the containers in a sanitary manner?
☐ ☐ ☐   8. Did the candidate clean the work area when finished?
☐ ☐ ☐   9. Were the knife and cutting board cleaned properly and safely?
☐ ☐ ☐ 10. Did the candidate cover and date the containers before placing them in the refrigerator?

Scoring:

Grade each evaluation criterion as it is observed (Y—Yes, N—No, ?—Maybe).
Give two points for each Y, one point for each ?, and no points for N.
A score of 16 or better means an overall evaluation of Yes.
A score of 10 to 15 means an overall evaluation of Maybe.
A score below 10 means an overall evaluation of No.

Total Score:

_____

Elapsed Time:

_____

OVERALL EVALUATION:

☐ Yes
☐ No
☐ Maybe

Professional Test

PRODUCTION STAFF
Answer Sheet

NAME: _____   SSN: _____

This test is designed to indicate how you view the restaurant industry. As a result, you will find that several questions may have more than one correct answer. Check the single answer you think is *MOST CORRECT* based on your point of view. Time is of the essence. The faster you complete the test, the better your index score.

HUMAN REL
A B C D E
1. ☐ ☐ ☐ ☐ ☐
2. ☐ ☐ ☐ ☐ ☐
3. ☐ ☐ ☐ ☐ ☐
4. ☐ ☐ ☐ ☐ ☐
5. ☐ ☐ ☐ ☐ ☐
6. ☐ ☐ ☐ ☐ ☐
7. ☐ ☐ ☐ ☐ ☐
8. ☐ ☐ ☐ ☐ ☐
9. ☐ ☐ ☐ ☐ ☐
10. ☐ ☐ ☐ ☐ ☐

SANITATION
11. ☐ ☐ ☐ ☐ ☐
12. ☐ ☐ ☐ ☐ ☐
13. ☐ ☐ ☐ ☐ ☐
14. ☐ ☐ ☐ ☐ ☐
15. ☐ ☐ ☐ ☐ ☐
16. ☐ ☐ ☐ ☐ ☐
17. ☐ ☐ ☐ ☐ ☐
18. ☐ ☐ ☐ ☐ ☐
19. ☐ ☐ ☐ ☐ ☐
20. ☐ ☐ ☐ ☐ ☐

IMPRESSIONS
21. ☐ ☐ ☐ ☐ ☐
22. ☐ ☐ ☐ ☐ ☐
23. ☐ ☐ ☐ ☐ ☐
24. ☐ ☐ ☐ ☐ ☐
25. ☐ ☐ ☐ ☐ ☐
26. ☐ ☐ ☐ ☐ ☐
27. ☐ ☐ ☐ ☐ ☐
28. ☐ ☐ ☐ ☐ ☐
29. ☐ ☐ ☐ ☐ ☐
30. ☐ ☐ ☐ ☐ ☐

OPERATIONS
A B C D E
31. ☐ ☐ ☐ ☐ ☐
32. ☐ ☐ ☐ ☐ ☐
33. ☐ ☐ ☐ ☐ ☐
34. ☐ ☐ ☐ ☐ ☐
35. ☐ ☐ ☐ ☐ ☐
36. ☐ ☐ ☐ ☐ ☐
37. ☐ ☐ ☐ ☐ ☐
38. ☐ ☐ ☐ ☐ ☐
39. ☐ ☐ ☐ ☐ ☐
40. ☐ ☐ ☐ ☐ ☐
41. ☐ ☐ ☐ ☐ ☐
42. ☐ ☐ ☐ ☐ ☐
43. ☐ ☐ ☐ ☐ ☐
44. ☐ ☐ ☐ ☐ ☐
45. ☐ ☐ ☐ ☐ ☐
46. ☐ ☐ ☐ ☐ ☐
47. ☐ ☐ ☐ ☐ ☐
48. ☐ ☐ ☐ ☐ ☐
49. ☐ ☐ ☐ ☐ ☐
50. ☐ ☐ ☐ ☐ ☐
51. ☐ ☐ ☐ ☐ ☐
52. ☐ ☐ ☐ ☐ ☐
53. ☐ ☐ ☐ ☐ ☐
54. ☐ ☐ ☐ ☐ ☐
55. ☐ ☐ ☐ ☐ ☐
56. ☐ ☐ ☐ ☐ ☐
57. ☐ ☐ ☐ ☐ ☐
58. ☐ ☐ ☐ ☐ ☐
59. ☐ ☐ ☐ ☐ ☐
60. ☐ ☐ ☐ ☐ ☐

ALCOHOL
A B C D E
61. ☐ ☐ ☐ ☐ ☐
62. ☐ ☐ ☐ ☐ ☐
63. ☐ ☐ ☐ ☐ ☐
64. ☐ ☐ ☐ ☐ ☐
65. ☐ ☐ ☐ ☐ ☐
66. ☐ ☐ ☐ ☐ ☐
67. ☐ ☐ ☐ ☐ ☐
68. ☐ ☐ ☐ ☐ ☐
69. ☐ ☐ ☐ ☐ ☐
70. ☐ ☐ ☐ ☐ ☐

T F
71. ☐ ☐
72. ☐ ☐
73. ☐ ☐
74. ☐ ☐
75. ☐ ☐
76. ☐ ☐
77. ☐ ☐
78. ☐ ☐
79. ☐ ☐
80. ☐ ☐

FINANCIAL
81. ☐ ☐ ☐ ☐ ☐
82. ☐ ☐ ☐ ☐ ☐
83. ☐ ☐ ☐ ☐ ☐
84. ☐ ☐ ☐ ☐ ☐
85. ☐ ☐ ☐ ☐ ☐
86. ☐ ☐ ☐ ☐ ☐
87. ☐ ☐ ☐ ☐ ☐
88. ☐ ☐ ☐ ☐ ☐
89. ☐ ☐ ☐ ☐ ☐
90. ☐ ☐ ☐ ☐ ☐

SALES
A B C D E
91. ☐ ☐ ☐ ☐ ☐
92. ☐ ☐ ☐ ☐ ☐
93. ☐ ☐ ☐ ☐ ☐
94. ☐ ☐ ☐ ☐ ☐
95. ☐ ☐ ☐ ☐ ☐
96. ☐ ☐ ☐ ☐ ☐
97. ☐ ☐ ☐ ☐ ☐
98. ☐ ☐ ☐ ☐ ☐
99. ☐ ☐ ☐ ☐ ☐
100. ☐ ☐ ☐ ☐ ☐

RECIPES
101. _____ _____ _____
102. _____ _____ _____
103. _____ _____ _____
104. _____ _____ _____
105. _____ _____ _____
106. _____ _____ _____
107. _____ _____ _____
108. _____ _____ _____
109. _____ _____ _____
110. _____ _____ _____
111. _____ _____ _____
112. _____ _____ _____
113. _____ _____ _____
114. _____ _____ _____
115. _____ _____ _____
116. _____ _____ _____
117. _____ _____ _____
118. _____ _____ _____
119. _____ _____ _____
120. _____ _____ _____

BEVERAGE
A B C D E
121. ☐ ☐ ☐ ☐ ☐
122. ☐ ☐ ☐ ☐ ☐
123. ☐ ☐ ☐ ☐ ☐
124. ☐ ☐ ☐ ☐ ☐
125. _____
126. _____
127. _____
128. _____
129. _____
130. _____
131. _____
132. _____
133. _____
134. _____
135. _____
136. _____
137. _____
138. _____
139. _____
140. _____
141. _____
142. _____
143. _____
144. _____
145. _____
146. _____
147. _____
148. _____
149. _____
150. _____

FOR OFFICE USE:

HR:___ SAN:___ IMP:___ OPS:___ ALC:___ FIN:___ SALE:___ REC:___ BEV:___ TOT:___ TIME:___ INDEX:___

Examen Profesional

EQUIPO TÉCNICO DE BEBIDAS

NOMBRE: _____   **NÚMERO DE SEGURIDAD SOCIAL:** _____

Esta prueba está diseñada para formar una opinión cómo es que usted ve a la industria de los restaurantes. Por lo tanto, usted encontrará que varias preguntas pueden tener más de una respuesta correcta. Marque la única respuesta que usted crea sea *MÁS CORRECTA* basándolo en su punto de vista personal. El tiempo es esencial. Entre más rápido complete usted la prueba, mejor será su puntuación.

REL HUMANAS
A B C D E
1. ☐ ☐ ☐ ☐ ☐
2. ☐ ☐ ☐ ☐ ☐
3. ☐ ☐ ☐ ☐ ☐
4. ☐ ☐ ☐ ☐ ☐
5. ☐ ☐ ☐ ☐ ☐
6. ☐ ☐ ☐ ☐ ☐
7. ☐ ☐ ☐ ☐ ☐
8. ☐ ☐ ☐ ☐ ☐
9. ☐ ☐ ☐ ☐ ☐
10. ☐ ☐ ☐ ☐ ☐

SANIDAD
11. ☐ ☐ ☐ ☐ ☐
12. ☐ ☐ ☐ ☐ ☐
13. ☐ ☐ ☐ ☐ ☐
14. ☐ ☐ ☐ ☐ ☐
15. ☐ ☐ ☐ ☐ ☐
16. ☐ ☐ ☐ ☐ ☐
17. ☐ ☐ ☐ ☐ ☐
18. ☐ ☐ ☐ ☐ ☐
19. ☐ ☐ ☐ ☐ ☐
20. ☐ ☐ ☐ ☐ ☐

IMPRESIONES
21. ☐ ☐ ☐ ☐ ☐
22. ☐ ☐ ☐ ☐ ☐
23. ☐ ☐ ☐ ☐ ☐
24. ☐ ☐ ☐ ☐ ☐
25. ☐ ☐ ☐ ☐ ☐
26. ☐ ☐ ☐ ☐ ☐
27. ☐ ☐ ☐ ☐ ☐
28. ☐ ☐ ☐ ☐ ☐
29. ☐ ☐ ☐ ☐ ☐
30. ☐ ☐ ☐ ☐ ☐

OPERACIONES
A B C D E
31. ☐ ☐ ☐ ☐ ☐
32. ☐ ☐ ☐ ☐ ☐
33. ☐ ☐ ☐ ☐ ☐
34. ☐ ☐ ☐ ☐ ☐
35. ☐ ☐ ☐ ☐ ☐
36. ☐ ☐ ☐ ☐ ☐
37. ☐ ☐ ☐ ☐ ☐
38. ☐ ☐ ☐ ☐ ☐
39. ☐ ☐ ☐ ☐ ☐
40. ☐ ☐ ☐ ☐ ☐
41. ☐ ☐ ☐ ☐ ☐
42. ☐ ☐ ☐ ☐ ☐
43. ☐ ☐ ☐ ☐ ☐
44. ☐ ☐ ☐ ☐ ☐
45. ☐ ☐ ☐ ☐ ☐
46. ☐ ☐ ☐ ☐ ☐
47. ☐ ☐ ☐ ☐ ☐
48. ☐ ☐ ☐ ☐ ☐
49. ☐ ☐ ☐ ☐ ☐
50. ☐ ☐ ☐ ☐ ☐
51. ☐ ☐ ☐ ☐ ☐
52. ☐ ☐ ☐ ☐ ☐
53. ☐ ☐ ☐ ☐ ☐
54. ☐ ☐ ☐ ☐ ☐
55. ☐ ☐ ☐ ☐ ☐
56. ☐ ☐ ☐ ☐ ☐
57. ☐ ☐ ☐ ☐ ☐
58. ☐ ☐ ☐ ☐ ☐
59. ☐ ☐ ☐ ☐ ☐
60. ☐ ☐ ☐ ☐ ☐

ALCOHOL
A B C D E
61. ☐ ☐ ☐ ☐ ☐
62. ☐ ☐ ☐ ☐ ☐
63. ☐ ☐ ☐ ☐ ☐
64. ☐ ☐ ☐ ☐ ☐
65. ☐ ☐ ☐ ☐ ☐
66. ☐ ☐ ☐ ☐ ☐
67. ☐ ☐ ☐ ☐ ☐
68. ☐ ☐ ☐ ☐ ☐
69. ☐ ☐ ☐ ☐ ☐
70. ☐ ☐ ☐ ☐ ☐

T F
71. ☐ ☐
72. ☐ ☐
73. ☐ ☐
74. ☐ ☐
75. ☐ ☐
76. ☐ ☐
77. ☐ ☐
78. ☐ ☐
79. ☐ ☐
80. ☐ ☐

FINANZAS
81. ☐ ☐ ☐ ☐ ☐
82. ☐ ☐ ☐ ☐ ☐
83. ☐ ☐ ☐ ☐ ☐
84. ☐ ☐ ☐ ☐ ☐
85. ☐ ☐ ☐ ☐ ☐
86. ☐ ☐ ☐ ☐ ☐
87. ☐ ☐ ☐ ☐ ☐
88. ☐ ☐ ☐ ☐ ☐
89. ☐ ☐ ☐ ☐ ☐
90. ☐ ☐ ☐ ☐ ☐

VENTAS
A B C D E
91. ☐ ☐ ☐ ☐ ☐
92. ☐ ☐ ☐ ☐ ☐
93. ☐ ☐ ☐ ☐ ☐
94. ☐ ☐ ☐ ☐ ☐
95. ☐ ☐ ☐ ☐ ☐
96. ☐ ☐ ☐ ☐ ☐
97. ☐ ☐ ☐ ☐ ☐
98. ☐ ☐ ☐ ☐ ☐
99. ☐ ☐ ☐ ☐ ☐
100. ☐ ☐ ☐ ☐ ☐

RECETAS
101. ____ ____ ____
102. ____ ____ ____
103. ____ ____ ____
104. ____ ____ ____
105. ____ ____ ____
106. ____ ____ ____
107. ____ ____ ____
108. ____ ____ ____
109. ____ ____ ____
110. ____ ____ ____
111. ____ ____ ____
112. ____ ____ ____
113. ____ ____ ____
114. ____ ____ ____
115. ____ ____ ____
116. ____ ____ ____
117. ____ ____ ____
118. ____ ____ ____
119. ____ ____ ____
120. ____ ____ ____

BEBIDAS
A B C D E
121. ☐ ☐ ☐ ☐ ☐
122. ☐ ☐ ☐ ☐ ☐
123. ☐ ☐ ☐ ☐ ☐
124. ☐ ☐ ☐ ☐ ☐
125. _____
126. _____
127. _____
128. _____
129. _____
130. _____
131. _____
132. _____
133. _____
134. _____
135. _____
136. _____
137. _____
138. _____
139. _____
140. _____
141. _____
142. _____
143. _____
144. _____
145. _____
146. _____
147. _____
148. _____
149. _____
150. _____

FOR OFFICE USE:

HR:__ SAN:__ IMP:__ OPS:__ ALC:__ FIN:__ SALE:__ REC:__ BEV:__ TOT:__ TIME:__ INDEX:__

Professional Test

BEVERAGE STAFF
Answer Sheet Overlay

NOTE: To save time when grading the Professional Test, make a copy of this sheet on clear transparency film and lay it over the candidate's completed test. This should enable you to easily note the number of questions marked correctly and incorrectly. You can then simply transfer the score to the blocks at the bottom of the answer sheet. The answer sheet and test are not returned to the applicant, so it is your choice whether to physically mark the answer to a specific question as correct or incorrect.

HUMAN REL

#	Answer
1.	E
2.	D
3.	D
4.	E
5.	D
6.	D
7.	B
8.	A
9.	A
10.	D

SANITATION

#	Answer
11.	E
12.	A
13.	C
14.	A
15.	B
16.	B
17.	B
18.	C
19.	B
20.	C

IMPRESSIONS

#	Answer
21.	D
22.	C
23.	B
24.	E
25.	C
26.	C
27.	D
28.	C
29.	E
30.	C

OPERATIONS

#	Answer
31.	C
32.	B
33.	C
34.	A
35.	B
36.	A
37.	B
38.	B
39.	B
40.	E
41.	A
42.	A
43.	B
44.	C
45.	D
46.	D
47.	A
48.	D
49.	C
50.	C
51.	D
52.	A
53.	E
54.	D
55.	B
56.	D
57.	D
58.	D
59.	D
60.	C

ALCOHOL

#	Answer
61.	C
62.	B
63.	D
64.	A
65.	D
66.	A
67.	A
68.	A
69.	E
70.	E

#	T/F
71.	T
72.	T
73.	F
74.	F
75.	F
76.	F
77.	T
78.	T
79.	T
80.	F

FINANCIAL

#	Answer
81.	E
82.	E
83.	D
84.	B
85.	A
86.	A
87.	C
88.	B
89.	C
90.	B

SALES

#	Answer
91.	E
92.	E
93.	E
94.	B
95.	D
96.	A
97.	C
98.	D
99.	E
100.	D

RECIPES

#			
101.	C	T	K
102.	E	T	ii
103.	B	M	xx
104.	F	L	kk
105.	H	J	xx
106.	A	V	jj
107.	A	S	xx
108.	E	cc	xx
109.	F	ii	kk
110.	C	Y	ll
111.	B	L	M
112.	G	ff	gg
113.	E	Z	dd
114.	A	S	gg
115.	A	Y	xx
116.	S	J	ff
117.	N	T	kk
118.	O	Y	xx
119.	D	M	kk
120.	Q	D	xx

BEVERAGE

#	Answer
121.	B
122.	C
123.	B
124.	D
125.	F
126.	I
127.	Y
128.	B
129.	U
130.	S
131.	K
132.	P
133.	V
134.	A
135.	X
136.	S
137.	E
138.	T
139.	M
140.	H
141.	Z
142.	D
143.	W
144.	L
145.	N
146.	G
147.	J
148.	O
149.	I
150.	Q

Professional Test

BEVERAGE STAFF

Pick the *MOST CORRECT* answer and mark your choice on the answer sheet. Please do not write on this test.

HUMAN RELATIONS

1. **What is the best measure of a supervisor's effectiveness?**
   A. Work skills.
   B. Health department scores.
   C. Profitability.
   D. Average check.
   E. Staff development.

2. **Which method of training would you use when showing someone how to clean a piece of equipment?**
   A. Written instructions.
   B. Classroom training.
   C. Role-playing.
   D. On-the-job instruction.
   E. None of the above.

3. **Who do you think makes the most effective trainer for operational subjects?**
   A. An outside consultant.
   B. The general manager.
   C. The department supervisor.
   D. A skilled co-worker.
   E. A company training director.

4. **In your experience, which statement is true about working with minorities?**
   A. They must be treated a little differently from other workers.
   B. They can be more difficult to motivate than other workers.
   C. It is more difficult to know what they really want from you.
   D. They tend to be less productive than other workers.
   E. They are no different from anyone else.

5. **How would you bring out the best in your co-workers?**
   A. Support them in following their job descriptions.
   B. Give them advice on how to do their jobs more effectively.
   C. Report substandard performance to your supervisor.
   D. Set a good personal example.
   E. All of the above.

6. **As a bartender on the restaurant staff, what is the best way to advance your career?**
   A. Do personal favors for the managers.
   B. Stand out from the competition.
   C. Take classes and attend seminars.
   D. Teach the cocktail servers how to tend bar.
   E. Make sure you get the credit when things go well.

7. **When it comes to guest complaints, which statement do you most agree with?**
   A. No news is good news.
   B. Complaints are special gifts.
   C. A satisfaction level of about 90% is realistic for a full-service restaurant.
   D. You can't expect to please all the people all the time.
   E. Some people complain just to get attention.

8. **What can you assume when a drink is returned by a guest?**
   A. The bartender screwed up the order.
   B. The cocktail server didn't understand what the guest wanted.
   C. Something is wrong with the drink.
   D. The guest is in a bad mood.
   E. You can't assume anything when a drink is returned.

9. **How would you deal with a complaint from an irate (sober) guest?**
    A. Apologize and immediately resolve the problem in favor of the guest.
    B. Try to keep the guest from disturbing the bar or dining room.
    C. Analyze market share data to determine if the problem is worth worrying about.
    D. Listen to the problem, explain what caused it, and negotiate a mutually acceptable solution.
    E. Help the guest to understand your side of the situation.

10. **When do you think it *not* appropriate to comp a guest's drink?**
    A. The server took a long time bringing the drinks.
    B. The guest did not care for the drink.
    C. The guests had an argument and decided to leave before finishing their drinks.
    D. Any of these situations could call for a comp.

SANITATION

11. **Which of the following is a *major* health department violation?**
    A. Cans without labels in the dry storeroom.
    B. No secondary thermometers in the reach-in refrigerator.
    C. A dirty floor under the bar.
    D. A dirty ice bin in the bar.
    E. An unlabeled spray bottle.

12. **A member of the staff has an open cut on her hand. How should the supervisor handle it?**
    A. Exclude her from all food-handling responsibilities until the cut heals.
    B. Send her home, without pay, until the cut heals.
    C. Send her home, with pay, until the cut heals.
    D. To avoid upsetting the guests, assign her to a workstation out of sight of the dining room.
    E. File a Workers' Compensation claim.

13. **What is the proper place for a secondary thermometer in a refrigerator?**
    A. In the lower back corner away from the door.
    B. In the middle of the refrigerator.
    C. In the upper front of the refrigerator by the door.
    D. On the back of the door.
    E. A secondary thermometer is not needed if the refrigerator has a built-in thermometer.

14. **Which practice is correct or acceptable?**
    A. Polishing glassware.
    B. Snacking in workstations.
    C. Using a glass to scoop ice.
    D. Washing utensils in the hand sink.
    E. Keeping wipe cloths in sanitizing solution.

15. **How often should sanitizing solution be checked?**
    A. At the start of each shift.
    B. At least twice each shift.
    C. At least once an hour.
    D. At least once every half hour.
    E. Every time you use it.

16. **How can you tell if the sanitizing solution is at the proper concentration?**
    A. Measure carefully when making new solution.
    B. Use a universal test kit.
    C. Dip a test strip in the solution and compare it with a scale.
    D. Dip a piece of paper towel in the solution and see if it darkens.
    E. Use a product thermometer.

17. **What happens if the sanitizing solution concentration is higher than recommended?**
    A. It will be more effective.
    B. It can be toxic.
    C. It will cost more money, but there is no real problem.

D. It won't work as well, if at all.

E. All of the above.

18. **What happens if the sanitizing solution concentration is lower than recommended?**

    A. It will kill bacteria more slowly.

    B. It can be toxic.

    C. It will save some money, and there is no real problem.

    D. It won't work as well, if at all.

    E. All of the above.

19. **You are the bartender in a full-service restaurant. It is mid-afternoon on a Tuesday and the bar is nearly empty. Suddenly, a glass breaks as you scoop it through the ice bin. What do you do?**

    A. Pick out the glass, being sure you get all the pieces.

    B. Fill the bin with fresh ice and use the ice on top.

    C. Empty the ice bin completely, wipe it dry, and refill it with fresh ice immediately.

    D. Empty the ice bin at the end of the shift.

    E. Use only ice that does not contain glass.

20. **You are the bartender in a busy restaurant. It is the Friday night happy hour and the bar is packed. You have been doing everything you can think of to save time and stay ahead of the crowd. Suddenly, a glass breaks as you scoop it through the ice bin. What do you do?**

    A. Pick out the glass, being sure to get all the pieces.

    B. Fill the bin with fresh ice and use the ice on top.

    C. Empty the ice bin completely, wipe it dry, and refill it with fresh ice immediately.

    D. Empty the ice bin at the end of the shift.

    E. Use only ice that does not contain glass.

FIRST IMPRESSIONS

21. **You are the bartender on duty. What is the first thing you do when a guest walks into the bar?**

    A. Find out how many people are in the party.

    B. Take care of the cocktail servers first.

    C. Ask the guest to wait until you finish what you are doing.

    D. Smile and welcome the guest to the restaurant.

22. **What do you do if you are talking on the phone when guests arrive?**

    A. It depends on who you are talking to.

    B. Pretend you don't see the new arrivals until you finish your conversation.

    C. Acknowledge the new arrivals with a smile and complete your call promptly.

    D. Point them to a table and bring them menus when you get off the phone.

    E. Hang up the phone immediately.

23. **The restaurant is really busy. Which of the following activities will help the restaurant be most successful?**

    A. Seating waiting guests as soon as a table is cleared.

    B. Making sure that every guest gets your personal attention.

    C. Selling guests appetizers while they wait.

    D. Helping the bussers clear and reset tables.

24. **What *must* you know before you can answer the phone in the restaurant?**

    A. Hours of operation.

    B. Daily specials.

    C. Directions on how to get to the restaurant.

    D. Description of the menu style and price levels.

    E. All of the above.

25. **Your operating hours state that you open at 4:00 P.M. A guest knocks on the locked front door and your watch says 3:50. What do you do?**

    A. Keep the door locked, show him the time on your watch, and ask him to wait 10 minutes.

    B. Pretend you don't see him.

    C. Let him in and have him wait in the lobby until 4:00.

    D. Invite him in, get him a seat, and take his order.

26. **Your restaurant hours state that you close at 10:00 P.M. The state closing hour is 2:00 A.M. A party of six arrives at 9:55. What do you do?**
    A. Explain that they cannot be served before the restaurant closes and ask them to come back tomorrow.
    B. Seat them and ask them to place their order before 10:00.
    C. Ask the bar crew if they want to serve another party.
    D. Seat them and serve them as you have any other guests that evening.

27. **You are showing a party of two to a table on a busy night. As you approach the deuce, they ask if you can seat them at the 4-top in the corner. What do you do?**
    A. Explain to them that the restaurant is very busy and seat them at the deuce.
    B. Ask them what is wrong with the deuce.
    C. Tell them you have a reservation for the 4-top and seat them at the deuce.
    D. Seat them at the 4-top.
    E. Call the manager.

28. **It is a busy Friday night and the greeter told the McPherson party to expect a 30-minute wait. Half an hour has almost passed and the greeter just told you there will not be a table available for another 10 minutes. What do you do?**
    A. Let it go and call them when their table is ready. Ten minutes is not worth worrying about.
    B. Inform them of the additional wait and apologize.
    C. Inform them of the additional wait and give them something to make up for the inconvenience.
    D. Inform of the additional wait and explain the reason for the delay.
    E. Call the manager.

29. **Which of the following will contribute to giving the guest an unpleasant experience?**
    A. Soiled or ill-fitting uniforms.
    B. Wet or sticky tabletops.
    C. Wobbly tables or chairs.
    D. Staff members with poor personal hygiene practices.
    E. All of the above.

30. **You are talking on the phone as guests are leaving the bar. What do you do?**
    A. Pretend you don't see them and continue with your call.
    B. Smile and wave to them while continuing to talk.
    C. Excuse yourself from the caller and thank them for coming.
    D. Hang up the phone immediately.
    E. Call the manager.

BAR OPERATIONS

31. **A party of four is getting ready to leave the bar. Three guests at a table have finished their drinks while a fourth is still finishing. What do you do?**
    A. Clear the glasses of the three guests who have finished.
    B. Ask guests who have finished if they would like their glasses cleared.
    C. Wait until the fourth guest finishes.
    D. Clear the glasses of the three guests who have finished, but only if they ask you to do so.
    E. None of the above.

32. **When serving wine, which of the following procedures is *incorrect*?**
    A. Presenting the bottle label to the person who ordered the wine.
    B. Placing the bottle on the table while cutting the foil.
    C. Pouring a taste for the host's approval before serving the rest of the table.
    D. Filling the ladies' glasses before filling those of the male guests.
    E. Filling wine glasses to the widest point of the glass.

33. **When should you change an ashtray at the table?**
    A. Whenever there is a cigarette butt in it.
    B. Before serving the main course.
    C. Whenever there are two cigarette butts in it.
    D. After serving cocktails.
    E. Whenever there are more than three cigarette butts in it.

34. What is the proper method for changing an ashtray?
  A. Capping a clean ashtray over the soiled one and remove it from the table.
  B. Removing the soiled ashtray with one hand while putting the clean one on the table with the other hand.
  C. Removing the soiled ashtray from the table, emptying the butts into a bus tub, and replacing it on the table.
  D. Any of the above is acceptable.

35. What is the first thing you do upon initially approaching the table?
  A. Introduce yourself.
  B. Welcome the guests to the restaurant.
  C. Place a cocktail napkin in front of each guest.
  D. Ask the guests if they would like a drink.

36. Which of the following is the most important factor in controlling pouring cost in a bar?
  A. The size of the glassware.
  B. The cost of the liquor.
  C. The shape of the ice cubes.
  D. The size of the shot.

37. You believe you have given excellent service to a party of three. After they leave, you notice that the credit card slip has been signed, but no tip has been added and the slip is not totaled. What do you do?
  A. Add 15% to the credit card slip and total it.
  B. Try to catch the guests before they drive away.
  C. Submit the slip as is.
  D. Check the table for a cash tip.
  E. Call the manager.

38. What is the most important thing in handling the rush effectively?
  A. Plan ahead and be sure adequate stocks are in place.
  B. Hire extra staff.
  C. Schedule only your best workers to work during the rush.
  D. Seat people only as fast as you can serve them.
  E. All of the above.

39. A party has a tab of $34.50. They give you two twenty-dollar bills in payment. What change do you bring back?
  A. Two quarters and a five-dollar bill.
  B. Two quarters and five ones.
  C. Five dimes, a one-dollar bill, and a five-dollar bill.
  D. None, because the change is about what they should leave for a tip.

40. What does courtesy mean?
  A. Liking people.
  B. Smiling and being polite.
  C. Being respectful to your guests.
  D. Making people aware that you like them.
  E. All of the above.

41. A guest asks you for directions to the restrooms. Which of the following do you *not* do?
  A. Point them toward the restrooms.
  B. Explain to them how to find the restrooms.
  C. Take them to the restrooms yourself.
  D. Any of the above is acceptable.

42. When is it important to indicate seat numbers on the guest check?
  A. When taking any order at the table.
  B. Only when taking the appetizer order.
  C. Only when you have enough time to do it.
  D. Seat numbers are not necessary if you have an elecronic ordering system.

43. How often do draft beer lines need to be cleaned?
  A. Every day.
  B. Once a week.
  C. Once a month.
  D. Once a year.
  E. Only when the beer starts excessive foaming.

44. When should a bartender cut fruit?
A. Only when business is slow.
B. Once a day.
C. Before every shift.
D. No more than a day ahead.
E. The kitchen should cut fruit, not the bartender.

45. Where should you store bottled beer?
A. In cases on the floor of the walk-in.
B. In the ice used for drinks.
C. Under the bar.
D. On shelves in the refrigerator.
E. All of the above.

46. Which of the following practices is stealing?
A. Overpouring.
B. Giving free drinks to good customers.
C. Forgetting to ring up drinks.
D. Giving free drinks to the restaurant staff.
E. All of the above.

47. What does it mean if a person has been "86'd?"
A. They are barred from the premises.
B. They are considered to be a special guest and have a charge account.
C. They are only allowed in the bar during daylight hours.
D. They may only come in if accompanied by a parent or other family members.
E. None of the above.

48. Who is allowed to drink at the bar after state closing time?
A. Management staff only.
B. Local law enforcement officials.
C. Customers finishing stacked drinks.
D. Staff members of legal drinking age.
E. No one is allowed to drink at the bar after state closing time.

49. Which of the following would be the best way to make regular bar patrons feel appreciated?
A. Giving them a drink on the house.
B. Giving them a heavier pour than other guests.
C. Buying them dinner in the dining room.
D. Inviting them to your home.
E. Giving them a drink and paying for it yourself.

50. Which of the following are inappropriate behaviors for beverage staff on duty?
A. Drinking or snacking at workstations.
B. Reading restaurant trade magazines.
C. Watching public affairs television programs.
D. All of the above are inappropriate behaviors.
E. None of the above are inappropriate behaviors.

51. What do you do when bar fruit gets old?
A. Soak it in soda water to revitalize it.
B. Serve it to drunks.
C. Make it into fruit punch.
D. Mix it with fresh stock.
E. Throw it out.

52. Which of the following is a proper way to open a bottle of champagne?
A. Hold the cork firmly and twist the bottle.
B. Point the bottle toward yourself and away from the guests.
C. Pop the cork across the room, being careful not to hit anyone.
D. Hold the bottle firmly and twist the cork.
E. Use a corkscrew to remove the cork.

53. **A cocktail server comes to the bar with a drink returned from a guest in the dining room. The server is obviously upset and a little rude. What do you do?**
    A. Reprimand the server for his rudeness.
    B. Find out what was wrong with the drink.
    C. Check the drink to see if it was properly prepared.
    D. Take the drink back to the guest yourself and explain how it is prepared.
    E. Fix or replace the drink without comment.

54. **What is the proper way to chill a glass?**
    A. Put it in the freezer for a few seconds.
    B. Put it in the refrigerator for a few seconds.
    C. Twist the glass in the ice bin for a few seconds.
    D. Fill the glass with ice and swirl it for a few seconds.
    E. It is not proper to chill a glass.

55. **You are the bartender in a midscale theme restaurant. It is 4:00 P.M. and you have four people sitting at the bar. A party comes in and heads for a corner table. There is no cocktail server working. What do you do?**
    A. Make the new guests come to the bar to get their drinks.
    B. Stay behind the bar and ask the new guests what they want.
    C. Leave the bar and go to the table to take the new guests' orders.
    D. Ask the new guests what they want before they sit down.
    E. Call a manager.

56. **You are the bartender in a full-service restaurant. It is a busy Friday night and the bar is packed. The sign over the service area says "Employees Only." A guest comes into the service area to order a drink. What do you do?**
    A. Request that the guest leave the service area and place his order from the front of the bar.
    B. Ask the guest to sit down and call a cocktail server to take his order.
    C. Make the drink and tell the manager about it.
    D. Make the drink.
    E. Call a manager.

57. **With which of the following statements do you most agree?**
    A. A good bartender knows how to make drinks without recipes.
    B. Good bartenders have their own drink recipes.
    C. To assure portion control, refer to the recipe every time you make a drink.
    D. Good bartenders memorize and follow prescribed bar recipes.
    E. All of the above.

58. **Your restaurant does not offer an appetizer menu in the bar. One night, some guests in the bar ask you for something to munch on. What do you do?**
    A. Find them a seat in the dining room.
    B. Tell them you do not have food service in the bar.
    C. Call a server from the dining room.
    D. Get them what they want to eat.
    E. Call a manager.

59. **You notice that your draft beer is not holding a head in the glass. Which of the following would you suspect is the cause of the problem?**
    A. The beer lines are dirty.
    B. The glasses are scratched.
    C. The beer is too warm.
    D. There is a detergent residue in the glasses.
    E. The beer kegs have been agitated.

60. **You are the bartender in a busy Mexican restaurant. A cocktail waitress returns a Margarita from the dining room because the guest did not want salt on the rim. Otherwise, the drink looks perfect and you sell a lot of Margaritas. What do you do with the returned drink?**
    A. Carefully wipe the salt from the rim and send it back to the dining room.
    B. Save the Margarita for the next order and serve it as is.
    C. Make a new drink without salt and throw the original drink away.
    D. Put it into the blender with the next batch of Margaritas.

ALCOHOL SERVICE

61. **Which of the following foods is most effective for *slowing* the rate of alcohol absorption?**
    A. Popcorn.
    B. Candy.
    C. Cheese.
    D. Black coffee.
    E. All are equally effective.

62. **Which of the following *increases* the rate of alcohol absorption in the body?**
    A. Water.
    B. Carbonated beverages.
    C. Protein foods.
    D. Sweets.
    E. None of the above.

63. **Which of the following is typically *not* considered a valid form of ID?**
    A. A birth certificate.
    B. A driver's license.
    C. An alien registration card.
    D. A Social Security card.
    E. All are valid for identification.

64. **Which of the following statements accurately describes the law?**
    A. It is legal to serve alcohol to intoxicated persons if they are not going to be driving.
    B. It is illegal to serve alcohol to intoxicated persons.
    C. It is illegal to serve more than three drinks per hour to a person.
    D. It is legal for a minor to drink if his parents purchase the alcoholic beverage.
    E. All of the above are accurate statements.

65. **You should stop alcohol service to a person exhibiting which of the following behaviors?**
    A. Flirting.
    B. Losing inhibitions.
    C. Being a nuisance.
    D. Spilling drinks.
    E. Being unusually quiet.

66. **Which of the following is *not* an equivalent drink to the others when considering alcohol content?**
    A. 12 ounces of beer.
    B. 8 ounces of wine.
    C. 1¼ ounces of 80 proof liquor.
    D. All are equal in alcohol content.

67. **A guest has definitely had too much to drink and is about to leave the restaurant. You approach him to offer a taxi home. He declines your offer and insists he is going to drive. What do you do?**
    A. Ask him to be careful and allow him to drive.
    B. If he gets into his car, call the police.
    C. Grab his keys and keep them.
    D. Continue to press your case.
    E. Call the owner.

68. **Which of the following practices will *not* help avoid overconsumption?**
    A. Serving one drink at a time.
    B. Making guests come to the bar to order.
    C. Serving rounds when most glasses are empty.
    D. Removing empty glasses from the table before serving a new round.
    E. Putting water on the table.

69. **A woman has definitely had too much to drink and wants another glass of wine. She swears she is not driving, a statement that is confirmed by her boyfriend. He is not drunk, assures you that he is driving her home, and will see that she gets there safely. He asks you to bring the wine. What do you do?**
    A. Bring the drink as requested.
    B. Call the police.

C. Call the owner.
D. Refuse to serve the drink.
E. Suggest nonalcoholic alternatives.

70. **A group of young people come into the restaurant and order alcoholic beverages. When you ask for proof of age, they tell you they have no IDs with them. They assure you they are over 21 years old. This is verified by an older guest who has overheard the conversation and whom you recognize as an off-duty police officer. What do you do?**
A. Bring the drinks.
B. Call the police department to confirm the identity of the older guest.
C. Call the owner.
D. Refuse to serve the drinks.
E. Suggest nonalcoholic alternatives.

Please answer the following questions TRUE or FALSE.
71. You may be held personally liable for the actions of intoxicated guests.
72. The use of cocaine or marijuana in conjunction with alcohol will intensify its effect.
73. A driver registering a .8% BAC is considered driving while impaired.
74. An out-of-state person of legal age to drink in his home state can drink in your restaurant.
75. High altitude lessens the effect of alcohol.
76. Alcohol is a depressant that decreases appetite.
77. A person with a higher percentage of fat will absorb alcohol faster than a more muscular person.
78. The body processes alcohol at the rate of one drink per hour, regardless of size.
79. When discontinuing service to intoxicated guests, it is best not to touch them.
80. A breathalizer measures the amount of alcohol in the blood.

FINANCIAL

81. **Let's say your restaurant *really* blows it with a party of four. Let's also say that the typical guest in your restaurant normally dines with you three times a month and that your average check is $20. What is this error likely to cost the company in lost business over the next five years?**
A. Under $4,000.
B. $10,000 to $12,000.
C. $25,000 to $30,000.
D. $50,000 to $60,000.
E. Over $85,000.

82. **What portion of a typical restaurant's sales is pretax income?**
A. 40% to 45%.
B. 30% to 35%.
C. 20% to 25%.
D. 10% to 15%.
E. Under 5%.

83. **Your beverage sales totaled $500 during your shift. You had a total of 50 guest checks representing drinks served to 100 people. There were 25 seats in your station. What was your average check for this shift?**
A. $500.
B. $20.
C. $10.
D. $5.

84. **You are a cocktail server in a busy hotel lounge and your tips for the shift were $80. Because she did a particularly great job today, you decide to give the bartender 15% of your tips. After taking care of the bartender, how much tip money will you take home?**
A. $80.
B. $68.
C. $58.
D. $12.

85. **Simply stated, what is an invoice?**
    A. A bill.
    B. A purchase order.
    C. A sales history.
    D. A statement of account.
    E. A production forecast.

86. **Your liquor salesperson has just offered you a deal: 20% off on orders of over three cases of Kahlua if you place the order today. You normally go through three to four bottles of Kahlua in a month. What do you do?**
    A. Pass.
    B. Buy three or more cases and save the restaurant some money.
    C. Buy three or more cases and invent a new specialty drink.
    D. Buy three or more cases and resell part of the stock at a profit.

87. **Your restaurant is having a contest to find a new drink special. In order to be eligible, an item has to be able to sell for $5 with a pouring cost of 25% or less. What is the highest pouring cost your entry can have?**
    A. $1.75.
    B. $1.50.
    C. $1.25.
    D. $1.00.

The following items are included on your restaurant's bar menu. Assume you are not running a premium well.

Well drinks	3.25	Domestic beer	2.75	Soft drinks	1.25
Call brands	3.75	Imported beer	3.50	Iced tea	.95
Premium brands	4.25	Long Island Iced Tea	4.25	Coffee	.50
House wines	2.75	Frozen Margarita	4.50	Orange juice	1.50

88. **A table of three orders Stolichnaya on the rocks, a Corona, and a glass of Chablis. What is the amount of their check before sales tax?**
    A. $8.75.
    B. $10.50.
    C. $11.50.
    D. $11.75.

89. **A table of four orders two rounds of drinks. The first includes a Margarita, a diet Coke, a bottle of Bud, and a Long Island Iced Tea. On the second round, they substitute J&B on the rocks for the diet Coke. If they leave a 15% tip based on the pretax total, how much will you get?**
    A. $3.50.
    B. $4.00.
    C. $4.25.
    D. $4.75.

90. **Last month, your restaurant's total receipts were $66,500, of which $4,100 was sales tax, $46,800 was food sales, and the rest was beverage sales. Your liquor purchases were $3,300, and your bar payroll was $2,900. You spent $550 on paper supplies. Opening liquor inventory was $4,400, and closing inventory was $3,900. What was your pouring cost for the month?**
    A. 21.2%.
    B. 24.4%.
    C. 25.9%.
    D. 20.2%.
    E. There is not enough information to answer the question.

SALES

91. **What practices will increase your sales?**
    A. Suggesting items that you like.
    B. Being able to describe what is in each drink and how it is prepared.
    C. Mentioning the signature drinks your restaurant offers.

D. Upselling.

E. All of the above.

92. Which of the following questions would best help sell alcoholic beverages effectively?

A. "May I bring you a cocktail?"

B. "Would you like to see the liquor menu?"

C. "What kind of cocktail can I bring you?"

D. "Are you ready to order?"

E. "Have you ever tried our famous rum punch?"

93. A guest comes into the bar late one night and orders a chocolate mousse. Which of the following drinks would you suggest to accompany that dessert?

A. A glass of Cabernet Sauvignon.

B. An Irish coffee.

C. Grand Marnier on the rocks.

D. Espresso.

E. Any of these goes well with chocolate mousse.

94. How does suggestive selling *most* help the restaurant?

A. By increasing sales.

B. By increasing guest satisfaction.

C. By increasing the server's tips.

D. By reducing food cost.

E. By getting rid of overstocked items.

95. Which of the following would you encourage your guests to purchase?

A. Well drinks.

B. Premium liquors.

C. Nonalcoholic specialties.

D. All of the above.

96. Which of the following would be an appropriate response when a guest orders scotch and water?

A. "Would you prefer Chivas Regal or Glenlivet in your scotch and water?"

B. "Would you prefer domestic or imported scotch?"

C. "You can get Glenlivet for another dollar."

D. "I'll be right back with your drink."

E. "Thank you."

97. What is upselling?

A. Charging the guest more than the menu price.

B. A pushy sales technique.

C. Suggesting premium brands.

D. Making the guest pay more than they planned.

E. None of the above.

98. What is the effect of upselling?

A. It will increase the average check.

B. The server will receive higher tips.

C. The guests will have a better time.

D. All of the above.

E. None of the above.

99. What is the best way to sell cocktails?

A. Knowing what is in each drink.

B. Knowing what each drink tastes like.

C. Knowing how each drink is made.

D. Knowing what your signature drinks are.

E. All of the above.

100. What would you suggest when a guest has been drinking in the bar for several hours?

A. Espresso.

B. Nonalcoholic specials.

C. Light beer.

D. Pizza.

E. Chocolate mousse.

RECIPES

For each of the following drinks, indicate its three principal ingredients.

101. Margarita	A. Vodka	T. Lime juice
102. Daiquiri	B. Gin	U. Lemon juice
103. Martini	C. Tequila	V. Tomato juice
104. Manhattan	D. Scotch	W. Cranberry juice
105. Stinger	E. Light rum	X. Grapefruit juice
106. Bloody Mary	F. Bourbon	Y. Orange juice
107. Black Russian	G. Irish whisky	Z. Pineapple juice
108. Cuba Libre	H. White creme de menthe	aa. Tonic water
109. Old Fashioned	I. White creme de cacao	bb. Club soda
110. Tequila Sunrise	J. Brandy	cc. Coca Cola
111. Perfect Martini	K. Triple sec	dd. Cream of coconut
112. Irish Coffee	L. Sweet vermouth	ee. Orgeat syrup
113. Piña Colada	M. Dry vermouth	ff. Coffee
114. White Russian	N. Dark rum	gg. Cream
115. Screwdriver	O. Peach schnapps	hh. Milk
116. Keoki Coffee	P. Peppermint schnapps	ii. Sugar
117. Planter's Punch	Q. Drambuie	jj. Tabasco
118. Fuzzy Navel	R. Grand Marnier	kk. Bitters
119. Rob Roy	S. Kahlua	ll. Grenadine
120. Rusty Nail	xx. There are no other ingredients in this drink.	

BEVERAGE KNOWLEDGE

121. If a guest orders Dewar's "neat," how do you serve it?

A. On the rocks.

B. In a shot glass.

C. With water.

D. With a twist.

122. Which of the following will bring a bottle of Merlot to the proper serving temperature?

A. Storing the bottle in the refrigerator at 38°F.

B. Keeping the bottle in a rack at the temperature of the dining room.

C. Cooling the bottle to 55°F.

D. Serving temperature is not an issue with Merlot.

123. How long can you hold coffee on a warmer before its quality starts to deteriorate?

A. No longer than 15 minutes.

B. No longer than 45 minutes.

C. No longer than 90 minutes.
D. No longer than 2½ hours.
E. Coffee can be held indefinitely if it is kept hot.

124. Ounce for ounce, which of the following is highest in alcohol content?
    A. Red wine.
    B. Fortified wine.
    C. 80 proof vodka.
    D. 100 proof bourbon.

Match the following beverages with their proper definitions. Assume you are not running a premium well.

125. Wild Turkey	A. Full-bodied red wine	138. Gamay Beaujolais	N. Imported cream liqueur
126. Smirnoff	B. Call scotch	139. Clausthaler	O. Blush wine
127. Myer's	C. Imported vodka	140. Harvey's	P. Call rum
128. Dewar's	D. Domestic blended whiskey	141. Triple sec	Q. Imported champagne
129. Sauza	E. Full-bodied white wine	142. Seagram's 7	R. Domestic scotch
130. Heineken	F. Premium bourbon	143. Kahlua	S. Imported beer
131. Port	G. Imported blended whiskey	144. Sauvignon Blanc	T. Light-bodied red wine
132. Bacardi Silver	H. Cream sherry	145. Bailey's	U. Imported tequila
133. Chivas Regal	I. Domestic vodka	146. Crown Royal	V. Imported scotch
134. Cabernet Sauvignon	J. Fruity, spicy white wine	147. Gewürztraminer	W. Imported coffee liqueur
135. Augsberger	K. Fortified wine	148. White Zinfandel	X. Domestic beer
136. Beck's	L. Light-bodied white wine	149. Wolfschmidt	Y. Imported dark rum
137. Chardonnay	M. Alcohol-free beer	150. Mumm's	Z. Orange liqueur

Examen Profesional

EQUIPO TÉCNICO DE BEBIDAS

Escoja la respuesta *MÁS CORRECTA* y marque su selección en la hoja de respuestas. Por favor, no escriba en el examen.

RELACIONES HUMANAS

1. **¿Cuál es la mejor medida de la efectividad de un supervisor?**
   A. Habilidades de trabajo.
   B. Calificaciones del departamento de salud.
   C. Ganacias.
   D. Promedio de revisión regular.
   E. Desarrollo del personal.

2. **¿Cuál método de entrenamiento utilizaría usted al mostrarle a alguien como limpiar una pieza del equipo?**
   A. Instrucciones escritas.
   B. Entrenamiento en clase.
   C. Demostración.
   D. Instrucción en el trabajo.
   E. Ninguno de los anteriores.

3. **¿Quien cree ud. que haría el papel más efectivo de entrenador de temas operacionales?**
   A. Un asesor.
   B. El administrador general.
   C. El supervisor del departamento.
   D. Un colega calificado.
   E. Un director de entrenamiento de la compañía.

4. **En su experiencia, ¿cuál de éstas declaraciones es verdadera acerca de trabajar con minorías?**
   A. Deberán ser tratados de un modo un poco diferente a los otros trabajadores.
   B. Puede que sean más difíciles de motivar que otros trabajadores.
   C. Es más difícil saber lo que ellos realmente esperan de usted.
   D. Tienden a ser menos productivos que otros trabajadores.
   E. No son diferentes de cualquier otro trabajador.

5. **¿Cómo haría usted para sacar lo mejor de sus colegas?**
   A. Apoyar a cada uno de ellos para que cumpla las descripciones de su trabajo.
   B. Darles asesoría de como hacer su trabajo con más efectividad.
   C. Informar a su supervisor de cualquier desempeño anormal.
   D. Establecer un buen ejemplo personal.
   E. Todo lo anterior.

6. **Como cantinero miembro del equipo técnico del restaurante, ¿cuál es la mejor manera de avanzar en su carrera?**
   A. Hacerle favores personales a los administradores.
   B. Resaltar en la competencia.
   C. Tomar clases y asistir a seminarios.
   D. Enseñarles a los meseros como atender el bar.
   E. Asegurarse de obtener crédito cuando las cosas van bien.

7. **Cuando hay quejas de los clientes, ¿con cuál declaración estará usted más de acuerdo?**
   A. No oír noticias son buenas noticias.
   B. Las quejas son regalos especiales.
   C. Un nivel de satisfacción cerca del 90% es realista para un restaurante con servicio completo.
   D. Usted no puede esperar complacer a toda la gente siempre.
   E. Algunos se quejan solamente para obtener atención.

8. **¿Qué puede usted asumir cuando un cliente regresa una bebida?**
   A. El cantinero se equivocó en la orden.
   B. El mesero no entendió lo que el cliente pidió al tomar la orden.
   C. Hay algo malo con la bebida.

D. El cliente está de mal humor.

E. Usted no puede asumir nada cuando se regresa una bebida.

9. **¿Cómo manejaría usted una queja de un cliente (sobrio) irritado?**
   A. Excúsese e inmediatamente resuelva el problema a favor del cliente.
   B. Intente mantener el bar o el comedor sin que sean molestados.
   C. Analice la información compartida en el mercado para determinar si vale la pena preocuparse del problema.
   D. Escuche el problema, explique qué lo causó y nogocie una solución aceptable mutua.
   E. Ayúdeles a entender su posición en la situación.

10. **¿Cuándo consideraría usted que no es apropiado compensar la bebida de un cliente?**
    A. El mesero se demoró mucho trayendo las bebidas.
    B. El cliente no quizo la bebida.
    C. Los clientes tuvieron una discusión y decidieron irse antes de terminar sus bebidas.
    D. Cualquiera de estas situaciones sería motivo de compensación.

SANIDAD

11. **¿Cuál de las siguientes es una de las mayores violaciones contra departamento de salud?**
    A. Latas sin etiquetas en la despensa.
    B. Falta de termómetros secundarios en el refrigerador de alcance.
    C. El piso sucio debajo del bar.
    D. El contenedor de hielo del bar sucio.
    E. Botellas de spray sin etiquetas.

12. **Una miembro del equipo técnico se ha cortado su mano. ¿Cómo deberá manejar la situación el supervisor?**
    A. Excluirla de todo el manejo de alimentos hasta que la herida esté completamente curada.
    B. Enviarla a su casa, sin pago, hasta que la herida esté completamente curada.
    C. Enviarla a su casa, con pago, hasta que la herida esté completamente curada.
    D. Para evitar que los clientes se sientan incómodos, asignarla a una sección aparte del comedor.
    E. Archiva un reclamo a la compensación de trabajadores.

13. **¿Cuál es el lugar más adecuado para el termómetro secundario en un refrigerador?**
    A. En la parte inferior de la esquina y más lejana de la puerta.
    B. En medio del refrigerador.
    C. En la parte superior del frente del refrigerador, por la puerta.
    D. Detrás de la puerta.
    E. Un termómetro secundario no es necesario si el refrigerador tiene un termómetro incorporado.

14. **¿Cuál de estas prácticas es correcta o aceptable?**
    A. Pulir la cristalería.
    B. Comer en las estaciones del trabajo.
    C. Utilizar un vaso para servir hielo.
    D. Lavar utensilios en el lavamanos.
    E. Mantener paños de limpiar en soluciones sanitarias.

15. **¿Cada cuánto debe ser revisada la solución sanitaria?**
    A. Al comienzo de cada turno.
    B. Por lo menos dos veces en cada turno.
    C. Por lo menos una vez por hora.
    D. Por lo menos una vez cada media hora.
    E. Cada vez que usted lo utiliza.

16. **¿Cómo determina usted si la solución sanitaria tiene la concentración adecuada?**
    A. Midiendo cuidadosamente cuando se prepara una nueva solución.
    B. Utilizando una prueba del equipo universal.
    C. Sumergiendo una tira de prueba en la solución y compararla con la escala.
    D. Sumergiendo un pedazo de papel toalla en la solución y ver si se oscurece.
    E. Utilizar el termómetro del producto.

17. **¿Qué ocurre si la concentración de la solución sanitaria está más alta de lo recomendado?**
    A. Será más efectiva.
    B. Puede ser tóxica.
    C. Costará más dinero, pero no es un problema real.
    D. No trabajará bien o en absoluto.
    E. Todo lo anterior.

18. **¿Qué ocurre si la concentración de la solución sanitaria es más baja de lo recomendado?**
    A. Matará la bacteria más lentamente.
    B. Puede ser tóxica.
    C. Ahorrará mas dinero y no será un problema real.
    D. No trabajará bien o en absoluto.
    E. Todo lo anterior.

19. **Usted es el cantinero en un restaurante de servicio completo. Es la tarde de un martes y el bar está casi vacío. De pronto, se rompe un vaso mientras usted está sacando hielo del contenedor. ¿Qué hace usted?**
    A. Recoge los vidrios, asegurándose de recoger todos los pedazos.
    B. Llena el contenedor con hielo fresco y usa el hielo de encima.
    C. Vacía el contenedor de hielo completamente, lo limpia y lo llena con hielo fresco inmediatamente.
    D. Vacía el contenedor de hielo al finalizar el turno.
    E. Utiliza solamente el hielo que no tenga vidrio.

20. **Usted es el cantinero en un restaurante muy ocupado. Es la "Happy Hour" de la noche del viernes y el bar está lleno. Usted ha estado haciendo todo lo posible por ahorrar tiempo y estar adelantado de la clientela. De pronto, se rompe un vaso mientras usted está sacando hielo del contenedor. ¿Qué hace usted?**
    A. Recoge los vidrios del hielo, asegurándose de recoger todos los pedazos.
    B. Llena el contenedor con hielo fresco y utiliza el hielo de encima.
    C. Vacía el contenedor de hielo completamente, lo limpia y lo llena con hielo fresco inmediatamente.
    D. Vacía el contenedor de hielo al finalizar el turno.
    E. Utiliza solamente hielo que no tenga vidrio.

PRIMERAS IMPRESIONES

21. **Usted es el cantinero en servicio. ¿Cuál es la primera cosa que usted hace cuando un cliente entra al bar?**
    A. Averigua cuantas personas hay en el grupo.
    B. Se preocupa por los meseros primero.
    C. Les pide que esperen hasta que usted termine lo que esté haciendo.
    D. Sonríe y les da la bienvenida al restaurante.

22. **¿Qué haría usted si cuando entran clientes al restaurante usted está hablando por teléfono?**
    A. Dependería de con quien está hablando.
    B. Finje que no se da cuenta que entraron hasta que termina la conversación.
    C. Recibe a los clientes nuevos con una sonrisa y completa la llamada rápidamente.
    D. Los sienta en una mesa y les lleva menúes cuando termina la llamada.
    E. Cuelga el teléfono inmediatamente.

23. **El restaurante está muy ocupado. ¿Cuál de las siguientes actividades podrían contribuir más al restaurante?**
    A. Sentar a los clientes que estén esperando tan pronto como haya una mesa libre.
    B. Asegurarse que cada cliente obtenga atención personal.
    C. Vender aperitivos a los clientes mientras esperan.
    D. Ayudar a los que limpian a aclarar a reorganizar las mesas.

24. **¿Qué debe usted saber antes de contestar el teléfono en el restaurante?**
    A. Las horas de servicio.
    B. Los especiales del día.
    C. Las instrucciones de cómo llegar al restaurante.
    D. La descripción y estilo del menú y la lista de precios.
    E. Todo lo anterior.

25. **Su horario de servicio estipula que usted abre a las 4:00 PM. Un cliente golpea en la puerta de enfrente que está cerrada y su reloj marca las 3:50 PM. ¿Qué hace usted?**
    A. Mantener la puerta cerrada, mostrarle la hora en pedir su reloj y pedirle que espere 10 minutos.
    B. Finje que usted no lo ha visto.
    C. Dejarlo entrar y hacerlo esperar en el lobby hasta las 4:00 PM.
    D. Invitarle a entrar, tomar asiento y pedir su orden.

26. **Su horario de servicio estipula que usted debe cerrar el restaurante a las 10:00 PM. El horario de cierre del estado es a las 2:00 AM. Un grupo de seis personas llega a las 9:55 PM. ¿Qué hace usted?**
    A. Explica que no les puede dar servicio a la hora de cierre del restaurante y les pide que regresen al otro día.
    B. Los sienta y les pide que ordenen antes de las 10:00 PM.
    C. Les pregunta a los que trabajan en la barra si quieren servirle a otro grupo.
    D. Los sienta y les sirve como a cualquier otro cliente esa noche.

27. **Usted le está mostrando a una pareja la mesa en una noche ocupada. A medida que usted se aproxima a la mesa para dos, ellos le preguntan si usted puede sentarlos en una mesa para cuatro en la esquina. ¿Qué hace usted?**
    A. Les explica que el restaurante está muy lleno y los sientan en la mesa para dos.
    B. Les pregunta cuál es el problema con la mesa para dos.
    C. Les dice que la mesa para 4 está reservada y los sienta en la de dos.
    D. Los sienta en la mesa para cuatro.
    E. Llama al administrador.

28. **Es una noche muy ocupada del viernes y el anfitrión le ha dicho al grupo McPherson que la espera será de 30 minutos. La media hora casi ha pasado y el anfitrión le ha dicho que la siguiente mesa estará disponible en 10 minutos. ¿Qué hace usted?**
    A. Los deja pasar y los llama cuando la mesa esté lista. Diez minutos no es motivo de preocupación.
    B. Les informa de la espera adicional y se excusa.
    C. Les informa de la espera adicional y les da algo para compensar la inconveniencia.
    D. Les informa de la espera adicional y les explica la razón de la demora.
    E. Llama al administrador.

29. **¿Cuál de los siguientes contribuirá a darle al cliente una experiencia desagradable?**
    A. Uniformes sucios o apretados.
    B. Mesas húmedas o pegajosas.
    C. Mesas o sillas inestables.
    D. Miembros de equipo técnico con malos hábitos de higiene personal.
    E. Todo el anterior.

30. **Usted está hablando por teléfono cuando los clientes se van del bar. ¿Qué hace usted?**
    A. Finje que no los ve y continúa su llamada.
    B. Sonríe y les saluda mientras continúa la conversación.
    C. Se excusa con el que está hablando y les agradece por su visita.
    D. Cuelga el teléfono inmediatamente.
    E. Llama al administrador.

OPERACIONES DEL BAR

31. **Un grupo de cuatro se está alistando para irse del bar. Tres clientes en otra mesa han terminado sus bebidas mientras la cuarta todavía está acabando. ¿Qué haría usted?**
    A. Recoge los vasos de los clientes que han terminado.
    B. Les pregunta a los clientes que han terminado si les gustaría que les recogiera sus vasos.
    C. Espera hasta que el cuarto cliente acabe.
    D. Recoge los vasos de los tres clientes que han terminado, siempre y cuando se lo hayan pedido.
    E. Ninguno de lo anterior.

32. **Al servir vino, ¿cuál de los siguientes procedimientos es *incorrecto*?**
    A. Presentar la etiqueta de la botella a la persona que la ordenó.
    B. Colocar la botella en la mesa mientras corta el aluminio.
    C. Servir un trago pequeño para la aprobación del cliente que lo pidió antes de servir al resto de la mesa.

D. Llenar las copas de las mujeres antes de llenar la de los hombres.

E. Llenar las copas de vino hasta la parte más ancha.

33. ¿Cuándo deberá usted cambiar los ceniceros en las mesas?

A. Cada vez que haya una colilla de cigarrillo en el cenicero.

B. Antes de servir el plato principal.

C. Cada vez que hayan dos colillas de cigarrillo en el cenicero.

D. Después de servir los cocteles.

E. Cada vez que hayan tres colillas de cigarrillos en el cenicero.

34. ¿Cuál es el método más adecuado para cambiar un cenicero?

A. Cubra el cenicero sucio con uno limpio y retírelo de la mesa.

B. Retire el cenicero sucio de la mesa con una mano mientras pone el limpio con la otra mano.

C. Retire el cenicero sucio de la mesa, vacíe las colillas en el contenedor y reemplácelo en la mesa.

D. Cualquiera de las anteriores es aceptable.

35. ¿Cuál es la primera cosa que usted haría al acercarse a una mesa?

A. Presentarse usted mismo.

B. Dar la bienvenida a los clientes del restaurante.

C. Colocar una servilleta de coctel frente a cada cliente.

D. Preguntarles a los clientes si les gustaría una bebida.

36. ¿Cuál de los siguientes es el factor más importante para el control de costo de servir en el bar?

A. El tamaño de la cristalería.

B. El costo del licor.

C. La forma de los cubos de hielo.

D. El tamaño del trago.

37. Usted cree que le ha dado excelente servicio a un grupo de tres. Cuando se han ido, usted nota que la cuenta de la tarjeta de crédito ha sido firmada, pero no hay propina incluída y la cuenta no fue sumada. ¿Qué hace usted?

A. Añade el 15% y pone el total de la cuenta en la tarjeta de crédito.

B. Intenta alcanzar a los clientes antes de que se vayan.

C. Presenta la cuenta como la dejaron.

D. Revisa la mesa en busca de la propina en efectivo.

E. Llama al administrador.

38. ¿Cuál es la cosa más importante al manejar la hora cumbre efectivamente?

A. Planee con tiempo asegurándose de tener el surtido adecuado en su lugar.

B. Contrate equipo técnico extra.

C. Planee que el horario incluya sus mejores trabajadores durante la hora cumbre.

D. Solamente siente gente tan rápido como usted pueda servirles.

E. Todo lo anterior.

39. Un grupo tiene un cuenta de $34.50. Ellos le dan dos billetes de veinte para pagar la cuenta. ¿Cuánto devuelve usted?

A. Dos monedas de 25 ctvs. y un billete de cinco dólares.

B. Dos monedas de 25 ctvs. y cinco billetes de uno.

C. Cinco monedas de 10 ctvs., un billete de un dólar y un billete de cinco dólares.

D. Nada, porque el cambio es más o menos lo que ellos deberían dejar de propina.

40. ¿Qué significa cortesía?

A. Que la gente le guste a usted.

B. Sonreír y ser cortés.

C. Ser respetuoso con sus clientes.

D. Asegurarse que la gente sepa que a usted le gusta la gente.

E. Todo lo anterior.

41. Un cliente le pide instrucciones de donde está el baño. ¿Cuál de lo siguiente usted no debe hacer?

A. Apunta hacia el baño.

B. Les explica como encontrar el baño.

C. Los lleva usted mismo al baño.

D. Cualquiera de los anteriores sería aceptable.

42. **¿Cuándo es importante indicar los números de los asientos en la cuenta del cliente?**
    A. Cuando se toma cualquier orden en la mesa.
    B. Solamente cuando se toma la orden de los aperitivos.
    C. Solamente cuando usted tiene tiempo suficiente para hacerlo.
    D. Los números no serán necesarios si usted tiene un sistema electrónico.

43. **¿Cada cuánto es necesario limpiar las líneas de la cerveza?**
    A. Todos los días.
    B. Una vez a la semana.
    C. Una vez al mes.
    D. Una vez al año.
    E. Solamente cuando la cerveza comienza a hacer espuma en exceso.

44. **¿Cuándo deberá cortar fruta el cantinero?**
    A. Solamente cuando el negocio esté lento.
    B. Una vez al día.
    C. Antes de cada turno.
    D. Menos de que un día por adelantado.
    E. Los cocineros deberán cortar la fruta, no el cantinero.

45. **¿Dónde debe guardar usted la cerveza embotellada?**
    A. En cajas en el piso del pasillo.
    B. En el hielo utilizado para las bebidas.
    C. Debajo del bar.
    D. En estantes en el refrigerador.
    E. Todo lo anterior.

46. **¿Cuál de las siguientes prácticas es robar?**
    A. Servir demasiado.
    B. Dar bebidas gratis a clientes buenos.
    C. Olvidar de marcar las bebidas en la caja registradora.
    D. Dar bebidas gratis al equipo técnico del restaurante.
    E. Todo el anterior.

47. **¿Qué significa si una persona ha sido "86 d"?**
    A. Ha sido hechada de las premisas.
    B. Es considerada un cliente especial y tiene una cuenta de crédito.
    C. Es solamente permitida en el bar durante el día.
    D. Solamente puede entrar acompañada por un padre u otros miembros familiares.
    E. Ninguno de los anteriores.

48. **¿Quién está autorizado a beber en el bar después de la hora de cierre por el estado?**
    A. Solamente el equipo técnico de administración.
    B. Los oficiales de policía locales.
    C. Clientes que estén terminando sus bebidas.
    D. Los miembros de equipo técnico de edad legal.
    E. Nadie está autorizado de beber en el bar después de la hora de cierre por el estado.

49. **¿Cuál de los siguientes sería el mejor modo de demostrarle a un cliente regular del bar que es apreciado?**
    A. Comprarle una bebida gratis de cortesía.
    B. Servirle los tragos más fuertes que a los otros clientes.
    C. Darles una cena en el comedor del restaurante.
    D. Invitarlos a su casa.
    E. Comprarle una bebida gratis y pagarla usted mismo.

50. **¿Cuál de los siguientes son comportamientos inapropiados del equipo técnico de bebida en servicio?**
    A. Beber o comer en las estaciones.
    B. Leer revistas comerciales de restaurantes.
    C. Ver programas de televisión de asuntos públicos.
    D. Todos los comportamientos anteriores son inapropiados.
    E. Ninguno de los comportamientos anteriores son inapropiados.

51. ¿Qué hace usted cuando la fruta del bar se pone vieja?
    A. Remójela en soda para revitalizarla.
    B. Sírvasela a los borrachos.
    C. Hace jugo de frutas.
    D. Mezclarla con fruta fresca.
    E. Tirarla.

52. ¿Cuál de las siguientes es una forma adecuada de abrir una botella de champaña?
    A. Sostenga el corcho firmemente y tuerza la botella.
    B. Apunte la botella hacia usted mismo y lejos de los clientes.
    C. Apunte el corcho a través del salón, teniendo cuidado de no golpear a nadie.
    D. Sostenga la botella firmemente y tuerza el corcho.
    E. Utilice un sacacorchos para sacar el corcho.

53. Un mesero llega al bar con una bebida que un cliente del comedor ha regresado. El mesero obviamente está un poco enfadado y es un poco grocero. ¿Qué hace usted?
    A. Llamarle la atención por su grocería.
    B. Averigue qué tenía de malo la bebida.
    C. Revise la bebida para ver si fue preparada adecuadamente.
    D. Devuelva la bebida al cliente usted mismo y explíquele como fue preparada.
    E. Arregle o reemplace la bebida sin comentarios.

54. ¿Cuál es la forma más adecuada de enfriar un vaso?
    A. Ponerlo en el congelador por algunos segundos.
    B. Ponerlo en el refrigerador por algunos segundos.
    C. Revuelva el vaso en el contenedor de hielo por algunos segundos.
    D. Llene el vaso con hielo y revuelvalo por algunos segundos.
    E. No es adecuado enfriar un vaso.

55. Usted es el cantinero en un restaurante de categoría media. Son las 4:00 PM y hay cuatro personas sentadas en el bar. Un grupo de gente llega y camina directo hacia una mesa en la esquina. No hay meseros trabajando. ¿Qué hace usted?
    A. Hacer que los clientes nuevos vayan al bar a pedir sus bebidas.
    B. Permanecer detrás de la barra y preguntarle a los nuevos clientes lo que quieren.
    C. Dejar la barra e ir a la mesa a tomar la orden de los clientes.
    D. Preguntarle a los clientes nuevos lo que quieren antes de que se sienten.
    E. Llamar al administrador.

56. Usted es el cantinero en un restaurante con servicio completo. Es una noche del viernes muy ocupada y el bar está lleno. El rótulo sobre el área de servicio dice "Empleados unicamente". Un cliente viene al área de servicio a ordenar una bebida. ¿Qué hace usted?
    A. Le solicita al cliente que deje el área de servicio y le dice que pida la orden en el bar.
    B. Le pide al cliente que se siente y llama a un mesero para que tome la orden.
    C. Prepara la bebida y le dice al administrador acerca de esto.
    D. Prepara la bebida.
    E. Llama al administrador.

57. ¿Con cuál de las siguientes declaraciones está usted más de acuerdo?
    A. Un buen cantinero sabe como preparar bebidas sin las recetas.
    B. Los buenos cantineros tienen sus propias recetas de las bebidas.
    C. Para asegurarse del control de tragos, refiérase a la receta cada vez que usted prepare una bebida.
    D. Los buenos cantineros memorizan y siguen recetas prescritas del bar.
    E. Todo lo anterior.

58. Su restaurante no ofrece un menú de aperitivos en el bar. Una noche, un cliente en el bar le pide algo de comer. ¿Qué hace usted?
    A. Le busca un puesto en el comedor.
    B. Les dice que usted no tiene servicio de comida en el bar.
    C. Llama a un mesero del comedor.
    D. Consigue lo que ellos quieren comer.
    E. Llama al administrador.

59. **Usted nota que la cerveza de barril no sostiene mucha espuma en los vasos. ¿Cuál de las siguientes usted sospecha que sea la causa del problema?**

    A. Las líneas de cerveza en el barril están sucias.

    B. Los vasos están rayados.

    C. La cerveza está caliente.

    D. Hay residuos de detergente en los vasos.

    E. Los barriles de cerveza han sido agitados.

60. **Usted es el cantinero en un restaurante mexicano muy ocupado. Una mesera regresa con una margarita del comedor porque el cliente no quería sal en el borde del vaso. Pero, la bebida está perfecta y usted vende muchas margaritas. ¿Qué hace usted con la bebida regresada?**

    A. Limpia cuidadosamente la sal del borde del vaso y lo devuelve al comedor.

    B. Guarda la margarita para la siguiente orden y la sirva como está.

    C. Prepara una nueva bebida sin sal y bota la primer bebida.

    D. La pone en el mezclador con el siguiente lote de margaritas.

EL SERVICIO DE ALCOHOL

61. **¿Cuál de los siguientes alimentos serían más efectivos para *retrazar* la absorción del alcohol?**

    A. Palomitas de maíz.

    B. Una barra de chocolate.

    C. Queso.

    D. Café negro.

    E. Todo tendría el mismo efecto.

62. **¿Cuál de los siguientes *aumentaría* la absorción de alcohol en el cuerpo?**

    A. El agua.

    B. Bebidas carbonatadas.

    C. Alimentos proteínicos.

    D. Dulces.

    E. Ninguno de los anteriores.

63. **¿Cuál de los siguientes típicamente *no* sería considerado una forma válida de indentificacíon?**

    A. Partida de nacimiento.

    B. Licencia de conducir.

    C. Tarjeta de la residencia extranjera.

    D. Tarjeta del seguro social.

    E. Todos son validos para identificación.

64. **¿Cuál de las siguientes declaraciones describen exactamente la ley?**

    A. Es legal servir alcohol a personas intoxicadas si no van a conducir.

    B. Es ilegal servir a alcohol a personas intoxicadas.

    C. Es ilegal servir más de tres bebidas por hora a una persona.

    D. Es legal que un menor beba si sus padres compran la bebida alcohólica.

    E. Todas las declaraciones anteriores son exactas.

65. **Usted deberá dejar de servirle alcohol a una persona que demuestre los siguientes comportamientos.**

    A. Coquetea.

    B. Pierde las inhibiciones.

    C. Es fastidiosa.

    D. Riega las bebidas.

    E. Es demasiado tranquila.

66. **¿Cuál de las siguientes no es una bebida equivalente a otras cuando se toma en cuenta el contenido de alcohol?**

    A. 12 onzas de cerveza.

    B. 8 onzas de vino.

    C. 1 onza de licor con 80 de prueba.

    D. Todo son iguales en contenido de alcohol.

67. **Un cliente definitivamente ha tomado demasiado y está listo para irse del restaurante. Usted se acerca para ofrecerle un taxi para que lo lleve a su casa. Rechaza su oferta e insiste que va a conducir a casa. ¿Qué hace usted?**
   A. Le pide que sea cuidadoso y le permite conducir.
   B. Si la persona entra al carro, llama a la policía.
   C. Agarra las llaves y no se las devuelva.
   D. Continúa insistiendo su punto de vista.
   E. Llama al dueño.

68. **¿Cuál de las siguientes prácticas no ayudarán a evitar el sobreconsumo?**
   A. Servir una bebida a la vez.
   B. Hacer que los clientes vayan al bar a ordenar.
   C. Servir las rondas cuando la mayoría de los vasos estén vacíos.
   D. Retirar los vasos vacíos de la mesa antes de servir la otra ronda.
   E. Poner agua en la mesa.

69. **Una mujer ha bebido demasiado y quiere otra copa de vino. Le jura que no va a conducir, una declaración confirmada por su novio. Él no ha bebido y le garantiza que él la llevará a casa y se asegurará de que llegue bien. Él le pide que traiga el vino. ¿Qué hace usted?**
   A. Lleva la bebida tal y como fue solicitada.
   B. Llama a la policía.
   C. Llama al dueño.
   D. Rehusa servir la bebida.
   E. Sugiere como alternativa bebidas sin alcohol.

70. **Un grupo de jóvenes entra al restaurante y ordena bebidas alcohólicas. Usted les pide identificación y ellos le dicen que no la tienen con ellos. Le aseguran que son mayores de 21 años de edad. Esto es verificado por otro cliente que oyó la conversación y a quien usted reconoce como un oficial de la policía en vestido civil. ¿Qué hace usted?**
   A. Sirve las bebidas.
   B. Llama al departamento de policía para confirmar la identidad del cliente mayor.
   C. Llama al dueño.
   D. Se rehusa a servir las bebidas.
   E. Sugiere otra alternativa a las bebidas alcohólicas.

Por favor responda las siguientes preguntas FALSO O VERDADERO.
71. Usted puede ser responsable de las acciones de los clientes intoxicados.
72. El uso de cocaína o marijuana junto con el alcohol intensifican el efecto.
73. Un conductor que registre .8% de BAC está considerado de manejar bajo la influencia del alcohol.
74. Si una persona de fuera del estado tiene la edad legal para beber en su estado podría beber en el restaurante.
75. La altitud disminuye el efecto del alcohol.
76. El alcohol es un depresivo que disminuye el apetito.
77. Una persona con un porcentaje de grasa alto absorbe el alcohol más rápido que una persona con más músculos.
78. El cuerpo procesa alcohol con un porcentaje de una bebida por hora, sin importar el tamaño.
79. Cuando descontinúa el servicio a un cliente intoxicado, es mejor no tocarlo.
80. Una máquina medidora del aliento mide la cantidad de alcohol en la sangre.

FINANZAS

81. **Vamos a decir que su restaurante *realmente* ha fallado con un grupo de cuatro. Vamos también a decir que el típico cliente de su restaurante come normalmente unas tres veces al mes y que su cuenta promedio es de $20.00. ¿Cuánto le costaría este error a la compañía en clientela perdida sobre los próximos cinco años?**
   A. Menos de $4,000.
   B. $10,000–$12,000.
   C. $25,000–$30,000.
   D. $50,000–$60,000.
   E. Más de $85,000.

82. ¿Que porción de ventas típicas del restaurante son ingresos antes del impuesto?
   A. 40–45%.
   B. 30–35%.
   C. 20–25%.
   D. 10–15%.
   E. Menos del 5%.

83. Sus ventas totales de bebidas fueron de $500.00 durante su turno. Usted tuvo un total de 50 cuentas que representan bebidas servidas a 100 personas. Había 25 asientos en su sección. ¿Cuál fué su cuenta promedio durante su turno?
   A. $500.00
   B. $20.00
   C. $10.00
   D. $5.00

84. Usted es un mesera en un bar de un hotel muy ocupado y sus propinas durante su turno suman $80.00. Como hizo un trabajo muy bueno hoy, usted decide darle al cantinero 15% de sus propinas. Después de haberle dado eso al cantinero, ¿cuánto dinero llevará usted a casa?
   A. $80.00
   B. $68.00
   C. $58.00
   D. $12.00

85. En pocas palabras, ¿qué es una factura?
   A. Una cuenta.
   B. Una orden de compra.
   C. Una historia de ventas.
   D. El estado de las cuentas.
   E. Una prognósis de producción.

86. Su vendedor de licor le acaba de ofrecer un trato: 20% de descuento en órdenes mayores a las 3 cajas de Kahlúa si usted pide la orden hoy. Usted utiliza normalmente de 3–4 botellas de Kahlúa en un mes. ¿Qué hace usted?
   A. Pasa.
   B. Compra 3+ cajas y le ahorra al restaurante dinero.
   C. Compra 3+ cajas e inventa una bebida especial nueva.
   D. Compra 3+ cajas y revende parte de las reservas con ganancia.

87. Su restaurante tiene un concurso para buscar una bebida especial nueva. Para ser elegible, la bebida tendrá que venderse por $5.00 con un costo de trago del 25% o menos. ¿Cuál sería el costo más alto de tragos que puede tener?
   A. $1.75
   B. $1.50
   C. $1.25
   D. $1.00

Las siguientes bebidas están incluidas en su menú del bar en el restaurante. Suponga que usted no tiene una reserva de licores caros.

Bebidas de la reserva	3.25	Cerveza local	2.75	Gaseosas	1.25
Marca barata	3.75	Cerveza importada	3.50	Té helado	.95
Marca de primera	4.25	Té helado Long Island	4.25	Café	.50
Vinos de la casa	2.75	Margarita helada	4.50	Jugo de naranja	1.50

88. Una mesa de tres ordena Stolichnaya en las rocas, una Corona y un vaso de Chablis. ¿A cuánto llega la cuenta antes del impuesto sobre la venta?
   A. $8.75
   B. $10.50
   C. $11.50
   D. $11.75

89. **Una mesa de cuatro ordena dos rondas de bebidas. La primera incluye una margarita, una Coca-Cola dietética, una botella de Budweiser y un té helado Long Island. En la segunda ronda, substituyen a la Coca-Cola dietética por un J & B en las rocas. Si dejaran el 15% de propina basado en el total antes del impuesto, ¿cuánto le darían?**
   A. $3.50
   B. $4.00
   C. $4.25
   D. $4.75

90. **El mes pasado sus recibos totales del restaurante fueron $66,500.00, de los cuales $4,100.00 fueron impuestos sobre la venta, $46,800.00 fueron ventas de comidas y el resto fueron ventas de bebidas. Su compra de licor fue de $3,300.00 y su nómina del bar fué de $2,900.00. Usted gastó $550 en materiales. El inventario de apertura del licor fué de $4,400.00 y el inventario de cierre fue de $3,900.00. ¿Cuál fue su costo de tragos en el mes?**
   A. 21.2%
   B. 24.4%
   C. 25.9%
   D. 28.2%
   E. No hay suficiente información para contestar ésta pregunta.

VENTAS

91. **¿Cuál práctica aumentaría sus ventas?**
   A. Sugerir artículos que le gusten.
   B. Poder describir cualquier bebida y como es preparada.
   C. Mencionar la firma de bebidas que su restaurante ofrece.
   D. Sugerir los mejores artículos.
   E. Todo el anterior.

92. **¿Cuál de las siguientes preguntas ayudarían efectivamente a vender bebidas alcohólicas?**
   A. "¿Puedo traerle un coctel?"
   B. "¿Le gustaría ver el menú de licores?"
   C. "¿Que clase de coctel puedo traerle?"
   D. "¿Está listo para ordenar?"
   E. "¿Alguna vez a probado nuestro famoso ponche de ron?"

93. **Una noche un cliente entra tarde al bar y ordena un mousse de chocolate. ¿Cuál de las siguientes bebidas sugeriría usted para acompañar el postre?**
   A. Una copa de Cabernet Sauvignon.
   B. Un café irlandés.
   C. Un Grand Marnier en las rocas.
   D. El café espresso.
   E. Cualquiera de estos irían bien con el mousse de chocolate.

94. **¿En qué ayuda *más* la venta sugerida al restaurante?**
   A. A incrementar las ventas.
   B. A incrementar la satisfacción de los clientes.
   C. A incrementar las propinas de los meseros.
   D. A reducir el costo de los alimentos.
   E. A usar los artículos almacenados.

95. **¿Cuál de los siguientes animaría usted a que sus clientes compren?**
   A. Bebidas de la reserva.
   B. Licores exclusivos.
   C. Especialidades sin alcohol.
   D. Todo lo anterior.

96. **¿Cuál de las siguientes sería una reacción apropiada cuando un cliente ordena un Scotch con agua?**
   A. "¿Qué prefiere, Chivas Regal o Glenlivet en su Scotch con agua?"
   B. "¿Qué prefiere, Scotch doméstico o importado?"
   C. "Usted puede tomar Glenlivet por un dolar más."

D. "Ya regreso con su bebida."

E. "Gracias."

97. ¿Que significa "upselling"?

A. Cobrándole al cliente más de lo del precio en el menú.

B. Un técnica de ventas obligatoria.

C. Sugerencias de marcas exclusivas.

D. Hacer que el cliente pague más de lo que planificó.

E. Ninguno de los anteriores.

98. ¿Cuál es el efecto de "upselling"?

A. Aumentará la cuenta promedio.

B. Los meseros recibirán propinas más altas.

C. Los clientes pasarán un rato mejor.

D. Todo lo anterior.

E. Ninguno de los anteriores.

99. ¿Cuál es la mejor manera de vender cocteles?

A. Saber que hay en cada bebida.

B. Saber a qué sabe cada bebida.

C. Saber cómo está hecha cada bebida.

D. Saber cuáles son las bebidas especiales de la casa.

E. Todo lo anterior.

100. ¿Cuál de estos sugeriría usted cuando un cliente ha estado bebiendo en el bar por varias horas?

A. Café espresso.

B. Bebidas especiales sin alcohol.

C. Cerveza suave.

D. Pizza.

E. Mousse de chocolate.

RECETAS

Para cada una de las siguientes bebidas, indique los tres ingredientes principales.

101. Margarita	A. Vodka	T. Jugo de lima
102. Daiquirí	B. Ginebra	U. Jugo de limón
103. Martini	C. Tequila	V. Jugo de tomate
104. Manhattan	D. Scotch	W. Jugo de "cranberry"
105. Stinger	E. Ron suave	X. Jugo de toronja
106. Bloody Mary	F. Bourbon	Y. Jugo de naranja
107. Black Russian	G. Irish Whisky	Z. Jugo de piña
108. Cuba libre	H. Crema de menta blanca	aa. Agua tónica
109. Old Fashioned	I. Crema de cacao blanca	bb. Club soda
110. Tequila Sunrise	J. Brandy	cc. Coca-Cola
111. Martini perfecto	K. Triple Sec	dd. Crema de coco
112. Café irlandés	L. Vermouth dulce	ee. Orgeat syrup
113. Piña colada	M. Vermouth seco	ff. Café
114. White Russian	N. Ron oro	gg. Crema
115. Screwdriver	O. Schnapps de melocotón	hh. Leche
116. Café keoki	P. Schnapps de menta	ii. Azúcar
117. Ponche de Planters	Q. Drambuie	jj. Tabasco
118. Fuzzy Navel	R. Grand Marnier	kk. Bitters
119. Rob Roy	S. Kahlúa	ll. Granada
120. Rusty Nail	xx. No hay otros ingredientes en esta bebida.	

CONOCIMIENTO DE BEBIDAS

121. ¿Si un cliente ordena un Dewar "neat," ¿cómo se lo sirve?
   A. En las rocas.
   B. En un vaso medidor.
   C. Con agua.
   D. Con limón.

122. ¿Cuál de las siguientes pondría una botella de Merlot a una temperatura adecuada?
   A. Ponga la botella en el refrigerador a 38°F.
   B. Mantenga la botella en un estante a la temperatura del comedor.
   C. Enfriar la botella a 55°F.
   D. La temperatura no es importante con un Merlot.

123. ¿Cuánto puede mantener el café en un calentador antes de que la calidad se deteriore?
   A. Menos de 15 minutos.
   B. Menos de 45 minutos.
   C. Menos de 90 minutos.
   D. Menos de 2½ horas.
   E. El café puede permanecer indefinidamente si se mantiene caliente.

124. Onza por onza, ¿cuál de las siguiente tiene el contenido de alcohol más alto?
   A. Vino tinto.
   B. Vino fortificado.
   C. Vodka de 80.
   D. Bourbon de 100.

Concuerde las siguientes bebidas con las definiciones adecuadas. Suponga que usted no tiene una reserva de bebidas exclusivas.

125. Wild Turkey	A. Vino tinto de buen cuerpo
126. Smirnoff	B. Scotch de marca barata
127. Myer's	C. Vodka importada
128. Dewar's	D. Whisky doméstico combinado
129. Suaza	E. Vino blanco de buen cuerpo
130. Heineken	F. Bourbon exclusivo
131. Port	G. Whiskey importado combinado
132. Bacardi Plata	H. Crema de jeréz
133. Chivas Regal	I. Vodka doméstica
134. Cabernet Sauvignon	J. Vino blanco de especies frutales
135. Augsberger	K. Vino fortificado
136. Beck's	L. Vino blanco de cuerpo suave
137. Chardonnay	M. Cerveza sin alcohol
138. Gamay Beaujolais	N. Cream de licor importada
139. Clausthaler	O. Vino blush
140. Harvey's	P. Ron de marca
141. Triple Sec	Q. Champaña importada
142. Seagram's 7	R. Scotch doméstico
143. Kahlúa	S. Cerveza importada
144. Sauvignon Blanc	T. Vino tinto de cuerpo suave
145. Bailey's	U. Tequila importada
146. Crown Royal	V. Scotch importada
147. Gewürztraminer	W. Licor de café importada
148. White Zinfandel	X. Cerveza doméstica
149. Wolfschmidt	Y. Ron oro importado
150. Mumm's	Z. Licor de naranja

Beverage Staff

PROFESSIONAL TEST
Answers

HUMAN RELATIONS

1. **E** **Staff development.** All of the factors are elements that an effective supervisor would do better on than an unskilled one. Still, the distinguishing factor of great supervisors is their ability to teach and bring out the best in those who work with and for them.

2. **D** **On-the-job instruction.** Anything that involves developing physical skills can only be effectively learned by doing.

3. **D** **A skilled co-worker.** The worker is always closer to the job and therefore knows more about its current intricacies than even the most experienced supervisor. Involving the staff in training is also an excellent way to eliminate the "them against us" mentality in a foodservice operation.

4. **E** **They are no different from anyone else.** Beware of generalizations about any group of people. Remember that somewhere in the world, *you* are a minority!

5. **D** **Set a good personal example.** What they see is what you will get. Anything else is wasted effort.

6. **D** **Teach the cocktail servers how to tend bar.** When you teach your crew to do your job, they get excited by the opportunity to improve their skills. As you eliminate tasks from your workload, it leaves you open to develop new skills yourself.

7. **B** **Complaints are special gifts.** Only one person in 25 will actually tell you about a complaint. The rest will simply go away, never return, and tell their friends to stay away, too. When you get a complaint, it is a rare insight into what may be killing your business. Accept the information with gratitude and fix the problem immediately.

8. **E** **You can't assume anything when a drink is returned.** There are thousands of reasons why a drink might be returned. Consider it an opportunity to give an extra level of service, replace or fix it immediately, and discuss the probable causes later. This is not to suggest that patterns of problems should not be identified and solved.

9. **A** **Apologize and immediately resolve the situation in favor of the guest.** The apology will help keep the guest from becoming more defensive. Resolving a complaint in favor of the guest is the only resolution that will be in the true long-term interests of the restaurant.

10. **D** **Any of these situations could call for a comp.** Guests come to the restaurant for a good time. Whenever they don't have that experience, regardless of whose "fault" it is, they will only remember that their last trip to your restaurant was not fun. In the case of the argument, comping the drink shows an unexpected compassion that will be memorable and might salvage what could otherwise be permanently lost patronage.

SANITATION

11. **E** **An unlabeled spray bottle in the service stand.**

12. **A** **Exclude her from all food-handling responsibilities until the cut heals.** This is the most correct choice of those offered. In practice, covering the wound with a surgical glove and having the staff member work out of sight of guests is a more likely solution. The important thing is that you never risk the wound or its bandage coming in contact with food.

13. **C** **In the upper front of the refrigerator by the door.** The secondary thermometer should be placed in the warmest part of the refrigerator. Most state health codes require all refrigerators to have a secondary thermometer easily visible when the door is opened.

14. **E** **Keeping wipe cloths in sanitizing solution.** This is the only practice on the list that is not a health department violation.

15. **C** **At least once an hour.** The effectiveness of sanitizing solution decreases over time and with use. To be safe, solutions should be tested at least once an hour.

16. **C** **Dip a test strip in the solution and compare it with a scale.** Typical sanitizers are usually either quaternary ammonia or chlorine bleach, and each requires a different test strip. There is no such thing as a universal test kit.

17. **B** **It can be toxic.** For the sake of illustration, consider the effect of using undiluted bleach to wipe down a cutting board. The *only* way to be sure you have a proper concentration is to measure the sanitizer into a known amount of water *and* verify the concentration with a test strip.

18. **D** **It won't work as well, if at all.** Too little sanitizer will be ineffective.

19. **C** **Empty the ice bin completely, wipe it dry, and refill it with fresh ice immediately.** There is no way to separate broken glass from ice. If guests swallow broken glass, they will suffer serious injury that will certainly bring massive legal action against the restaurant.

20. **C** **Empty the ice bin completely, wipe it dry, and refill it with fresh ice immediately.** The time of day or pace of business does not give you permission to risk injury to your guests.

FIRST IMPRESSIONS

21. **D** **Smile and welcome the guest to the restaurant.** Your first words should thank your guests for coming and welcome them to the restaurant. After that you can address details such as how many are in the party, seating preferences, reservations, etc.

22. **C** **Acknowledge the new arrivals with a smile and complete your call promptly.**

23. **B** **Making sure that every guest gets your personal attention.** Taking care of guests is what makes the operation successful. It is your level of personal connection with the guest that best demonstrates the degree of your caring.

24. **E** **All of the above.** If guest service is your first priority, you will not allow yourself or the restaurant to be embarrassed when a guest calls.

25. **D** **Invite him in, get him a seat, and take his order.** It is not worth inconveniencing a guest to prove a point about whose watch is correct. The bar may not be totally ready to go, but it is rude to leave a guest waiting in the cold. Breaking the rules in the interests of guest service is no crime.

26. **D** **Seat them and serve them as you have any other guests that evening.** Closing time is when you stop seating people, *not* the time when everyone on the staff should expect to go home. They were clearly there before closing and are entitled to your full service—with a smile!

27. **D** **Seat them at the 4-top.** Guests come to the restaurant to have a good time. If they will have a better time at a larger table, give it to them.

28. **C** **Inform them of the additional wait and give them something to make up for the inconvenience.** You must always keep the guests informed of the status of the wait—most of them are probably checking their watches anyway. If your estimate was off, do something to make up for the inconvenience. Your guests will be delighted.

29. **E** **All of the above.** Any distraction will intrude on the guests' experience and cause them to enjoy themselves less. In the extreme, these sorts of irritations may cause them to take their patronage elsewhere.

30. **C** **Excuse yourself from the caller and thank them for coming.** People never get enough gratitude. It is important to show your guests that you appreciate their patronage.

BAR OPERATIONS

31. **C/D** **Wait until the fourth guest finishes (or) clear the glasses of the three guests who have finished, but only if they ask you to do so.** Either of these choices is correct. Many guests who are slow eaters or drinkers feel rushed when their companions' glasses are cleared before everyone at the table has finished.

32. **B** **Placing the bottle on the table while cutting the foil.** Hold the bottle while cutting the foil. The table is the guest's territory, and many diners will resent your trespassing.

33. **C** **Whenever there are two cigarette butts in it.**

34. **A** **Capping a clean ashtray over the soiled one and removing it from the table.** The cap keeps ashes from flying about as the full container is removed. Be sure to replace it with a clean ashtray rather than just emptying the dirty one and returning it to the table.

35. **B** **Welcome the guests to the restaurant.** As with the arrival in the restaurant, a server should first thank guests for coming and welcome them to the restaurant. After that, they can deal with the particulars of the meal. Personal introductions are seldom appreciated by diners.

36. **A** **The size of the glassware.** A proper cocktail has the right ratio of ice, liquor, and mixer. If the glasses are too large, there will be a tendency to pour a heavier shot to create the proper balance.

37. **C** **Submit the slip as is.** It may be that the guest simply forgot, but you do not have the right to add the tip. Without the cardholder's permission, such an act will cost you that person's patronage forever.

38. **A** **Plan ahead and be sure adequate stocks are in place.** The only effective way to get through the rush is never to get behind. Key to staying ahead of the crowd is to be sure you know what you are doing and not to have to interrupt the flow of service to restock.

39. **B** **Two quarters and five ones.** This combination gives the guests the change they need to leave a tip if they choose. While you may get it all back, never presume a tip or you risk losing a guest's business forever.

40. **E** **All of the above.**

41. **A** **Point them toward the restrooms.** Many people find pointing to be rude. When it comes to the restrooms, pointing can embarrass your guests by making everyone in the dining room aware of the nature of their request.

42. **A** **When taking any order at the table.** Table and seat numbers will enable anyone on the staff to properly serve an order if you are occupied. It will also help you split the check should the party ask for separate checks later in the meal.

43. **B** **Once a week.** Many suppliers will do this for you, but one way or another it must be done every week. Dirty draft lines will cause the beer to be excessively foamy, increasing waste, mess, and pouring cost.

44. **C** **Before every shift.** To be attractive as a garnish, fruit must be fresh and moist. Fruit that is stored too long can become slimy and detract from the guests' enjoyment.

45. **D** **On shelves in the refrigerator.** Proper storage requires air circulation and the ability to keep the storage area clean.

46. **E** **All of the above.**

47. **A** **They are barred from the premises.**

48. **E** **No one is allowed to drink at the bar after state closing time.** In most states, this is a violation of the law that can cause serious problems for the restaurant's liquor license.

49. **C** **Buying them dinner in the dining room.** This encourages them to regard you more as a restaurant and less as a bar. Since you cannot build loyalty with alcohol, it can help keep regular guests coming back.

50. **D** **All of the above are inappropriate behaviors.**

51. **E** **Throw it out.** There is no valid way to salvage old bar fruit.

52. **A** **Hold the cork firmly and twist the bottle.** This will provide better leverage and keep the cork under control.

53. **E** **Fix or replace the drink without comment.** Remember that you work for the server in creating guest delight. If a guest has a problem, take care of it and don't waste a lot of energy being righteous.

54. **D** **Fill the glass with ice and swirl it for a few seconds.** A few seconds in the refrigerator or freezer will not chill the glass, and placing the glass in the service ice is a health department violation. Chilled glasses can be a nice touch for a cold beer or glass of chilled wine at the bar.

55. **C** **Leave the bar and go to the table to take the new guests' orders.** Good service is focused on giving the guests a great time every time. Beware of anything that is done for the convenience of the staff rather than for the enjoyment of the guest.

56. **D** **Make the drink.** It's not worth the aggravation, and going on a power trip will only irritate the guest. If this happens regularly, it might be appropriate to look at the coverage being provided by the cocktail staff.

57. **D** **Good bartenders memorize and follow prescribed bar recipes.** Just as good cooks follow standardized recipes, legendary bartenders in legendary restaurants ensure that their drinks have a consistent taste.

58. **D** **Get them what they want to eat.** The only reason the restaurant exists is to make its guests happy. If food will make them happy, there is really no decision to make.

59. **D** **There is detergent residue in the glasses.** A detergent film on the glass will prevent a head from forming. Sometimes this happens when bar glassware is washed in the kitchen dish machine.

60. **C** **Make a new drink without salt and throw the original drink away.** You cannot reuse any product returned from the dining room. There is no way to be certain that a product has not been tainted in some way by the guest.

ALCOHOL SERVICE

61. C **Cheese.** Protein foods slow the absorption rate of alcohol.

62. B **Carbonated beverages.**

63. D **A Social Security card.** It does not show a birth date and is not valid ID for the purchase of alcohol.

64. B **It is illegal to serve alcohol to intoxicated persons.**

65. D **Spilling drinks.** This is one of the signs of someone in the "red zone."

66. B **8 ounces of wine.** The equivalent amount of wine is four ounces.

67. B **If he gets into his car, call the police.** In many states, this is the law. Good guest relations notwithstanding, I would rather have a guest angry at me than dead.

68. B **Making guests come to the bar to order.** This will not slow consumption and only provides poor service to the guest.

69. E **Suggest nonalcoholic alternatives.** This will keep the situation focused on positive factors rather than negative ones. In general, it is always preferable to tell people what you *can* do for them rather than what you *can't*!

70. E **Suggest nonalcoholic alternatives.** The reasoning is the same as in the previous question.

71. T In most states, the person who serves alcohol to an intoxicated person is personally liable.

72. T This can be a dangerous combination both for the individual and the restaurateur.

73. F The legal limit for DWI will depend on your state, but anyone with a BAC of .8 is most likely *dead*! Now if the question said *.08*, that would be a different story!

74. F It's your state and your liquor license.

75. F High altitude intensifies the effects of alcohol.

76. F Alcohol is a depressant, but one that initially increases appetite—that's why we serve it in restaurants!

77. T Fat absorbs alcohol faster than muscle.

78. T The rate of alcohol absorption varies with body composition, but the rate at which the liver eliminates alcohol from the system is fairly constant for all people.

79. T While occasionally a light touch can be calming, it is not a wise idea to touch intoxicated people because you can never be sure how they are going to react.

80. F A breathalizer measures the amount of alcohol in the lungs, which is then converted to a BAC (blood alcohol content) reading.

FINANCIAL

81. E **Over $85,000.** There is a slight trick in this question to prove a point. Each person you lose will cost you $3,600 over 5 years (3 visits per month times $20 per visit times 60 months). For the party of 4, the loss is $14,400. The trick is that the typical dissatisfied guest will tell 8 to 10 other people. One in 5 will tell 20 others. The people who hear the horror story are not likely to come to your restaurant. If each of the 4 original guests only told 5 others, it would mean 20 more lost guests. At $3,600 each, this represents another $72,000 in lost business. The total cost to you is already $86,400!

82. E **Under 5%.** According to statistical studies by the National Restaurant Association, the typical full-service restaurant earns a median pretax profit of 3.5% to 4.0% of sales.

83. D **$5.** Average check is sales divided by the number of guests served—in this case, $500 divided by 100.

84. B **$68.** Fifteen percent of $80 is $12. Subtracting that from $80 leaves you with $68.

85. A **A bill.** The company is obligated to pay the amount of the invoice. Whenever someone on the staff signs an invoice, they are effectively signing a check.

86. A **Pass.** One of the keys to foodservice profitability is to maintain minimal inventories and turn them frequently. There is no deal good enough (and no storeroom big enough) to warrant tying up excess money and space for products that do not move.

87. **C** **$1.25.** 25% of $5.00 is $1.25.

88. **B** **$10.50.** This is a simple addition problem.

89. **C** **$4.25.** The check total is $28.00, and 15% of that amount is $4.20.

90. **B** **24.4%.** Beverage sales were $15,600 ($66,500 total sales less $4,100 sales tax less $46,800 food sales). Cost of beverages consumed was $3,300 in purchases plus $500 worth of beverages consumed from inventory ($4,400 opening value less $3,900 closing value), a total of $3,800. Beverages consumed divided by beverage sales equals the pouring cost percentage for this example of 24.4%.

SALES

91. **E** **All of the above.** The point is that suggestive selling is an overt activity on the part of the server. Unless the staff member takes the initiative to tell the guest something, no additional sales will be made.

92. **E** **"Have you ever tried our famous rum punch?"** This is a specific suggestion that leaves a sales opportunity no matter which way the guest answers the question. Many diners find the words "cocktail" and "liquor" to have connotations of alcoholism, yet they will readily order a frozen Margarita. Go figure.

93. **E** **Any of these goes well with Chocolate Mousse.**

94. **B** **By increasing guest satisfaction.** Suggestive selling helps guests have a better time by making their meal decisions easier and allowing them to try some menu items they might otherwise have missed. Suggestive selling also increases the restaurant's sales and the server's tips. Whether or not it decreases food cost depends on the items suggested and the structure of the menu.

95. **D** **All of the above.** Any of these will produce profit for the house and satisfaction for the guest.

96. **A** **"Would you prefer Chivas Regal or Glenlivet in your Scotch and water?"** This is an example of upselling and can help both sales and guest satisfaction.

97. **C** **Suggesting premium brands.** The national trend is for people to drink less but order higher-quality brands. Upselling is just another form of suggestive selling in the bar.

98. **D** **All of the above.** Upselling works well for everyone.

99. **E** **All of the above.** There is no substitute for product knowledge.

100. **D** **Pizza.** Protein foods will slow the rate of alcohol absorption.

RECIPES

101.	C	T	K	Tequila, lime juice, and triple sec.
102.	E	T	ii	Light rum, lime juice, and sugar.
103.	B	M	xx	Gin and dry vermouth.
104.	F	L	kk	Bourbon, sweet vermouth, and bitters.
105.	H	J	xx	White creme de menthe and brandy.
106.	A	V	jj	Vodka, tomato juice, and tabasco.
107.	A	S	nn	Vodka and Kahlua (over ice).
108.	E	cc	xx	Rum and Coca Cola (with a wedge of lime).
109.	F	ii	kk	Bourbon, sugar, and bitters (with a splash of soda).
110.	C	Y	ll	Tequila, orange juice, and grenadine.
111.	B	L	M	Gin, sweet vermouth, and dry vermouth.
112.	G	ff	gg	Irish whisky, coffee, and cream.
113.	E	Z	dd	Light rum, pineapple juice, and cream of coconut.
114.	A	S	gg	Vodka, Kahlua, and cream (over ice).

115. A Y xx Vodka and orange juice.

116. S J ff Kahlua, brandy, and coffee (with cream).

117. N T kk Dark rum, lime juice, and bitters.

118. O Y xx Peach schnapps and orange juice.

119. D M kk Scotch, dry vermouth, and bitters.

120. Q D xx Drambuie and Scotch (over ice).

BEVERAGE KNOWLEDGE

121. B **In a shot glass.** The drink could also be served in a regular glass. In either event, it is served without ice.

122. C **Cooling the bottle to 55°F.** Merlot is a red wine and should be served at "room temperature." When speaking of wine, room temperature means the temperature found in old castles or wine cellars, or about 55°F.

123. B **No longer than 45 minutes.**

124. D **100 proof bourbon.** Proof is a measure of alcohol content. Pure alcohol is 200 proof.

125. F **Premium bourbon.**

126. I **Domestic vodka.**

127. Y **Imported dark rum.**

128. B **Call Scotch.**

129. U **Imported tequila.**

130. S **Imported beer.**

131. K **Fortified wine.**

132. P **Call rum.**

133. V **Imported scotch.**

134. A **Full-bodied red wine.**

135. X **Domestic beer.**

136. S **Imported beer.**

137. E **Full-bodied white wine.**

138. T **Light-bodied red wine.**

139. M **Alcohol-free beer.**

140. H **Cream sherry.**

141. Z **Orange liqueur.**

142. D **Domestic blended whiskey.**

143. W **Imported coffee liqueur.**

144. L **Light-bodied white wine.**

145. N **Imported cream liqueur.**

146. G **Imported blended whiskey.**

147. J **Fruity, spicy white wine.**

148. O **Blush wine.**

149. I **Domestic vodka.**

150. Q **Imported champagne.**

Beverage Situations

1. It is a busy Friday night during Happy Hour and the bar is packed. When clearing a table, you notice a glass is missing. Although you didn't see anyone take it, one of the guests has a huge purse at her feet and is looking uncomfortable as you clear the table.

   A. What would you do?

   B. How would you handle it if you saw her put the glass in her purse?

   C. If glassware theft became enough of an issue to prompt a staff meeting about it, what would you recommend to the group?

2. You are the bar manager in a neighborhood restaurant noted for its giant hamburgers and the skimpy costumes of its cocktail waitresses. Murray has been a steady customer of your bar, coming in several days a week for a few drinks after work and bringing noticeable business from his company. In short, he is a good customer and you need every one of those you can find.

   In the last week, however, you have noticed that Murray's habits have started to change. Instead of his usual two draft beers, he has started ordering Wild Turkey with a Heineken back and is drinking more of them. He seems to have developed a fondness for Karen, a newly hired (vegetarian) cocktail server who just turned 21. You were off yesterday, but according to the daily communication log, Murray came in last night and after five or six bourbons, allegedly started grabbing at Karen and making off-color remarks to her. He said he was only joking, but the report was that Karen was uncomfortable, as were Murray's friends, who calmed him down and drove him home.

   Today he came in alone at 6:00, asked to be seated at Karen's station, and started drinking doubles. At 7:00, Karen comes to you, visibly upset, and says, "He's doing it again."

   A. Describe your conversation with Karen at this point.

   B. What, if anything, do you do tonight?

   C. What, if anything, do you do over the next few days?

1. **Es la noche de un viernes muy ocupado durante la "Happy Hour" y el bar está lleno. Al limpiar una mesa, usted nota que falta un vaso. Aunque usted no vió a nadie tomarlo, uno de los clientes tiene una cartera muy grande a sus pies y se ve incómoda mientras usted limpia la mesa.**

   A. ¿Qué hace usted?

   B. ¿Cómo reaccionaría usted si la ve a ella guardando el vaso en su cartera?

   C. Si el robo de cristalería llegara a un punto que una reunión del equipo técnico fuera necesaria, ¿qué le recomendaría usted al grupo?

2. **Usted es el administrador del bar de un restaurante de la vecindad famoso por sus hamburguesas gigantes y los uniformes "cortos" de las meseras. Murray ha sido un cliente constante en su bar, llendo varios días a la semana a tomarse unos tragos después del trabajo y trayendo sobresaliente clientela de su compañía. En breve, es un buen cliente y usted necesita cada uno de los clientes que usted pueda encontrar.**

   La semana pasada, sin embargo, usted ha notado que los hábitos de Murray han comenzado a cambiar. En lugar de sus dos cervezas diarias, ha comenzado a ordenar Wild Turkey con una Heineken y está bebiendo aún más. Parece que ha desorrollado un cariño especial por Karen, una nueva mesera (vegetariana) que acaba de cumplir 21. Usted tuvo su día libre ayer, pero de acuerdo con el diario de entradas, Murray estuvo la noche anterior y después de cinco o seis bourbons, según las declaraciones comenzó a agarrar a Karen y a hacerle comentarios grotescos. El dijo que solamente estaba bromeando, pero el informe aclaró que Karen estaba incómoda, al igual que sus amigos que lo calmaron y lo llevaron a su casa.

   Hoy llegó sólo a las 6:00, pidió sentarse en la sección de Karen y ha comenzado a tomar tragos dobles. A las 7:00, Karen va a usted obviamente alterada y le dice, "Lo está haciendolo de nuevo."

   A. Describa su conversación con Karen.

   B. ¿Qué, si cualquier cosa, hace usted esta noche?

   C. ¿Qué, si cualquier cosa, haría usted a los pocos días?

Situation Test Evaluation

BEVERAGE STAFF

Name: _____   **Evaluated By:** _____

Scoring:

Grade each evaluation criterion as it is observed (Y—Yes, N—No, ?—Maybe).
Give two points for each Y, one point for each ?, and no points for N.
A score of 16 or better means an overall evaluation of Yes.
A score of 10 to 15 means an overall evaluation of Maybe.
A score of 9 or below means an overall evaluation of No.

SITUATION 1:

Y N ?

☐ ☐ ☐ 1. Did the candidate come up with a solution without hesitation?
☐ ☐ ☐ 2. Would the solution retain the good will of the guest?
☐ ☐ ☐ 3. Would the solution work for the house?
☐ ☐ ☐ 4. Did the candidate take control of the situation?
☐ ☐ ☐ 5. Were the candidate's priorities appropriate?
☐ ☐ ☐ 6. Did the candidate maintain a sense of humor?
☐ ☐ ☐ 7. Did the candidate take a positive (rather than negative) approach to the situation?
☐ ☐ ☐ 8. Did the candidate accept personal responsibility for the situation?
☐ ☐ ☐ 9. Did the solution avoid embarrassment to all parties?
☐ ☐ ☐ 10. Would the long-term approach be likely to prevent a similar occurrence in the future?

Total Score:

_____

OVERALL EVALUATION:

☐ Yes
☐ No
☐ Maybe

SITUATION 2:

Y N ?

☐ ☐ ☐ 1. Did the candidate come up with a solution without hesitation?
☐ ☐ ☐ 2. Did the candidate clarify just what it was that Murray was "doing again"?
☐ ☐ ☐ 3. Would the solution avoid embarrassment to all parties?
☐ ☐ ☐ 4. Would the solution retain Murray's good will?
☐ ☐ ☐ 5. Did the candidate take control of the situation?
☐ ☐ ☐ 6. Were the candidate's priorities appropriate?
☐ ☐ ☐ 7. Did the candidate grasp the real causes underlying the situation?
☐ ☐ ☐ 8. Did the candidate take a positive (rather than negative) approach to the situation?
☐ ☐ ☐ 9. Would the solution be likely to work for Karen?
☐ ☐ ☐ 10. Would the long-term approach be likely to prevent a similar occurrence in the future?

Total Score:

_____

OVERALL EVALUATION:

☐ Yes
☐ No
☐ Maybe

Demonstration Test 2

BEVERAGE STAFF

Name: _____ **Evaluated By:** _____

RECIPE TEST

Procedure:

Candidates receive recipes for your four most popular drinks. They study the recipes overnight, then make the drinks from memory the following day.

Materials:

Standard bar setup, drink recipes.

Setup:

Include several pieces of blemished or miscut fruit garnishes on the top of the fruit containers. They should be the pieces most likely to be selected first.

Evaluation Criteria:

Y N ?

☐ ☐ ☐   1. Did the candidate memorize the recipe for Drink 1?
☐ ☐ ☐   2. Did the candidate follow the recipe for Drink 1?
☐ ☐ ☐   3. Did the candidate memorize the recipe for Drink 2?
☐ ☐ ☐   4. Did the candidate follow the recipe for Drink 2?
☐ ☐ ☐   5. Did the candidate memorize the recipe for Drink 3?
☐ ☐ ☐   6. Did the candidate follow the recipe for Drink 3?
☐ ☐ ☐   7. Did the candidate memorize the recipe for Drink 4?
☐ ☐ ☐   8. Did the candidate follow the recipe for Drink 4?
☐ ☐ ☐   9. Did the candidate wash his hands before starting work?
☐ ☐ ☐ 10. Did the candidate use proper handwashing technique?
☐ ☐ ☐ 11. Did the candidate organize the materials provided before starting?
☐ ☐ ☐ 12. Were the candidate's moves smooth and pleasant to watch?
☐ ☐ ☐ 13. Did the candidate have a pleasant expression while working?
☐ ☐ ☐ 14. Did the candidate observe proper sanitation standards?
☐ ☐ ☐ 15. Did the candidate discard blemished or miscut garnishes?
☐ ☐ ☐ 16. Did the candidate keep the work area clean while working?
☐ ☐ ☐ 17. Did the candidate demonstrate confidence while working?
☐ ☐ ☐ 18. Did the candidate properly clean the work area when finished?
☐ ☐ ☐ 19. Was the candidate's personal appearance up to company standards?
☐ ☐ ☐ 20. Did the candidate converse with the observer while working?

Scoring:

Grade each evaluation criterion as it is observed (Y—Yes, N—No, ?—Maybe).
Give two points for each Y, one point for each ?, and no points for N.
A score of 32 or better means an overall evaluation of Yes.
A score of 20 to 31 means an overall evaluation of Maybe.
A score of 19 or below means an overall evaluation of No.

Total Score:

_____

Elapsed Time:

_____

OVERALL EVALUATION:

☐ Yes
☐ No
☐ Maybe

A P P E N D I X   G

Production Staff Tests

Lifting Test (English)   **G-1**

Demonstration Test 1—Production Staff (English)   **G-2**

Demonstration Test 1—Dishwashing Staff (English)   **G-3**

Professional Test Answer Sheet (English)   **G-4**

Professional Test Answer Sheet (Spanish)   **G-5**

Professional Test Answer Sheet Overlay (English)   **G-6**

Professional Test (English)   **G-7**

Professional Test (Spanish)   **G-22**

Professional Test Answers (English)   **G-38**

Production Situations (English)   **G-46**

Production Situations (Spanish)   **G-47**

Situation Test Evaluation (English)   **G-48**

Demonstration Test 2 (English)   **G-49**

Lifting Test

PRODUCTION STAFF

Name: _____ **Evaluated By:** _____

Procedure:

The candidate lifts the heaviest object likely to be encountered on the job from where it is normally found to the most difficult location at which it could logically be placed. This is *not* a timed test.

Materials:

Select an item that has figured in on-the-job lifting injuries. Consider what tasks the candidate will typically perform in the position as well as situations likely to be encountered in the normal course of business while assisting co-workers.

Demonstration Specification:

Item to be lifted: _____ Weight: _____

Lift from: _____

Lift to: _____

Evaluation Criteria:

Y N ?

☐ ☐ ☐ 1. Could the candidate lift the object?
☐ ☐ ☐ 2. Did the lift show lack of strain?
☐ ☐ ☐ 3. Did the candidate lift with a straight back?
☐ ☐ ☐ 4. Did the candidate lift with the legs?
☐ ☐ ☐ 5. Did the candidate keep the load close to the body?
☐ ☐ ☐ 6. Did the candidate use a proper ladder or stool (if appropriate)?
☐ ☐ ☐ 7. Was the object safely under control at all times?
☐ ☐ ☐ 8. Was the candidate alert to the physical surroundings during the lift?
☐ ☐ ☐ 9. Did the final placement of the object allow for proper air circulation?
☐ ☐ ☐ 10. Did the candidate handle the object with care and respect?

Scoring:

Grade each evaluation criterion as it is observed (Y—Yes, N—No, ?—Maybe).
Give two points for each Y, one point for each ?, and no points for N.
If use of a ladder or stool was not appropriate, score Item 6 as Y.
If Item 1 is marked N, the overall evaluation must be No.
If Item 1 is marked ?, the overall evaluation must be Maybe.
If Item 2 is marked N or ?, the overall evaluation must be Maybe.
A score of 16 or better means an overall evaluation of Yes.
A score of 10 to 15 means an overall evaluation of Maybe.
A score of 9 or below means an overall evaluation of No.

Total Score:

_____

Elapsed Time:

_____

OVERALL EVALUATION:

☐ Yes
☐ No
☐ Maybe

Demonstration Test 1

PRODUCTION STAFF

Name: **Evaluated By:**

KNIFE TEST
Procedure:

The candidate dices an onion and places it in the refrigerator. This is a timed test.

Materials:

French knife, onion, steel, cutting board, container, clear wrap, marking pen.

Setup:

The knife, onion, cutting board, and container are placed in obvious positions. The clear wrap and marking pen are on the periphery of the work area in a position that makes them less obvious as being part of the test.

Evaluation Criteria:

Y N ?

☐ ☐ ☐ 1. Did the candidate wash his hands before starting work?
☐ ☐ ☐ 2. Did the candidate use proper hand-washing technique?
☐ ☐ ☐ 3. Was the onion diced evenly (not minced or chopped)?
☐ ☐ ☐ 4. Was the work accomplished with a minimum of wasted effort?
☐ ☐ ☐ 5. Did the candidate use a safe cutting technique?
☐ ☐ ☐ 6. Did the candidate exhibit a smooth cutting technique?
☐ ☐ ☐ 7. Did the candidate hold the knife properly?
☐ ☐ ☐ 8. Did the candidate clean the work area when finished?
☐ ☐ ☐ 9. Were the knife and cutting board cleaned properly and safely?
☐ ☐ ☐ 10. Did the candidate cover and date the container before placing it in the refrigerator?

Scoring:

Grade each evaluation criterion as it is observed (Y—Yes, N—No, ?—Maybe).
Give two points for each Y, one point for each ?, and no points for N.
A score of 16 or better means an overall evaluation of Yes.
A score of 10 to 15 means an overall evaluation of Maybe.
A score of 9 or below means an overall evaluation of No.

Total Score:

_____

Elapsed Time:

_____

OVERALL EVALUATION:

☐ Yes
☐ No
☐ Maybe

Demonstration Test 1

DISHWASHING STAFF

Name: _____ **Evaluated By:** _____

NOTE: The following demonstration tests can be used to appraise job skills if you have a position called "dishwasher" in which the principal duties are washing dishes and cleaning. DO NOT employ these tests if your entry-level production position is called "Assistant Production Manager." Doing so will create an erroneous impression of the job content.

PART I—DISHWASHING TEST
Procedure:

Ask the candidate to load, wash, and unload several racks of soiled china, glassware, and flatware. This is *not* a timed test.

Materials:

Dish machine, soiled china, glassware and flatware, dish racks.

Evaluation Criteria:

Y N ?

☐ ☐ ☐ 1. Did the candidate arrange items on the rack for best cleaning?
☐ ☐ ☐ 2. Did the candidate maximize the rack space?
☐ ☐ ☐ 3. Were dishes handled so as to minimize breakage?
☐ ☐ ☐ 4. Was the work accomplished quickly and quietly?
☐ ☐ ☐ 5. Did the candidate observe proper sanitation practices?

PART II—MOPPING TEST
Procedure:

Ask the candidate to mop a section of floor. This is *not* a timed test.

Materials:

Mop, bucket, wringer, detergent, and wet-floor signs.

Setup:

The mop, bucket, wringer, and detergent are placed in an obvious position. The wet-floor signs are on the periphery of the work area in a position that makes them less obvious as being part of the test.

Evaluation Criteria:

Y N ?

☐ ☐ ☐ 1. Did the candidate determine the proper detergent concentration?
☐ ☐ ☐ 2. Did the candidate put out wet-floor signs before proceeding?
☐ ☐ ☐ 3. Did the candidate rinse the floor with clear water?
☐ ☐ ☐ 4. Was the work accomplished with a minimum of wasted effort?
☐ ☐ ☐ 5. Did the candidate properly clean the equipment and put it away?

Scoring:

Grade each evaluation criterion as it is observed (Y—Yes, N—No, ?—Maybe).
Give two points for each Y, one point for each ?, and no points for N.
A score of 16 or better means an overall evaluation of Yes.
A score of 10 to 15 means an overall evaluation of Maybe.
A score of 9 or below means an overall evaluation of No.

Total Score:

_____

OVERALL EVALUATION:

☐ Yes
☐ No
☐ Maybe

Professional Test

PRODUCTION STAFF
Answer Sheet

NAME: _____ SSN: _____

This test is designed to indicate how you view the restaurant industry. As a result, you will find that several questions may have more than one correct answer. Check the single answer you think is *MOST CORRECT* based on your point of view. Time is of the essence. The faster you complete the test, the better your index score.

TERMINOLOGY

1. _____
2. _____
3. _____
4. _____
5. _____
6. _____
7. _____
8. _____
9. _____
10. _____
11. _____
12. _____
13. _____
14. _____
15. _____
16. _____
17. _____
18. _____
19. _____
20. _____
21. _____
22. _____
23. _____
24. _____
25. _____
26. _____
27. _____
28. _____
29. _____
30. _____

EQUIP/SAFETY

A B C D E

31. ☐ ☐ ☐ ☐ ☐
32. ☐ ☐ ☐ ☐ ☐
33. ☐ ☐ ☐ ☐ ☐
34. ☐ ☐ ☐ ☐ ☐
35. ☐ ☐ ☐ ☐ ☐
36. ☐ ☐ ☐ ☐ ☐
37. ☐ ☐ ☐ ☐ ☐
38. ☐ ☐ ☐ ☐ ☐
39. ☐ ☐ ☐ ☐ ☐
40. ☐ ☐ ☐ ☐ ☐

SANITATION

41. ☐ ☐ ☐ ☐ ☐
42. ☐ ☐ ☐ ☐ ☐
43. ☐ ☐ ☐ ☐ ☐
44. ☐ ☐ ☐ ☐ ☐
45. ☐ ☐ ☐ ☐ ☐
46. ☐ ☐ ☐ ☐ ☐
47. ☐ ☐ ☐ ☐ ☐
48. ☐ ☐ ☐ ☐ ☐
49. ☐ ☐ ☐ ☐ ☐
50. ☐ ☐ ☐ ☐ ☐
51. ☐ ☐ ☐ ☐ ☐
52. ☐ ☐ ☐ ☐ ☐
53. ☐ ☐ ☐ ☐ ☐
54. ☐ ☐ ☐ ☐ ☐
55. ☐ ☐ ☐ ☐ ☐
56. ☐ ☐ ☐ ☐ ☐
57. ☐ ☐ ☐ ☐ ☐
58. ☐ ☐ ☐ ☐ ☐
59. ☐ ☐ ☐ ☐ ☐
60. ☐ ☐ ☐ ☐ ☐

HUMAN REL

A B C D E

61. ☐ ☐ ☐ ☐ ☐
62. ☐ ☐ ☐ ☐ ☐
63. ☐ ☐ ☐ ☐ ☐
64. ☐ ☐ ☐ ☐ ☐
65. ☐ ☐ ☐ ☐ ☐
66. ☐ ☐ ☐ ☐ ☐
67. ☐ ☐ ☐ ☐ ☐
68. ☐ ☐ ☐ ☐ ☐
69. ☐ ☐ ☐ ☐ ☐
70. ☐ ☐ ☐ ☐ ☐

FINANCIAL

71. ☐ ☐ ☐ ☐ ☐
72. ☐ ☐ ☐ ☐ ☐
73. ☐ ☐ ☐ ☐ ☐
74. ☐ ☐ ☐ ☐ ☐
75. ☐ ☐ ☐ ☐ ☐
76. ☐ ☐ ☐ ☐ ☐
77. ☐ ☐ ☐ ☐ ☐
78. ☐ ☐ ☐ ☐ ☐
79. ☐ ☐ ☐ ☐ ☐
80. ☐ ☐ ☐ ☐ ☐

OPERATIONS

81. ☐ ☐ ☐ ☐ ☐
82. ☐ ☐ ☐ ☐ ☐
83. ☐ ☐ ☐ ☐ ☐
84. ☐ ☐ ☐ ☐ ☐
85. ☐ ☐ ☐ ☐ ☐
86. ☐ ☐ ☐ ☐ ☐
87. ☐ ☐ ☐ ☐ ☐
88. ☐ ☐ ☐ ☐ ☐
89. ☐ ☐ ☐ ☐ ☐
90. ☐ ☐ ☐ ☐ ☐

OPERATIONS

A B C D E

91. ☐ ☐ ☐ ☐ ☐
92. ☐ ☐ ☐ ☐ ☐
93. ☐ ☐ ☐ ☐ ☐
94. ☐ ☐ ☐ ☐ ☐
95. ☐ ☐ ☐ ☐ ☐
96. ☐ ☐ ☐ ☐ ☐
97. ☐ ☐ ☐ ☐ ☐
98. ☐ ☐ ☐ ☐ ☐
99. ☐ ☐ ☐ ☐ ☐
100. ☐ ☐ ☐ ☐ ☐
101. ☐ ☐ ☐ ☐ ☐
102. ☐ ☐ ☐ ☐ ☐
103. ☐ ☐ ☐ ☐ ☐
104. ☐ ☐ ☐ ☐ ☐
105. ☐ ☐ ☐ ☐ ☐
106. ☐ ☐ ☐ ☐ ☐
107. ☐ ☐ ☐ ☐ ☐
108. ☐ ☐ ☐ ☐ ☐
109. ☐ ☐ ☐ ☐ ☐
110. ☐ ☐ ☐ ☐ ☐

FOOD PREP

111. ☐ ☐ ☐ ☐ ☐
112. ☐ ☐ ☐ ☐ ☐
113. ☐ ☐ ☐ ☐ ☐
114. ☐ ☐ ☐ ☐ ☐
115. ☐ ☐ ☐ ☐ ☐
116. ☐ ☐ ☐ ☐ ☐
117. ☐ ☐ ☐ ☐ ☐
118. ☐ ☐ ☐ ☐ ☐
119. ☐ ☐ ☐ ☐ ☐
120. ☐ ☐ ☐ ☐ ☐

FOOD PREP

A B C D E

121. ☐ ☐ ☐ ☐ ☐
122. ☐ ☐ ☐ ☐ ☐
123. ☐ ☐ ☐ ☐ ☐
124. ☐ ☐ ☐ ☐ ☐
125. ☐ ☐ ☐ ☐ ☐
126. ☐ ☐ ☐ ☐ ☐
127. ☐ ☐ ☐ ☐ ☐
128. ☐ ☐ ☐ ☐ ☐
129. ☐ ☐ ☐ ☐ ☐
130. ☐ ☐ ☐ ☐ ☐
131. ☐ ☐ ☐ ☐ ☐
132. ☐ ☐ ☐ ☐ ☐
133. ☐ ☐ ☐ ☐ ☐
134. ☐ ☐ ☐ ☐ ☐
135. ☐ ☐ ☐ ☐ ☐
136. ☐ ☐ ☐ ☐ ☐
137. ☐ ☐ ☐ ☐ ☐
138. ☐ ☐ ☐ ☐ ☐
139. ☐ ☐ ☐ ☐ ☐
140. ☐ ☐ ☐ ☐ ☐
141. ☐ ☐ ☐ ☐ ☐
142. ☐ ☐ ☐ ☐ ☐
143. ☐ ☐ ☐ ☐ ☐
144. ☐ ☐ ☐ ☐ ☐
145. ☐ ☐ ☐ ☐ ☐
146. ☐ ☐ ☐ ☐ ☐
147. ☐ ☐ ☐ ☐ ☐
148. ☐ ☐ ☐ ☐ ☐
149. ☐ ☐ ☐ ☐ ☐
150. ☐ ☐ ☐ ☐ ☐

FOR OFFICE USE:

TRM:____ E/S:____ SAN:____ HR:____ FIN:____ OPS:____ PREP:____ TOTAL:____ TIME:____ INDEX:_____

Examen Profesional

EQUIPO TÉCNICO DE PRODUCCIÓN
Haja de las Respuestas

NOMBRE: **NÚMERO DE SEGURIDAD SOCIAL:**

Este examen está diseñado para formar una opinión de cómo usted ve la industria de los restaurantes. Por lo tanto, usted encontrará que varias preguntas pueden tener más de una respuesta correcta. Marque la única respuesta que usted piense sea la *MÁS CORRECTA* basándolo en su punto de vista personal. El tiempo es esencial. Entre más rápido complete el exámen, mejor será su índice de puntuación.

TERMINOLOGÍA

1. _____
2. _____
3. _____
4. _____
5. _____
6. _____
7. _____
8. _____
9. _____
10. _____
11. _____
12. _____
13. _____
14. _____
15. _____
16. _____
17. _____
18. _____
19. _____
20. _____
21. _____
22. _____
23. _____
24. _____
25. _____
26. _____
27. _____
28. _____
29. _____
30. _____

EQUIP/SEGURIDAD — A B C D E

31–40, then **SANIDAD** 41–60

REL HUMANAS — A B C D E

61–70, then **FINANZAS** 71–80, then **OPERACIONES** 81–90

OPERACIONES — A B C D E

91–110, then **PREP DE COMIDA** 111–120

PREP DE COMIDA — A B C D E

121–150

FOR OFFICE USE:

TRM:____ E/S:____ SAN:____ HR:____ FIN:____ OPS:____ PREP:____ TOTAL:____ TIME:____ INDEX:_____

Professional Test

PRODUCTION STAFF
Answer Sheet Overlay

NOTE: To save time when grading the Professional Test, make a copy of this sheet on clear transparency film and lay it over the candidate's completed test. This should enable you to easily note the number of questions marked correctly and incorrectly, and you can then simply transfer the score to the blocks at the bottom of the answer sheet. The answer sheet and test are not returned to the applicant, so it is your choice whether or not to physically mark the answer to a specific question as correct or incorrect.

TERMINOLOGY

1. F	16. J
2. S	17. C
3. b	18. R
4. d	19. W
5. N	20. c
6. Q	21. E
7. P	22. a
8. A	23. X
9. Z	24. K
10. B	25. E
11. L	26. O
12. U	27. I
13. Y	28. G
14. T	29. V
15. D	30. M

EQUIP/SAFETY (A B C D E)

Q	Answer
31.	E
32.	C
33.	E
34.	A
35.	D
36.	C
37.	A
38.	D
39.	A
40.	D

SANITATION

Q	Answer
41.	C
42.	A
43.	C
44.	C
45.	C
46.	B
47.	D
48.	E
49.	B
50.	D
51.	B
52.	D
53.	B
54.	B
55.	E
56.	C
57.	C
58.	B
59.	D
60.	E

HUMAN REL

Q	Answer
61.	E
62.	D
63.	D
64.	A
65.	E
66.	B
67.	A
68.	C
69.	B
70.	B

FINANCIAL

Q	Answer
71.	A
72.	D
73.	C
74.	E
75.	C
76.	C
77.	B
78.	D
79.	E
80.	B

OPERATIONS

Q	Answer
81.	C
82.	A
83.	B
84.	C
85.	B
86.	E
87.	C
88.	E
89.	E
90.	A

OPERATIONS

Q	Answer
91.	E
92.	E
93.	A
94.	A
95.	D
96.	B
97.	D
98.	E
99.	D
100.	C
101.	C
102.	E
103.	D
104.	D
105.	D
106.	B
107.	D
108.	D
109.	B
110.	A

FOOD PREP

Q	Answer
111.	D
112.	D
113.	C
114.	E
115.	B
116.	C
117.	C
118.	C
119.	A
120.	B

FOOD PREP

Q	Answer
121.	A
122.	C
123.	D
124.	E
125.	C
126.	A
127.	E
128.	E
129.	D
130.	B
131.	E
132.	C
133.	C
134.	A
135.	A
136.	C
137.	A
138.	D
139.	C
140.	C
141.	E
142.	A
143.	C
144.	C
145.	B
146.	D
147.	C
148.	B
149.	D
150.	B

Professional Test

PRODUCTION STAFF

Choose the *MOST CORRECT* answer and mark your choice on the answer sheet. Please do not write on this test.

TERMINOLOGY

Match the following cooking terms with their proper definitions.

1. Chop	A. Use a knife or fork to cut shallow lines into the product.		
2. Dice	B. Mix ingredients with a vigorous rotating motion.		
3. Grate	C. Add a liquid to dissolve the solid particles left in the bottom of a pan after cooking.		
4. Grind	D. Clear butter, soup, or other liquid of solid particles.		
5. Julienne	E. Cook in a pan with a small amount of fat or oil.		
6. Mince	F. Cut into pieces of irregular shape.		
7. Puree	G. Cook in hot air.		
8. Score	H. Coat an item thoroughly with flour or other finely ground substance.		
9. Whip	I. Cook in liquid at a high temperature.		
10. Beat	J. Cover with a thick, sugary syrup or sauce and (usually) brown under a broiler.		
11. Blend	K. Cook with little or no fat or oil on a polished metal surface.		
12. Fold	L. Mix ingredients evenly using a gentle motion.		
13. Bread	M. Cook (usually a protein product) gently in hot liquid.		
14. Barbecue	N. Cut into long, thin strips.		
15. Clarify	O. Cook in liquid at a temperature at which slow bubbling occurs.		
16. Glaze	P. Turn into a somewhat grainy liquid using a blender or food processor.		
17. Deglaze	Q. Cut into fine pieces.		
18. Knead	R. Work dough by hand.		
19. Marinate	S. Cut into ¼- to ¾-inch cubes.		
20. Deep-Fry	T. Cook over an open flame.		
21. Sauté	U. Gently combine a light ingredient with a heavier one using a spatula or spoon.		
22. Braise	V. Cook with moist heat with the product not submerged in liquid.		
23. Broil	W. Soak in a pungent or tenderizing solution.		
24. Grill	X. Cook without fat or oil under a heat source.		
25. Panfry	Y. Cover with flour, eggs, and crumbs.		
26. Simmer	Z. Beat at a high speed to add air.		
27. Boil	a. Use a combination of dry and moist cooking methods.		
28. Bake	b. Use an implement or machine to make flakelike pieces.		
29. Steam	c. Cook submerged in fat or oil.		
30. Poach	d. There is no proper definition listed for this term.		

EQUIPMENT AND SAFETY

31. Generally, what is the most cost-effective way to maintain equipment?
   A. Replacing equipment as soon as it breaks.
   B. Employing a full-time equipment troubleshooter.
   C. Maintaining all equipment yourself.
   D. Hiring an outside maintenance firm.
   E. Practicing preventive maintenance.

32. What would be your first question when considering the purchase of a new piece of equipment?
   A. How much will it cost to buy?
   B. What is its rate of energy consumption?
   C. How will it improve guest satisfaction?
   D. How much labor will it save?
   E. What is the experience of others using it?

33. What is the proper procedure for cleaning kitchen machines?
   A. Unplugging electrical equipment before cleaning.
   B. Using a solution of detergent and water.

C. Using baking soda and water to clean refrigerators.
D. Asking for an inspection of your work when you finish.
E. All of the above.

34. What should you do if the dish machine is not functioning properly?
A. Stop using the machine and tell the supervisor or manager immediately.
B. Slow down the rate at which dishes are passed through the machine.
C. Mention it to a supervisor or manager once you get caught up.
D. Don't worry about it because all machines malfunction from time to time.
E. Call the health department.

35. What do you do after applying a cleaning solution?
A. Scrub lightly with a soft brush.
B. Use a squeegee to remove the solution.
C. Allow it to dry.
D. Wait for the solution to work.
E. Scrub with a steel sponge and rinse with clear water.

36. What do you think is the biggest barrier to effective cleaning?
A. Improper training.
B. Inadequate tools.
C. Clutter and junk.
D. Lack of time.
E. Lack of adequate staffing.

37. Which of the following practices would you correct *immediately*?
A. A fry cook juggling ice cubes at his workstation, out of guests' sight.
B. A dishwasher cutting vegetables with a very sharp French knife.
C. A busser placing a bus tub on a prep table.
D. A sous-chef standing on a folding ladder to reach a high shelf in the storeroom.
E. A server using an aluminum tray to carry food.

38. What is the proper first aid for a minor burn in the kitchen?
A. Calling 911.
B. Putting ice on the burned area.
C. Putting butter on the burned area.
D. Holding the burned area under cool water.
E. Holding the burned area under warm water.

39. If the criterion is the most frequent cause of accidents, what is the most dangerous item in the kitchen?
A. The floor.
B. The deep fat fryer.
C. The French knife.
D. The slicing machine.
E. The dish machine.

40. Which of the following is proper procedure when mopping floors?
A. Moving the mop bucket as little as possible while you work.
B. Using bleach and ammonia in the water to boost the cleaning action.
C. Frequently wringing the mop by hand.
D. Placing wet-floor signs where the floor goes from dry to wet.
E. All of the above.

SANITATION

41. Which of the following procedures is most likely to cause foodborne illness?
A. Reheating a previously cooked food product on the range.
B. Initial cooking of a food product.
C. Cooling a cooked food product in the walk-in.
D. Food preparation activities (cutting, mixing, etc.).

42. **You notice that one of your staff has an open cut on her hand. What is the best way to handle it?**
   A. Exclude her from all food-handling responsibilities until the cut heals.
   B. Send her home, without pay, until the cut heals.
   C. Send her home, with pay, until the cut heals.
   D. To avoid upsetting the guests, assign her to a workstation out of sight of the dining room.
   E. File a Worker's Compensation claim.

43. **What is the proper place for a secondary thermometer in a refrigerator?**
   A. In the lower back corner, away from the door.
   B. In the middle.
   C. In the upper front, by the door.
   D. On the back of the door.
   E. A secondary thermometer is not needed if the refrigerator has a built-in thermometer.

44. **What is the minimum temperature of hot food being held for service?**
   A. 200°F.
   B. 165°F.
   C. 140°F.
   D. 120°F.
   E. 45°F.

45. **What is the proper wash temperature for the dish machine?**
   A. 120°F.
   B. 140°F.
   C. 160°F.
   D. 180°F.
   E. 200°F.

46. **What is the proper rinse temperature for a low-temperature dish machine?**
   A. 65°F.
   B. 120°F.
   C. 140°F.
   D. 160°F.

47. **What is the proper rinse temperature for a high-temperature dish machine?**
   A. 120°F.
   B. 140°F.
   C. 160°F.
   D. 180°F.

48. **Which practice is correct or acceptable?**
   A. Polishing silverware.
   B. Snacking in food preparation areas.
   C. Using a glass to scoop ice.
   D. Thawing covered food on a clean kitchen counter.
   E. Keeping wipe cloths in sanitizing solution.

49. **What is a product thermometer?**
   A. The pop-up indicator in a turkey that tells when it is done.
   B. A small pocket thermometer used to check food temperatures.
   C. The wall-mounted thermometer that monitors refrigeration temperatures.
   D. The thermostat that controls the temperature in the kitchen.
   E. None of the above.

50. **Which of the following may be served in a commercial foodservice establishment?**
   A. Produce from your neighbor's home garden.
   B. Untouched rolls returned from the dining room.
   C. The lasagna that one of your cooks made at home.
   D. Organic vegetables.
   E. All of the above.

51. **Within what time limit must potentially hazardous foods be chilled to an internal temperature of 45°F?**
   A. 1 hour.
   B. 2 hours.

C. 6 hours.
D. 4 hours.
E. As quickly as possible.

52. **In which of the following foods would botulism grow best?**
   A. Fresh tomatoes.
   B. Raw chicken.
   C. Frozen salmon.
   D. Canned tuna.
   E. Homemade chili.

53. **Which of the following is a foodborne illness often associated with poultry?**
   A. Lactobacillus bulgarius.
   B. Salmonella.
   C. Staphylococcus.
   D. Clostridium perfringens.
   E. Botulism.

54. **Which of the following is the rule of thumb for the maximum total time potentially hazardous food products may be in the "danger zone"?**
   A. 2 hours.
   B. 4 hours.
   C. 6 hours.
   D. 8 hours.
   E. It doesn't matter.

55. **Which of the following forms of food poisoning is fatal over half the time?**
   A. Lactobacillus bulgarius.
   B. Salmonella.
   C. Staphylococcus.
   D. Clostridium perfringens.
   E. Botulism.

56. **How often should sanitizing solution be checked?**
   A. At the start of each shift.
   B. At least twice each shift.
   C. At least once an hour.
   D. At least once every half hour.
   E. Every time you use it.

57. **How can you tell if the sanitizing solution is at the proper concentration?**
   A. Measure carefully when making a new solution.
   B. Use a universal test kit.
   C. Dip a test strip in the solution and compare it with a scale.
   D. Dip a piece of paper towel in the solution and see if it darkens.
   E. Use a product thermometer.

58. **What happens if the sanitizing solution concentration is higher than recommended?**
   A. It will be more effective.
   B. It can be toxic.
   C. It will cost more money, but there is no real problem.
   D. It won't work as well, if at all.
   E. All of the above.

59. **What happens if the sanitizing solution concentration is lower than recommended?**
   A. It will kill bacteria more slowly.
   B. It can be toxic.
   C. It will save some money and there is no real problem.
   D. It won't work as well, if at all.
   E. All of the above.

60. **To what internal temperature must you heat food to kill staphylococcus toxins?**
   A. 120°F.
   B. 165°F.

C. 180°F.
D. 200°F.
E. Staphylococcus toxins cannot be killed.

HUMAN RELATIONS

61. **What is the best measure of a supervisor's effectiveness?**
   A. Work skills.
   B. Health department scores.
   C. Profitability.
   D. Average check.
   E. Staff development.

62. **Which method of training would you use when showing someone how to clean a piece of equipment?**
   A. Written instructions.
   B. Classroom training.
   C. Role-playing.
   D. On-the-job instruction.

63. **Who do you think makes the most effective trainer for operational subjects?**
   A. An outside consultant.
   B. The general manager.
   C. The department supervisor.
   D. A skilled co-worker.
   E. A company training director.

64. **What do you think your staff wants most from their jobs?**
   A. Appreciation for the work they do.
   B. Higher wages.
   C. Being "in" on things.
   D. Health insurance and benefits.
   E. Job security.

65. **In your experience, which statement is true about working with minorities?**
   A. They must be treated a little differently from other workers.
   B. They can be more difficult to motivate than other workers.
   C. It is more difficult to know what they really want from you.
   D. They tend to be less productive than other workers.
   E. They are no different from anyone else.

66. **Where does the primary responsibility lie for high staff turnover in restaurants?**
   A. With the individual workers.
   B. With the management of the restaurant.
   C. With the rate of pay in restaurants.
   D. With prevailing values in our society.
   E. With increased competition from other industries.

67. **How would you bring out the best in your crew?**
   A. Set a personal example that reflects everything you expect of your staff.
   B. Set high standards and manage your crew's activities.
   C. Develop standard procedures in all major areas.
   D. Conduct extensive and consistent skill training for all positions.

68. **As a member of the restaurant staff, what is the best way to advance your career?**
   A. Do personal favors for the managers.
   B. Stand out from the competition.
   C. Take classes and attend seminars.
   D. Teach your subordinates how to do your job.
   E. Make sure you get the credit when things go well.

69. **It is going to be a busy Saturday night. One of your cooks reports for work at 3:00 P.M. in a soiled uniform. How do you handle it?**
   A. Assign him to his regular station.
   B. Send him home to get a clean uniform before allowing him to go on the clock.
   C. Reprimand him and be sure he works out of sight of the guests.
   D. Assign him to the dish machine and have the dishwasher work the line.
   E. Send him home without pay.

70. **It is going to be a busy Saturday night. One of your cooks reports for work at 4:30 P.M. in a soiled uniform. How do you handle it?**
   A. Assign her to her regular station.
   B. Send her home to get a clean uniform before allowing her to go on the clock.
   C. Reprimand her and be sure she works out of sight of the guests.
   D. Assign her to the dish machine and have the dishwasher work the line.
   E. Send her home without pay.

FINANCIAL

71. **Your grocery salesman has just offered you a deal: 20% off on orders of over three cases of truffles if you place the order immediately. You normally go through two to three cans of truffles a month. What do you do?**
   A. Pass.
   B. Buy over three cases and save the restaurant some money.
   C. Buy over three cases and invent a new specialty item to use it up.
   D. Buy over three cases and resell part of the stock to a competitor at a profit.

72. **Last month, your restaurant's total receipts were $66,500, of which $4,100 was sales tax, $15,600 was beverage sales, and the rest was food sales. Your food purchases were $16,800, and your kitchen payroll was $9,900. You spent $550 on paper supplies. Opening food inventory was $5,400, and closing inventory was $4,000. What was your food cost percentage for the month?**
   A. 27.3%.
   B. 32.9%.
   C. 35.9%.
   D. 38.9%.
   E. There is not enough information to answer the question.

You want to find a daily special for next week and have been searching through your cookbook collection looking for a likely menu item. You come upon the following recipe for Hungarian Goulash that looks interesting:

2½ lb. top round	2 T. paprika
3 T. flour	4 t. butter
1 t. salt	1 c. tomato puree
1 t. pepper	1 c. beef stock

You call your suppliers and receive the following cost information:

Top round	$2.75/1 lb.	Paprika	$3.00/1 lb.
Flour	$7.50/50 lb.	Butter	$1.50/1 lb.
Salt	$0.40/1 lb.	Tomato puree	$19.50/6/10
Pepper	$9.00/1 lb.	Beef stock	$30.50/12/49 oz.

73. **The recipe as written makes 5 servings. You plan to produce 55 servings if you offer it as a special. Approximately how much flour will you need for the larger quantity?**
   A. 1 c.
   B. 30 t.
   C. 2 c.
   D. 1 lb.
   E. None of the above.

74. **How much salt will you use for 55 servings?**
   A. 11 t.
   B. 11 T.

C. ¼ c.
D. ½ c.
E. None of the above.

75. What will be the approximate meat portion per serving at 55 servings?
A. 4 ounces.
B. 6 ounces.
C. 8 ounces.
D. 12 ounces.
E. None of the above.

76. What is the portion cost on Hungarian Goulash?
A. $1.23.
B. $1.53.
C. $1.82.
D. $2.10.
E. None of the above.

77. You have a product that you sell as a takeout item for $6.95. The food on the plate costs $2.50, and the packaging costs another 25¢. It takes about $2.00 in labor to prepare the item. What is your food cost percentage on this product?
A. 34.4%.
B. 36.0%.
C. 38.8%.
D. 68.3%.
E. None of the above.

78. You have a product that you sell for $8.50. Its portion cost is $3.00. What is your gross margin on the item?
A. 35.3%.
B. 64.7%.
C. $3.00.
D. $5.50.
E. None of the above.

79. Let's say the restaurant *really* blows it with a typical party of four. Let's also say that the typical guest in your restaurant normally dines with you three times a month and that your average check is $20. What is this error likely to cost the company in lost business over the next five years?
A. Under $4,000.
B. $10,000–$12,000.
C. $25,000–$30,000.
D. $50,000–$60,000.
E. Over $85,000.

80. You are planning to add a smoked salmon appetizer to the menu. You expect a 75% EP yield from a whole 12-pound smoked salmon that you can purchase for $100.00. You can also purchase sliced smoked salmon for $11.75 a pound. You have been told (in no uncertain terms!) to keep your operating costs as low as possible. You expect to use about 50 pounds of salmon a week. Based on your experience, which product do you buy?
A. Whole salmon.
B. Sliced salmon.
C. There is not enough information to answer the question.

OPERATIONS

81. What does "first in, first out" refer to?
A. Changing suppliers regularly to keep them honest.
B. Traffic control for trucks in the loading area.
C. Using food supplies in the order they were received.
D. Determining who gets laid off based on seniority.
E. None of the above.

82. **What is the best document to use when receiving the grocery order?**
    A. The purchase order.
    B. The supplies requisition.
    C. The purveyor's invoice.
    D. The standardized recipe.
    E. The DICE System book.

83. **What information do USDA grades on meat provide?**
    A. The plant where the meat was processed.
    B. The quality of the meat.
    C. The date the meat was processed.
    D. The sanitary or wholesome condition of the meat.
    E. The cut of the meat.

84. **Which of the following shows the characteristics of a particular food product you buy?**
    A. The vendor's cost-plus sheet.
    B. The tying agreement.
    C. The specification sheet.
    D. The rebate certificate.
    E. The DICE System book.

85. **How does forecasting help to control production?**
    A. It ensures that food will be produced according to standard procedures.
    B. It helps avoid under- or overproduction.
    C. It guarantees that there will be sufficient inventories to meet production needs.
    D. It helps determine job assignments.
    E. Forecasting relates to sales—it has nothing to do with production.

86. **Let's say your target food cost is 34%. You are evaluating a new menu item with a portion cost of 82¢. How would you price it on the menu?**
    A. $1.95.
    B. $2.25.
    C. $2.41.
    D. $2.50.
    E. There is not enough information to answer the question.

87. **Which item is *not* normally part of portion control?**
    A. Purchasing specifications.
    B. Standardized recipes.
    C. Properly adjusted cooking equipment.
    D. Waste control.
    E. Putting the proper amount on the plate.

88. **What is your best course of action when a government official arrives to inspect the restaurant?**
    A. Ask the official to communicate only with you and not to talk to your staff.
    B. Insist on your right to advance notice and reschedule the inspection.
    C. Allow the official to conduct the inspection alone.
    D. Follow the official at a distance and make notes on how the inspection is conducted.
    E. Accompany the official on the inspection.

89. **What does a yield analysis determine?**
    A. The price of a menu item.
    B. The tasks involved in preparing a menu item.
    C. The raw cost of a menu item.
    D. How long a menu item can be safely held before service.
    E. How much usable food is contained in a purchased quantity.

90. **What is the first action you would take if you thought your food cost was too high?**
    A. Check portion control procedures.
    B. Substitute less expensive ingredients.
    C. Change the menu to use lower-cost entrees.
    D. Raise the menu prices.
    E. Look for evidence of theft.

91. What is the first action you would take if you thought your labor cost was too high?
    A. Reduce hours equally across the board.
    B. Cut back the hours for part-time workers.
    C. Lay off marginal workers.
    D. Raise menu prices.
    E. Concentrate on increasing productivity.

92. If food is coming out of the kitchen too slowly, what is the most likely cause of the problem?
    A. The cooks are incompetent.
    B. The orders are not being placed properly.
    C. The kitchen equipment is inadequate.
    D. The kitchen manager is not paying attention.
    E. None of the above.

93. How do you control theft in the restaurant?
    A. Expect the best from your staff and create an environment in which they won't want to steal.
    B. Watch everyone like a hawk.
    C. Have very tight control systems and monitor them continually.
    D. Double-check every transaction.
    E. Conduct unannounced locker and bag inspections.

94. Simply stated, what is an invoice?
    A. A bill.
    B. A purchase order.
    C. A sales history.
    D. A statement of account.
    E. A production forecast.

95. Which of the following actions is most likely to decrease energy consumption?
    A. Not tampering with the heat settings on kitchen equipment once they have been turned on.
    B. Cooking foods rapidly at high heat.
    C. Using cold water for cooking.
    D. Cooking foods in large quantities.
    E. Cooking foods in small batches.

96. What is your goal when creating a staff schedule?
    A. To minimize labor cost.
    B. To ensure a high level of guest service.
    C. To match the labor schedule to the budget.
    D. To distribute the available hours equitably among the staff.
    E. To accommodate the special requests of the workers.

97. What is the first thing to do when there has been an injury on the job?
    A. Try to have the injured worker use their own health insurance for treatment.
    B. Unless you witnessed the accident, be suspicious that it happened at work.
    C. File a Workers' Compensation claim.
    D. Arrange for immediate treatment under your Workers' Compensation policy.
    E. If the injury is minor, have the restaurant pay the costs and don't file a Workers' Compensation claim.

98. You are receiving the grocery order. The invoice lists 12 cases of strip loin, but the driver has only delivered 11 to you and has not noticed the difference. What do you do?
    A. Since it is within 10% of the invoice quantity, sign the invoice.
    B. Sign the invoice and tell the driver to change the strip loin quantity to 11 cases.
    C. Sign the invoice and have the driver bring an extra case on his next trip.
    D. Notify the driver of the discrepancy and change the strip loin quantity to 11 cases yourself.
    E. Call the manager.

99. You are receiving the grocery order. The invoice lists 12 cases of strip loin, but the driver has delivered 13 to you and has not noticed the difference. What do you do?
    A. Since it is within 10% of the invoice quantity, sign the invoice and say nothing.
    B. Sign the invoice and tell the driver to change the strip loin quantity to 13 cases.
    C. Sign the invoice and take the extra case home.
    D. Notify the driver of the discrepancy and change the strip loin quantity to 13 cases yourself.
    E. Call the manager.

100. **Doing which of the following will most help improve the working relationship between the kitchen and the dining room staff?**
    A. Holding a class to explain kitchen operations to the dining room staff.
    B. Installing an electronic POS system.
    C. Conducting cross-training for all staff members.
    D. Yelling at the service staff and ridiculing them when they make a mistake in the kitchen.
    E. Using an expediter.

101. **As a member of the production staff, whom do you work for?**
    A. The general manager.
    B. The guests.
    C. The dining room staff.
    D. The health department.
    E. Yourself.

102. **A server comes into the kitchen with a food item returned from a guest in the dining room. The server is obviously upset and a little rude. What do you do?**
    A. Reprimand the server for his rudeness.
    B. Find out what was wrong with the food.
    C. Check the food to see if it was properly prepared.
    D. Take the item back to the guest yourself and explain how it is prepared.
    E. Fix or replace the item without comment.

103. **It is Saturday night and you are in the middle of the rush. A server comes in and orders an item that is offered on the lunch menu but not on the dinner menu. What do you have the server tell the guest?**
    A. The item is not available at dinner.
    B. You are too busy to accommodate the request.
    C. You will make the item when you are caught up with your other orders.
    D. You will be pleased to prepare the item as requested.

104. **What can you assume when an item is returned to the kitchen by a guest?**
    A. Someone in the kitchen screwed up the order.
    B. The server didn't explain the item properly to the guest.
    C. Something is wrong with the food.
    D. The guest is in a bad mood.
    E. You can't assume anything when an item is returned.

105. **What is the best way to identify the operating problems of your restaurant?**
    A. Call in a consultant.
    B. Talk to your guests.
    C. Talk with the supervisors.
    D. Talk to your staff.
    E. Attend a restaurant management seminar.

106. **When it comes to guest complaints, which statement do you most agree with?**
    A. No news is good news.
    B. Complaints are special gifts.
    C. A satisfaction level of about 90% is realistic for a full-service restaurant.
    D. You can't expect to please all the people all the time.
    E. Some people complain just to get attention.

107. **It is a typical Monday night and you are in the middle of dinner. A server comes in and asks for an item that is not on your menu. You do not even have all the ingredients in stock. What do you have the server tell the guest?**
    A. That you cannot prepare the item.
    B. That you are too busy to accommodate the request.
    C. That you will make the item for the guests the next time they come in.
    D. That you will be pleased to prepare the item (and immediately send someone to the supermarket).

108. **What portion of a typical restaurant's sales is pretax income?**
    A. 40–45%.
    B. 30–35%.
    C. 20–25%.

D. 10–15%.

E. Under 5%.

109. **The average check is the restaurant's total food sales divided by what number?**
   A. The average value of a typical guest check.
   B. The number of guests served.
   C. The number of entrees sold.
   D. The average number of people in the party.
   E. The number of seats in the restaurant.

110. **If you wish to allow for labor costs in establishing menu prices, which of these items probably has the highest cost percentage?**
   A. Chef's Salad.
   B. Scrambled eggs with bacon and toast.
   C. Cheeseburger with french fries.
   D. Pork chop with apple sauce.

FOOD PREP

111. **Which of the following sauces is not a "mother sauce"?**
   A. Espagnole.
   B. Velouté.
   C. Béchamel.
   D. Béarnaise.
   E. Hollandaise.

112. **What is a roux?**
   A. A slurry of milk and flour.
   B. A small bag of herbs added for flavor during cooking.
   C. A butter sauce for fish.
   D. A mixture of butter and flour.
   E. A double boiler.

113. **What is a "bouquet garni"?**
   A. The vegetables used to season a sauce.
   B. Flowers traditionally placed in a kitchen to bring luck.
   C. A bag of spices.
   D. Fresh flowers placed on the plate as decoration.
   E. A coloring agent used in brown sauces.

114. **What starch is used extensively in thickening sweet sauces and desserts?**
   A. Arrowroot.
   B. Pastry flour.
   C. Gelatin.
   D. Tapioca.
   E. Cornstarch.

115. **In the purchase of fresh fish, which condition would *not* be acceptable?**
   A. Protruding eyes.
   B. Soft, pliable flesh.
   C. Mild, nonfishy odor.
   D. Shiny skin.
   E. Bright red gills.

116. **Which of the following foods should be stored under refrigeration?**
   A. Bananas.
   B. Unripe avocados.
   C. Oranges.
   D. Potatoes.
   E. Yellow onions.

117. **You are preparing a spaghetti sauce and accidentally add too much salt. How would you correct it?**
    A. Add more tomato puree.
    B. Add more water.
    C. Drop in a potato.
    D. Add oregano.
    E. Throw it out and start again.

118. **Which of the following is an AP weight?**
    A. 4 pounds of sliced roast beef.
    B. 1 pound of chopped onion.
    C. 2 pounds of raw broccoli.
    D. 2 cups of béchamel sauce.

119. **Which of the following is an EP weight?**
    A. 2 pounds of cleaned spinach leaves.
    B. 20 pounds of whole frozen turkey.
    C. 12 pounds of standing rib roast.
    D. 1 pound of unshelled walnuts.

120. **You are cooking a 20-pound prime rib. At what temperature should you remove it from the oven if you want to serve it medium?**
    A. 100°F.
    B. 120°F.
    C. 130°F.
    D. 140°F.
    E. 160°F.

121. **You are cooking a 20-pound prime rib. What is the best way to cook it?**
    A. At 325°F for 2½ hours.
    B. At 375°F for 2 hours.
    C. At 425°F for 1½ hours.
    D. At 500°F for 1 hour.
    E. All these combinations produce equal results.

122. **You have made Hollandaise sauce for breakfast. At the end of the meal period, you still have about a quart of sauce left. You also use Hollandaise on your lunch menu. What do you do with the excess sauce?**
    A. Keep it hot and use it for lunch.
    B. Add new sauce to the leftover product to freshen it for lunch.
    C. Throw the sauce out and make new product for lunch.
    D. Freeze the leftover Hollandaise to kill the bacteria before reusing it.
    E. All of the above are acceptable solutions.

123. **Which of the following ingredients is *not* normally part of a white sauce?**
    A. Cream.
    B. Butter.
    C. Flour.
    D. Water.
    E. Milk.

124. **Which of the following ingredients is *not* normally part of a brown sauce?**
    A. Beef stock.
    B. Flour.
    C. Mirepoix.
    D. Fat.
    E. Milk.

125. **Which of the following ingredients is *not* normally part of a tomato sauce?**
    A. Onion.
    B. Tomato paste.
    C. Court bouillon.
    D. Herbs.
    E. Tomato puree.

126. You are cooking a spaghetti sauce and accidentally scorch it. What do you do?
   A. Throw the sauce out and start again.
   B. Drop in a potato.
   C. Stir the sauce thoroughly and strain it through a china cap.
   D. Add more tomatoes.
   E. Add some sugar.

127. Which of the following sauces *cannot* be reheated?
   A. Brown.
   B. White.
   C. Tomato.
   D. Velouté.
   E. Hollandaise.

128. Which piece of equipment would you use to reheat 5 gallons of New England Clam Chowder?
   A. The steam table.
   B. The oven.
   C. The steamer.
   D. The microwave.
   E. The range.

129. You are preparing a fresh vegetable noodle soup. Which of the following ingredients would you add *last*?
   A. Onion.
   B. Carrot.
   C. Celery.
   D. Egg noodles.
   E. Add everything at once.

130. Which of the following would you use to activate yeast before using?
   A. Boiling water.
   B. Lukewarm water.
   C. Ice water.
   D. Butter.

131. You are broiling a steak when a fire starts in the broiler. What do you do first?
   A. Throw water on the fire.
   B. Activate the Ansul system.
   C. Try to save the steak.
   D. Shut off the hood fan.
   E. None of the above.

132. How can you tell when a steak is cooked to medium rare?
   A. Time how long it has been on the grill.
   B. Check the degree of exterior charring.
   C. Cut it slightly and look.
   D. Press it with your fingers.
   E. Refer to the DICE System book.

133. Where would you look for the ingredients you need to prepare a hollandaise sauce?
   A. The canned goods section of the dry storeroom.
   B. The dry goods section of the dry storeroom.
   C. The refrigerator.
   D. The freezer.

134. Which cut of meat would you expect to be the most tender?
   A. Top sirloin steak.
   B. Filet mignon.
   C. Flank steak.
   D. T-bone steak.
   E. New York strip.

135. Which cut of meat would you expect to have the most flavor?
   A. Veal chop.
   B. Top sirloin steak.

    C. Filet mignon.
    D. Ground round.
    E. Flank steak.

136. **Which of the following is a proper way to thaw frozen food?**
    A. Placing it under warm running water.
    B. Stirring it in an ice bath.
    C. Leaving it in the refrigerator.
    D. Placing it in a tub of cold water.
    E. All of these are proper procedures.

137. **When preparing a sauté item, how much fat is placed in the pan?**
    A. Enough to cover the item.
    B. Enough to just coat the bottom of the pan.
    C. About ¼ inch.
    D. About ½ inch.
    E. Fat is not used when you sauté an item.

138. **You have been holding food in a bain marie and the water boils dry. What do you do?**
    A. Throw out the food.
    B. Add liquid to the food.
    C. Add liquid to the bain marie.
    D. Turn down the heat.
    E. Taste the product to see if it is still acceptable.

139. **Which of the following is *not* a consideration in the preparation of pasta?**
    A. The size of the pot used to cook the pasta.
    B. The amount of water used to boil the pasta.
    C. The sauce to be used on the pasta.
    D. The temperature of the water in which the pasta is cooked.
    E. The amount of time the pasta is cooked.

140. **To what internal breast temperature should you cook a whole roast turkey?**
    A. 100°F.
    B. 130°F.
    C. 170°F.
    D. 200°F.
    E. 250°F.

141. **What would you expect to happen to the internal temperature of a 20-pound roast for the first half hour or so after you remove it from the oven?**
    A. It will drop 5 to 10 degrees.
    B. It will drop 15 to 20 degrees.
    C. It will remain stable.
    D. It will increase 5 to 10 degrees.
    E. It will increase 15 to 20 degrees.

142. **What is the proper way to store peeled, uncooked potatoes?**
    A. Under water.
    B. In plastic bags.
    C. In a cool, dry place.
    D. In the freezer.
    E. Peeled potatoes cannot be stored.

143. **Which of the following is the safest way to cover a tomato sauce while it cools in the refrigerator?**
    A. With aluminum foil.
    B. With a tight-fitting lid.
    C. Loosely with parchment.
    D. With a solid piece of clear wrap.
    E. Tomato sauce should not be covered in the refrigerator until after it has cooled.

144. **Which of the following will *not* cause lettuce to turn rusty?**
    A. Improper drying.
    B. Soaking the leaves in water.

C. Tearing the leaves.
D. Excessive age.

145. You have just prepared 20 gallons of chili for a special promotion. As always, refrigeration space in the restaurant is very limited. In which container do you place the chili to cool it in the walk-in?
A. A 5-gallon plastic pail.
B. A 4″ stainless steel pan filled to 1½″ full.
C. A 1½″ stainless steel pan filled to the top.
D. A stainless steel stockpot.
E. A plastic bus tub.

146. How do you most effectively cool hot soup for storage?
A. Place it in the freezer immediately.
B. Place it in the refrigerator immediately.
C. Allow it to cool naturally to room temperature before placing it in the walk-in.
D. Cool it to 45°F while stirring it in an ice bath.
E. Any of the above is acceptable.

147. In checking the walk-in this morning, you find that the escarole is quite rusty. What do you do?
A. Soak it in an oxidizing solution.
B. Throw it out.
C. Save it for soup.
D. Scrub off the rust with a stainless steel sponge.
E. Tear off the rusty spots.

148. Which of the following procedures is the most wasteful when cleaning lettuce?
A. Removing the core with a paring knife.
B. Removing the core with a French knife.
C. Smashing the head on the counter and removing the core by hand.
D. Cutting the head in half before removing the core.
E. None of the above are acceptable procedures.

149. Which of the following procedures will maximize your production of frozen french fries?
A. Filling the fryer baskets as full as possible.
B. Blanching the french fries before cooking.
C. Turning up the heat on the fryer.
D. Keeping the french fries frozen and cooking them in small batches.

150. Which of the following would you *not* put in a gelatin dessert?
A. Crushed walnuts.
B. Fresh pineapple.
C. Sliced bananas.
D. Canned mandarin oranges.
E. Miniature marshmallows.

Examen Profesional

EQUIPO TÉCNICO DE PRODUCCIÓN

Escoja la respuesta *MÁS CORRECTA* y marque su opción en la hoja de respuestas. Por favor, no escriba en este examen.

TERMINOLOGÍA

Concuerde los siguientes términos de cocina con las definiciones adecuadas.

1. Chop	A.	Utilizar un cuchillo o tenedor para cortar líneas profundas en el producto.
2. Dice	B.	Mezclar los ingredientes con un movimiento de rotación vigoroso.
3. Grate	C.	Agregar líquido para disolver las partículas sólidas que quedan en el fondo de la olla.
4. Grind	D.	Quitarle a la mantequilla, la sopa o cualquier otro líquido las partículas sólidas.
5. Julienne	E.	Cocinar en una sartén con muy poca grasa o aceite.
6. Mince	F.	Cortar en pedazos de diferentes tamaños.
7. Puree	G.	Cocinar en aire caliente.
8. Score	H.	Cubrir un artículo completamente con harina u otra substancia en polvo.
9. Whip	I.	Cocinar en líquido a temperaturas altas.
10. Beat	J.	Cubrir con un almíbar o salsa espesa y azucarada y generalmente dorada al horno.
11. Blend	K.	Cocinar con poca grasa o aceite en una plataforma lisa de metal.
12. Fold	L.	Mezclar los ingredientes uniformemente con un movimiento suave.
13. Bread	M.	Cocinar (generalmente un producto vitamínico) suavemente en líquido caliente.
14. Barbecue	N.	Cortar en pedazos finos y largos.
15. Clarify	O.	Cocinar en líquido a una temperatura que produzca poco burbujeo.
16. Glaze	P.	Convertir en un líquido granuloso utilizando una batidora o un procesador de comida.
17. Deglaze	Q.	Cortar en pedazos finos.
18. Knead	R.	Trabajar la masa con las manos.
19. Marinate	S.	Cortar en cubos (¼–¾ pulgadas).
20. Deep Fry	T.	Cocinar en brasas.
21. Sauté	U.	Combinar un ingrediente suave delicadamente con uno más pesado utilizando una espátula o cuchara.
22. Braise	V.	Cocinar un producto en el vapor del calor y sin sumergirlo en el líquido.
23. Broil	W.	Sumergir por un rato en una solución suavizadora o potente.
24. Grill	X.	Cocinar sin grasa o aceite bajo el fuego.
25. Pan Fry	Y.	Cubrir con harina, huevos y migajas de pan.
26. Simmer	Z.	Batir a una velocidad alta para que adquiera cuerpo.
27. Boil	a.	Utilizar una combinación de productos secos y húmedos.
28. Bake	b.	Utilizar un implemento o máquina para hacer hojuelas.
29. Steam	c.	Cocinar sumergiendo en manteca o aceite.
30. Poach	d.	No existe una definición apropiada para este término.

EQUIPO Y SEGURIDAD

31. Generalmente, ¿cuál es la manera más eficiente de mantener el equipo con efectividad de costo?
   A. Reemplazar el equipo tan pronto como se rompa.
   B. Contratar a un especialista del equipo a tiempo completo.
   C. Mantener todo el equipo usted mismo.
   D. Contratar a una firma exterior para el mantenimiento.
   E. Practicar mantenimiento preventivo.

32. ¿Cuál sería su primera pregunta al considerar la compra de una pieza nueva de equipo?
   A. ¿Cuánto costará?
   B. ¿Cuál es la tasa de consumo de energía?
   C. ¿Cómo mejorará la satisfacción del cliente?
   D. ¿Cuánto trabajo ahorrará?
   E. ¿Cuál es la experiencia de otros con el uso de ésta máquina?

33. **¿Cuál es el procedimiento adecuado para limpiar la maquinaria de la cocina?**
    A. Desconecte el equipo eléctrico antes de limpiarlo.
    B. Utilice una solución de detergente y agua.
    C. Utilice bicarbonato de soda y agua para limpiar los refrigeradores.
    D. Pida una inspección de su trabajo cuando haya acabado.
    E. Todo lo anterior.

34. **¿Qué deberá hacer si la máquina lavadora de platos no funciona adecuadamente?**
    A. No utilice la máquina y avísele al supervisor o administrador inmediatamente.
    B. Disminuya el ritmo en que los platos estén pasando a través de la máquina.
    C. Menciónelo a un supervisor o administrador una vez que usted haya terminado con todo.
    D. No se preocupe de ello porque todas las máquinas dejan de funcionar de vez en cuando.
    E. Llama al departamento de salud.

35. **¿Qué hace usted después de aplicar una solución limpiadora?**
    A. Cepilla ligeramente con un cepillo suave.
    B. Utiliza una esponja para retirar la solución.
    C. Permitirle que se seque.
    D. Espera que la solución haga efecto.
    E. Restriegua con una esponja de metal y enjuaga con agua limpia.

36. **¿Cuál piensa usted que sea la barrera más grande para una limpieza efectiva?**
    A. Entrenamiento impropio.
    B. Herramientas inadecuadas.
    C. Desorden y basura.
    D. Falta de tiempo.
    E. Falta de personal adecuado.

37. **¿Cuál de las siguientes prácticas corregiría usted *inmediatamente*?**
    A. Un cocinero encargado de freír que juega con cubos de hielo fuera de la vista de los clientes.
    B. Un lavador de platos que corta verduras con un cuchillo francés muy afilado.
    C. Un conserge que coloca un balde de limpieza en una mesa de preparación.
    D. Un chef de sous parado en una escalera desplegable para alcanzar un estante alto en la despensa.
    E. Un mesero que utiliza una bandeja de aluminio para llevar la comida.

38. **¿Cuáles son los primeros auxilios adecuados para una quemadura de primer grado en la cocina?**
    A. Llamar al 911.
    B. Poner hielo en el área quemada.
    C. Poner mantequilla en el área quemada.
    D. Mantener el área quemada bajo agua fría.
    E. Mantener el área quemada bajo agua tibia.

39. **Si el criterio fuera la causa más frecuente de accidentes, ¿cuál sería el artículo más peligroso en la cocina?**
    A. El piso.
    B. El freidor de grasa.
    C. El cuchillo francés.
    D. La máquina rebanadora.
    E. La lavadora de platos.

40. **¿Cuál de las siguientes es el procedimiento adecuado para trapear los pisos?**
    A. Mover el balde del trapeador lo menos posible mientras limpia.
    B. Utilizar blanqueador y amoníaco en el agua para aumentar la acción limpiadora.
    C. Torcer el trapeador frecuentemente.
    D. Colocar avisos de "Piso mojado" en donde comience el piso húmedo y donde termina el piso seco.
    E. Todo lo anterior.

SALUBRIDAD

41. **¿Cuál de los siguientes procedimientos tienen el potencial más alto de provocar una enfermedad transmitida por la comida?**
    A. Recalentando un producto alimenticio previamente cocinado en la estufa.
    B. En la primera etapa en que se cocina el producto alimenticio.

C. Enfriando una comida en el comedor.

D. Las actividades de preparación (corte, mezcla, etc.) de un producto alimenticio.

42. **Usted nota que un miembro de su equipo técnico tiene una cortada abierta en su mano. ¿Cuál es la mejor forma de manejar esto?**

A. Excluirla de toda la responsabilidad de manejo de comida hasta que la cortada esté curada.

B. La envía a su casa sin pago hasta que la cortada esté curada.

C. La envía a su casa con pago hasta que la cortada esté curada.

D. Para evitar molestar a los clientes, le asigna a una estación de trabajo fuera de la vista del comedor.

E. Archiva un reclamo al compensador de trabajadores.

43. **¿Cuál es el lugar adecuado para un termómetro secundario en un refrigerador?**

A. En la esquina inferior lejos de la puerta.

B. En medio del refrigerador.

C. En la parte superior de enfrente del refrigerador, por la puerta.

D. Detrás de la puerta.

E. Un termómetro secundario no es necesario si el refrigerador tiene un termómetro incorporado.

44. **¿Cuál es la temperatura mínima de comida caliente mantenida por el servicio?**

A. 200°F.

B. 165°F.

C. 140°F.

D. 120°F.

E. 45°F.

45. **¿Cuál es la temperatura adecuada para la lavadora de platos?**

A. 120°F.

B. 140°F.

C. 160°F.

D. 180°F.

E. 200°F.

46. **¿Cuál es la temperatura de enjuague adecuado para una máquina lavadora de platos de baja temperatura?**

A. 65°F.

B. 120°F.

C. 140°F.

D. 160°F.

47. **¿Cuál es la temperatura de enjuague adecuada para una máquina lavadora de platos de alta temperatura?**

A. 120°F.

B. 140°F.

C. 160°F.

D. 180°F.

48. **¿Cuál práctica es correcta o aceptable?**

A. Pulir los cubiertos.

B. Comer en áreas de la preparación de comida.

C. Utilizar un vaso como cuchara para servir hielo.

D. Descongelar comida en los muebles de la cocina.

E. Mantener paños de limpieza en una solución sanitaria.

49. **¿Cuál es un termómetro de producto?**

A. El indicador en un pavo que salta cuando este está listo.

B. Un termómetro pequeño de bolsillo utilizado para medir las temperaturas de los alimentos.

C. El termómetro montado en la pared que mide la temperatura de refrigeración.

D. El termostato que controla la temperatura de la cocina.

E. Ninguno de los anteriores.

50. **¿Cuál de los siguientes puede ser servido en un establecimiento comercial de servicio de comidas?**

A. Productos de la huerta de su vecino.

B. Panesillos devueltos del comedor.

C. La lasagna que uno de sus cocineros hizo en casa.

D. Verduras orgánicas.

E. Todo lo anterior.

51. **¿Entre cuáles límites de tiempo deberá ser refrigerada a una temperatura interna de 45°F comida con peligro de ponerse mala?**
   A. 1 hora.
   B. 2 horas.
   C. 6 horas.
   D. 4 horas.
   E. Tan rápido como sea posible.

52. **¿En cuál de las siguientes comidas crece mejor el botulismo?**
   A. Tomates frescos.
   B. Pollo crudo.
   C. Salmón congelado.
   D. Atún enlatado.
   E. Chile picante casero.

53. **¿Cuál de las siguientes enfermedades es frecuentemente causada y asociada con aves?**
   A. Lactobacillus bulgarius.
   B. Salmonella.
   C. Staphylococcus.
   D. Clostridium perfringens.
   E. Botuliom.

54. **¿Cuál de las siguientes es la regla general para el máximo tiempo total que los productos alimenticios con peligro de ponerse malos pueden estar en la "zona de peligro"?**
   A. 2 horas.
   B. 4 horas.
   C. 6 horas.
   D. 8 horas.
   E. No importa.

55. **¿Cuál de las siguientes formas de envenenamiento por alimento es fatal más de la mitad de las veces?**
   A. Lactobacillus bulgarius.
   B. Salmonella.
   C. Staphylococcus.
   D. Clostridium perfringens.
   E. Botulism.

56. **¿Cada cuánto deberá ser revisada la solución sanitaria?**
   A. Al comienzo de cada turno.
   B. Por lo menos dos veces por turno.
   C. Por lo menos una vez por hora.
   D. Por lo menos una vez por media hora.
   E. Cada vez que usted la utilice.

57. **¿Cómo puede saber usted si la solución sanitaria tiene la concentración adecuada?**
   A. Midiendo cuidadosamente al preparar una nueva solución.
   B. Utilizando un equipo de prueba universal.
   C. Sumergiendo una tira de prueba en la solución y comparándola con una escala.
   D. Sumergiendo un pedazo de papel toalla en la solución y ver si se oscurece.
   E. Utilizando un termómetro de producto.

58. **¿Qué ocurre si la concentración de la solución sanitaria es más alta de lo recomendado?**
   A. Puede ser más efectiva.
   B. Puede ser tóxica.
   C. Costará más dinero, pero no hay problema real.
   D. No trabajará del todo o en lo absoluto.
   E. Todo lo anterior.

59. **¿Qué ocurre si la concentración de la solución sanitaria es menor de lo recomendado?**
   A. Matará la bacteria lentamente.
   B. Puede ser tóxico.
   C. Ahorrará dinero y no hay problema real.
   D. No trabajará del todo o en lo absoluto.
   E. Todo el anterior.

60. **¿A qué temperatura interna tiene usted que calentar la comida para matar toxinas del staphylococcus?**
   A. 120°F.
   B. 165°F.
   C. 180°F.
   D. 200°F.
   E. A las toxinas del staphylococcus no se les puede matar.

RELACIONES HUMANAS

61. **¿Cuál es la mejor forma de medir la efectividad de un supervisor de cocina?**
   A. Que tan bien cocina.
   B. El puntaje del departamento de salud.
   C. Ganancias.
   D. La cuenta promedio.
   E. El desarrollo personal y profesional de sus subalternos.

62. **¿Cuál método de entrenamiento utiliza usted al mostrarle a alguien cómo limpiar una pieza del equipo?**
   A. Instrucciones escritas.
   B. Entrenamiento en clase.
   C. Demostración.
   D. Instrucción en el trabajo.

63. **¿Quién piensa ud. que sería un entrenador más efectivo para temas operacionales?**
   A. Un asesor.
   B. Un administrador general.
   C. El supervisor del departamento.
   D. Un colega calificado.
   E. Un director de entrenamiento de la compañía.

64. **¿Qué piensa ud. que su equipo técnico quiere sacar de su trabajo?**
   A. Aprecio por el trabajo que hacen.
   B. Sueldos más altos.
   C. Estar enterado de las cosas.
   D. Los beneficios y el seguro de salud.
   E. Seguridad de tener trabajo.

65. **Basado en su experiencia, ¿qué declaración es verdadera acerca de trabajar con minorías?**
   A. Deben ser tratados un poco diferente a los otros trabajadores.
   B. Pueden ser más difíciles de motivar que otros trabajadores.
   C. Es más difícil de saber lo que ellos realmente quieren de usted.
   D. Tienden a ser menos productivos que otros trabajadores.
   E. No son diferentes a cualquier otro trabajador.

66. **¿Dónde yace la responsabilidad principal de retener un volumen alto de equipo técnico en los restaurantes?**
   A. En los trabajadores individuales involucrados.
   B. En la administración del restaurante.
   C. En la tasa de pago de los restaurantes.
   D. En los valores que prevalecen en nuestra sociedad.
   E. En la competencia aumentada a causa de otras industrias.

67. **¿Cómo saca usted lo mejor de su tripulación?**
   A. Al establecer un ejemplo personal que refleje todo lo que usted espera de su equipo técnico.
   B. Al establecer normas altas y manejar las actividades de su equipo técnico.
   C. Al desarrollar procedimientos en las áreas mayores.
   D. Al conducir entrenamiento extensivo y consistente de las habilidades necesarias en todas las posiciones.

68. **Como un miembro del equipo técnico del restaurante, ¿cuál es la mejor forma de avanzar en su carrera?**
   A. Hacer favores personales a los administradores.
   B. Resaltar en la competencia.
   C. Tomar clases y asistir a seminarios.

D. Enseñarle a sus subalternos cómo hacer su trabajo.

E. Asegurarse de que usted obtenga el crédito cuando las cosas van bien.

69. **Va a ser una noche del sábado muy ocupada. Uno de los cocineros se reporta al trabajo a las 3:00 PM con su uniforme sucio. ¿Cómo maneja usted esto?**

A. Lo asigna a su estación regular.

B. Le envía a su casa a recoger un uniforme limpio antes de permitirle que continúe.

C. Lo regaña y se asegura de que trabaje fuera de la vista de los clientes.

D. Lo asigna a la lavadora de platos y asigna al lavador de platos a trabajar en la línea.

E. Lo envía a su casa sin pago.

70. **Va a ser una noche del sábado muy ocupada. Uno de sus cocineros se presenta al trabajo a las 4:30 PM con el uniforme sucio. ¿Cómo maneja usted esto?**

A. Lo asigna a su estación regular.

B. Lo envía a su casa a recoger un uniforme limpio antes de permitirle que continúe.

C. Lo regaña y se asegura que trabaje fuera de la vista de los clientes.

D. Lo asigna a la lavadora de platos y asigna al lavador de platos a trabajar en la línea.

E. Le envía a su casa sin pago.

FINANZAS

71. **Su vendedor de comestibles le acaba de ofrecer un trato: 20% de descuento en órdenes de más de 3 cajas de trufas si hace la orden inmediatamente. Usted normalmente utiliza 2 o 3 latas de trufas por mes. ¿Qué hace usted?**

A. Pasa.

B. Compra 3+ cajas y le ahorra dinero al restaurante.

C. Compra 3+ cajas e inventa una nueva especialidad para poder usarlo.

D. Compra 3+ cajas y revende parte de las existencias a un competidor obteniendo así ganancias.

72. **El mes pasado, los recibos totales del restaurante fueron de $66,500 de los cuales $4,100 fueron impuestos sobre la venta, $15,600 fueron ventas de bebidas y el resto fueron ventas de alimento. Sus compras de alimento fueron de $16,800 y su nómina de la cocina fue de $9,900. Usted gastó $550 en suministros de papel. El inventario de comida inicial fue $5,400 y el inventario de cierre fue de $4,000. ¿Cuál fue el costo de los alimentos para el mes?**

A. 27.3%

B. 32.9%

C. 35.9%

D. 38.9%

E. No hay suficiente información para responder la pregunta.

Usted quiere encontrar un especial del día para la siguiente semana y sigue buscando a través de su colección de libros de cocina un artículo del menú que sea suceptible. Usted se atraviesa con la siguiente receta para goulash húngaro que se ve muy interesante:

2 lb. de filete de res	2 cucharadas de paprika
3 cucharadas de harina	4 cucharaditas de mantequilla
1 cucharadita de sal	1 taza de puré de tomate
1 cucharadita de pimienta	1 taza de consomé de carne

Usted llama a su proveedor y recibe la siguiente información del costo:

filete	$2.75/1 lb.	paprika	$3.00/1 lb.
harina	$7.50/50 lb.	mantequilla	$1.50/1 lb.
sal	$0.40/1 lb.	puré de tomate	$19.50/6/10
pimienta	$9.00/1 lb.	consomé de carne	$30.50/12/49 oz.

73. **La receta como está escrita hace 5 porciones. Usted planifica producir 55 porciones, si lo ofreciera como un especial. Aproximadamente, ¿cuánta harina necesitará para esta gran cantidad?**

A. 1 taza

B. 30 cucharaditas

C. 2 tazas

D. 1 lb.

E. Ninguno de los anteriores.

74. ¿Cuánta sal utilizaría para 55 porciones?

A. 11 cucharaditas

B. 11 cucharadas

C. ¼ taza

D. ½ taza

E. Ninguno de los anteriores.

75. ¿Cuál será la porción aproximada de carne de 55 porciones?

A. 4 onzas

B. 6 onzas

C. 8 onzas

D. 12 onzas

E. Ninguno de los anteriores.

76. ¿Cuál es el costo de la porción de goulash húngaro?

A. $1.23

B. $1.53

C. $1.82

D. $2.10

E. Ninguno de los anteriores.

77. Usted tiene un producto que se vende como un artículo de servicio a domicilio por $6.95. La comida en el plato cuesta $2.50 y los costos de empaque cuestan 25¢. Se gasta por lo menos $2.00 en la preparación. ¿Cuál es el porcentaje de costo de alimento en este producto?

A. 34.4%

B. 36.0%

C. 38.8%

D. 68.3%

E. Ninguno de los anteriores.

78. Usted tiene un producto que se vende a $8.50 con un costo por porción de $3.00. ¿Cuál es su márgen de ganancias totales?

A. 35.3%

B. 64.7%

C. $3.00

D. $5.50

E. Ninguno de los anteriores.

79. Digamos que el restaurante realmente se ha equivocado con un grupo típico de cuatro. También vamos a decir que el típico cliente de su restaurante come normalmente tres veces al mes y la cuenta promedio es de $20.00. Probablemente, ¿cuánto le sale costando este error a la compañía por el negocio perdido los siguientes cinco años?

A. Menos de $4,000

B. $10,000–$12,000

C. $25,000–$30,000

D. $50,000–$60,000

E. Más de $85,000

80. Usted está planificando un aperitivo de salmón ahumado para el menú. Usted espera que un 75% del producto sea comestible con un rendimiento de un salmón ahumado de 12 lbs. que puede comprar a $100.00. También puede comprar salmón ahumado rebanado por $11.55 la libra. A usted le han dicho (¡en términos exactos!) que mantenga sus costos operativos tan bajos como le sea posible. Usted espera utilizar cerca de 50 lbs. de salmón por semana. Basado en su experiencia, ¿qué producto compra usted?

A. Salmón entero.

B. Salmón rebanado.

C. No hay suficiente información para responder a esa pregunta.

OPERACIONES

81. **¿A qué se refiere el dicho "primero adentro, primero afuera"?**
    A. Al cambio de suministradores regular para mantenerlos honestos.
    B. Al control de tráfico de los camiones en el área de cargamento.
    C. Al utilizar los víveres en el orden en que fueron recibidos.
    D. Al determinar a quien se despide basado en la antigüedad del empleado.
    E. Ninguno de los anteriores.

82. **¿Cuál sería el mejor documento que se puede utilizar al recibir la orden del mercado?**
    A. La orden de compra.
    B. La orden de las provisiones.
    C. La factura del proveedor.
    D. La receta normal.
    E. El libro de sistema DICE.

83. **¿Qué información provee el puntaje del USDA en la carne?**
    A. La planta de donde la carne fue procesada.
    B. La calidad de la carne.
    C. La fecha que la carne fue procesada.
    D. La condición sanitaria de la carne.
    E. El corte de la carne.

84. **¿Cuál de las siguientes sirve de descripción de un producto alimenticio deseado?**
    A. Hoja de costo de los vendedores.
    B. El acuerdo del sindicato.
    C. La hoja de especificación.
    D. El certificado de reembolso.
    E. El libro de sistema de DICE.

85. **¿Cómo ayuda la pronosticación a controlar la producción?**
    A. Asegura que el alimento sea producido de acuerdo con los procedimientos dictados por las normas.
    B. Ayuda a evitar la baja o la superproducción.
    C. Garantiza que habrá suficientes inventarios para alcanzar las necesidades de producción.
    D. Ayuda a determinar asignaciones de trabajo.
    E. La pronosticación se relaciona a las ventas; no tiene nada que ver con la producción.

86. **Digamos que el costo proyectado de la comida es de un 34%. Usted está evaluando a un nuevo artículo en el menú con un costo por porción de 82¢. ¿Cómo lo cobraría en el menú?**
    A. $1.95
    B. $2.25
    C. $2.41
    D. $2.50
    E. No hay suficiente información para responder la pregunta.

87. **¿Cuál artículo _no_ es normalmente parte de la porción de control?**
    A. Especificaciones de compra.
    B. Recetas normalizadas.
    C. Equipo de cocina ajustado apropiadamente.
    D. Control de desperdicio.
    E. Poner la cantidad adecuada en el plato.

88. **¿Cuál es el mejor plan de acción cuando un oficial del gobierno llega a inspeccionar el restaurante?**
    A. Pedirle al oficial de comunicarse solamente con usted y de no hablar con su equipo técnico.
    B. Insistir en su derecho de aviso previo a la visita y cambiar la fecha de la inspección.
    C. Permite al oficial que conduzca la inspección sólo.
    D. Sigue el oficial de lejos y toma nota de cómo conduce la inspección.
    E. Acompaña al oficial durante la inspección.

89. **¿Qué determina un análisis de rendimiento?**
    A. El precio de un artículo en el menú.
    B. Las tareas involucradas en preparar un artículo del menú.

C. El costo bruto de un artículo del menú.

D. Cuánto tiempo se puede mantener un artículo del menú en buenas condiciones antes de servirlo.

E. Cuánta cantidad de alimento es utilizable en el contenido de una cantidad comprada.

90. **¿Cuál sería la primera medida que usted tomaría si usted pensara que el costo del alimento es demasiado alto?**

A. Revisar los procedimientos de control de porciones.

B. Substituir los ingredientes menos caros.

C. Cambiar el menú para utilizar entradas de costo más bajo.

D. Subir los precios del menú.

E. Buscar evidencia de robo.

91. **¿Cuál sería la primer medida que usted tomaría si pensara que el costo del trabajo es demasiado alto?**

A. Reducir las horas por igual.

B. Disminuir las horas de los trabajadores de medio tiempo.

C. Despedir a los trabajadores marginales.

D. Subir los precios del menú.

E. Concentrarse en el entrenamiento de ventas.

92. **Si la comida estuviera saliendo de la cocina demasiado lenta, ¿cuál sería probablemente la causa del problema?**

A. Los cocineros son incompetentes.

B. Las órdenes no se están pidiendo adecuadamente.

C. El equipo de cocina es inadecuado.

D. El administrador de cocina no está prestando atención.

E. Ninguno de los anteriores.

93. **¿Cómo controlaría los robos en los restaurantes?**

A. Espera lo mejor de su equipo técnico y crea un ambiente en donde no quieren robar.

B. Supervisa a todos los empleados como un halcón.

C. Mantiene sistemas de control cercano y los vigila continuamente.

D. Revisa todas las transacciones.

E. Conduce inspecciones de casilleros y bolsas sin ser anunciadas.

94. **Simplemente, ¿qué es una factura?**

A. Una cuenta.

B. Una orden de compra.

C. Una historia de ventas.

D. El estado de las cuentas.

E. Un proyecto de producción.

95. **¿Cuál de las siguientes acciones es más probable que disminuya el consumo de energía?**

A. Evite el juego con las temperaturas del equipo de cocina una vez que hayan sido encendidos.

B. Cocine alimentos a fuego alto rápidamente.

C. Utilice agua fría para cocinar.

D. Cocine alimentos en grandes cantidades.

E. Cocine alimentos en pequeñas cantidades.

96. **¿Cuál es su objetivo al crear un horario para el equipo técnico?**

A. Minimizar el costo del trabajo.

B. Asegurar un nivel alto de servicio para los clientes.

C. Concordar el horario de trabajo con el presupuesto.

D. Distribuir las horas disponibles equitativamente entre el equipo técnico.

E. Acomodar las solicitudes especiales de los trabajadores.

97. **¿Cuál es la primera cosa que hace usted cuando hay una lesión en el trabajo?**

A. Intenta que el trabajador utilice su propio seguro de salud para el tratamiento.

B. A menos que usted haya sido testigo del accidente, sospeche que no ocurrió en el trabajo.

C. Archive un reclamo a la compensadora de trabajadores.

D. Arregle para que haya tratamiento inmediato bajo su póliza de la compensadora de trabajadores.

E. Si la lesión es menor, haga que el restaurante pague los costos y no archive un reclamo a la compensadora de trabajadores.

98. **Usted recibe la orden de la tienda de comestibles. La factura tiene en la lista 12 cajas de lomo de res pero el conductor solamente ha entregado 11 y no ha notado la diferencia. ¿Qué hace usted?**

A. Como está entre el límite del 10% de la cantidad de factura, firma la factura.

B. Firma la factura y le dice al conductor que cambie la cantidad de cajas de lomo de res a 11.

C. Firma la factura y le pide al conductor un caja extra en su próximo viaje.
D. Notifique al conductor de la discrepancia y cambie la cantidad de cajas de lomo de res a 11 usted mismo.
E. Llama al administrador.

99. **Usted recibe la orden de la tienda de comestibles. La factura tiene en la lista 12 cajas de lomo de res pero el conductor ha entregado 13 y no ha notado la diferencia. ¿Qué hace usted?**
A. Ya que está en un límite del 10% de la cantidad de la factura, firma la factura y no dice nada.
B. Firma la factura y le dice al conductor que cambie la cantidad de cajas de lomo de res a 13.
C. Firma la factura y se lleva la cajas extra a casa.
D. Notifica al conductor de la discrepancia y cambia la cantidad de cajas de lomo de res a 13 usted mismo.
E. Llama el administrador.

100. **¿Cuál de las siguientes ayudaría más a mejorar la relación laboral entre la cocina y el equipo técnico del comedor?**
A. Da una clase para explicar las operaciones de la cocina al equipo técnico del comedor.
B. Instala un sistema electrónico de POS.
C. Conduce entrenamiento intercambiando a todos los miembros del equipo técnico.
D. Gritarle al equipo técnico de servicio y ridiculizarlo cuando comete un error en la cocina.
E. Utiliza a un despachador.

101. **Como miembro del equipo técnico de producción, ¿para quién trabaja usted?**
A. El administrador general.
B. Los clientes.
C. El equipo técnico de comedor.
D. El departamento de salud.
E. Usted mismo.

102. **Un mesero entra en la cocina con un plato que un cliente del comedor ha regresado. El mesero obviamente está alterado y es un poco grocero. ¿Qué hace usted?**
A. Regaña al mesero por su grocería.
B. Averigua qué hay de malo con el alimento.
C. Revisa el alimento para ver si está preparado adecuadamente.
D. Devuelve el plato al cliente usted mismo y le explica cómo está preparado.
E. Lo arregla o reemplaza sin comentario.

103. **Es la noche del sábado y usted está en plena hora pique. Un mesero viene y ordena un plato que se ofrece en el menú del almuerzo pero no en el menú de la cena. ¿Qué le dice al mesero que le diga al cliente?**
A. El plato no se ofrece en la cena.
B. Usted está demasiado ocupado para satisfacer la orden.
C. Usted prepara el plato cuando usted haya terminado con las otras órdenes.
D. Usted prepara el plato tal y como fue pedido.

104. **¿Qué puede suponer usted cuando un cliente regresa un plato a la cocina?**
A. Alguien en la cocina se equivocó con la orden.
B. El mesero no explicó adecuadamente el plato al cliente.
C. Hay algo malo con el alimento.
D. El cliente está de mal humor.
E. Usted no puede suponer nada cuando alguien regresa un plato.

105. **¿Cuál es la mejor forma de identificar los problemas operativos de su restaurante?**
A. Llama a un asesor.
B. Habla con sus clientes.
C. Habla con los supervisores.
D. Habla con el equipo técnico.
E. Asiste a un seminario de administración de restaurantes.

106. **En cuanto a lo que se refiere a quejas de los clientes, ¿con cuál declaración está usted más de acuerdo?**
A. No oir noticias significa buenas noticias.
B. Las quejas son regalos especiales.
C. Un nivel de satisfacción de cerca del 90% es realista para un restaurante de servicio completo.
D. Usted no puede esperar complacer a toda la gente siempre.
E. Algunos se quejan solamente para llamar la atención.

107. **Es una noche típica del lunes y usted está en medio de la cena. Un mesero viene y le pide un plato que no está en el menú. Usted ni siquiera tiene todos los ingredientes en la despensa. ¿Qué le dice usted al mesero que le diga al cliente?**
   A. Que usted no puede preparar el plato.
   B. Que usted está demasiado ocupado para preparar la solicitud.
   C. Que usted prepará el plato la siguiente vez que vengan.
   D. Que usted con mucho gusto preparará el plato (e inmediatamente envía a alguien al supermercado).

108. **¿Qué porción de las ventas típicas del restaurante tiene pre-impuesto?**
   A. 40–45%
   B. 30–35%
   C. 20–25%
   D. 10–15%
   E. Menos del 5%

109. **La cuenta promedio es las ventas totales de alimento del restaurante divididas por cuál número?**
   A. El valor promedio de la cuenta típica del cliente.
   B. La cantidad de clientes servidos.
   C. La cantidad de entradas vendidas.
   D. El número promedio de gente en grupo.
   E. La cantidad de asientos en el restaurante.

110. **Si usted permite que el costo del trabajo establezca los precios del menú, ¿cuál de estos detalles probablemente tendrían el porcentaje más alto de costo?**
   A. La ensalada del chef.
   B. Los huevos revueltos con tocineta y tostada.
   C. Hamburguesa con queso y papas fritas.
   D. Chuleta de cerdo con salsa de manzana.

PREPARACIÓN DE ALIMENTOS

111. **¿Cuál de las siguientes salsas no es una "salsa madre"?**
   A. Española.
   B. Velouté.
   C. Bechamel.
   D. Bearnaise.
   E. Holandesa.

112. **¿Qué es un "roux"?**
   A. Una mezcla de leche y harina.
   B. Una bolsa pequeña de hierbas agregada para darle sabor durante la coción.
   C. La salsa de mantequilla para el pescado.
   D. Una mezcla de mantequilla y harina.
   E. Baño maría.

113. **¿Qué es un "Bouquet Garni"?**
   A. Las verduras utilizadas para darle sabor a una salsa.
   B. Flores tradicionalmente puestas en la mesa de la cocina para que traigan buena suerte.
   C. Una bolsa de especias.
   D. Flores frescas situadas en los platos como decoración.
   E. Un agente de color utilizado en salsas oscuras.

114. **¿Qué clase de almidón es utilizado extensivamente para espesar salsas dulces y postres?**
   A. Arrurruz.
   B. Harina de pastelería.
   C. Gelatina.
   D. Tapioca.
   E. Maicena.

115. **Cuando compra pescado fresco, ¿cuál condición no es aceptable?**
    A. Ojos resaltados.
    B. Carne suave y flexible.
    C. Olor suave y sin olor a pescado.
    D. Piel brillante.
    E. Agallas rojas brillantes.

116. **¿Cuál de los siguientes alimentos deberán estar refrigerados?**
    A. Bananos.
    B. Aguacates verdes.
    C. Naranjas.
    D. Papas.
    E. Cebollas amarillas.

117. **Usted está preparando una salsa de spaguetti y accidentalmente añade demasiada sal. ¿Cómo corrige usted esto?**
    A. Añade más puré de tomate.
    B. Añade más agua.
    C. Pone una papa.
    D. Añade oregano.
    E. La tira y comienza de nuevo.

118. **¿Cuál de las siguientes es una pesa AP?**
    A. 4 lb. de carne asada rebanada.
    B. 1 lb. cebolla picada.
    C. 2 lb. broccoli crudo.
    D. 2 tazas de salsa bechamel.

119. **¿Cuál de las siguientes es una pesa EP?**
    A. 2 lb. hojas de espinaca limpias.
    B. 20 lb. un pavo entero congelado.
    C. 12 lb. costillas rostizadas.
    D. 1 lb. nueces en su cáscara.

120. **Usted está cocinando una costilla de 20 lbs. ¿A qué temperatura deberá usted retirarla del horno si quiere servirla a término medio?**
    A. 100°F.
    B. 120°F.
    C. 130°F.
    D. 140°F.
    E. 160°F.

121. **Usted está cocinando una costilla de 20 lbs. ¿Cuál sería la mejor forma de cocinarla?**
    A. Cocinarla a 325°F durante 2 horas.
    B. Cocinarla a 375°F durante 2 horas.
    C. Cocinarla a 425°F durante 1 hora.
    D. Cocinarla a 500°F durante 1 hora.
    E. Todas estas combinaciones producirán resultados iguales.

122. **Usted ha preparado salsa holandesa para el desayuno. Al final de la comida, usted aún tiene cerca de un cuarto de salsa de sobra. Usted también utiliza salsa holandesa en su menú del almuerzo. ¿Qué hace usted con la salsa sobrante?**
    A. La mantiene caliente y la utiliza para el almuerzo.
    B. Agrega salsa nueva al producto sobrante para refrescarla para el almuerzo.
    C. Tira la salsa y hace una nueva para el almuerzo.
    D. Congela el sobrante para matar cualquier bacteria antes de ser reutilizada.
    E. Todas las anteriores son soluciones aceptables.

123. **¿Cuál de los siguientes ingredientes normalmente no sería parte de una salsa blanca?**
    A. Crema.
    B. Mantequilla.
    C. Harina.

D. Agua.

E. Leche.

124. **¿Cuál de los siguientes ingredientes normalmente no sería parte de una salsa oscura?**

  A. Consomé de res.

  B. Harina.

  C. Mirepoix.

  D. Manteca.

  E. Leche.

125. **¿Cuál de los siguientes ingredientes normalmente no sería parte de una salsa de tomate?**

  A. Cebolla.

  B. Pasta de tomate.

  C. Consomé court.

  D. Hierbas.

  E. Puré de tomate.

126. **Usted está cocinando una salsa de spaguetti y accidentalmente la quema. ¿Qué hace usted?**

  A. La tira y comienza de nuevo.

  B. Agrega una papa.

  C. Revuelve la salsa completamente y la cuela por una malla china.

  D. Añade más tomates.

  E. Añade más azúcar.

127. **¿Cuál de las siguientes salsas no puede ser recalentada?**

  A. Oscura.

  B. Blanca.

  C. Tomate.

  D. Veloute.

  E. Holandesa.

128. **¿Cuál pieza del equipo utilizaría usted para recalentar 5 galones de sopa de almejas inglesa?**

  A. La mesa de vapor.

  B. El horno.

  C. El vaporizador.

  D. El horno de microonda.

  E. La estufa.

129. **Usted está preparando una sopa de verduras frescas con fideos. ¿Cuál de los siguientes ingredientes agregaría usted al final?**

  A. Cebolla.

  B. Zanahoria.

  C. Apio.

  D. Fideos de huevo.

  E. Agrega todo al mismo tiempo.

130. **¿Cuál de lo siguiente utilizaría usted para activar la levadura antes de utilizarla?**

  A. Agua hirviendo.

  B. Agua tibia.

  C. Agua con hielo.

  D. Mantequilla.

131. **Usted está asando a la parrilla cuando comienza un incendio en la parrilla. ¿Qué es lo primero que usted hace?**

  A. Lanza agua al fuego.

  B. Activa el sistema Ansul.

  C. Intenta salvar el filete.

  D. Apaga el ventilador.

  E. Ninguno de los anteriores.

132. **¿Cómo puede usted saber cuando un filete está cocinado a punto medio?**

  A. Cuanto tiempo ha estado en la parrilla.

  B. Por el grado de carbonización en el exterior.

  C. Lo corta ligeramente y mira.

D. Lo presiona con sus dedos.

E. Se refiere al libro de Sistema DICE.

133. **¿Dónde buscaría usted los ingredientes que necesita para preparar salsa holandesa?**

A. En la sección de alimentos enlatados de la despensa.

B. En la sección de provisiones de la despensa seca.

C. El refrigerador.

D. El congelador.

134. **¿Cuál corte de carne creería usted que es más suave?**

A. Filete de lomo.

B. Filet mignon.

C. Filete de costado.

D. Filete de T-Bone.

E. Tira de Nueva York.

135. **¿Cuál corte de carne cree usted que tiene más sabor?**

A. Chuleta de ternera.

B. Filete de lomo.

C. Filet mignon.

D. Molida.

E. Filete del costado.

136. **¿Cuál de los siguientes es el modo más adecuado de descongelar un alimento?**

A. Lo coloca bajo la llave del agua caliente.

B. Lo agita en un baño de hielo.

C. Lo deja en el refrigerador.

D. Lo coloca en una bañera con agua fría.

E. Todos estos procedimientos son adecuados.

137. **Cuando se prepara una comida sofrita, ¿cuánta manteca pone en el sartén?**

A. Suficiente para cubrir el artículo.

B. Suficiente para cubrir justamente la base del sartén.

C. Como un ¼ de pulgada.

D. Como ½ pulgada.

E. No se utiliza manteca para sofreir comida.

138. **Usted ha estado cocinando un alimento a baño maría y el agua que hierve se seca. ¿Qué hace usted?**

A. Tira el alimento.

B. Añade líquido al alimento.

C. Añade líquido al baño maría.

D. Baja la temperatura.

E. Prueba el producto para ver si todavía es aceptable.

139. **¿Cuál de las siguientes no sería una consideración al planificar la preparación de pasta?**

A. El tamaño de la vasija para cocinar la pasta.

B. La cantidad de agua utilizada para hervir la pasta.

C. La salsa que será utilizada para la pasta.

D. La temperatura del agua en que se cocinará la pasta.

E. La cantidad de tiempo que se cocina la pasta.

140. **¿A qué temperatura interna de la pechuga deberá cocinar un pavo entero?**

A. 100°F.

B. 130°F.

C. 170°F.

D. 200°F.

E. 250°F.

141. **¿Qué cree usted que le ocurre a la temperatura interna de un pernil asado durante la primera media hora aproximadamente después que la retira del horno?**

A. Baja de 5 a 10 grados.

B. Baja de 15 a 20 grados.

C. Permanece estable.

D. Aumenta de 5 a 10 grados.

E. Aumenta de 15 a 20 grados.

142. ¿Cuál es el mejor método para almacenar papas crudas y peladas?

A. Guardarlas bajo el agua.

B. Guardarlas en una bolsa plástica.

C. Guardarlas en un lugar seco y fresco.

D. Guardarlas en el refrigerador.

E. Las papas peladas no pueden ser almacenadas.

143. ¿Cuál de los siguientes sería la forma más segura de cubrir una salsa de tomate mientras se enfría en el refrigerador?

A. La cubre con papel aluminio.

B. La cubre con una tapa apretada.

C. La cubre cuidadosamente con pergamino.

D. La cubre con un pedazo de papel plástico.

E. La salsa de tomate no debe ser cubierta en el refrigerador hasta después que haya sido enfriada.

144. ¿Cuál de las siguientes prácticas no causará que la lechuga se oxide?

A. Secado impropio.

B. Remojar las hojas en agua.

C. Romper las hojas.

D. La edad excesiva.

145. Usted ha preparado justamente 20 galones de chile picante para una promoción especial. Como siempre, el espacio del refrigerador en el restaurante es muy limitado. ¿En qué recipiente colocaría el chile picante para enfriarlo en el corredor?

A. Un balde de plástico de 5 galones.

B. Ollas de acero inoxidable de 4″ llenas con un 1½″.

C. Ollas de acero inoxidable de 1½″ llenas hasta arriba.

D. Olla de acero inoxidable para consomé.

E. Un balde plástico con los que limpian.

146. ¿Cuál es el modo más efectivo de enfriar una sopa caliente para poder guardarla?

A. La coloca en el congelador inmediatamente.

B. La coloca en el refrigerador inmediatamente.

C. Permitirle que se enfríe a termperatua ambiental antes de colocarla en el corredor.

D. Enfríela a 45°F mientras la revuelve en un baño de hielo.

E. Cualquiera de los anteriores sería aceptable.

147. Al revisar el congelador de tamaño grande, usted encontró escarola (lechuga) bastante oxidada. ¿Qué hace usted?

A. La remoja en una solución oxidante.

B. La tira.

C. La guarda para sopa.

D. Quitar el óxido de las hojas con una esponja metálica.

E. Romper las partes con óxido.

148. ¿Cuál de los siguientes procedimientos serían malgastados al limpiar lechuga?

A. Quitar el corazón con un cuchillo.

B. Quitar el corazón con un cuchillo francés.

C. Romper la lechuga con el mueble de la cocina y quitarle el corazón con la mano.

D. Corte la cabeza por la mitad antes de quitarle el corazón.

E. Ninguno de los anteriores son procedimientos aceptables.

149. ¿Cuál de los siguientes procedimientos aumentaría la producción de papas fritas congeladas?

A. Llene los cestos de metal para freír tan llenos como sea posible.

B. Blanquee las papas fritas antes de cocinarlas.

C. Aumente la temperatura del freidor.

D. Mantenga las papas fritas congeladas y cocine en porciones pequeñas.

150. ¿Cuál de las siguientes no pondría usted en un postre de gelatina?

A. Nueces partidas.

B. Piña fresca.

C. Bananos rebanados.
D. Naranjas-mandarinas enlatadas.
E. Malvaviscos miniaturas.

Production Staff

PROFESSIONAL TEST
Answers

TERMINOLOGY

---

1. F Cut into pieces of irregular shape.

2. S Cut into ¼- to ¾-inch cubes.

3. b Use an implement or machine to make flakelike pieces.

4. d There is no proper definition listed for this term.

5. N Cut into long, thin strips.

6. Q Cut into fine pieces.

7. P Turn into a somewhat grainy liquid using a blender or food processor.

8. A Use a knife or fork to cut shallow lines into the product.

9. Z Beat at a high speed to add air.

10. B Mix ingredients with a vigorous rotating motion.

11. L Mix ingredients evenly using a gentle motion.

12. U Gently combine a light ingredient with a heavier one using a spatula or spoon.

13. Y Cover with flour, eggs, and crumbs.

14. T Cook over an open flame.

15. D Clear butter, soup, or other liquid of solid particles.

16. J Cover with a thick, sugary syrup or sauce and (usually) brown under a broiler.

17. C Add a liquid to dissolve the solid particles left in the bottom of a pan after cooking.

18. R Work dough by hand.

19. W Soak in a pungent or tenderizing solution.

20. c Cook submerged in fat or oil.

21. E Cook in a pan with a small amount of fat or oil.

22. a Use a combination of dry and moist cooking methods.

23. X Cook without fat or oil under a heat source.

24. K Cook with little or no fat on a polished metal surface.

25. E Cook in a pan with a small amount of fat or oil.

26. O Cook in liquid at a temperature at which slow bubbling occurs.

27. I Cook in liquid at a high temperature.

28. G Cook in hot air.

29. V Cook with moist heat with the product not submerged in liquid.

30. M Cook (usually a protein product) gently in hot liquid.

EQUIPMENT AND SAFETY

---

31. E **Practicing preventive maintenance.** The best way to maintain equipment is to not have it break down at all. This means keeping it clean and lubricated. It also means staying ahead of problems by replacing seals, keeping screws tight, and so forth.

---

32. **C** **How will it improve guest satisfaction?** While all of the possible answers bear on an equipment decision, the primary consideration has to be its impact on making your guests happy, since that is job #1 in a restaurant.

33. **E** **All of the above.** Cleaning equipment involves safety considerations as well as the simple removal of dirt and grease. It is also appropriate to be sure the job is done to the supervisor's satisfaction before considering the task completed.

34. **A** **Stop using the machine and tell the supervisor or manager immediately.** A dish machine that is not functioning properly is a major health department violation, since it means that dishes are not being properly cleaned and sanitized. If you do not have sufficient clean serviceware to carry you over until the machine can be fixed, you must either switch to disposable ware or stop serving.

35. **D** **Wait for the solution to work.** The liquid and chemical action of the cleaner will loosen and dissolve the dirt if you give it a chance. Allowing your cleaning solution to work will speed cleaning and reduce damage to equipment and facilities caused by hard scrubbing.

36. **C** **Clutter and junk.** Junk makes every job harder and makes cleaning take forever. An empty shelf can be quickly wiped clean. A shelf piled with chipped china, mismatched glassware, and broken kitchen utensils will never be cleaned.

37. **A** **A fry cook juggling ice cubes at his work station, out of guests' sight.** The reason you stop this practice immediately is that should an ice cube fall into the fryer, it will instantly vaporize. Essentially, it explodes, throwing hot oil all over the cook and the kitchen.

38. **D** **Holding the burned area under cool water.** A burn is an overload of heat on body tissue. The logical cure is to remove the excess heat. Neither butter nor warm water can accomplish this. Ice will remove heat, but is eliminated as a correct answer because it can permanently damage tender tissue.

39. **A** **The floor.** Primarily because it is taken for granted, the floor causes more lost-time accidents through falls than any of the other choices.

40. **D** **Placing wet-floor signs where the floor goes from dry to wet.** This ties in with the previous question. Wet-floor signs put others on notice that footing could be slippery and reminds them to walk with caution.

SANITATION

41. **C** **Cooling a cooked food product in the walk-in.** All of the other choices are activities conducted under close observation by the kitchen staff. Because cooling takes place out of sight, food can remain out of temperature the longest, and food out of temperature is the primary cause of foodborne illness.

42. **A** **Exclude her from all food-handling responsibilities until the cut heals.** This is the most correct choice of those offered. In practice, covering the wound with a surgical glove and having the staff member work out of sight of guests is a more likely solution. The important thing is that you never risk the wound or its bandage coming in contact with food.

43. **C** **On the upper front, by the door.** The secondary thermometer should be placed in the warmest part of the refrigerator. Most state health codes require all refrigerators and freezers to have a secondary thermometer easily visible when the door is opened.

44. **C** **140°F.** Previously prepared food must be reheated to at least 165°F before serving, but can be held at 140°F. However, it is preferable to hold food at 165°F or higher to be sure it is perceived as hot when it reaches the table.

45. **C** **160°F.** A lower temperature will not permit proper cleaning action, while a higher temperature will actually cook food onto the plates.

46. **B** **120°F.** This is the service temperature of a legal hot-water system. In a low-temp dish machine, sanitizing is accomplished by a chemical additive in the final rinse water, not by the water temperature.

47. **D** **180°F.** If the temperature is lower, it will not properly sanitize serviceware. If it is higher (particularly at high altitudes), the water will start to turn to steam and will not completely remove detergent residues from the serviceware.

48. **E** **Keeping wipe cloths in sanitizing solution.** This is the only practice on the list that is not a health department violation.

49. B **A small pocket thermometer used to check food temperatures.** Every member of the food preparation staff and every attendant on a cafeteria line or salad bar should have a product thermometer to monitor food temperatures.

50. D **Organic vegetables.** Most health codes require that all food served to the public must be from an approved source, eliminating produce grown by a stranger. Once unwrapped products have been served, they cannot be reused, striking out the rolls as a possibility. Most local codes stipulate that food served to the public must be prepared in an inspected and approved kitchen, so truly "homemade" products are illegal. Organic vegetables from an approved source are fine.

51. B **2 hours.** While the less time food remains in the "danger zone" the better, the goal is to bring cooked foods to below 45°F within two hours. Four hours is the maximum total time an item can be out of temperature, and "As soon as possible" does not address the question of time and so is not a proper answer.

52. D **Canned tuna.** Botulism is an anaerobic bacteria, meaning that it thrives in the absence of air. Canned tuna is the only choice in which the bacteria would find this condition.

53. B **Salmonella.** Poultry products should be washed as soon as they are received, and certainly before they are prepared, to reduce the possibility of passing salmonella infection to the guests.

54. B **4 hours.** This means the total time out of temperature in the product's life cycle—including at the purveyor's facilities, in the delivery truck, and on various loading docks.

55. E **Botulism.**

56. C **At least once an hour.** The effectiveness of sanitizing solution decreases over time and with use. To be safe, solutions should be tested at least once an hour.

57. C **Dip a test strip in the solution and compare it with a scale.** Typical sanitizers are usually either quaternary ammonia or chlorine bleach, and each type requires a different test strip. There is no such thing as a universal test kit.

58. B **It can be toxic.** For the sake of illustration, consider the effect of using undiluted bleach to wipe down a cutting board. The *only* way to be sure you have a proper concentration is to measure the sanitizer into a known amount of water *and* verify the concentration with a test strip.

59. D **It won't work as well, if at all.** The comments about question 58 apply.

60. E **Staphylococcus toxins cannot be killed.** Toxins are poisons created by staph bacteria under proper conditions of heat, moisture, and time. While heat will kill the bacteria, it will not kill the poisons once they have grown.

HUMAN RELATIONS

61. E **Staff development.** All of the factors are elements that an effective supervisor would do better on than an unskilled one. Still, the distinguishing factor of great supervisors is their ability to teach and bring out the best in those who work with and for them.

62. D **On-the-job instruction.** Anything that involves developing physical skills can only be effectively learned by doing.

63. D **A skilled co-worker.** The worker is always closer to the job and therefore knows more about its current intricacies than even the most experienced supervisor. Involving the staff in training is also an excellent way to eliminate the "them against us" mentality in a foodservice operation.

64. A **Appreciation for the work they do.** When you ask most managers this question, the majority usually answer that their crew is looking for the money. When you ask hourly staff, money takes fifth place. If you want to lower turnover, it helps to know what your staff wants.

65. E **They are no different from anyone else.** Beware of generalizations about any group of people. Remember that somewhere in the world, *you* are a minority!

66. B **With the management of the restaurant.** Remember that people stay or go because they want to. The more unpleasant the working atmosphere, the less time people will want to spend in your organization.

67. A **Set a personal example that reflects everything you expect of your staff.** What they see is what you will get. Anything else is wasted effort.

68. D **Teach your subordinates how to do your job.** When you teach your crew to do your job, they get excited by the opportunity to improve their skills. As you eliminate tasks from your workload, you have more time to develop new skills yourself.

69. B **Send him home to get a clean uniform before allowing him to go on the clock.** A legendary restaurant has clear standards that are never compromised. Failure to enforce your standards is the same as having no standards at all.

70. B **Send her home to get a clean uniform before allowing her to go on the clock.** This situation is no different from the one in question 69. It will certainly make everyone's job a little harder for a while, but it will deliver a clear message to all that you mean what you say. In my experience, people do not resent tough standards as much as they dislike inconsistent enforcement.

FINANCIAL

71. A **Pass.** One of the keys to foodservice profitability is maintaining minimal inventories and turning them frequently. There is no deal good enough (and no storeroom big enough) to warrant tying up excess money and space for products that do not move.

72. D **38.9%.** Food sales were $46,800 ($66,500 total sales less $4,100 sales tax less $15,600 beverage sales). The cost of food consumed was $16,800 in purchases plus $1,400 worth of food consumed from inventory ($5,400 opening value less $4,000 closing value), for a total of $18,200. Food consumed divided by food sales equals food cost percentage—for this example, 38.9%.

73. C **2 cups.** There are 16 tablespoons in a cup. The expanded recipe requires 33 tablespoons of flour, which is approximately 2 cups.

74. E **None of the above.** Salt does not increase or decrease proportionately with the recipe. The proper amount of salt has to be determined by taste.

75. C **8 ounces.** The meat ingredient of the recipe is 2½ pounds and yields 5 servings. Converting the meat portion to ounces (2½ times 16 ounces per pound) equals 40 ounces. This result, divided by 5 servings, gives a portion size of 8 ounces.

76. C **$1.82.** Applicants should be able to figure this out without conversion tables. For the recipe as listed, the meat cost is $8.25 (2½ × $2.75); the flour costs a penny; salt and pepper costs are negligible; paprika adds 7.5¢ (1 tablespoon of paprika equals ⅜ ounce); and butter cost is about 6¢ (1 pound equals 2 cups). The tomato puree portion is 27¢ (a #10 can contains 12–13 cups, 6 cans per case), and the beef stock adds an additional 41.5¢ (12 cans per case at 49 ounces each). The total cost to produce the recipe is approximately $9.08, or $1.82 per portion.

77. B **36.0%.** Food cost is only the edible portion of the meal, in this case $2.50. Dividing the cost by the selling price of $6.95 gives a food cost percentage of 36.0%.

78. D **$5.50.** Gross margin is the dollar difference between the sales price and the cost.

79. E **Over $85,000.** There is a slight trick in this question to prove a point. Each person you lose will cost you $3,600 over 5 years (3 visits per month times $20 per visit times 60 months). For the party of 4, the loss is $14,400. The trick is that the typical dissatisfied guest will tell 8 to 10 other people, and 1 in 5 will tell 20 others. And the people who hear the horror story are also unlikely to come to your restaurant. If each of the 4 original guests only told 5 others, it would mean 20 more lost guests. At $3,600 each, this represents another $72,000 in lost business. The total cost to you is already $86,400!

80. B **Sliced salmon.** The whole salmon works out to $11.11 per pound ($100 cost divided by 12 pounds divided by the 75% yield). While this is 44¢ per pound less than the sliced product, the labor involved in slicing whole salmon offsets the lower product cost. If you use 50 pounds of salmon a week, that will mean slicing over 5½ whole salmon. The total cost differential is $22.00 (50 pounds times 44¢ per pound) or about $4.00 per salmon. If you can slice salmon accurately for less than $4.00 per fish, you can work for me anytime!

OPERATIONS

81. C **Using food supplies in the order they were received.** This is an important part of kitchen management because it helps ensure that fresh product will always be served to the guests. If items are not properly rotated, older products can easily deteriorate to a point where they must be discarded.

82. A **The purchase order.** The purchase order tells you what was ordered, while the purveyor's invoice only tells you what the driver has on the truck. Using a purchase order for receiving will alert you if an item you wanted is *not* in the shipment.

83. B **The quality of the meat.** The carcass roll identifies the plant where the meat was processed, but the USDA grade (prime, choice, etc.) deals only with meat quality.

84. C **Specification sheet.** The spec sheet is the purchasing blueprint for the food items used in the restaurant.

85. B **It helps avoid over- or underproduction.** Forecasting is simply an educated guess as to how much of every product you think you will sell on a given day. Forecasting also provides a basis for ordering. While the forecast seldom exactly equals demand, it is much closer than just preparing (or ordering) based on the whim of the kitchen manager.

86. E **There is not enough information to answer the question.** An item with a portion cost of 82¢ has to sell at $2.41 to have a 34% cost. I doubt that you will price a menu item at $2.41. In the real world, there are a number of factors that determine selling price, including what the item typically sells for in your market, the price points of the rest of your menu, and the presentation. Without knowing the impact of these other factors, you don't have enough information to answer the question.

87. C **Properly adjusted cooking equipment.** Keeping cooking equipment properly calibrated is a factor in food quality but not *necessarily* an element of portion control. All of the other choices combine to permit an operator to consistently know (and control) the cost of each portion served.

88. E **Accompany the official on the inspection.** The health department, fire department, and OSHA, among others, all have a need (and the right!) to see what you are doing. Your best approach is just to accept official inspections as a fact of life, like gravity. When inspectors arrive unannounced, as they usually will, accompany them on their tour and listen to what they have to say. Ask for their suggestions as to how best to remedy the problems they find. They can make your life miserable if you get defensive, and they can often be among your best allies if you meet them halfway.

89. E **How much usable food is contained in a purchased quantity.** An example of a yield analysis is carving a 20-pound turkey and weighing the amount of servable meat.

90. A **Check portion control procedures.** This question will give you an idea of how the applicant responds to problems. Someone whose solution is to check portion control is likely a person with a positive, action-oriented response to problems. In contrast, someone who would first check for theft may be the sort who expects the worst of people (and probably gets it!). Changing the menu might be an option, but not before determining that portion control is not lax.

91. E **Concentrate on increasing productivity.** The general comments about question 90 apply here. The most positive response is to assume that productivity is too low rather than that labor cost is too high! All other responses might address the symptoms but not the underlying problem.

92. E **None of the above.** There is seldom a single cause of a problem, and it is dangerous to jump to conclusions.

93. A **Expect the best from your staff and create an environment in which they won't want to steal.** This is the only effective way to control theft because it addresses the cause of the problem from the perspective of a coach rather than that of a cop. This is not to minimize the need for control systems and due diligence. Just don't make a career of it or you will stifle creativity and foster the very behavior you are trying to eliminate.

94. A **A bill.** The company is obligated to pay the amount of the invoice. Whenever someone on the staff signs an invoice, they are effectively signing a check.

95. D **Cooking foods in large quantities.** Larger quantities take less energy per portion to prepare. While energy conservation is always a worthwhile pursuit, be careful not to prepare larger quantities than you can use in a timely manner.

96. B **To ensure a high level of guest service.** Guest service is the reason the operation exists and the only reason you have staff in the first place! If you want to minimize hours, fire everybody!

97. **D** **Arrange for immediate treatment under your Worker's Compensation policy.** Your first priority is always getting treatment for the injured worker. Paperwork comes later. Generally, personal insurance will not pay for on-the-job injuries.

98. **D** **Notify the driver of the discrepancy and change the strip loin quantity to 11 cases yourself.** Remember that the invoice is a bill and the amount must be correct. Pay for what you get, and don't trust anyone else to make corrections after the fact.

99. **D** **Notify the driver of the discrepancy and change the strip loin quantity to 13 cases yourself.** It has to work both ways. Honest business requires that you pay for what you get and that the company gets everything it pays for.

100. **C** **Conducting cross-training for all staff members.** The more your staff understands about the demands of each other's jobs, the more supportive the work environment will become. Nothing serves to create this awareness more than actually doing some of the work.

101. **C** **The dining room staff.** Since the restaurant exists to please the guests and the dining room staff is the principal point of guest contact, it stands to reason that the role of the kitchen is to support the dining room staff.

102. **E** **Fix or replace the item without comment.** Remember that you work for the server in creating guest delight. If a guest has a problem, take care of it and don't waste a lot of energy being righteous.

103. **D** **You will be pleased to prepare the item as requested.** Since the restaurant exists to please the guest, there is really little question. Besides, it will be faster and involve less work for you if you just do it than if you get into a hassle about it.

104. **E** **You can't assume anything when an item is returned.** There are thousands of reasons why an item might be returned. Consider it an opportunity to give an extra level of service, fix it, and discuss the probable causes later. This is not to suggest that patterns of problems should not be identified and solved.

105. **D** **Talk to your staff.** In 25 years of consulting, I have yet to run into an operating problem that couldn't be precisely identified by the staff. They may not know how to fix it, but they always know what is making their jobs difficult.

106. **B** **Complaints are special gifts.** Only 1 person in 25 will actually tell you when he has a complaint. The rest will simply go away, never return, and tell their friends to stay away, too. When you get a complaint, it is a rare insight into what may be killing your business. Accept the information with gratitude and fix the problem immediately.

107. **D** **That you will be pleased to prepare the item (and immediately send someone to the supermarket).** Legendary service comes from going beyond what is convenient for the operator and doing whatever it takes to delight the guest.

108. **E** **Under 5%.** According to statistical studies by the National Restaurant Association, the typical full-service restaurant earns a median pretax profit of 3.5% to 4.0% of sales.

109. **B** **The number of guests served.**

110. **A** **Chef's Salad.** The labor involved in preparing a chef's salad is significantly more than that for any of the other choices.

FOOD PREP

111. **D** **Béarnaise.** A "mother sauce" is the base from which other sauces are made. Béarnaise is a derivation of hollandaise sauce.

112. **D** **A mixture of butter and flour.** A roux is cooked and used as a thickening agent for certain sauces.

113. **C** **A bag of spices.** The bouquet garni is typically a cheesecloth sack containing spices. It is removed once the item has finished cooking.

114. **E** **Cornstarch.** While all the choices are agents used for thickening, cornstarch is particularly common in desserts because it gives body to such items as pie fillings, preventing them from running onto the plate when the pie is portioned.

115. **B** **Soft, pliable flesh.** All of the other choices are characteristics of fresh fish.

116. **C** **Oranges.** Under refrigeration, bananas will turn brown, unripe avocados will not ripen, and potatoes and yellow onions will rot.

117. C **Drop in a potato.** The potato will absorb the extra salt and should be removed when the desired effect has been achieved.

118. C **2 pounds of raw broccoli.** AP stands for "As Purchased."

119. A **2 pounds of cleaned spinach leaves.** EP stands for "Edible Portion."

120. B **120°F.** The roast will be cooked medium when its internal temperature reaches 140°F. A roast this size will experience an internal temperature rise of from 15 to 25 degrees after it is removed from the oven.

121. A **At 325°F for 2½ hours.** Low and slow will provide the least shrinkage (highest yield).

122. C **Throw the sauce out and make new product for lunch.** Hollandaise cannot be safely reheated and is extremely hazardous if held too long. Make Hollandaise in small batches as needed.

123. D **Water.**

124. E **Milk.**

125. C **Court bouillon.** Court bouillon is another name for fish stock.

126. A **Throw the sauce out and start again.** A scorched taste will permeate the sauce and cannot be removed. Whatever money you hope to save by salvaging the sauce is nothing compared to the money you stand to lose by disappointing guests who may never return.

127. E **Hollandaise.** The ingredients are so potentially hazardous that reheating is dangerous.

128. E **The range.** This is the only piece of equipment that can bring five gallons of thick chowder from 45°F to 165°F within a short period of time.

129. D **Egg noodles.** The texture of the noodles will suffer most from overcooking.

130. B **Lukewarm water.**

131. E **None of the above.**

132. D **Press it with your fingers.** With a little experience, you can tell the degree of doneness by feel.

133. C **The refrigerator.** Hollandaise is made from egg yolks, lemon juice, and butter. Other answers may indicate "chefs" whose knowledge of sauces consists of opening mixes.

134. B **Filet mignon.** This is considered the most naturally tender cut of beef.

135. B **Top sirloin steak.** Ground round is relatively mild, and all the other choices typically require marinades or sauces to impart flavor. In general, the more tender the cut, the less natural flavor it will have.

136. C **Leaving it in the refrigerator.** Thawing food under refrigeration is the safest procedure. Thawing by stirring in an ice bath works, but involves too much time and effort to be practical. Thawing under warm running water or in a tub of standing cold water can be dangerous.

137. B **Enough to just coat the bottom of the pan.** Any more fat than this starts to become frying.

138. E **Taste the product to see if it is still acceptable.** That the bain marie (water bath) has run dry does not automatically mean the product has been damaged. Check out the product quality before proceeding to more involved solutions.

139. C **The sauce to be used on the pasta.** All of the other choices are variables that affect pasta preparation.

140. C **170°F.** The internal temperature of a properly cooked turkey should be 185°F. The internal temperature rise after the turkey is removed from the oven will bring the internal temperature from 170°F to 185°F.

141. E **It will increase 15 to 20 degrees.** Meat continues to cook once it is removed from the oven. The larger the piece of meat, the greater the temperature rise.

142. A **Under water.** This will prevent the oxidation that turns peeled potatoes brown.

143. C **Loosely with parchment.** All items in the refrigerator should be covered. Hot items should be loosely covered to allow the heat to dissipate.

144. C **Tearing the leaves.**

145. B **A 4-inch stainless steel pan filled 1½" full.** Thick products should be cooled in shallow pans. If a number of full 1½-inch pans are stacked on top of each other, the effect is the same as a tall column of product, and the interior of the column will not cool to below 45°F for days! In this case, the best answer is the one that will still provide for proper cooling if the pans are stacked.

146. D **Cool it to 45°F while stirring it in an ice bath.** This is the safest (and fastest) way to cool a hot product. Cooling in the freezer can cause partial thawing of other products. Cooling in the refrigerator takes more time. Allowing the product to cool naturally is dangerous, as the product stays in the danger zone for an unacceptable length of time.

147. C **Save it for soup.** Escarole is a tasty lettucelike product. Getting *some* use from the product is preferable to throwing it out. It cannot be served in salad once it gets rusty, at least not in a legendary restaurant.

148. B **Removing the core with a French knife.** This method will remove more usable product than any of the other choices.

149. D **Keeping the french fries frozen and cooking them in small batches.** Overfilling the baskets will drop the temperature of the oil and slow down the cooking process. Frozen french fries are already blanched. Blanching a raw product speeds up the final cooking time, but the total production time (blanching plus finishing) does not decrease. Turning up the heat will only break the oil down more quickly.

150. B **Fresh pineapple.** It contains an enzyme that prevents gelatin from setting.

Production Situations

1. **You are the Kitchen Manager of a full-service restaurant in the Midwest. It is Super Bowl Sunday, and the restaurant has a big party planned featuring Danish baby back ribs. You are taking the weekend off and come into the restaurant at about 1:15 P.M. on Sunday to pick up a few pounds of ribs for your own Super Bowl party at home. Kickoff for the game is at 4:15, and you are expecting close to 250 guests to start arriving when the restaurant opens at 3:00.**

   When you arrive at the restaurant, there are no ribs to pick up. In fact, there are no Danish baby backs in the house! You find that the sous-chef on duty has been into the beer in the walk-in and is too drunk to cook. Not that there is much to cook today—the sous-chef reluctantly tells you that your rib supplier didn't deliver as scheduled yesterday. Of course, all your purveyors are closed for the weekend.

   Your restaurant is noted for its barbecued chicken, but Danish baby back ribs are not a regular item on your menu. You had been planning to cook them slowly overnight, baste them with your famous barbecue sauce, and finish them off on the charbroiler. However, the big batch of barbecue sauce that your sous-chef had been making for the day is burned on the bottom of the pan because the cook got a little scorched himself! Plus, the hors d'oeuvres he was supposed to be preparing for the party are nowhere to be found.

   The restaurant's General Manager is on vacation. The Assistant Manager is scheduled to arrive at about 2:00, but he lives 30 miles away and is probably already in transit. The rest of your kitchen crew is starting to arrive. It appears that the success or failure of Super Sunday is squarely in your hands!

   A. How would you handle things? What would you do—how and in what order? Please note that suicide or resignation is not an option!

   B. What do you see as the factors that created the problem?

   C. How would you handle things over the next few days? What would you do—how and in what order?

2. **You are the Kitchen Manager of a full-service restaurant. It is a busy Saturday night, and you are in the middle of the rush. The wheel is starting to back up; the pace is getting frantic. Your kitchen crew is yelling at each other trying to get the plates out. At 7:30, you hear a scream and see that your prep cook has nearly severed his right thumb on the slicing machine.**

   A. How would you handle things tonight? What would you do—how and in what order?

   B. What do you see as the factors that created the problem?

   C. How would you handle things over the next few days? What would you do—how and in what order?

Situaciones de Producción

1. Usted es el administrador de cocina de un restaurante con servicio completo en el medio oeste. Es el domingo de "super bowl" y el restaurante tiene una fiesta grande planificada con costillitas a la danesa. Usted se tomó el fin de semana libre y fue al restaurante a eso de la 1:15 PM del domingo a recoger algunas libras de costillitas para su propia fiesta de "super bowl" que usted tendrá en su casa esa tarde. El partido comienza a las 4:15 PM y usted espera que cerca de 250 clientes lleguen cuando el restaurante abra a las 3:00 PM para la fiesta.

   Cuando usted llega al restaurante, no hay costillas que recoger. De hecho, ¡no hay costillitas danesas por ninguin lado! Usted encuentra que el chef de sous de turno ha estado tomando cerveza en el congelador grande y está muy bebido como para cocinar. Como si no hubiera mucho que cocinar hoy—e chef de sous sin la menor gana le dice que su proveedor de costillas no las trajo tal y como estaba programado. Por supuesto, todos sus proveedores están cerrados durante el fin de semana.

   Su restaurante es famoso por su pollo a la barbacoa, pero las costillitas danesas no son un artículo regular en su menú. Usted había planeado cocinarlas lentamente durante toda la noche, cubrirlas con su salsa de barbacoa famosa y acabarlas en la parrilla. La olla de salsa de barbacoa que su chef de sous estaba haciendo ese día está quemada en la parte inferior de la olla debido a que el cocinero se quemó también. Los aperitivos que supuestamente se iban a preparar para la fiesta no están por ninguna parte tampoco.

   El administrador general del restaurante está de vacaciones. El administrador auxiliar está programado para llegar cerca de las 2:00 PM. Vive a 30 millas y está probablemente de camino. El resto de su equipo técnico de cocina está comenzando a llegar. Al parecer, el éxito o fallo de la fiesta de "super bowl" del domingo está en sus manos.

   A. ¿Cómo maneja usted ésto? ¿Qué haría usted, cómo lo haría y en qué orden lo haría? ¡Por favor observe que el suicidio o renunciar no son opciones!

   B. ¿Qué ve usted como los factores que crearon el problema?

   C. ¿Cómo manejaría usted las cosas los días siguientes? ¿Qué haría usted, cómo lo haría y en qué orden lo haría?

2. Usted es el administrador de cocina de un restaurante con servicio completo. Es la noche del sábado, está muy ocupada y usted está en plena hora pique. La rueda se está retrasando. La marcha se está poniendo frenética. Su equipo técnico de cocina está gritando el uno a otro intentando sacar los platos. A las 7:30, usted oye un grito y ve que su cocinero de preparación se ha cortado el dedo pulgar de la mano derecha con la máquina rebanadora.

   A. ¿Cómo manejaría usted las cosas esta noche? ¿Qué hace usted, cómo lo hace y en qué orden lo haría?

   B. ¿Qué ve usted como los factores que crearon el problema?

   C. ¿Cómo manejaría usted las cosas en los días siguientes? ¿Qué haría usted, cómo lo haría y en qué orden?

Situation Test Evaluation

PRODUCTION STAFF

Name: **Position:**

Scoring:

Grade each evaluation criterion as it is observed (Y—Yes, N—No, ?—Maybe).
Give two points for each Y, one point for each ?, and no points for N.
A score of 16 or better means an overall evaluation of Yes.
A score of 10 to 15 means an overall evaluation of Maybe.
A score of 9 or below means an overall evaluation of No.

SITUATION 1:

Y N ?

☐ ☐ ☐ 1. Did the candidate come up with a solution without hesitation?
☐ ☐ ☐ 2. Was it a guest-oriented solution?
☐ ☐ ☐ 3. Would the solution work for the house?
☐ ☐ ☐ 4. Did the candidate take control of the situation?
☐ ☐ ☐ 5. Were the candidate's priorities appropriate?
☐ ☐ ☐ 6. Did the candidate grasp the real causes underlying the situation?
☐ ☐ ☐ 7. Did the candidate take a positive (rather than negative) approach to the situation?
☐ ☐ ☐ 8. Did the candidate accept personal responsibility for the situation?
☐ ☐ ☐ 9. Did the candidate delegate responsibility as part of the solution?
☐ ☐ ☐ 10. Would the candidate's long-term approach be likely to prevent a similar occurrence in the future?

Total Score:

_____

OVERALL EVALUATION:

☐ Yes
☐ No
☐ Maybe

SITUATION 2:

Y N ?

☐ ☐ ☐ 1. Did the candidate come up with a solution without hesitation?
☐ ☐ ☐ 2. Did the candidate put the welfare of the injured worker first?
☐ ☐ ☐ 3. Is the solution likely to retain the good will of the restaurant's patrons?
☐ ☐ ☐ 4. Would the solution work for the house?
☐ ☐ ☐ 5. Did the candidate take control of the situation?
☐ ☐ ☐ 6. Were the candidate's priorities appropriate?
☐ ☐ ☐ 7. Did the candidate grasp the real causes underlying the situation?
☐ ☐ ☐ 8. Did the candidate take a positive (rather than negative) approach to the situation?
☐ ☐ ☐ 9. Did the candidate accept personal responsibility for the situation?
☐ ☐ ☐ 10. Would the candidate's long-term approach be likely to prevent a similar occurrence in the future?

Total Score:

_____

OVERALL EVALUATION:

☐ Yes
☐ No
☐ Maybe

Demonstration Test 2
PRODUCTION STAFF

Name: _____ **Evaluated By:** _____

PREP TEST—PART I
Procedure:

The candidate receives the recipe for an item on your menu that calls for prepreparation and preportioning (such as enchiladas). Under the supervision of a member of the production staff, the candidate prepares the item. This is *not* a timed test.

Materials:

As required by the recipe.

Evaluation Criteria:

Y N ?

□ □ □   1. Did the candidate wash his hands before starting work?
□ □ □   2. Did the candidate follow the recipe correctly (weighed, measured)?
□ □ □   3. Was the work accomplished with a minimum of food waste?
□ □ □   4. Did the candidate demonstrate safe work habits?
□ □ □   5. Did the candidate demonstrate proper sanitation techniques?
□ □ □   6. Was the candidate receptive to direction from the supervisor?
□ □ □   7. Did the candidate converse with the supervisor while working?
□ □ □   8. Did the candidate's actions reflect professional confidence?
□ □ □   9. Did the candidate keep a clean work area while working?
□ □ □ 10. Did the candidate clean the work area when finished?

PREP TEST—PART II
Procedure:

The candidate receives the recipe for the plate presentation of a popular item from your menu that calls for assembly, garnishing, and finishing (such as an enchilada platter). Under the supervision of a member of the production staff, the candidate prepares the item. This is *not* a timed test.

Materials:

As required by the recipe.

Evaluation Criteria:

Y N ?

□ □ □   1. Did the candidate wash his hands before starting work?
□ □ □   2. Did the candidate follow the recipe correctly (weighed, measured)?
□ □ □   3. Was the plate properly and neatly arranged?
□ □ □   4. Was the plate clean and free of spills?
□ □ □   5. Did the candidate demonstrate safe work habits?
□ □ □   6. Did the candidate demonstrate proper sanitation techniques?
□ □ □   7. Was the candidate receptive to direction from the supervisor?
□ □ □   8. Did the candidate converse with the supervisor while working?
□ □ □   9. Did the candidate keep the work area clean while working?
□ □ □ 10. Was the work accomplished with a minimum of wasted motion?

Scoring:

Grade each evaluation criterion as it is observed (Y—Yes, N—No, ?—Maybe).
Give two points for each Y, one point for each ?, and no points for N.
A score of 32 or better means an overall evaluation of Yes.
A score of 20 to 31 means an overall evaluation of Maybe.
A score of 19 or below means an overall evaluation of No.

Total Score:

_____

OVERALL EVALUATION:

☐ Yes
☐ No
☐ Maybe

APPENDIX H

Service Staff Tests

Lifting Test (English)   **H-1**

Demonstration Test 1 (English)   **H-2**

Professional Test Answer Sheet (English)   **H-3**

Professional Test Answer Sheet (Spanish)   **H-4**

Professional Test Answer Sheet Overlay (English)   **H-5**

Professional Test (English)   **H-6**

Professional Test (Spanish)   **H-18**

Professional Test Answers (English)   **H-30**

Service Situations (English)   **H-37**

Service Situations (Spanish)   **H-38**

Situation Test Evaluation—Service (English)   **H-39**

Floor Situations (English)   **H-40**

Floor Situations (Spanish)   **H-41**

Situation Test Evaluation—Floor (English)   **H-42**

Demonstration Test 2 (English)   **H-43**

Lifting Test

SERVICE STAFF

Name: _____ **Evaluated By:** _____

Procedure:

The candidate lifts the heaviest object likely to be encountered on the job from where it would normally be found to the most difficult location at which it could logically be placed. This is *not* a timed test.

Materials:

Select an item that has figured in on-the-job lifting injuries. Consider what tasks the person will typically perform in the position as well as situations likely to be encountered in the normal course of business while assisting co-workers.

Demonstration Specification:

Item to be lifted: _____ Weight: _____

Lift from: _____

Lift to: _____

Evaluation Criteria:

Y N ?

☐ ☐ ☐ 1. Could the candidate lift the object?
☐ ☐ ☐ 2. Did the lift show lack of strain?
☐ ☐ ☐ 3. Did the candidate lift with a straight back?
☐ ☐ ☐ 4. Did the candidate lift with the legs?
☐ ☐ ☐ 5. Did the candidate keep the load close to the body?
☐ ☐ ☐ 6. Did the candidate use a proper ladder or stool (if appropriate)?
☐ ☐ ☐ 7. Was the object safely under control at all times?
☐ ☐ ☐ 8. Was the candidate alert to the physical surroundings during the lift?
☐ ☐ ☐ 9. Did the final placement of the object allow for proper air circulation?
☐ ☐ ☐ 10. Did the candidate handle the object with care and respect?

Scoring:

Grade each evaluation criterion as it is observed (Y—Yes, N—No, ?—Maybe).
Give two points for each Y, one point for each ?, and no points for N.
If use of a ladder or stool was not appropriate, score Item 6 as Y.
If Item 1 is marked N, the overall evaluation must be No.
If Item 1 is marked ?, the overall evaluation must be Maybe.
If Item 2 is marked N or ?, the overall evaluation must be Maybe.
A score of 16 or better means an overall evaluation of Yes.
A score of 10 to 15 means an overall evaluation of Maybe.
A score of 9 or below means an overall evaluation of No.

Total Score:

_____

OVERALL EVALUATION:

☐ Yes
☐ No
☐ Maybe

Demonstration Test 1

SERVICE STAFF

Name: _____ **Evaluated By:** _____

PART I—TRAY TEST
Procedure:

Applicants load and carry a tray through an "obstacle course" set in the dining room. This is *not* a timed test.

Materials:

Table, tray, tray stand, filled water glasses, weighted plates.

Evaluation Criteria:

Y N ?

☐ ☐ ☐   1. Was the tray properly balanced when loaded?
☐ ☐ ☐   2. Were proper ware handling techniques used when loading the tray?
☐ ☐ ☐   3. Was the tray under control at all times?
☐ ☐ ☐   4. Did the candidate demonstrate safe lifting techniques?
☐ ☐ ☐   5. Was the tray carried in a proper position (balanced above the shoulder)?
☐ ☐ ☐   6. Did the candidate have a pleasant facial expression while working?

PART II—TABLE TEST
Procedure:

Applicants visually check a table setting and make required adjustments. This is *not* a timed test.

Situation:

Crooked silverware, china and glassware misplaced, missing pieces, wrinkled napkins, dirty ashtrays, etc. (*Note*: Operators should standardize and document the number and type of discrepancies in this test to ensure fairness.)

Materials:

4-top with standard place settings.

Evaluation Criteria:

Y N ?

☐ ☐ ☐   7. Were all the discrepancies noted?
☐ ☐ ☐   8. Were the discrepancies properly corrected?
☐ ☐ ☐   9. Were the errors corrected quickly?
☐ ☐ ☐ 10. Did the candidate have a pleasant facial expression while working?

Scoring:

Grade each evaluation criterion as it is observed (Y—Yes, N—No, ?—Maybe).
Give two points for each Y, one point for each ?, and no points for N.
A score of 16 or better means an overall evaluation of Yes.
A score of 10 to 15 means an overall evaluation of Maybe.
A score of 9 or below means an overall evaluation of No.

Total Score:

_____

OVERALL EVALUATION:

☐ Yes
☐ No
☐ Maybe

Professional Test

SERVICE STAFF
Answer Sheet

NAME: _____ SSN: _____

This test is designed to indicate how you view the restaurant industry. As a result, you will find that several questions may have more than one correct answer. Check the single answer you think is *MOST CORRECT* based on your point of view. Time is of the essence. The faster you complete the test, the better your index score.

HUMAN REL
A B C D E
1. ☐ ☐ ☐ ☐ ☐
2. ☐ ☐ ☐ ☐ ☐
3. ☐ ☐ ☐ ☐ ☐
4. ☐ ☐ ☐ ☐ ☐
5. ☐ ☐ ☐ ☐ ☐
6. ☐ ☐ ☐ ☐ ☐
7. ☐ ☐ ☐ ☐ ☐
8. ☐ ☐ ☐ ☐ ☐
9. ☐ ☐ ☐ ☐ ☐
10. ☐ ☐ ☐ ☐ ☐

SANITATION
11. ☐ ☐ ☐ ☐ ☐
12. ☐ ☐ ☐ ☐ ☐
13. ☐ ☐ ☐ ☐ ☐
14. ☐ ☐ ☐ ☐ ☐
15. ☐ ☐ ☐ ☐ ☐
16. ☐ ☐ ☐ ☐ ☐
17. ☐ ☐ ☐ ☐ ☐
18. ☐ ☐ ☐ ☐ ☐
19. ☐ ☐ ☐ ☐ ☐
20. ☐ ☐ ☐ ☐ ☐

IMPRESSIONS
21. ☐ ☐ ☐ ☐ ☐
22. ☐ ☐ ☐ ☐ ☐
23. ☐ ☐ ☐ ☐ ☐
24. ☐ ☐ ☐ ☐ ☐
25. ☐ ☐ ☐ ☐ ☐
26. ☐ ☐ ☐ ☐ ☐
27. ☐ ☐ ☐ ☐ ☐
28. ☐ ☐ ☐ ☐ ☐
29. ☐ ☐ ☐ ☐ ☐
30. ☐ ☐ ☐ ☐ ☐

OPERATIONS
A B C D E
31. ☐ ☐ ☐ ☐ ☐
32. ☐ ☐ ☐ ☐ ☐
33. ☐ ☐ ☐ ☐ ☐
34. ☐ ☐ ☐ ☐ ☐
35. ☐ ☐ ☐ ☐ ☐
36. ☐ ☐ ☐ ☐ ☐
37. ☐ ☐ ☐ ☐ ☐
38. ☐ ☐ ☐ ☐ ☐
39. ☐ ☐ ☐ ☐ ☐
40. ☐ ☐ ☐ ☐ ☐
41. ☐ ☐ ☐ ☐ ☐
42. ☐ ☐ ☐ ☐ ☐
43. ☐ ☐ ☐ ☐ ☐
44. ☐ ☐ ☐ ☐ ☐
45. ☐ ☐ ☐ ☐ ☐
46. ☐ ☐ ☐ ☐ ☐
47. ☐ ☐ ☐ ☐ ☐
48. ☐ ☐ ☐ ☐ ☐
49. ☐ ☐ ☐ ☐ ☐
50. ☐ ☐ ☐ ☐ ☐
51. ☐ ☐ ☐ ☐ ☐
52. ☐ ☐ ☐ ☐ ☐
53. ☐ ☐ ☐ ☐ ☐
54. ☐ ☐ ☐ ☐ ☐
55. ☐ ☐ ☐ ☐ ☐
56. ☐ ☐ ☐ ☐ ☐
57. ☐ ☐ ☐ ☐ ☐
58. ☐ ☐ ☐ ☐ ☐
59. ☐ ☐ ☐ ☐ ☐
60. ☐ ☐ ☐ ☐ ☐

ALCOHOL
A B C D E
61. ☐ ☐ ☐ ☐ ☐
62. ☐ ☐ ☐ ☐ ☐
63. ☐ ☐ ☐ ☐ ☐
64. ☐ ☐ ☐ ☐ ☐
65. ☐ ☐ ☐ ☐ ☐
66. ☐ ☐ ☐ ☐ ☐
67. ☐ ☐ ☐ ☐ ☐
68. ☐ ☐ ☐ ☐ ☐
69. ☐ ☐ ☐ ☐ ☐
70. ☐ ☐ ☐ ☐ ☐
T F
71. ☐ ☐
72. ☐ ☐
73. ☐ ☐
74. ☐ ☐
75. ☐ ☐
76. ☐ ☐
77. ☐ ☐
78. ☐ ☐
79. ☐ ☐
80. ☐ ☐

FINANCIAL
81. ☐ ☐ ☐ ☐ ☐
82. ☐ ☐ ☐ ☐ ☐
83. ☐ ☐ ☐ ☐ ☐
84. ☐ ☐ ☐ ☐ ☐
85. ☐ ☐ ☐ ☐ ☐
86. ☐ ☐ ☐ ☐ ☐
87. ☐ ☐ ☐ ☐ ☐
88. ☐ ☐ ☐ ☐ ☐
89. ☐ ☐ ☐ ☐ ☐
90. ☐ ☐ ☐ ☐ ☐

SALES
A B C D E
91. ☐ ☐ ☐ ☐ ☐
92. ☐ ☐ ☐ ☐ ☐
93. ☐ ☐ ☐ ☐ ☐
94. ☐ ☐ ☐ ☐ ☐
95. ☐ ☐ ☐ ☐ ☐
96. ☐ ☐ ☐ ☐ ☐
97. ☐ ☐ ☐ ☐ ☐
98. ☐ ☐ ☐ ☐ ☐
99. ☐ ☐ ☐ ☐ ☐
100. ☐ ☐ ☐ ☐ ☐

FOOD
101. ☐ ☐ ☐ ☐ ☐
102. ☐ ☐ ☐ ☐ ☐
103. ☐ ☐ ☐ ☐ ☐
104. ☐ ☐ ☐ ☐ ☐
105. _____
106. _____
107. _____
108. _____
109. _____
110. _____
111. _____
112. _____
113. _____
114. _____
115. _____
116. _____
117. _____
118. _____
119. _____
120. _____

BEVERAGE
A B C D E
121. ☐ ☐ ☐ ☐ ☐
122. ☐ ☐ ☐ ☐ ☐
123. ☐ ☐ ☐ ☐ ☐
124. ☐ ☐ ☐ ☐ ☐
125. _____
126. _____
127. _____
128. _____
129. _____
130. _____
131. _____
132. _____
133. _____
134. _____
135. _____
136. _____
137. _____
138. _____
139. _____
140. _____
141. _____
142. _____
143. _____
144. _____
145. _____
146. _____
147. _____
148. _____
149. _____
150. _____

FOR OFFICE USE:

HR:___ SAN:___ IMP:___ OPS:___ ALC:___ FIN:___ SALE:___ FOOD:___ BEV:___ TOT:___ TIME:___ INDEX:___

Examen Profesional

EQUIPO TÉCNICO DE SERVICIO

NOMBRE: **NÚMERO DE SEGURIDAD SOCIAL:**

Esta prueba está diseñada para formar una opinión cómo usted ve a la industria de los restaurantes. Por lo tanto, usted encontrará que varias preguntas pueden tener más de una respuesta correcta. Marque la única respuesta que usted crea sea *MÁS CORRECTA* basándolo en su punto de vista personal. El tiempo es esencial. Entre más rápido complete usted la prueba, mejor será su puntuación.

REL HUMANAS — A B C D E
1. – 10.

SANIDAD — A B C D E
11. – 20.

IMPRESIONES — A B C D E
21. – 30.

OPERACIONES — A B C D E
31. – 60.

ALCOHOL — A B C D E
61. – 70.

T F
71. – 80.

FINANZAS — A B C D E
81. – 90.

VENTAS — A B C D E
91. – 100.

COMIDA — A B C D E
101. – 104.
105. – 120. _____

BEBIDAS — A B C D E
121. – 124.
125. – 150. _____

FOR OFFICE USE:

HR:___ SAN:___ IMP:___ OPS:___ ALC:___ FIN:___ SALE:___ FOOD:___ BEV:___ TOT:___ TIME:___ INDEX:___

Professional Test

SERVICE STAFF
ANSWER SHEET OVERLAY

NOTE: To save time when grading the Professional Test, make a copy of this sheet on clear transparency film and lay it over the candidate's completed test. This should enable you to easily note the number of questions marked correctly and incorrectly. You can then simply transfer the score to the blocks on the bottom of the answer sheet. The answer sheet and test are not returned to the applicant, so it is your choice whether to physically mark the answer to a specific question as correct or incorrect.

HUMAN REL

#	Answer
1.	E
2.	D
3.	C
4.	E
5.	C
6.	C
7.	B
8.	D
9.	A
10.	E

SANITATION

#	Answer
11.	E
12.	A
13.	C
14.	E
15.	A
16.	B
17.	C
18.	C
19.	B
20.	D

IMPRESSIONS

#	Answer
21.	D
22.	B
23.	E
24.	D
25.	D
26.	B
27.	D
28.	C
29.	D
30.	C

OPERATIONS

#	Answer
31.	A
32.	A
33.	E
34.	E
35.	A
36.	B
37.	A
38.	E
39.	D
40.	B
41.	C
42.	A
43.	B
44.	B
45.	B
46.	A
47.	A
48.	B
49.	C
50.	A
51.	E
52.	A
53.	D
54.	B
55.	C
56.	D
57.	A
58.	E
59.	C
60.	B

ALCOHOL

#	Answer
61.	C
62.	B
63.	D
64.	B
65.	D
66.	B
67.	A
68.	E
69.	E
70.	B

#	T/F
71.	T
72.	T
73.	T
74.	F
75.	F
76.	F
77.	T
78.	T
79.	F
80.	F

FINANCIAL

#	Answer
81.	E
82.	E
83.	D
84.	C
85.	A
86.	A
87.	C
88.	B
89.	C
90.	A

SALES

#	Answer
91.	A
92.	B
93.	D
94.	E
95.	E
96.	D
97.	C
98.	B
99.	D
100.	B

FOOD

#	Answer
101.	B
102.	A
103.	A
104.	D
105.	M
106.	O
107.	J
108.	H
109.	G
110.	K
111.	I
112.	E
113.	A
114.	N
115.	E
116.	L
117.	B
118.	F
119.	D
120.	C

BEVERAGE

#	Answer
121.	D
122.	B
123.	C
124.	B
125.	F
126.	I
127.	Y
128.	B
129.	U
130.	S
131.	K
132.	P
133.	V
134.	A
135.	X
136.	S
137.	E
138.	T
139.	M
140.	H
141.	Z
142.	D
143.	W
144.	L
145.	N
146.	G
147.	J
148.	O
149.	I
150.	Q

Professional Test

SERVICE STAFF

Pick the *MOST CORRECT* answer and mark your choice on the answer sheet. Please do not write on this test.

HUMAN RELATIONS

1. **What is the best measure of a supervisor's effectiveness?**
   A. Work skills.
   B. Health department scores.
   C. Profitability.
   D. The average check.
   E. Staff development.

2. **Which method of training would you use when showing someone how to clean a piece of equipment?**
   A. Written instructions.
   B. Classroom training.
   C. Role-playing.
   D. On-the-job instruction.
   E. None of the above.

3. **Who do you think makes the most effective trainer for operational subjects?**
   A. An outside consultant.
   B. The general manager.
   C. The department supervisor.
   D. A skilled co-worker.
   E. A company training director.

4. **In your experience, which statement is true about working with minorities?**
   A. They must be treated a little differently from other workers.
   B. They can be more difficult to motivate than other workers.
   C. It is more difficult to know what they really want from you.
   D. They tend to be less productive than other workers.
   E. They are no different from anyone else.

5. **How would you bring out the best in your co-workers?**
   A. Support them in following their job descriptions.
   B. Give them advice on how to do their jobs more effectively.
   C. Report substandard performance to your supervisor.
   D. Set a good personal example.
   E. All of the above.

6. **As a server on the restaurant staff, what is the best way to advance your career?**
   A. Do personal favors for the managers.
   B. Stand out from the competition.
   C. Take classes and attend seminars.
   D. Teach your bussers how to do your job.
   E. Make sure you get the credit when things go well.

7. **When it comes to guest complaints, which statement do you most agree with?**
   A. No news is good news.
   B. Complaints are special gifts.
   C. A satisfaction level of about 90% is realistic for a full-service restaurant.
   D. You can't expect to please all the people all the time.
   E. Some people complain just to get attention.

8. **What can you assume when an order is returned to the kitchen by the guest?**
   A. Someone in the kitchen screwed up the order.
   B. The guest didn't properly understand what the item was when he ordered it.
   C. Something is wrong with the food.
   D. The guest is in a bad mood.
   E. You can't assume anything when an item is returned.

9. **How should you deal with a complaint from an irate guest?**
    A. Apologize and immediately resolve the problem in favor of the guest.
    B. Try to keep the guest from disturbing the dining room.
    C. Analyze market share data to determine if the problem is worth worrying about.
    D. Listen to the problem, explain what caused it, and negotiate a mutually acceptable solution.
    E. Help the guest understand your side of the situation.

10. **When do you think it *not* appropriate to comp all (or part) of a guest's meal?**
    A. The guest had a longer wait than you had led him to expect.
    B. The server was late bringing the salad.
    C. The guest did not care for the entree.
    D. The guests had an argument and decided to leave before finishing their meals.
    E. All of these situations could call for a comp.

SANITATION

11. **Which of the following is a major health department violation?**
    A. Cans without labels in the dry storeroom.
    B. No secondary thermometers in the reach-in refrigerator.
    C. A dirty floor under the salad bar.
    D. A dish machine wash temperature of 160°F.
    E. An unlabeled spray bottle in the service stand.

12. **A member of the staff has an open cut on her hand. How should the supervisor handle it?**
    A. Exclude her from all food-handling responsibilities until the cut heals.
    B. Send her home, without pay, until the cut heals.
    C. Send her home, with pay, until the cut heals.
    D. To avoid upsetting the guests, assign her to a workstation out of sight of the dining room.
    E. File a Worker's Compensation claim.

13. **What is the proper place for a secondary thermometer in a refrigerator?**
    A. In the lower back corner away from the door.
    B. In the middle of the refrigerator.
    C. In the upper front of the refrigerator by the door.
    D. On the back of the door.
    E. A secondary thermometer is not needed if the refrigerator has a built-in thermometer.

14. **Which practice is correct or acceptable?**
    A. Polishing silverware.
    B. Snacking in workstations.
    C. Using a glass to scoop ice.
    D. Thawing covered food on a clean kitchen counter.
    E. Keeping wipe cloths in sanitizing solution.

15. **What is a product thermometer?**
    A. The pop-up indicator in a turkey that tells you when it is done.
    B. A small pocket thermometer used to check food temperatures.
    C. The wall-mounted thermometer that monitors refrigeration temperatures.
    D. The thermostat that controls the temperature in the walk-ins.

16. **Which of the following is the rule of thumb for the maximum total time potentially hazardous food products may be in the "danger zone"?**
    A. 2 hours.
    B. 4 hours.
    C. 6 hours.
    D. 8 hours.
    E. It doesn't matter.

17. **How often should sanitizing solution be checked?**
    A. At the start of each shift.
    B. At least twice each shift.

  C. At least once an hour.
  D. At least once every half hour.
  E. Every time you use it.

18. **How can you tell if the sanitizing solution is at the proper concentration?**
  A. Measure carefully when making new solution.
  B. Use a universal test kit.
  C. Dip a test strip in the solution and compare it with a scale.
  D. Dip a piece of paper towel in the solution and see if it darkens.
  E. Use a product thermometer.

19. **What happens if the sanitizing solution concentration is higher than recommended?**
  A. It will be more effective.
  B. It can be toxic.
  C. It will cost more money, but there is no real problem.
  D. It won't work as well, if at all.
  E. All of the above.

20. **What happens if the sanitizing solution concentration is lower than recommended?**
  A. It will kill bacteria more slowly.
  B. It can be toxic.
  C. It will save some money, and there is no real problem.
  D. It won't work as well, if at all.
  E. All of the above.

FIRST IMPRESSIONS

21. **What is the first thing you would do when a guest walks into the restaurant?**
  A. Find out how many people are in the party.
  B. Ask if they prefer smoking or nonsmoking.
  C. Ask them to wait in the bar.
  D. Smile and welcome them to the restaurant.
  E. Ask them if they have a reservation.

22. **You are at the greeter stand talking on the phone when guests arrive. What do you do?**
  A. It depends on who you are talking to.
  B. Pretend you don't see the new arrivals until you finish your conversation.
  C. Acknowledge the new arrivals with a smile and complete your call promptly.
  D. Point them to a table and bring them menus when you get off the phone.
  E. Hang up the phone immediately.

23. **What *must* you know before you can answer the phone in the restaurant?**
  A. Hours of operation.
  B. Daily specials.
  C. Directions on how to get to the restaurant.
  D. The description of the menu style and price levels.
  E. All of the above.

24. **Your operating hours state that you open at 6:00 AM. A guest knocks on the locked front door early in the morning and your watch says 5:50. What do you do?**
  A. Keep the door locked, show him the time on your watch, and ask him to wait 10 minutes.
  B. Pretend you don't see him.
  C. Let him in and have him wait in the lobby until 6:00.
  D. Invite him in, get him a seat, a menu, and a cup of coffee.
  E. Call the manager.

25. **Your restaurant hours state that you close at 10:00 PM. A party of six arrives at 9:55 and you know it will take at least an hour for them to eat. What do you do?**
  A. Explain that they cannot be served before the restaurant closes and ask them to come back tomorrow.
  B. Seat them and tell them to get their order placed before 10:00.

C. Ask the kitchen crew if they want to serve another party.
D. Seat them and serve them as you have any other guests that evening.
E. Call the manager.

26. **You are the greeter and the restaurant is really busy. Which of the following activities will help the restaurant be most successful?**
    A. Seating waiting guests as soon as a table is cleared.
    B. Making sure that every guest gets your personal attention.
    C. Selling guests drinks while they wait.
    D. Helping the bussers clear and reset tables.

27. **You are showing a party of two to their table on a busy night. As you approach the deuce, they ask if you can seat them at the 4-top in the corner. You know there is no reservation for the larger table. What do you do?**
    A. Explain to them that the restaurant is very busy and seat them at the deuce.
    B. Ask them what is wrong with the deuce.
    C. Tell them you have a reservation for the 4-top and seat them at the deuce.
    D. Seat them at the 4-top.
    E. Call the manager.

28. **It is a busy Friday night and you told the McPherson party to expect a 30-minute wait. Half an hour has almost passed, and now it appears that you will not have a table available for another 10 minutes. What do you do?**
    A. Let it go and call them when their table is ready. Ten minutes is not worth worrying about.
    B. Inform them of the additional wait and apologize.
    C. Inform them of the additional wait and give them something to make up for the inconvenience.
    D. Inform them of the additional wait and explain the reason for the delay.
    E. Call the manager.

29. **It is a busy night and there is a wait. A family comes in with several children in tow and looks obviously disappointed that they cannot be immediately seated. What would you do?**
    A. Call them when their table is ready.
    B. You can't do much because you have to treat everyone the same.
    C. Offer the parents a drink.
    D. Get the children something to play with.
    E. Call the manager.

30. **You are talking on the phone as guests are leaving the restaurant. What do you do?**
    A. Pretend you don't see them and continue with your call.
    B. Smile and wave to them while continuing to talk.
    C. Excuse yourself from the caller and thank them for coming.
    D. Hang up the phone immediately.
    E. Call the manager.

DINING ROOM OPERATIONS

From which side of the guest would you do the following?

31. Serve soup.	A. Left side with the left hand.
32. Serve entrees.	B. Left side with the right hand.
33. Serve beverages.	C. Either side with either hand.
34. Clear plates.	D. Right side with the left hand.
	E. Right side with the right hand.

On which side of the guest would you set the following?

35. Knives.	A. Right side.
36. Forks.	B. Left side.
37. Glasses.	C. Either side.
38. Guest check.	D. Whichever side is most comfortable for you.
	E. Whichever side is most comfortable for the guest.

39. Three guests at a table have finished their main courses while a fourth is still eating. What would you do?
    A. Clear the plates of the three guests who have finished.
    B. Ask guests who have finished if they would like their plates cleared.
    C. Wait until the fourth guest finishes.
    D. Clear the plates of the three guests who have finished, but only if they ask you to do so.
    E. None of the above.

40. When serving wine, which of the following procedures is *incorrect*?
    A. Presenting the bottle label to the person who ordered the wine.
    B. Placing the bottle on the table while cutting the foil.
    C. Pouring a taste for the host's approval before serving the rest of the table.
    D. Filling the ladies' glasses before filling those of the male guests.
    E. Filling wine glasses to the widest point of the glass.

41. When should you change an ashtray at the table?
    A. Whenever there is a cigarette butt in it.
    B. Before serving the main course.
    C. Whenever there are two cigarette butts in it.
    D. After serving cocktails.
    E. Whenever there are more than three cigarette butts in it.

42. What is the proper method for changing an ashtray?
    A. Capping a clean ashtray over the soiled one and removing it from the table.
    B. Removing the soiled ashtray with one hand while putting the clean one on the table with the other hand.
    C. Removing the soiled ashtray from the table, emptying the butts into a bus tub, and replacing it on the table.
    D. Any of the above is acceptable.

43. What items should be left on the table after clearing the main course?
    A. Bread, butter, water glasses, ashtrays, and unused silverware.
    B. Ashtrays and unused silverware.
    C. Water glasses, ashtrays, unfinished drinks, and silverware needed for dessert.
    D. Nothing. The table should be clear.

44. What actions are appropriate on your first trip to the table?
    A. Introducing yourself.
    B. Welcoming the guests to the restaurant.
    C. Unfolding the napkins and placing them in the guests' laps.
    D. Asking the guests if they would like a drink.

45. What is the safest way to pour coffee at the table?
    A. Pour the coffee while holding the cup in your hand or on a tray.
    B. Pour the coffee into the cup without removing the cup from the table.
    C. Have the busperson pour the coffee.
    D. Whichever method above is most convenient for the guest.

46. You have an order up in the kitchen and new guests have just been seated at your station. What do you do?
    A. Pick up the food in the kitchen, serve it, then greet the new guests.
    B. Greet the new guests, excuse yourself, then pick up the food in the kitchen.
    C. Ask your busperson to pick up and serve the order while you greet the new guests.
    D. Ask the manager to greet the guests while you pick up the order.
    E. It depends on the situation.

47. When is it important to indicate seat numbers on the guest check?
    A. When taking the order for drinks, appetizers, entrees, or desserts.
    B. Only when taking the entree order.
    C. Only when you have enough time to do it.
    D. Seat numbers are not necessary if you have an electronic ordering system.

48. Which of the following is proper salad bar procedure?
    A. Keeping food containers topped off with fresh, refrigerated product.
    B. Replacing nearly empty food containers with full ones.
    C. Reusing serving utensils when food containers are refilled.
    D. Allowing guests to refill their salad bowls.
    E. Placing ice on salad greens to keep them cold and crisp.

49. **Although nobody wanted steak sauce when you served the T-bones to a party of businesspeople, someone asks for it when you check back. What do you do?**
   A. Ask what kind of steak sauce.
   B. Bring your full selection of steak sauces.
   C. Ask if the steaks are satisfactory.
   D. Replace the steaks at once.
   E. Call the manager.

50. **What is the most important thing in handling the rush effectively?**
   A. Planning ahead and being sure adequate stocks are in place.
   B. Hiring extra staff.
   C. Scheduling only your best workers to work during the rush.
   D. Seating people only as fast as you can serve them.
   E. All of the above.

51. **What does courtesy mean?**
   A. Liking people.
   B. Smiling and being polite.
   C. Being respectful to your guests.
   D. Making people aware that you like them.
   E. All of the above.

52. **A guest asks you for directions to the restrooms. Which of the following should you *not* do?**
   A. Point them toward the restrooms.
   B. Explain to them how to find the restrooms.
   C. Take them to the restrooms yourself.
   D. Any of the above is acceptable.

53. **What is salmonella?**
   A. An Italian pasta dish made with salmon.
   B. A full-bodied red wine.
   C. A baby salmon, usually served whole.
   D. A type of foodborne illness.

54. **A party of four has a lunch tab totaling $34.50. They give you two twenty-dollar bills in payment. What change do you bring back?**
   A. Two quarters and a five-dollar bill.
   B. Two quarters and five ones.
   C. Five dimes, a one-dollar bill, and a five-dollar bill.
   D. None, because the change is about what they should leave for a tip.

55. **You believe you have given excellent service to a party of three. After they leave, you notice that the credit card slip has been signed, but no tip has been added, and the slip has not been totaled. What do you do?**
   A. Add 15% to the credit card slip and total it.
   B. Try to catch the guests before they drive away.
   C. Submit the slip as is.
   D. Check the table for a cash tip.
   E. Call the manager.

Match the following terms with their proper definitions:

56. **American service.**   A. Food is brought on platters and served at the table.
57. **Russian service.**   B. Guests help themselves from a long table or tables filled with food.
58. **Banquet service.**   C. Food is brought in bowls and on platters, and guests help themselves at the table.
59. **Family service.**   D. Food is portioned in the kitchen and brought out to guests on plates.
60. **Buffet service.**   E. There is no such term.

ALCOHOL SERVICE

61. **Which of the following foods is most effective for *slowing* the rate of alcohol absorption?**
   A. Popcorn.
   B. Candy.

C. Cheese.
D. Black coffee.
E. All are equally effective.

62. **Which of the following *increases* the rate of alcohol absorption in the body?**
   A. Water.
   B. Carbonated beverages.
   C. Protein foods.
   D. Sweets.
   E. None of the above.

63. **Which of the following is typically *not* considered a valid form of ID?**
   A. A birth certificate.
   B. A driver's license.
   C. An alien registration card.
   D. A Social Security card.
   E. All are valid for identification.

64. **Which of the following statements accurately describes the law?**
   A. It is legal to serve alcohol to intoxicated persons if they are not going to be driving.
   B. It is illegal to serve alcohol to intoxicated persons.
   C. It is illegal to serve more than three drinks per hour to a person.
   D. It is legal for a minor to drink if her parents purchase the alcoholic beverage.
   E. All of the above are accurate statements.

65. **You should stop alcohol service to a person exhibiting which of the following behaviors?**
   A. Flirting.
   B. Losing inhibitions.
   C. Being a nuisance.
   D. Spilling drinks.
   E. Being unusually quiet.

66. **Which of the following is *not* an equivalent drink to the others when considering alcohol content?**
   A. 12 ounces of beer.
   B. 8 ounces of wine.
   C. 1¼ ounces of 80 proof liquor.
   D. All are equal in alcohol content.

67. **A guest has definitely had too much to drink and is about to leave the restaurant. You approach him to offer a taxi home. He declines your offer and insists he is going to drive. What do you do?**
   A. Ask him to be careful and allow him to drive.
   B. If he gets into his car, call the police.
   C. Grab his keys and keep them.
   D. Continue to press your case.
   E. Call the owner.

68. **A woman has definitely had too much to drink and wants another glass of wine. She swears she is not driving, a statement that is confirmed by her boyfriend. He is not drunk, and assures you that he is driving her home and will see that she gets there safely. He asks you to bring the wine. What do you do?**
   A. Bring the drink as requested.
   B. Call the police.
   C. Call the owner.
   D. Refuse to serve the drink.
   E. Suggest nonalcoholic alternatives.

69. **A group of young people comes into the restaurant and orders alcoholic beverages. When you ask for proof of age, they tell you they have no IDs with them. They assure you they are over 21 years old. This is verified by an older guest who has overheard the conversation and whom you recognize as an off-duty police officer. What do you do?**
   A. Bring the drinks.
   B. Call the police department to confirm the identity of the older guest.
   C. Call the owner.
   D. Refuse to serve the drinks.
   E. Suggest nonalcoholic alternatives.

70. Which of the following practices will *not* help avoid overconsumption?
  A. Serving one drink at a time.
  B. Making guests come to the bar to order.
  C. Serving rounds when most glasses are empty.
  D. Removing empty glasses from the table before serving a new round.
  E. Putting water on the table.

Please answer the following questions TRUE or FALSE.

71. You may be held personally liable for the actions of intoxicated guests.
72. The use of cocaine or marijuana in conjunction with alcohol will intensify its effect.
73. A driver registering a .8% BAC is considered driving while impaired.
74. If an out-of-state person is of legal age to drink in their home state, they can drink in your restaurant.
75. High altitude lessens the effect of alcohol.
76. Alcohol is a depressant that decreases appetite.
77. A person with a higher percentage of fat will absorb alcohol faster than a more muscular person.
78. The body processes alcohol at the rate of one drink per hour, regardless of size.
79. When discontinuing service to an intoxicated guest, a hand on the shoulder will help keep them calm.
80. A breathalizer measures the amount of alcohol in the blood.

FINANCIAL

81. Let's say you *really* blow it with a typical party of four. Let's also say that the typical guest in your restaurant normally dines with you three times a month and that your average check is $20. What is this error likely to cost the company in lost business over the next five years?
  A. Under $4,000.
  B. $10,000 to $12,000.
  C. $25,000 to $30,000.
  D. $50,000 to $60,000.
  E. Over $85,000.

82. What portion of a typical restaurant's sales is pretax income?
  A. 40 to 45%.
  B. 30 to 35%.
  C. 20 to 25%.
  D. 10 to 15%.
  E. Under 5%.

83. Your food and beverage sales totaled $500 during your shift. You had a total of 20 guest checks representing meals served to 50 people. There were 25 seats in your station. What was your average check for this shift?
  A. $500.
  B. $25.
  C. $20.
  D. $10.
  E. There is not enough information to answer this question.

84. You are a server in a high-volume restaurant. You customarily give your busperson 15% of the tips you receive. Your tips for the shift were $150. After taking care of your busperson, how much tip money will you take home?
  A. $100.00.
  B. $115.00.
  C. $127.50.
  D. $135.00.
  E. $150.00.

85. Simply stated, what is an invoice?
  A. A bill.
  B. A purchase order.
  C. A sales history.

D. A statement of account.

E. A production forecast.

86. **You are filling in for the dining room manager. A chemical salesman has just offered you a deal: 20% off on orders of over three cases of carpet shampoo if you place the order today. You normally go through a case of carpet shampoo in three months. What do you do?**

A. Pass.

B. Buy over three cases and save the restaurant some money.

C. Buy over three cases and clean the carpets more frequently.

D. Buy over three cases and resell part of the stock at a profit.

87. **Your restaurant is having a contest to find a new lunch special. In order to be eligible, an item has to be able to sell for $6 with a food cost of 30% or less. What is the highest portion cost your entry could have?**

A. $3.20.

B. $2.40.

C. $1.80.

D. $1.20.

The following items are included on your restaurant's lunch menu:

Hamburger	4.25	Chef's salad	5.25	Soft drinks	.95
w/cheese add:	.75	Bowl of chili	3.95	Iced tea	.75
Turkey sandwich	4.95	Spaghetti w/sauce	4.50	Coffee	.50
Chicken enchiladas	5.95	Veal Parmigiana	5.75	Apple pie	1.95
Roast beef platter	6.95	French fries	1.25	w/ice cream add:	.95

88. **A table orders a cheeseburger, two bowls of chili, an order of fries, enchiladas, two iced teas, a cup of coffee, and apple pie. What is the amount of the check before sales tax?**

A. $22.20.

B. $24.05.

C. $25.00.

D. $26.25.

E. None of the above.

89. **A table of four orders roast beef, veal Parmigiana, a chef's salad, and spaghetti. They also order an iced tea and two coffees. If they leave a 15% tip based on the pretax total, how much are you likely to get?**

A. $2.50.

B. $3.15.

C. $3.50.

D. $4.25.

E. None of the above.

90. **A group of teenagers has only $10.25 between them. They get two orders of fries and 3 cokes. They are still hungry and want one more thing to eat. Disregarding sales tax, what item do you suggest?**

A. A hamburger.

B. A cheeseburger.

C. A turkey sandwich.

D. Ice cream a la mode.

E. French fries.

SALES

You are a server in a full-service restaurant. You have not been suggesting menu items to your guests. The menu includes the following items:

Dessert	$ 3.00
Bottle of wine (for 4)	$10.00
Side dishes	$ 2.00
Coffee, after-dinner drinks	$ 1.50

91. **Based on these average prices, how much potential revenue are you losing from a table of four?**
    A. $36.
    B. $44.
    C. $52.
    D. $76.

92. **Based on a 15% gratuity, how much in tips are you potentially losing on this 4-top?**
    A. $3.90.
    B. $5.40.
    C. $6.60.
    D. $11.40.

93. **To maximize the restaurant's profit, which one of the following items would you sell?**
    A. An enchilada plate selling for $6.95 with a 20% food cost.
    B. A chicken sandwich selling for $4.95 with a 32% food cost.
    C. A fried catfish platter selling for $8.95 with a 38% food cost.
    D. A steak dinner selling for $12.95 with a 50% food cost.

94. **What practices will increase your sales?**
    A. Suggesting items that you like.
    B. Being able to describe what is in each dish and how it is prepared.
    C. Making it a point to mention certain specific selections your restaurant offers.
    D. Knowing which wines go with each main course.
    E. All of the above.

95. **Which of the following questions will best help sell alcoholic beverages effectively?**
    A. "May I bring you a cocktail?"
    B. "Would you like to see the liquor menu?"
    C. "What kind of cocktail can I bring you?"
    D. "Are you ready to order?"
    E. "Have you ever tried our famous rum punch?"

96. **Which of the following would you suggest to a guest who has ordered a Chocolate Mousse?**
    A. A glass of Cabernet Sauvignon.
    B. An Irish coffee.
    C. Grand Marnier on the rocks.
    D. Espresso.
    E. Any of these go well with Chocolate Mousse.

97. **Which of the following wines would you suggest to a guest ordering prime rib?**
    A. Port.
    B. Gewürtztraminer.
    C. Pinot Noir.
    D. French Sauterne.
    E. Cream sherry.

98. **How does suggestive selling *most* help the restaurant?**
    A. By increasing sales.
    B. By increasing guest satisfaction.
    C. By increasing the server's tips.
    D. By reducing food cost.
    E. All of the above.

99. **A party of two has been waiting in the bar for 45 minutes. Upon finishing their cocktails at the table, they order a bottle of wine. When should you suggest a second bottle of wine to them?**
    A. When the first one is one-third full.
    B. When you empty the first one.
    C. After clearing the entree plates.
    D. I would not suggest a second bottle of wine.

100. **You are a vegetarian. A guest asks if you would recommend the Beef Wellington. What is the best thing to tell them?**
    A. "I don't eat meat, so I really don't know."
    B. "We sell a lot of Beef Wellington."

C. "It's really nice."
D. "My friends who eat meat tell me it's very good."
E. "It's filet mignon covered with pate and cooked in pastry."

FOOD KNOWLEDGE

101. Which cut of meat would you expect to be most tender?
A. Top sirloin steak.
B. Filet mignon.
C. Flank steak.
D. T-bone steak.
E. New York strip.

102. Which cut of meat would you expect to have the most flavor?
A. Veal chop.
B. Top sirloin steak.
C. Filet mignon.
D. Ground round.
E. Flank steak.

103. Which of the following colors would you expect to find if you cut open a medium-rare filet mignon?
A. Brown.
B. Red.
C. Purple.
D. Pink.

104. How would you expect a poached salmon to be cooked?
A. Over (or under) a direct flame.
B. Sautéed in a pan with butter.
C. Wrapped in parchment and baked in the oven.
D. Simmered in a liquid.
E. Steamed with herbs.

Match the following foods with their proper definitions.

105. Burrito	A. A salad using romaine leaves
106. Fettuccine	B. Meatless tomato sauce
107. Seviche	C. A stuffed corn tortilla in sauce
108. Hollandaise	D. A sauce of vinegar and oil
109. Cocktail sauce	E. A preparation using shrimp
110. Linguini	F. With spinach
111. Escargot	G. Chili sauce and horseradish
112. Scampi	H. A sauce served on Eggs Benedict
113. Caesar	I. Snails, usually cooked in garlic butter
114. Béarnaise	J. Marinated seafood
115. Prawns	K. Pasta noodles approximately ⅛-inch wide
116. Salsa	L. Chopped tomatoes, onions, and chilies
117. Marinara	M. A stuffed flour tortilla
118. Florentine	N. A sauce served on steak
119. Vinaigrette	O. Pasta noodles approximately ¼-inch wide
120. Enchilada	P. This is not a food item

BEVERAGE KNOWLEDGE

121. What are the ingredients in a Margarita?
A. Rum, triple sec, lime juice.
B. Tequila, grenadine, orange juice.

    C. Vodka, lime juice, club soda.

    D. Tequila, triple sec, lime juice.

    E. Whiskey, lemon juice, sugar.

122. If a guest ordered Dewar's "neat," how would you expect to serve it?

    A. On the rocks.

    B. In a shot glass.

    C. With water.

    D. With club soda.

    E. With a twist.

123. Which of the following brings a bottle of Merlot to the proper serving temperature?

    A. Storing the bottle in the refrigerator at 38°F.

    B. Keeping the bottle in a rack at the temperature of the dining room.

    C. Cooling the bottle to 55°F.

    D. Serving temperature is not an issue with Merlot.

124. How long can you hold coffee on a warmer before its quality starts to deteriorate?

    A. No longer than 10 minutes.

    B. No longer than 45 minutes.

    C. No longer than 90 minutes.

    D. No longer than 2½ hours.

    E. Coffee can be held indefinitely if it is kept hot.

Match the following beverages with their proper definitions. Assume you are not running a premium well.

125. Wild Turkey	A. Full-bodied red wine
126. Smirnoff	B. Call scotch
127. Myer's	C. Imported vodka
128. Dewar's	D. Domestic blended whiskey
129. Sauza	E. Full-bodied white wine
130. Heineken	F. Premium bourbon
131. Port	G. Imported blended whiskey
132. Bacardi Silver	H. Cream sherry
133. Chivas Regal	I. Domestic vodka
134. Cabernet Sauvignon	J. Fruity, spicy white wine
135. Augsberger	K. Fortified wine
136. Beck's	L. Light-bodied white wine
137. Chardonnay	M. Alcohol-free beer
138. Gamay Beaujolais	N. Imported cream liqueur
139. Clausthaler	O. Blush wine
140. Harvey's	P. Call rum
141. Triple sec	Q. Imported champagne
142. Seagram's 7	R. Domestic scotch
143. Kahlua	S. Imported beer
144. Sauvignon Blanc	T. Light-bodied red wine
145. Bailey's	U. Imported tequila
146. Crown Royal	V. Imported scotch
147. Gewürztraminer	W. Imported coffee liqueur
148. White Zinfandel	X. Domestic beer
149. Wolfschmidt	Y. Imported dark rum
150. Mumm's	Z. Orange liqueur

Examen Profesional

EQUIPO TÉCNICO DE SERVICIO

Escoja la respuesta *MÁS CORRECTA* y marque su opción en la hoja de respuestas. Por favor, no escriba en el examen.

RELACIONES HUMANAS

1. **¿Cuál es la mejor medida de la efectividad de su supervisor?**
   A. Habilidades en el trabajo.
   B. Las calificaciones del departamento de salud.
   C. Ganancias.
   D. La cuenta promedio.
   E. El desarrollo del equipo técnico.

2. **¿Cuál método de entrenamiento utiliza usted al mostrarle a alguien como limpiar una pieza del equipo?**
   A. Instrucciones escritas.
   B. Entrenamiento en clase.
   C. Demostración.
   D. Instrucción en el trabajo
   E. Ninguno de los anteriores.

3. **¿Quién cree ud. que sea el entrenador más efectivo de temas operacionales?**
   A. Un asesor.
   B. El administrador general.
   C. El supervisor del departamento.
   D. Un colega calificado.
   E. El director de entrenamiento de la compañía.

4. **Basado en su experiencia, ¿qué declaración es verdadera acerca de trabajar con minorías?**
   A. Tienen que ser tratados de un modo diferente a los otros trabajadores.
   B. Pueden ser más difíciles de motivar que los otros trabajadores.
   C. Es más difícil saber lo que ellos esperan realmente de usted.
   D. Tienden a ser menos productivos que otros trabajadores.
   E. No son diferentes de los otros trabajadores.

5. **¿Cómo haría usted para sacar lo mejor de sus colegas?**
   A. Apoyar a todos con el desempeño las descripciones de sus trabajos.
   B. Darles asesoría de cómo desempeñar su trabajo con mas efectividad.
   C. Informar a su supervisor de casos de desempeño bajo.
   D. Establecer un buen ejemplo personal.
   E. Todo lo anterior.

6. **Como mesero en el equipo técnico del restaurante, ¿cuál es la mejor forma de avanzar en su carrera?**
   A. Hacerle favores personales a los administradores.
   B. Sobresalir en la competencia.
   C. Tomar clases y asistir a seminarios.
   D. Enseñarle a los encargados de la limpieza como hacer su trabajo.
   E. Asegurarse de obtener buen crédito cuando las cosas van bien.

7. **Cuando se trata de quejas de un cliente, ¿con cuál declaración está usted más de acuerdo?**
   A. No oir noticias es buenas noticias.
   B. Las quejas son regalos especiales.
   C. Un nivel de satisfacción cerca del 90% es realista para un restaurante con servicio completo.
   D. Usted no puede esperar complacer a todo el mundo siempre.
   E. Algunos se quejan solamente para llamar la atención.

8. **¿Qué puede asumir usted cuando un cliente regresa una orden a la cocina?**
   A. Alguien en la cocina se equivocó con la orden.
   B. El cliente no entendió exactamente cómo era el plato al momento de ordenar.
   C. Hay algo malo con la comida.
   D. El cliente está de mal humor.
   E. Usted no puede asumir nada cuando se regresa un plato.

9. **¿Cómo manejaría usted una queja de un cliente irritado?**
    A. Se excusa e inmediatamente resuelve el problema a favor del cliente.
    B. Intenta mantenerlo sin molestar el restaurante.
    C. Analiza la información de participación en el mercado para determinar si vale la pena preocuparse por el problema.
    D. Escucha su problema, explica qué lo provocó y negocia una solución aceptable mutua.
    E. Le ayuda a que él entienda su parte en la situación.

10. **¿Cuándo *no* consideraría apropiado recompensar toda (o parte) de una comida a un cliente?**
    A. El cliente tuvo que esperar más de lo que usted le dijo.
    B. El mesero llevó la ensalada tarde.
    C. El cliente no quizo su plato.
    D. Los clientes tuvieron una discusión y decidieron irse antes de acabar sus alimentos.
    E. Todas estas situaciones son motivo de recompensa.

SANIDAD

11. **¿Cuál de las siguientes es una violación mayor del departamento de salud?**
    A. Latas sin etiqueta en la despensa de alimento seco.
    B. El refrigerador de alcance sin termómetros secundarios.
    C. El piso sucio debajo del bar de ensalada.
    D. La temperatura de la máquina lavadora de platos a 160° grados.
    E. Una botella de spray sin etiqueta en el puesto de servicio.

12. **Un miembro del equipo técnico se cortó la mano. ¿Cómo deberá manejar la situación el supervisor?**
    A. La excluye de toda responsabilidad de manejo de comida hasta que la cortada esté curada.
    B. La envía a su casa, sin pago, hasta que la cortada esté curada.
    C. La envía a su casa, con pago, hasta que la cortada esté curada.
    D. Para evitar molestar a los demás clientes, la asigna a una estación fuera de la vista del comedor.
    E. Archiva un reclamo a la compensadora de trabajadores.

13. **¿Cuál es el lugar adecuado para un termómetro secundario en un refrigerador?**
    A. En la esquina inferior lejos de la puerta.
    B. En medio del refrigerador.
    C. En la parte superior del frente del refrigerador cerca de la puerta.
    D. Detrás de la puerta.
    E. Un termómetro secundario no es necesario si el refrigerador tiene uno incorporado.

14. **¿Cuál práctica es correcta o aceptable?**
    A. Pulir los cubiertos.
    B. Comer en las estaciones de trabajo.
    C. Utilizar un vaso como cuchara para servir hielo.
    D. Descongelar comida tapada en el mueble limpio de la cocina.
    E. Mantener los paños de limpieza en una solución sanitaria.

15. **¿Qué es un termómetro de producto?**
    A. El indicador que salta en un pavo cuando está listo.
    B. Un termómetro de bolsillo pequeño utilizado para medir las temperaturas en las comidas.
    C. El termómetro de pared que controla las temperaturas de refrigeración.
    D. El termostato que controla la temperatura en los pasillos.

16. **¿Cuál de las siguientes es la regla general con respecto al tiempo máximo total que los productos alimenticios con potencial de ponerse maleos pueden estar en la "zona de peligro"?**
    A. 2 horas.
    B. 4 horas.
    C. 6 horas.
    D. 8 horas.
    E. No importa.

17. **¿Cada cuánto deberá revisar la solución sanitaria?**
    A. Al comienzo de cada turno.
    B. Por lo menos dos veces en cada turno.

C. Por lo menos una vez por hora.

D. Por lo menos una vez cada media hora.

E. Cada vez que la utiliza.

18. **¿Cómo sabe usted si la solución sanitaria tiene la concentración adecuada?**

A. Mide cuidadosamente al hacer una nueva solución.

B. Utiliza el equipo universal de prueba.

C. Sumerge una tira reactiva en la solución y la compara con la escala.

D. Sumerge un pedazo de papel toalla en la solución y vea si oscurece.

E. Utiliza un termómetro de producto.

19. **¿Qué ocurre si la concentración de la solución sanitaria es más alta de lo recomendado?**

A. Será más efectiva.

B. Puede ser tóxica.

C. Costará más dinero, pero no hay mucho problema.

D. No trabajaría bien o en lo absoluto.

E. Todo lo anterior.

20. **¿Qué ocurre si la concentración de la solución sanitaria es menor de lo recomendado?**

A. Matará a la bacteria más lentamente.

B. Puede ser tóxica.

C. Ahorrará algún dinero y no habrá un problema real.

D. No trabajaría bien o en lo absoluto.

E. Todo lo anterior.

PRIMERAS IMPRESIONES

21. **¿Cuál es la primera cosa que usted haría cuando un grupo de clientes entra al restaurante?**

A. Averigua cuántas personas hay en el grupo.

B. Les pregunta si prefieren la sección de fumar o de no fumar.

C. Les pide que esperen en el bar.

D. Sonríe y les da la bienvenida al restaurante.

E. Les pregunta si tienen una reservación.

22. **Usted está en el puesto de anfitrión hablando por teléfono cuando unos clientes llegan. ¿Qué hace usted?**

A. Depende con quién esté hablando.

B. Disimula que usted no los ve, hasta que usted acabe su conversación.

C. Los saluda con una sonrisa y termina su llamada rápidamente.

D. Les apunta a una mesa y les lleva menúes cuando termina de hablar por teléfono.

E. Cuelga el teléfono inmediatamente.

23. **¿Qué *debe* usted saber antes de contestar el teléfono en el restaurante?**

A. Las horas de servicio.

B. Los especiales del día.

C. Instrucciones de cómo llegar al restaurante.

D. Descripción del estilo y precio del menú.

E. Todo lo anterior.

24. **Sus horas de servicio estipulan que usted abra a las 6:00 AM. Un cliente toca la puerta de enfrente, que está cerrada porque es muy temprano en la mañana y su reloj marca las 5:50 AM. ¿Qué hace usted?**

A. Mantiene la puerta cerrada, le muestra la hora en el reloj y le pide que espere 10 minutos.

B. Disimula que usted no le ve.

C. Le permite entrar y lo hace esperar en el lobby hasta las 6:00 AM.

D. Le invita a que entre, le consigue una mesa, un menú y una taza de café.

E. Llama al administrador.

25. **El horario de su restaurante estipula que usted debe cerrar a las 10:00 PM. Un grupo de seis llega a las 9:55 PM y usted sabe que les tomará por lo menos una hora para que coman. ¿Qué hace usted?**

A. Las explica que no pueden ser servidos antes del cierre del restaurante y les pide que regresen mañana.

B. Los sienta y les dice que den su orden antes de las 10:00 PM.

C. Le pregunta al equipo técnico de cocina si quieren servirle a otro grupo.
D. Los sienta y les sirve como a cualquier otro cliente de esa noche.
E. Llama al administrador.

26. Usted es el anfitrión y el restaurante está muy ocupado. ¿Cuál de las siguientes actividades le ayudará al restaurante a tener más éxito?
A. Sienta a los clientes que están esperando tan pronto como una mesa esté libre.
B. Asegurarse que cada cliente tenga atención personal.
C. Les vende bebidas a los clientes mientras esperan.
D. Ayuda a los encargados de la limpieza a limpiar y a reorganizar a las mesas.

27. Usted lleva a un grupo de dos a su mesa en una noche muy ocupada. Al acercarse a la pareja, ellos le piden que los siente en la mesa para 4 en la parte superior de la esquina. Usted sabe que no hay una reservación para esa mesa. ¿Qué hace usted?
A. Les explica que el restaurante está muy ocupado y los sienta en la de dos.
B. Les pregunta qué tiene de malo la mesa para dos.
C. Les dice que usted tiene una reservación para la mesa de 4 en la parte superior y los sienta en la de dos.
D. Los sientan en la mesa para 4 en la parte superior.
E. Llama al administrador.

28. Es una noche del viernes muy ocupada y usted le dice al grupo Mcpherson que la espera será de 30 minutos. La media hora casi ha pasado y ahora parece que usted no tendrá una mesa disponible por otros 10 minutos. ¿Qué hace usted?
A. Los deja pasar y los llama cuando la mesa está lista. Diez minutos no son motivo de preocupación.
B. Les informa de la espera adicional y se excusa.
C. Les informa de la espera adicional y les da algo para compensar la inconveniencia.
D. Les informa de la espera adicional y les explica la razón de la demora.
E. Llama al administrador.

29. Es una noche muy ocupada y hay espera. Una familia llega con varios niños en grupo y los clientes obviamente quedan decepcionados al saber que no pueden ser sentados inmediatamente. ¿Qué hace usted?
A. Los llama cuando la mesa está lista.
B. Usted no puede hacer mucho porque debe tratar a cada cliente por igual.
C. Les ofrece una bebida a los padres.
D. Les da a los niños algo con que jugar.
E. Llama al administrador.

30. Usted está hablando por teléfono cuando un cliente sale del restaurante. ¿Qué hace usted?
A. Disimula que no lo ve y continúa con su llamada.
B. Sonríe y lo saluda mientras continúa hablando.
C. Se excusa con la persona que está hablando y le agradece por su visita.
D. Cuelga el teléfono inmediatamente.
E. Llama al administrador.

OPERACIONES DEL COMEDOR

¿De qué lado del cliente haría usted lo siguiente?

31. Sirve la sopa
32. Sirve el plato principal
33. Sirve las bebidas
34. Retira los platos

A. El lado izquierdo con la mano izquierda.
B. El lado izquierdo con la mano derecha.
C. Cualquier lado con cualquier mano.
D. El lado derecho con la mano izquierda.
E. El lado derecho con la mano derecha.

¿A cuál lado del cliente colocaría usted lo siguiente?

35. Los cuchillos
36. Los tenedores
37. Los vasos
38. La cuenta del cliente

A. Al lado derecho.
B. Al lado izquierdo.
C. Cualquier lado.
D. Al lado más cómodo para usted.
E. Al lado más cómodo para el cliente.

39. **Tres clientes en una mesa han terminado sus entradas principales mientras el cuarto todavía está comiendo. ¿Qué hace usted?**
    A. Retira los platos de los tres clientes que han terminado.
    B. Pregunta a los clientes que terminaron si quieren que sus platos sean retirados.
    C. Espera hasta que el cuarto cliente acabe.
    D. Retira los platos de los tres clientes que han terminado solamente si ellos se lo piden.
    E. Ninguno de los anteriores.

40. **Cuando sirve vino, ¿cuál de los siguientes procedimientos es incorrecto?**
    A. Presentar la etiqueta de la botella a la persona que ordenó el vino.
    B. Colocar la botella en la mesa mientras corta el aluminio.
    C. Servir un poco para la aprobación del cliente que lo ordenó, antes de servirle al resto de la mesa.
    D. Llenar las copas de las damas antes de llenar las de los clientes masculinos.
    E. Llenar las copas hasta la parte ancha de la copa.

41. **¿Cuándo deberá cambiar el cenicero en la mesa?**
    A. Siempre que haya una colilla de cigarrillo.
    B. Antes de servir el plato principal.
    C. Siempre que haya dos colillas de cigarrillos.
    D. Después de servirle los cocteles.
    E. Siempre que haya más de tres colillas de cigarrillos.

42. **¿Cuál es el método más adecuado de cambiar un cenicero?**
    A. Cubre el cenicero sucio con uno limpio y lo retira de la mesa.
    B. Retira el cenicero sucio de la mesa con una mano mientras pone el limpio con la otra mano.
    C. Retira el cenicero sucio de la mesa, vacía las colillas en el balde de los encargados de la limpieza y lo reemplaza en la mesa.
    D. Cualquiera de los anteriores es aceptable.

43. **¿Cuáles artículos deberán permanecer en la mesa después de haber quitado el plato principal?**
    A. Pan, mantequilla, vasos con agua, ceniceros y los cubiertos que no han sido utilizados.
    B. Los ceniceros y los cubiertos que no han sido utilizados.
    C. Vasos con agua, ceniceros, bebidas sin terminar y el cubierto necesario para el postre.
    D. Nada. La mesa deberá estar completamente limpia.

44. **¿Cuáles acciones son apropiadas en su primera visita a la mesa?**
    A. Se presenta usted mismo.
    B. Les da la bienvenida a los clientes del restaurante.
    C. Desenvuelve las servilletas y las coloca en el regazo de los clientes.
    D. Les pregunta a los clientes si les gustaría una bebida.

45. **¿Cuál es el procedimiento más seguro de servir café en la mesa?**
    A. Sirve el café sosteniendo la taza en su mano o en una bandeja.
    B. Sirve el café en la taza sin retirar la taza de la mesa.
    C. Hace que el encargado de la limpieza sirva el café.
    D. Cualquier método mencionado anteriormente que sea más cómodo para el cliente.

46. **Usted tiene una orden en la cocina y clientes nuevos han sido sentados en su estación. ¿Qué hace usted?**
    A. Recoge la comida en la cocina, la sirve, y después saluda a los nuevos clientes.
    B. Saluda a los nuevos clientes, se excusa, y recoge la comida en la cocina.
    C. Le pide a su encargado de la limpieza que recoja y sirva la orden mientras que saluda a los nuevos clientes.
    D. Le pide al administrador que salude a los clientes mientras que usted recoge la orden.
    E. Depende de la situación.

47. **¿Cuándo es importante indicar los números de los asientos en la cuenta del cliente?**
    A. Cuando se toma la orden de las bebidas, aperitivos, platos principales o postres.
    B. Solamente cuando se toma la orden de los platos principales.
    C. Solamente cuando usted tiene tiempo suficiente para hacerlo.
    D. Los números en los asientos no son necesarios si usted tiene un sistema de ordenador electrónico.

48. **¿Cuál de los siguientes son procedimientos adecuados del bar de ensaladas?**
    A. Mantener los contenedores de alimentos llenos de productos frescos y refrigerados.
    B. Reemplazar contenedores de alimento casi vacíos con llenos.

C. Reutilizar utensilios de servir cuando se rellenan los contenedores de alimento.

D. Permitiéndole a los clientes rellenar sus platos de ensalada.

E. Colocar hielo en la ensalada verde para mantenerla fresca y crocante.

49. **Aunque nadie quiso salsa cuando usted sirvió filetes T-bone a un grupo de hombres de negocio, uno de ellos se la pide cuando usted regresó. ¿Qué hace usted?**

A. Les pregunta qué clase de salsa de filete desean.

B. Les trae su selección de salsas de filete completa.

C. Les pregunta si los filetes están bien.

D. Reemplaza los filetes de inmediato.

E. Llama al administrador.

50. **¿Cuál es la cosa más importante al manejar efectivamente la hora más ocupada?**

A. Planifica por adelantado y se asegura de tener los surtidos adecuados en su lugar.

B. Contrata equipo técnico extra.

C. Planifica solamente que sus mejores trabajadores trabajen durante la hora más ocupada.

D. Sienta a gente solamente tan rápido como pueda servirlos.

E. Todo lo anterior.

51. **¿Qué significa cortesía?**

A. Que le guste la gente.

B. Sonreir y ser cortés.

C. Ser respetuoso con los clientes.

D. Hacer que la gente sea consciente de que a usted le agrada.

E. Todo lo anterior.

52. **Un cliente le pregunta por instrucciones para ir al baño. ¿Cuál de las siguientes *no* haría usted?**

A. Les apunta hacia el baño.

B. Les explica como encontrar el baño.

C. Los lleva al baño usted mismo.

D. Cualquiera de los anteriores sería aceptable.

53. **¿Qué es salmonella?**

A. Un plato de pasta italiana hecha con salmón.

B. Un vino tinto con buen cuerpo.

C. Un salmón tierno, generalmente servido completo.

D. Un tipo de enfermedad causada por la comida.

54. **Un grupo de cuatro tiene un total de $34.50 en su cuenta. Ellos le dan dos billetes de veinte como pago. ¿Qué cambio le trae usted?**

A. Dos monedas de veinticinco ctvs. y un billete de cinco dólares.

B. Dos monedas de veinticinco ctvs. y cinco billetes de un dólar.

C. Cinco monedas de 10 ctvs., un billete de un dólar y un billete de cinco dólares.

D. Nada porque el cambio es más o menos lo que deben dejar de propina.

55. **Usted cree que le ha dado servicio excelente a un grupo de tres. Cuando se han ido, usted nota que el recibo de la tarjeta de crédito ha sido firmado, pero no añadió propina y la cuenta no fue sumada. ¿Qué hace usted?**

A. Añade 15% al recibo de la tarjeta de crédito y hace la suma.

B. Intenta alcanzar a los clientes antes de que se vayan.

C. Presenta el recipo tal y como está.

D. Revisa la mesa para ver si dejaron propina.

E. Llama al administrador.

Concuerde los siguientes términos con las definiciones adecuadas:

56. **Servicio americano**	A. La comida es llevada en bandejas y servida en la mesa.
57. **Servicio ruso**	B. Los invitados se sirven de una mesa larga o de una mesa con toda la comida.
58. **Servicio de banquete**	C. La comida es llevada en moldes y bandejas y los invitados se sirven en la mesa.
59. **Servicio familiar**	D. La comida es servida en la cocina y llevada en el plato al invitado que está en la mesa.
60. **Servicio de buffet**	E. No existe tal término.

SERVICIO DE ALCOHOL

61. **¿Cuál de los siguientes alimentos sería más efectivo para retrasar la absorción del alcohol?**
    A. Palomitas de maíz.
    B. Una barra de caramelo.
    C. Queso.
    D. Café negro.
    E. Todo tendrá el mismo efecto.

62. **¿Cuál de los siguientes artículos aumenta la absorción del alcohol en el cuerpo?**
    A. Agua.
    B. Bebidas carbonatadas.
    C. Alimentos proteínicos.
    D. Dulces.
    E. Ninguno de los anteriores.

63. **¿Cuál de las siguientes no son típicamente consideradas como una forma válida de identificación?**
    A. Partida de nacimiento.
    B. Licencia de conducir.
    C. Tarjeta del registro de extranjeros.
    D. Tarjeta del seguro social.
    E. Todas son formas válidas de identificación.

64. **¿Cuál de las siguientes declaraciones describe exactamente la ley?**
    A. Es legal servirle bebidas alcohólicas a personas intoxicadas si no van a conducir.
    B. Es ilegal servirle bebidas alcohólicas a personas intoxicadas.
    C. Es ilegal servirle más de tres bebidas alcóholicas a una persona en una hora.
    D. Es legal que un menor beba si sus padres compran la bebida alcohólica.
    E. Todas las anteriores son declaraciones exactas.

65. **¿Usted deberá parar el servicio de alcohol a una persona que exhiba cuál de los siguientes comportamientos?**
    A. Coquetea.
    B. Pierde las inhibiciones.
    C. Es una molestia.
    D. Riega bebidas.
    E. Actuá extraordinariamente tranquila.

66. **¿Cuál de los siguientes *no* es una bebida equivalente a las otras cuando se considera el contenido de alcohol?**
    A. 12 onzas de cerveza.
    B. 8 onzas de vino.
    C. 1 onza de licor de 80 de prueba.
    D. Todas son iguales en el contenido de alcohol.

67. **Un cliente definitivamente ha bebido demasiado y está listo para irse del restaurante. Usted se acerca para ofrecerle un taxi que lo lleve a casa, rechaza su oferta e insiste en conducir a casa. ¿Qué haría usted?**
    A. Le pide que tenga cuidado y le permite conducir.
    B. Si la persona entra en su carro, llama a la policía.
    C. Agarra sus llaves y las guarda.
    D. Continúa insistiendo su caso.
    E. Llama al dueño.

68. **Una mujer definitivamente ha bebido demasiado y quiere otra copa de vino. Jura que no va a conducir, una declaración que es confirmada por su novio. Él no está bebido y le garantiza que él la llevará y se asegurará de que llegue a casa. Le pide que traiga el vino. ¿Qué hace usted?**
    A. Trae la bebida tal y como fue solicitada.
    B. Llama a la policía.
    C. Llama al dueño.
    D. Rehusa servirle la bebida.
    E. Sugiere bebidas sin alcohol como alternativa.

69. **Un grupo de seis jóvenes entra al restaurante y ordena bebidas alcohólicas. Usted les pide tarjetas de identificación pero ellos le dicen que no las tran consigo. Le aseguran que son mayores de 21 años de edad. Esto es**

verificado por un cliente mayor que oyó la conversación y a quien usted reconoce como un oficial de la policía. ¿Qué hace usted?

A. Trae las bebidas.

B. Llama al departamento de policía para confirmar la identidad del cliente mayor.

C. Llama al dueño.

D. Se rehusa a servir a las bebidas.

E. Sugiere bebidas sin alcohol como alternativa.

70. **¿Cuál de las siguientes prácticas no ayuda a evitar el sobreconsumo?**

A. Sirve una bebida a la vez.

B. Hace que los clientes vayan al bar para ordenar.

C. Sirve las rondas cuando los vasos están casi vacíos.

D. Retira los vasos vacíos de la mesa antes de servir otra ronda.

E. Pone agua en la mesa.

Por favor responda a las siguientes preguntas FALSO O VERDADERO.

71. Usted puede ser responsable personalmente de las acciones de un cliente intoxicado.

72. El uso de cocaína o marihuana junto con alcohol intensifica su efecto.

73. Un conductor que registre .8% de BAC se considera estar conduciendo bajo los efectos del alcohol.

74. Si una persona de fuera del estado tiene la edad legal para beber en su estado de origen, puede beber en su restaurante.

75. La altitud aumenta el efecto del alcohol.

76. El alcohol es un deprimente que disminuye el apetito.

77. Una persona con un porcentaje alto de grasa absorbe el alcohol más rápido que una persona con más musculos.

78. El cuerpo procesa alcohol a un ritmo de una bebida por hora, sin importar el tamaño.

79. Al descontinuar el servicio a un cliente intoxicado, una mano en su hombro le ayudará a mantenerlo más calmado.

80. Una máquina "breathalizer" mide la cantidad de alcohol en la sangre.

FINANZAS

81. **Vamos a decir que usted realmente se equivoca con un grupo típico de cuatro. También vamos a decir que el típico cliente en su restaurante come normalmente tres veces al mes y que su cuenta promedio es de $20.00. ¿Cuál será el costo de la pérdida del negocio en los siguientes cinco años?**

A. Menos de $4,000.

B. $10,000–$12,000.

C. $25,000–$30,000.

D. $50,000–$60,000.

E. Más de $85,000.

82. **¿Qué porción de las ventas típicas de un restaurante son ingresos sin impuestos?**

A. 40–45%.

B. 30–35%.

C. 20–25%.

D. 10–15%.

E. Menos del 5%.

83. **Sus ventas de alimento y bebidas suman $500 durante su turno. Usted tuvo un total de 20 cuentas de clientes representando alimentos servidos a 50 personas. Había 25 asientos en su estación. ¿Cuál fue su cuenta promedio en este turno?**

A. $500.00.

B. $25.00.

C. $20.00.

D. $10.00.

E. No hay suficiente información para responder esta pregunta.

84. **Usted es un mesero en un restaurante de alto volumen y sus propinas en su turno fueron de $150. Por haber desempeñado un buen trabajo hoy, usted decide darle a su encargado de la limpieza el 15% de sus propinas. Después de arreglarse con él, ¿cuánto dinero de propinas llevará usted a casa?**

A. $100.00.

B. $115.00.

C. $122.50.
D. $135.00.
E. $150.00.

85. **Simplemente, ¿qué es una factura?**
   A. Una recibo.
   B. Una orden de compra.
   C. Una historia de ventas.
   D. El estado de las cuentas.
   E. Un proyecto de producción.

86. **Usted reemplaza al administrador del comedor. Un vendedor de productos químicos le ofrece un negocio: 20% de descuento en las órdenes de más de 3 cajas de champú para alfombras si usted hace la orden hoy. Usted normalmente utiliza una caja de champú para alfombra cada 3 meses. ¿Qué hace usted?**
   A. Pasa.
   B. Compra 3+ cajas y le ahorra dinero al restaurante.
   C. Compra 3+ cajas y limpia las alfombras con más frecuencia.
   D. Compra 3+ cajas y revende parte de las existencias con ganancia.

87. **Su restaurante tiene un concurso para encontrar un almuerzo especial nuevo. Para poder ser elegible, el plato tiene que venderse a $6.00 con un costo del alimento de 30% o menos. ¿Cuál es el costo de porción más alto que su plato puede tener?**
   A. $3.20.
   B. $2.40.
   C. $1.80.
   D. $1.20.

Los siguientes platos están incluidos en su menú del almuerzo en el restaurante:

Hamburguesa	$4.25	Ensalada del chef	$5.25
\con queso agregue:	$ .75	Plato de chili	$3.95
Sandwich de pavo	$4.95	Spaguetti con salsa	$4.50
Enchilada de pollo	$5.95	Carne a la parmigiana	$5.75
Bandeja con roast beef	$6.95	Papas a la francesa	$1.25
Bebidas gaseosas	$ .95	Té helado	$ .75
Café	$ .50	Pastel de manzana	$1.95
		\con helado agregue:	$ .95

88. **Una mesa ordena una hamburguesa con queso, dos platos de chili, una orden de papas a la francesa, enchiladas, dos té helados, una taza de café, y un pastel de manzana. ¿Cuánto es la cuenta antes del impuesto?**
   A. $22.50.
   B. $24.05.
   C. $25.00.
   D. $26.25.
   E. Ninguno de lo anterior.

89. **Una mesa de cuatro ordena roast beef, carne a la parmigiana, una ensalada del chef y spaguetti con salsa. También ordena un té helado y 2 cafés. Si dejara un 15% de propina basado en el total antes del impuesto, ¿cuánto recibirá usted probablemente?**
   A. $2.50.
   B. $3.15.
   C. $3.50.
   D. $4.25.
   E. Ninguno de lo anterior.

90. **Un grupo de jóvenes solamente tiene $10.25 entre todos. Pide dos órdenes de papas a la francesa y 3 Coca-Colas. Todavía tienen hambre y quieren algo más de comer. Sin contar el impuesto, ¿qué sugeriría usted?**
   A. Una hamburguesa.
   B. Un hamburguesa con queso.
   C. Un sandwich de pavo.
   D. El helado con pastel.
   E. Papas a la francesa.

VENTAS

Usted es un mesero en un restaurante con servicio completo. Usted no ha estado sugiriendo platos del menú a sus clientes. El menú incluye los siguientes platos:

Postre	$ 3.00
Botella de vino (para 4)	$10.00
Platos adicionales	$ 2.00
Café, bebidas digestivas	$ 1.50

91. ¿Basados en los precios promedio, ¿cuánta ganancia potencial pierde con una mesa de cuatro?
   A. $36.00.
   B. $44.00.
   C. $52.00.
   D. $76.00.

92. Basado en un 15% de propina, ¿cuánto en propinas potencialmente pierde en esta mesa para cuatro?
   A. $3.90.
   B. $5.40.
   C. $6.60.
   D. $11.40.

93. Para maximizar las ganancias del restaurante, ¿cuál de los siguientes platos vendería usted?
   A. Un plato de enchiladas a $6.95 con un 20% de costo de alimento.
   B. Un sandwich de pollo a $4.95 con un 32% de costo de alimento.
   C. Una bandeja de bagre frito a $8.95 con un 38% de costo de alimento.
   D. Una cena de filete de res a $12.95 con un 50% de costo de alimento.

94. ¿Cuáles prácticas aumentarían sus ventas?
   A. Sugerir detalles que le gustan.
   B. Poder describir qué hay en cada plato y cómo está preparado.
   C. Proponerse mencionar selecciones específicas que el restaurante ofrece.
   D. Saber cuáles vinos van con cada plato principal.
   E. Todo lo anterior.

95. ¿Cuál de las siguientes preguntas ayudarían mejor a vender bebidas alcohólicas efectivamente?
   A. "¿Puedo traerle un coctel?"
   B. "¿Le gustaría ver nuestro menú de licores?"
   C. "¿Qué clase de coctel puedo traerle?"
   D. "¿Está listo para ordenar?"
   E. "¿Ha probado alguna vez nuestro famoso ponche de ron?"

96. ¿Cuál de las siguientes bebidas sugeriría a un cliente que ha ordenado un mousse de chocolate?
   A. Una copa de Cavernet Sauvignon.
   B. Un café irlandés.
   C. Grand Marnier en las rocas.
   D. Café espresso.
   E. Cualquiera de estos iría bien con mousse de chocolate.

97. ¿Cuál de los siguientes vinos sugeriría usted a un cliente que ha ordenado filete de res?
   A. Port.
   B. Gewurztraminer.
   C. Pinot Noir
   D. Sauterne francés.
   E. Vino de jerez.

98. ¿De qué ayuda *más* al restaurante la venta sugerida?
   A. Incremento de ventas.
   B. Incrementando la satisfacción al cliente.
   C. Incrementando las propinas de los meseros.
   D. Reduciendo el costo del alimento.
   E. Todo lo anterior.

99. **Un grupo de dos ha estado esperando en el bar 45 minutos. Después de acabar sus cocteles en la mesa, ordenan una botella de vino. ¿Cuándo les sugeriría una segunda botella de vino?**
   A. Cuando la primera esté un tercio llena.
   B. Cuando usted vacíe la primera.
   C. Después de retirar el servicio del plato principal.
   D. No sugeriría una segunda botella de vino.

100. **Usted es un vegetariano. Un cliente le pregunta si usted recomendaría carne a la Wellington. ¿Cuál sería su mejor respuesta?**
   A. "No como carne, de modo que realmente no sé."
   B. "Vendemos mucha carne a la Wellington."
   C. "Es muy buena."
   D. "Mis amigos que comen carne dicen que es muy buena."
   E. "Es un filet mignon cubierto con paté y cocinado como un pastel."

CONOCIMIENTO DE COMIDAS

101. **¿Cuál corte de carne cree usted que sea más suave?**
   A. Filete principal de lomo.
   B. Filet mignon.
   C. Filete de costado.
   D. Filete de T-bone.
   E. Filete de Nueva York.

102. **¿Cuál corte de carne cree usted que tenga más sabor?**
   A. Chuleta de ternera.
   B. Filete principal de lomo.
   C. Filet mignon.
   D. Carne molida.
   E. Filete de costado.

103. **¿Cuál de los siguientes colores esperaría usted encontrar si usted cortara un Filet mignon medio asado?**
   A. Café.
   B. Rojo.
   C. Morado.
   D. Rosado.

104. **¿Cómo esperaría usted que un salmón cocido sea cocinado?**
   A. Sobre (o debajo) de una llama directa.
   B. Sofrito en un sartén con mantequilla.
   C. Envuelto en pergamino y horneado en el horno.
   D. Hervido a fuego lento en un líquido.
   E. Al vapor con hierbas.

Concuerde los siguientes alimentos con sus definiciones adecuadas.

105. Burrito	A.	Ensalada que usa hojas de lechuga romana
106. Fetuccini	B.	Salsa de tomate sin carne
107. Seviche	C.	Tortillas de maíz rellenas en salsa
108. Holandesa	D.	Salsa de vinagre y aceite
109. Salsa de coctel	E.	Una preparación que usa camarones
110. Linguini	F.	Con espinacas
111. Escargot	G.	Salsa de chili con rábano
112. Scampi	H.	Salsa servida con huevos a la benedict
113. César	I.	Caracoles, generalmente cocinados en mantequilla con ajo
114. Bearnaise	J.	Mariscos Marinados
115. Camarones	K.	Fideos de un octavo de ancho
116. Salsa	L.	Tomates picados, cebollas y chiles
117. Marinara	M.	Tortilla de harina rellena
118. Florentina	N.	Salsa servida en filetes
119. Vinagreta	O.	Fideos de aproximadamente un ¼" de ancho
120. Enchilada	P.	Esto no es un artículo de comida

CONOCIMIENTO DE BEBIDAS

121. ¿Cuáles son los ingredientes en una margarita?
A. Ron, triple sec y jugo de limón.
B. Tequila, granadina y jugo de naranja.
C. Vodka, jugo de limón, gaseosa.
D. Tequila, triple sec, jugo de limón.
E. Whiskey, jugo limón y azúcar.

122. Si un cliente ordenó un Dewar "neat," ¿cómo lo sirve usted?
A. En las rocas.
B. En un vaso de trago.
C. Con agua.
D. Con gaseosa.
E. Con un poquito de limón.

123. ¿Cuál de las siguientes pondría a una botella de Merlot a la temperatura adecuada?
A. Guarde la botella en el refrigerador a 38° grados.
B. Mantenga la botella en un estante a la temperatura del comedor.
C. Enfríe la botella a 55° grados.
D. La temperatura no es un problema con el Merlot.

124. ¿Cuánto tiempo puede mantener el café en un calentador antes que comience a deteriorarse?
A. Menos de 10 minutos.
B. Menos de 45 minutos.
C. Menos de 90 minutos.
D. Menos de 2 horas.
E. El café puede ser mantenido indefinidamente si se mantiene caliente.

Concuerde las siguientes bebidas con las definiciones adecuadas. Asuma que usted no tiene una reserva de primera.

125. Wild Turkey	A. Vino tinto de buen cuerpo
126. Smirnoff	B. Scotch de marca barata
127. Myer's	C. Vodka importada
128. Dewar's	D. Whiskey de mezcla doméstica
129. Sauza	E. Vino blanco de buen cuerpo
130. Heineken	F. Bourbon premium
131. Port	G. Whiskey de mezcla importada
132. Bacardi plata	H. Crema de vino de jerez
133. Chivas Regal	I. Vodka domestica
134. Cabernet Sauvignon	J. Vino blanco con frutas y especies
135. Augsberger	K. Vino fortificado
136. Beck's	L. Vino blanco de cuerpo suave
137. Chardonnay	M. Cerveza sin alcohol
138. Gamay Beaujolais	N. Crema de licor importada
139. Clausthaler	O. Vino rosado
140. Harvey's	P. Ron de marca barata
141. Triple sec	Q. Champaña importada
142. Seagram's 7	R. Scotch doméstico
143. Kahlúa	S. Cerveza importada
144. Sauvignon blanc	T. Vino tinto de cuerpo suave
145. Bailey's	U. Tequila importada
146. Crown Royal	V. Scotch importado
147. Gewürztraminer	W. Licor de café importado
148. Zinfandel Blanco	X. Cerveza doméstica
149. Wolfschmidt	Y. Ron oro importado
150. Mumm's	Z. Licor de naranja

Service Staff

PROFESSIONAL TEST
Answers

HUMAN RELATIONS

1. **E** **Staff development.** All of the factors are elements that an effective supervisor would do better on than an unskilled one. Still, the distinguishing characteristic of great supervisors is their ability to teach and bring out the best in those who work with and for them.

2. **D** **On-the-job instruction.** Anything that involves developing physical skills can only be effectively learned by doing.

3. **D** **A skilled co-worker.** The worker is always closer to the job and therefore knows more about its current intricacies than even the most experienced supervisor. Involving the staff in training is also an excellent way to eliminate the "them against us" mentality in a foodservice operation.

4. **E** **They are no different from anyone else.** Beware of generalizations about any group of people. Remember that somewhere in the world, *you* are a minority!

5. **D** **Set a good personal example.** What they see is what you will get. Anything else is wasted effort.

6. **D** **Teach your bussers how to do your job.** When you teach your crew to do your job, they get excited by the opportunity to improve their skills. As you eliminate tasks from your workload, it leaves you open to develop new skills yourself.

7. **B** **Complaints are special gifts.** Only one person in 25 will actually tell you about a complaint. The rest will simply go away, never return, and tell their friends to stay away, too. When you get a complaint, it is a rare insight into what may be killing your business. Accept the information with gratitude and fix the problem immediately.

8. **E** **You can't assume anything when an item is returned.** There are thousands of reasons why an item might be returned. Consider it an opportunity to give an extra level of service, fix it, and discuss the probable causes later. This is not to suggest that patterns of problems should not be identified and solved.

9. **A** **Apologize and immediately resolve the situation in favor of the guest.** The apology will help keep the guest from becoming more defensive. Resolving a complaint in favor of the guest is the only resolution that will be in the true long-term interests of the restaurant.

10. **E** **All of these situations could call for a comp.** Guests come to the restaurant for a good time. Whenever they don't have that experience, regardless of whose "fault" it is, they will only remember that their last trip to your restaurant was not fun. In the case of the argument, comping the meal shows an unexpected compassion that will be memorable and might salvage what could otherwise be permanently lost patronage.

SANITATION

11. **E** **An unlabeled spray bottle in the service stand.**

12. **A** **Exclude her from all food-handling responsibilities until the cut heals.** This is the most correct choice of those offered. In practice, covering the wound with a surgical glove and having the staff member work out of sight of guests is a more likely solution. The important thing is that you never risk the wound or its bandage coming in contact with food.

13. **C** **In the upper front of the refrigerator by the door.** The secondary thermometer should be placed in the warmest part of the refrigerator. Most state health codes require all refrigerators and freezers to have a secondary thermometer easily visible when the door is opened.

14. **E** **Keeping wipe cloths in sanitizing solution.** This is the only practice on the list that is not a health department violation.

15. **A** **A small pocket thermometer used to check food temperatures.** Every member of the food preparation staff and every attendant on a cafeteria line or salad bar should have a product thermometer to monitor food temperatures.

16. **B** **4 hours.** This means the total time out of temperature in the product's life cycle—including at the purveyor's facilities, in the delivery truck, and on various loading docks.

17. **C** **At least once an hour.** The effectiveness of sanitizing solution decreases over time and with use. To be safe, solutions should be tested at least once an hour.

18. **C** **Dip a test strip in the solution and compare it with a scale.** Typical sanitizers are usually either quaternary ammonia or chlorine bleach, and each requires a different test strip. There is no such thing as a universal test kit.

19. **B** **It can be toxic.** For the sake of illustration, consider the effect of using undiluted bleach to wipe down a cutting board. The *only* way to be sure you have a proper concentration is to measure the sanitizer into a known amount of water *and* verify the concentration with a test strip.

20. **D** **It won't work as well, if at all.** The comments above apply.

FIRST IMPRESSIONS

21. **D** **Smile and welcome them to the restaurant.** Your first words should thank the guests for coming and welcome them to the restaurant. After that you can address the details like how many are in the party, seating preferences, reservations, and so forth.

22. **C** **Acknowledge the new arrivals with a smile and complete your call promptly.**

23. **E** **All of the above.** If guest service is your first priority, you will not allow yourself or the restaurant to be embarrassed when a guest calls.

24. **D** **Invite him in, get him a seat, a menu, and a cup of coffee.** It is not worth inconveniencing a guest to prove a point about whose watch is correct. The kitchen may not be ready to go, but you know there will be hot coffee ready. Breaking the rules in the interests of guest service is no crime.

25. **D** **Seat them and serve them as you have any other guests that evening.** Closing time is when you stop seating people, *NOT* the time when everyone on the staff should expect to go home. They were clearly there before closing and are entitled to your full service—with a smile!

26. **B** **Making sure that every guest gets your personal attention.** Undistracted personal attention will make your guests feel well cared for. You should never seat anyone at an unset table. While you may offer waiting guests a drink or give the dining room staff a hand, it is the level of guest service that determines how successful a restaurant will be.

27. **D** **Seat them at the 4-top.** Guests come to the restaurant to have a good time. If they will have a better time at a larger table, give it to them.

28. **C** **Inform them of the additional wait and give them something to make up for the inconvenience.** You must always keep the guests informed of the status of the wait—most of them are probably checking their watches anyway. If your estimate was off, do something to make up for the inconvenience. Your guests will be delighted.

29. **D** **Get the children something to play with.** Parents are happy when their kids are happy. If the children don't have something to play with, they will turn the restaurant into a playground!

30. **C** **Excuse yourself from the caller and thank them for coming.** People never get enough gratitude. It is important to show your guests that you appreciate their patronage.

DINING ROOM OPERATIONS

31. **A** **Left side with the left hand.**

32. **A** **Left side with the left hand.**

33. **E** **Right side with the right hand.**

34. **E** **Right side with the right hand.**

35. **A** **Right side.**

36. **B** **Left side.**

37. A   **Right side.**

38. E   **Whichever side is most comfortable for the guest.**

39.C/D **Wait until the fourth guest finishes (or) clear the plates of the three guests who have finished, but only if they ask you to do so.** Either of these choices is correct. Many guests who are slow eaters or drinkers feel rushed when their companions' glasses are cleared before everyone at the table has finished.

40. B   **Placing the bottle on the table while cutting the foil.** Hold the bottle while cutting the foil. The table is the guest's territory, and many diners will resent your trespassing.

41. C   **Whenever there are two cigarette butts in it.**

42. A   **Capping a clean ashtray over the soiled one and removing it from the table.** The cap keeps ashes from flying about as the full container is removed. Be sure to replace it with a clean ashtray rather than just emptying the dirty one and returning it to the table.

43. C   **Water glasses, ashtrays, unfinished drinks, and silverware needed for dessert.** Everything not being used by the guests or needed for the next course should be removed.

44. B   **Welcoming the guests to the restaurant.** As with the arrival in the restaurant, a server should first thank guests for coming and welcome them to the restaurant. After that, they can deal with the particulars of the meal. Personal introductions are seldom appreciated by diners.

45. A   **Pour the coffee while holding the cup in your hand or on a tray.** This procedure reduces the possibilities of splashing hot coffee on the table or on your guests.

46. B   **Greet the new guests, excuse yourself, then pick up the food in the kitchen.** Hot food must be served while it is hot, but acknowledging the guests will only take a few seconds of undistracted attention and keep them content while you pick up the food from the kitchen. Guests often get confused when too many people appear at the table. Having a busser pick up the order and bring it out to the dining room would be a better option than having them serve it, unless that's what it took to make sure it was hot when it hit the table.

47. A   **When taking the order for drinks, appetizers, entrees, or desserts.** Table and seat numbers will enable anyone on the staff to properly serve an order if you are occupied. It will also help you split the check should the party ask for separate checks later in the meal.

48. B   **Replacing nearly empty food containers with full ones.** Of the choices offered, topping off containers, reusing serving utensils, or allowing salad bowls to be refilled are all forms of cross-contamination. Placing ice on the salad greens may help keep them crisp, but will also make for soggy salads.

49. C   **Ask if the steaks are satisfactory.** After all, *something* prompted the request. It may just be that you or the guests forgot to mention steak sauce when the order was placed, but it is always best to make sure.

50. A   **Planning ahead and being sure adequate stocks are in place.** The only effective way to get through the rush is never to get behind. The key to staying ahead of the crowd is to be sure you know what you are doing and not to have to interrupt the flow of service to restock.

51. E   **All of the above.**

52. A   **Point them toward the restrooms.** Many people find pointing to be rude. When it comes to the restrooms, pointing can embarrass your guests by making everyone in the dining room aware of the nature of their request.

53. D   **A type of foodborne illness.**

54. B   **Two quarters and five ones.** This combination gives the guests the change they need to leave a tip, if they choose. While you may get it all back, never presume a tip or you risk losing a guest's business forever.

55. C   **Submit the slip as is.** It may be that the guest simply forgot, but you do not have the right to add the tip. Without the cardholder's permission, such an act will cost you that person's patronage forever.

56. D   **Food is portioned in the kitchen and brought out to guests on plates.**

57. A   **Food is brought on platters and served at the table.**

58. D   **Food is portioned in the kitchen and brought out to guests on plates.**

59. C   **Food is brought in bowls and on platters, and guests help themselves at the table.**

60. B   **Guests help themselves from a long table or tables filled with food.**

ALCOHOL SERVICE

61. C Cheese. Protein foods slow the absorption rate of alcohol.

62. B Carbonated beverages.

63. D A Social Security card. It does not show a birth date and is not a valid ID for the purchase of alcohol.

64. B It is illegal to serve alcohol to intoxicated persons.

65. D Spilling drinks. This is one of the signs of someone in the "red zone."

66. B 8 ounces of wine. The equivalent amount of wine is four ounces.

67. B If he gets into his car, call the police. In many states, this is the law. Good guest relations notwithstanding, I would rather have a guest angry at me than dead.

68. E Suggest nonalcoholic alternatives. This will keep the situation focused on positive factors rather than negative ones. In general, it is always preferable to tell people what you *can* do for them rather than what you *can't*!

69. E Suggest nonalcoholic alternatives. The reasoning is the same as in the previous question.

70. B Making the guests come to the bar to order. This will not slow consumption and only provides poor service to the guest.

71. T In most states, the person who serves alcohol to an intoxicated person is personally liable.

72. T This can be a dangerous combination both for the individual and the restaurateur.

73. F The legal limit for DWI will depend on your state, but anyone with a BAC of .8 is most likely *dead*! Now if the question said .08, that would be a different story!

74. F It's your state and your liquor license.

75. F High altitude intensifies the effects of alcohol.

76. F Alcohol is a depressant, but one that initially increases appetite—that's why we serve it in restaurants!

77. T Fat absorbs alcohol faster than muscle.

78. T The rate of alcohol absorption varies with body composition, but the rate at which the liver eliminates alcohol from the system is constant for everyone.

79. F While occasionally a light touch can be calming, it is not a wise idea to touch intoxicated persons because you can never be sure how they are going to react.

80. F A breathalizer measures the amount of alcohol in the lungs which is then converted to a BAC (blood alcohol content) reading.

FINANCIAL

81. E Over $85,000. There is a slight trick in this question to prove a point. Each person you lose will cost you $3,600 over 5 years (3 visits per month times $20 per visit times 60 months). For the party of 4, the loss is $14,400. The trick is that the typical dissatisfied guest will tell 8 to 10 other people, and 1 in 5 will tell 20 others. The people who hear the horror story are also not likely to come to your restaurant. If each of the 4 original guests only told 5 others, it would mean 20 more lost guests. At $3,600 each, this represents another $72,000 in lost business. The total cost to you is already $86,400!

82. E Under 5%. According to statistical studies by the National Restaurant Association, the typical full-service restaurant earns a median pretax profit of 3.5% to 4.0% of sales.

83. D $10.00. The average check is sales divided by the number of guests served. In this case, $500 divided by 50.

84. C $127.50. Fifteen percent of $150 is $22.50. Subtracting that from $150 leaves you with $127.50.

85. A A bill. The company is obligated to pay the amount of the invoice. Whenever someone on the staff signs an invoice, she is effectively signing a check.

86. **A** **Pass.** One of the keys to foodservice profitability is to maintain minimal inventories and turn them frequently. There is no deal good enough (and no storeroom big enough) to warrant tying up excess money and space for products that do not move.

87. **C** **$1.80.** 30% of $6.00 is $1.80.

88. **B** **$24.05.** This is a simple addition problem.

89. **C** **$3.50.** The check total is $23.20, and 15% of that amount is $3.48.

90. **A** **A hamburger.** Their initial orders total $5.35, leaving $4.90. A hamburger is the highest-priced item they can order with that amount. It will be interesting to see if any applicants suggest a lower-cost item to give themselves the possibility of a higher tip.

SALES

91. **A** **$36.** This calculation assumes a bottle of wine for the table plus a side dish, dessert, and after-dinner drink per diner. Even if you only get diners to share some of these add-ons, the increase in the average check can be considerable.

92. **B** **$5.40.**

93. **D** **A steak dinner selling for $12.95 with a 50% food cost.** This question tests the applicant's understanding of the fact that you don't pay bills with percentages. While the steak has the highest food cost percentage, its gross margin (the amount of money you get to keep every time you sell it) is $6.48. Gross margin on the other choices is as follows: enchiladas, $5.56; chicken sandwich, $3.37; and catfish, $5.55.

94. **E** **All of the above.** The point is that suggestive selling is an overt activity on the part of the seller. Unless the staff member takes the initiative to tell the guest something, no additional sales will be made.

95. **E** **"Have you ever tried our famous rum punch?"** This is a specific suggestion that leaves a sales opportunity no matter which way the guest answers the question. Many diners find the words "cocktail" and "liquor" to have connotations of alcoholism, yet they will readily order a frozen Margarita. Go figure.

96. **E** **Any of these go well with Chocolate Mousse.**

97. **C** **Pinot Noir.** Pinot Noir is a medium-bodied red wine that is excellent with prime rib. Of the other choices, Port is too sweet and heavy, Gewürztraminer is too light and spicy, and French sauterne and cream sherry are too sweet. Of course, the most appropriate wine is whatever one the guest wants.

98. **B** **By increasing guest satisfaction.** Suggestive selling helps guests have a better time by making their meal decisions easier and allowing them to try some menu items they might have missed. Suggestive selling also increases the restaurant's sales and the server's tips. Whether or not it decreases food cost depends on the items suggested and the structure of the menu.

99. **D** **I would not suggest a second bottle of wine.** The issue here is alcohol consumption, not sales. Two bottles of wine after 45 minutes of cocktails will put them well over the legal BAC limit.

100. **B** **"We sell a lot of Beef Wellington."** The server's personal diet preferences are of no interest or concern to the diners and should not even come up. Describing the item as "nice" is no recommendation at all. While the ingredients in Beef Wellington are good to know, it does not answer the guest's question. Confirming the popularity of the dish reinforces the guest's decision to order.

101. **B** **Filet mignon.**

102. **B** **Top sirloin steak.**

103. **B** **Red.**

104. **D** **Simmered in a liquid.**

105. **M** **A stuffed flour tortilla.**

106. **O** **Pasta noodles approximately ¼-inch wide.**

107. **J** **Marinated seafood.**

108. **H** A sauce served on Eggs Benedict.

109. **G** Chili sauce and horseradish.

110. **K** Pasta noodles approximately ⅛-inch wide.

111. **I** Snails, usually cooked in garlic butter.

112. **E** A preparation using shrimp.

113. **A** A salad using romaine leaves.

114. **N** A sauce served on steak.

115. **E** A preparation using shrimp.

116. **L** Chopped tomatoes, onions and chilis.

117. **B** Meatless tomato sauce.

118. **F** With spinach.

119. **D** A sauce of vinegar and oil.

120. **C** A stuffed corn tortilla in sauce.

BEVERAGE KNOWLEDGE

121. **D** **Tequila, triple sec, lime juice.** The other drink ingredients would make a Daiquiri, a Tequila Sunrise, a Vodka Collins and a Whiskey Sour.

122. **B** **In a shot glass.** The drink could also be served in a regular glass. In either event, it is served without ice.

123. **C** **Cooling the bottle to 55°F.** Merlot is a red wine and should be served at "room temperature." When speaking of wine, room temperature means the temperature found in old castles or wine cellars, or about 55°F.

124. **B** **No longer than 45 minutes.**

125. **F** **Premium bourbon.**

126. **I** **Domestic vodka.**

127. **Y** **Imported dark rum.**

128. **B** **Call Scotch.**

129. **U** **Imported tequila.**

130. **S** **Imported beer.**

131. **K** **Fortified wine.**

132. **P** **Call rum.**

133. **V** **Imported Scotch.**

134. **A** **Full-bodied red wine.**

135. **X** **Domestic beer.**

136. **S** **Imported beer.**

137. **E** **Full-bodied white wine.**

138. **T** **Light-bodied red wine.**

139. **M** **Alcohol-free beer.**

140. **H** **Cream sherry.**

141. **Z** **Orange liqueur.**

142. **D**   **Domestic blended whiskey.**

143. **W**   **Imported coffee liqueur.**

144. **L**   **Light-bodied white wine.**

145. **N**   **Imported cream liqueur.**

146. **G**   **Imported blended whiskey.**

147. **J**   **Fruity, spicy white wine.**

148. **O**   **Blush wine.**

149. **I**   **Domestic vodka.**

150. **Q**   **Imported champagne.**

Service Situations

1. You are a server in a full-service restaurant. The situation at your station is as follows:

TABLE	GUESTS	STATUS
21	3	Entrees just came up in the kitchen.
22	2	Drinks being made at the bar.
23	4	Just seated.
24	4	Waiting for the check.
25	6	Just finished entrees—need to be cleared and coffee/dessert order taken.

   A. How would you handle your station? What would you do—how and in what order?

   B. Would you handle things any differently if the party at Table 24 were angry and starting to get up to walk out? If so, what would you do differently, assuming that everything else at your station stayed the same as outlined above?

2. You are a server at McNeal's, a classic steak house that has been serving your community for over 60 years. The restaurant is located in an older part of the city that is experiencing a renaissance. The area now contains several trendy restaurants, a fish market, a custom butcher shop, and two gourmet food stores.

   Every year, Harold and Binnie Smith come to your restaurant to celebrate their anniversary. They always sit at Table 22, they always order the same meal they had the night they got engaged over half a century ago . . . and they never tip. They live 75 miles away, and tonight is their 50th wedding anniversary. They have a reputation for being hard to please, and for new servers, waiting on Harold and Binnie has become your restaurant's equivalent of fraternity hazing. Table 22 is in your section tonight. There is no escape.

   Harold and Binnie shuffle in at 5:00 PM. You patiently listen as they tell the story of how it was in this very restaurant at this very table that Harold first "popped the question." They go on to say how important the evening is to them, how much they have been looking forward to dining at McNeal's tonight, and how important it is that you do a good job for them. They order their "traditional" dinner: Coquilles St. Jacques, Caesar Salad, a bottle of burgundy, and your famous double-cut steak for two, medium rare.

   As soon as you hear the order, you realize you may be in trouble. Coquilles St. Jacques was taken off the menu three months ago, and there are no scallops in the house. When you get back to the kitchen, the blackboard tells you that there are no more double-cut steaks. The manager has gone to do an errand and is not expected back for 45 minutes. It appears that Harold and Binnie's evening is squarely in your hands.

   A. Describe your conversation with the chef.

   B. Describe your conversation with the Smiths.

   C. What other questions does this situation raise in your mind?

Situaciones de Servicio

1. **Usted es un mesero en un restaurante con servicio completo. La situación en su estación es la siguiente:**

MESAS	CLIENTES	CONDICION
21	3	Las entradas están listas en la cocina.
22	2	Las bebidas preparadas están en el bar.
23	4	Acaban de sentarse.
24	4	Esperando la cuenta.
25	6	Acaban de terminar las entradas—necesitan ser retiradas y la orden del postre o café tomadas.

A. ¿Cómo manejaría su estación? ¿Qué haría usted, cómo lo haría y en qué orden lo haría?

B. ¿Manejaría las cosas de manera diferente si el grupo en la mesa #24 estuviera enfadado y se levantaran de la mesa para irse? Si es así, ¿qué haría de forma diferente? Asuma que todo lo demás en su estación ha quedado de la misma manera.

2. **Usted es un mesero en McNeal's, un restaurante clásico de carne asada que ha estado sirviéndole a su comunidad por más de 60 años. El restaurante está localizado en la parte más vieja de la ciudad que recientemente ha pasado por un renacimiento. El área ahora tiene varios restaurantes de moda, una pescadería, una carnicería y dos tiendas de comida gourmet.**

Cada año, Harold y Binnie Smith van a su restaurante para celebrar su aniversario. Siempre se sientan en la mesa 22, siempre ordenan el mismo plato que ordenaron la noche que se comprometieron hace más de medio siglo . . . y nunca dejan propina. Ellos viven a 75 millas de distancia y esta noche celebran 50 años de casados. Tienen una reputación de ser difíciles de complacer y, para los nuevos meseros, servir a Harold y Binnie se ha vuelto el equivalente de una prueba en el restaurante. La mesa 22 está en su sección esta noche. No hay escape.

Harold y Binnie llegaron a las 5:00 PM. Usted escucha pacientemente como le cuentan la historia de cómo fue que en este restaurante, en esta misma mesa, que Harold "le hizo la pregunta". Continúan diciéndole lo importante que es esta noche para ellos, cuánto han estado esperando comer en McNeal's esta noche y lo importante que es el que usted haga un buen trabajo. Le dan la orden de la cena "tradicional": Coquillas St. Jacques, ensalada césar, una botella de Burgundy y su famoso filete de doble corte para dos, término medio.

Tan pronto oye usted la orden, usted sabe que puede estar en problemas. Coquillas St. Jacques fueron quitadas del menú hace tres meses y no hay veneras en la casa. Cuando usted regresa a la cocina, la pizarra dice que no hay más filetes de corte doble. El administrador ha salido a dar una vuelta y no lo esperan sino hasta dentro de 45 minutos. Aparentemente la noche de Harold y Binnie está completamente en sus manos.

A. Le describe su conversación con el chef.

B. Le describe su conversación con los Smiths.

C. ¿Qué otras preguntas surgen en su mente sobre ésta situación?

Situation Test Evaluation

SERVICE STAFF

Name: _____ **Position:** _____

Scoring:

Grade each evaluation criterion as it is observed (Y—Yes, N—No, ?—Maybe).
Give two points for each Y, one point for each ?, and no points for N.
A score of 16 or better means an overall evaluation of Yes.
A score of 10 to 15 means an overall evaluation of Maybe.
A score of 9 or below means an overall evaluation of No.

SITUATION 1:

Y N ?

☐ ☐ ☐ 1. Did the candidate come up with a solution without hesitation?
☐ ☐ ☐ 2. Did the solution show an understanding of dining room operations?
☐ ☐ ☐ 3. Would the solution work for the house?
☐ ☐ ☐ 4. Did the candidate take control of the situation?
☐ ☐ ☐ 5. Were the candidate's priorities appropriate?
☐ ☐ ☐ 6. Did the candidate put the well-being of the guests first at all times?
☐ ☐ ☐ 7. Did the candidate take a positive (versus negative) approach to the situation?
☐ ☐ ☐ 8. Did the candidate accept personal responsibility for the situation?
☐ ☐ ☐ 9. Did the candidate ask someone else for help?
☐ ☐ ☐ 10. Did the candidate handle the potential walk-out in a way that would be likely to retain the party's future patronage and good will?

Total Score:

_____

OVERALL EVALUATION:

☐ Yes
☐ No
☐ Maybe

SITUATION 2:

Y N ?

☐ ☐ ☐ 1. Did the candidate come up with a solution without hesitation?
☐ ☐ ☐ 2. Did the candidate put the welfare of the Smiths first?
☐ ☐ ☐ 3. Is the solution likely to retain the good will of the Smiths?
☐ ☐ ☐ 4. Did the candidate's conversation with the chef help resolve the situation?
☐ ☐ ☐ 5. Did the candidate take control of the situation?
☐ ☐ ☐ 6. Were the candidate's priorities appropriate?
☐ ☐ ☐ 7. Did the candidate maintain a sense of humor?
☐ ☐ ☐ 8. Did the candidate take a positive (versus negative) approach to the situation?
☐ ☐ ☐ 9. Did the candidate accept personal responsibility for the situation?
☐ ☐ ☐ 10. Did the solution get the Smiths the steak and scallops they wanted?

Total Score:

_____

OVERALL EVALUATION:

☐ Yes
☐ No
☐ Maybe

Floor Situations

1. **It is a busy night and the wait is running long. You have a table that has just been cleared but has not yet been reset. An irate guest comes up and demands that you seat his party at that table immediately. His party is the second one on your list.**

   A. What are your options for handling the situation? How would you deal with this man's demand? What would you do and how would you do it?

   B. Would you handle the situation any differently if the man's name was not on your waiting list at all? If so, how?

2. **It is a busy night and there is about a 45-minute wait. At 7:20 a well-dressed party of four arrives. They say they called that afternoon and made a reservation for 7:30. You have nothing in your reservation book. Since you have been the principal person answering the phone since 3:00, you suspect they may be trying to scam you.**

   A. How would you handle the situation? What would you do and how would you do it?

   B. Would you handle the situation any differently if you had not come to work until 5:00 today? If so, how?

Situaciones de los Anfitriones

1. **Es una noche muy ocupada y la espera es larga. Usted tiene una mesa que ha sido desocupada, pero todavía no ha sido limpiada. Un cliente irritado va a usted y le demanda que siente a su grupo en esa mesa inmediatamente. El grupo está de segundo en su lista.**

    A. ¿Cuáles son sus opciones al manejar la situación? ¿Cómo manejaría la demanda del cliente? ¿Qué haría usted y cómo lo haría?

    B. ¿Manejaría la situación usted de otra manera si el nombre del cliente no estuviera en su lista de espera en absoluto? Si es así, ¿cómo?

2. **Es una noche muy ocupada y hay cerca de 45 minutos de espera. A las 7:20 PM un grupo de cuatro, vestidos de fiesta, entran. Le dicen que llamaron esa tarde e hicieron una reservación para las 7:30 PM. Usted no tiene nada en su libro de reservaciones. Como usted ha sido la persona principal en contestar el teléfono desde las 3:00 PM, usted sospecha que pueden estar intentando engañarlo.**

    A. ¿Cómo manejaría la situación? ¿Qué haría usted y cómo lo haría?

    B. ¿Manejaría usted la situación de forma diferente si usted hubiera empezado a trabajar a las 5:00 PM ese día? Si es así, ¿cómo?

Situation Test Evaluation

FLOOR STAFF

Name: **Evaluated By:**

Scoring:

Grade each evaluation criterion as it is observed (Y—Yes, N—No, ?—Maybe).
Give two points for each Y, one point for each ?, and no points for N.
A score of 16 or better means an overall evaluation of Yes.
A score of 10 to 15 means an overall evaluation of Maybe.
A score of 9 or below means an overall evaluation of No.

SITUATION 1:

Y N ?

☐ ☐ ☐ 1. Did the candidate come up with a solution without hesitation?
☐ ☐ ☐ 2. Did the candidate maintain a sense of humor?
☐ ☐ ☐ 3. Would the solution present the house in the best light?
☐ ☐ ☐ 4. Did the candidate take control of the situation?
☐ ☐ ☐ 5. Were the candidate's priorities appropriate?
☐ ☐ ☐ 6. Did the candidate keep the well-being of the guest first at all times?
☐ ☐ ☐ 7. Did the candidate take a positive (versus negative) approach to the situation?
☐ ☐ ☐ 8. Did the candidate accept personal responsibility for the situation?
☐ ☐ ☐ 9. Would the solution maintain the good will of the other guests?
☐ ☐ ☐ 10. Did the candidate give the guest the benefit of the doubt?

Total Score:

_____

OVERALL EVALUATION:

☐ Yes
☐ No
☐ Maybe

SITUATION 2:

Y N ?

☐ ☐ ☐ 1. Did the candidate come up with a solution without hesitation?
☐ ☐ ☐ 2. Did the candidate maintain a sense of humor?
☐ ☐ ☐ 3. Would the solution present the house in the best light?
☐ ☐ ☐ 4. Did the candidate take control of the situation?
☐ ☐ ☐ 5. Were the candidate's priorities appropriate?
☐ ☐ ☐ 6. Did the candidate keep the well-being of the guests first at all times?
☐ ☐ ☐ 7. Did the candidate take a positive (versus negative) approach to the situation?
☐ ☐ ☐ 8. Did the candidate accept personal responsibility for the situation?
☐ ☐ ☐ 9. Would the solution maintain the good will of the other guests?
☐ ☐ ☐ 10. Did the candidate give the guests the benefit of the doubt?

Total Score:

_____

OVERALL EVALUATION:

☐ Yes
☐ No
☐ Maybe

Demonstration Test 2

SERVICE STAFF

Name: _____ **Evaluated By:** _____

MENU TEST

Procedure:

Applicants receive a written description of your four most popular menu items. The following day, they observe the preparation of these items and taste the products. They then explain the items to a table of "guests." This is *not* a timed test.

Materials:

Menu descriptions.

Evaluation Criteria:

Y N ?

☐ ☐ ☐ 1. Did the candidate show interest while the products were prepared?
☐ ☐ ☐ 2. Did the candidate accurately describe Product 1?
☐ ☐ ☐ 3. Was the description of Product 1 animated?
☐ ☐ ☐ 4. Was the description of Product 1 appetizing?
☐ ☐ ☐ 5. Could the candidate answer basic questions about Product 1?
☐ ☐ ☐ 6. Did the candidate accurately describe Product 2?
☐ ☐ ☐ 7. Was the description of Product 2 animated?
☐ ☐ ☐ 8. Was the description of Product 2 appetizing?
☐ ☐ ☐ 9. Could the candidate answer basic questions about Product 2?
☐ ☐ ☐ 10. Did the candidate accurately describe Product 3?
☐ ☐ ☐ 11. Was the description of Product 3 animated?
☐ ☐ ☐ 12. Was the description of Product 3 appetizing?
☐ ☐ ☐ 13. Could the candidate answer basic questions about Product 3?
☐ ☐ ☐ 14. Did the candidate accurately describe Product 4?
☐ ☐ ☐ 15. Was the description of Product 4 animated?
☐ ☐ ☐ 16. Was the description of Product 4 appetizing?
☐ ☐ ☐ 17. Could the candidate answer basic questions about Product 4?
☐ ☐ ☐ 18. Did the candidate appear at ease while at the table?
☐ ☐ ☐ 19. Did the candidate appear distracted while at the table?
☐ ☐ ☐ 20. Did the candidate make smiling eye contact while speaking with the guests?

Scoring:

Grade each evaluation criterion as it is observed (Y—Yes, N—No, ?—Maybe).
Give two points for each Y, one point for each ?, and no points for N.
A score of 32 or better means an overall evaluation of Yes.
A score of 20 to 31 means an overall evaluation of Maybe.
A score of 19 or below means an overall evaluation of No.

Total Score:

_____

OVERALL EVALUATION:

☐ Yes
☐ No
☐ Maybe

APPENDIX I

Legal Summaries

Fair Labor Standards Act	I-1
Sources of Employee Protection	I-3
Summary of State Legislation	I-5
Pre-Employment Inquiries	I-8

The Fair Labor Standards Act of 1938, as Amended (FLSA)

(COMMONLY CALLED THE FEDERAL WAGE AND HOUR LAW)

DESCRIPTION	REQUIREMENT
Who is subject to FLSA?	1. Individual employee coverage—if the employee's job duties involve the production or handling of goods crossing the state lines. 2. Enterprise coverage—a business is subject to FLSA (with respect to its employees) if two or more employees are engaged in interstate commerce, in the production of goods for interstate commerce, or in the handling of goods or materials that have been moved in or produced for commerce.
Minimum Wage: April 1, 1990	1. Current minimum wage is $4.25 per hour. 2. Training wage: $3.35 per hour or 85% of the minimum wage ($3.62 per hour). • Applies to first-time workers age 16 to 19. • Applicable for 90 days only. • A second employer may hire the employee at the same wage for an additional 90 days. • The employer must obtain a certificate of employment for the worker from the Secretary of Labor. • The training wage expires April 1, 1993. 3. Tipped employees: Tips received may be counted as part of minimum wage. The employer may take a credit up to 50% of minimum wage or tipped employees may receive $2.13 per hour so long as tips received equal $2.12 per hour.
Employee Classification	1. Nonexempt Employees—commonly called "hourly." The employee must be compensated at minimum wage (can be greater) for the first 40 hours worked and at time and one-half for time worked greater than 40 hours. 2. Exempt Employees—commonly called "salaried." The employee is exempt (not entitled) to overtime pay.
Overtime Pay	1. Must be paid for time worked in excess of 40 hours worked. 2. Must be paid at 1½ times the regular base rate of pay. 3. Must be paid on the next regularly scheduled pay date. 4. An employee is eligible for overtime pay if the employee has actually "suffered or was permitted" to work extra hours, whether or not extra hours were authorized by the employer. 5. Generally, overtime worked in one week cannot be offset by reduced hours in the following week.
Poster Display	A prescribed poster must be displayed in a conspicuous place and must state the minimum wage, that time and one-half is paid for all hours worked over 40 in a work week, and must explain how back wages may be recovered. Note: The Equal Opportunity Commission issues a poster which is required to be displayed in a conspicuous place which contains the prohibition against sex discrimination in the payment of wages to women and men performing substantially equal work in the same establishment.
Inspection/Investigation	Representatives of the Wage and Hour Division of the Department of Labor are authorized to inspect records and gather information. The Wage and Hour Division can issue a subpoena to the employer to produce the records for inspection. Investigation usually takes place because: 1. A complaint about a FLSA violation is received. 2. A previous offender (employer) is reinspected. 3. Random spot checks of firms in industries where high rates of violations have occurred.

Source: Compiled by Benefit & Personnel Resources, Colorado Springs, Colorado, used by permission.

The Fair Labor Standards Act of 1938, as Amended (FLSA) *(continued)*

DESCRIPTION	REQUIREMENT
Recordkeeping	1. Employee's full name and number or identifying symbol. 2. Home address. 3. Date of Birth (if employee is under age 19). 4. Sex. 5. Occupation in which employed. 6. Time and day on which work week begins and ends. 7. Rate of pay and the basis on which wages are paid. 8. Hours worked each workday and the total hours worked each work week. 9. Total daily or weekly straight-time earnings (wages). 10. Total overtime (excess) compensation for the work week. 11. Total additions to or deductions from wages paid in each pay period. 12. Total wages paid each pay period. 13. Date of payment and the pay period covered by the payment. 14. Retroactive wage payment under government supervision. 15. Factors which are the basis for payment of any wage differential to employees of differing sex which may be pertinent to determining whether the differential is based on a factor other than sex. Note: Records are required to be retained by the employer for three years.
Record Format	Forms are not provided. Records kept must contain the essential information and must present the required information in an accurate, complete and intelligible manner. Essential information can be carried on more than one set of records.
Time limit for FLSA violation	1. Nonwillful violations—charges must be brought within two years of the date the employer allegedly failed to pay employees in accordance with FLSA. 2. Willful violations—charges must be brought within three years of the date the employer allegedly failed to pay employees in accordance with FLSA.
Penalties for FLSA violation	Civil Penalties: Willful, repeated violations are subject to a civil penalty not to exceed $1,000 for each violation. Injunction: The Secretary of Labor has the power to restrain (hold) goods that were produced in violation of the statute out of interstate commerce and to collect back wages by obtaining an injunction in federal district court. Contempt proceedings can be brought against an employer who fails to comply with an injunction. Damages: Employees can recover unpaid wages and overtime wages, plus attorney's fees and court costs. Additional "liquidated damages" (double damages) equal to the unpaid wages can be awarded. Criminal Penalties: Criminal penalties can be imposed for willful and flagrant violations of the FLSA.
Retaliation	It is illegal for an employer to discipline or terminate an employee who has reported, complained or brought suit alleging a FLSA violation.

Source: Compiled by Benefit & Personnel Resources, Colorado Springs, Colorado, used with permission.

Note: The FLSA descriptions contained in this text are brief summaries and do not include the detail or complete text or requirements of the FLSA.

Sources of Employee Protection

FEDERAL LAW

Title VII of the Civil Rights Act of 1964	Prohibits discrimination on the basis of race, color, religion, national origin and sex.
Age Discrimination in Employment Act of 1967 (ADEA)	Prohibits discrimination against workers over age 40.
Occupational Safety and Health Act	Employees have the right to a safe and healthful working environment. Prohibits discharge of employees in retaliation for exercising rights under the act.
Labor Management Relations Act of 1986 (LMRA)	Employees have the right to engage in concerted, protected activity, including but not limited to, union activities.
Employee Retirement Income Security Act of 1974 (ERISA)	Intent is to protect benefit plan participants and beneficiaries. A comprehensive statute regulating every aspect of private sector employee benefit plan administration, operation, reporting and disclosure.
Immigration Reform and Control Act of 1986 (IRCA)	Prohibits discrimination with respect to hiring, recruitment, referral or discharge against all individuals except unauthorized aliens because of national origin and against U.S. citizens or aliens eligible for citizenship because of citizen status.
Drug-Free Workplace Act of 1988	Employers who are federal contractors with contracts of $25,000 or more must certify to the contracting agency that they provide and maintain a drug-free workplace.
Worker Adjustment and Retraining Notification Act of 1989 (WARN)	Applies to employers employing 100 or more employees (all sites) requiring a 60-day notice to employees of plant closing or layoff affecting 50 to 499 employees (33% of all employees) or the layoff of 500 or more employees at one location.
Employee Polygraph Protection Act of 1988	Prohibits employers from requiring applicants or employees to submit to a lie detector test except whereby the employer is conducting investigations of economic loss or injury to their business.
Section 89 of the Internal Revenue Code as amended by the Technical and Miscellaneous Revenue Act of 1988 (TAMRA)	Rules preventing discrimination in favor of highly compensated employees with respect to accident, health and group term life insurance plans. Excess benefits under the plan are taxable income.
Rehabilitation Act of 1973	Any contract or subcontract in excess of $2,500 entered into by any federal agency is required to contain a clause that the employer will take affirmative action to employ and advance in employment qualified handicapped individuals.
Executive Order #11,246 of 1965 as amended 1968	Prohibits race and sex discrimination by all contractors with a federal contract of more than $10,000 in any 12 months, to require affirmative action to employ and advance minorities and women.
Vietnam Era Veterans Readjustment Assistance Act of 1974 as amended.	Prohibits the discrimination against Vietnam Era and other disabled veterans by government contractors and subcontractors.

Source: Compiled by Benefit & Personnel Resources, Colorado Springs, Colorado, used with permission.

Sources of Employee Protection *(continued)*

Hostile Working Environment Title VII	A working environment overrun by racial antagonism may constitute a Title VII violation—racial harassment.
1866 Civil Rights Act (Section 1981)	All persons in the United States have the same right in every state . . . as enjoyed by white citizens. Primarily relates to ancestry or ethnic background.
Sexual Harassment Title VII	Harassment on the basis of sex—unwelcomed sexual advances, requests for sexual favors, verbal or physical conduct of a sexual nature causing unreasonable interference with work performance/relationship or a hostile, intimidating or offensive work environment.
Pregnancy Discrimination Act of 1978 (PDA)	Provides that women affected by pregnancy, childbirth or related medical conditions be treated the same as other individuals with temporary disabilities, in leave and benefit plans. Prohibits discrimination on the basis of pregnancy, childbirth or related medical conditions.
Consumer Credit Protection Act (1982)	Prohibits the discharge of employees because of garnishment of wages for any one indebtedness.
Judiciary and Judicial Procedure Act	Prohibits the discharge of employees for service on grand or petit jury.
Fair Labor Standards Act—1938, as amended (Commonly known as Federal Wage and Hour Act)	Prohibits discharge for an individual exercising their rights under the act. Specifies a minimum wage, requires overtime pay and restricts child labor.
Equal Pay Act of 1963	Prohibits wage differentials based upon sex for workers covered under the FLSA.
Energy Reorganization Act of 1974	Prohibits discharge of employees who assist in any proceeding under the act.
Clean Air Act	Prohibits discharge of employees who assist in any proceeding under the act.
Federal Water Pollution Control Act	Prohibits discharge of employees who assist in any proceeding under the act.
Railroad Safety Act	Prohibits discharge of employees who assist in any proceeding under the act.
Consolidated Omnibus Budget Reconciliation Act of 1985 (COBRA)	Applies to employers with 20 or more employees. Employees whose employment terminates or whose work hours are reduced or dependents who are no longer eligible for coverage, are eligible to elect continuation of group employee health plan coverage, at cost, for either 18 months or 36 months in certain situations. Employer has certain notification requirements and the employee has certain response and payment requirements.
Americans with Disabilities Act—1990 (ADA)	Prohibits discrimination against the disabled in employment, public services, public accommodations and services operated by private entities and telecommunications. ADA notices must be posted. Covers employers with 25 or more employees in the first two years of the act and then employers with 15 or more employees.

Source: Compiled by Benefit & Personnel Resources, Colorado Springs, Colorado, used with permission.

Summary of State Legislation

	Release of Medical Records	Military Service and Leave	Homework	Lie Detector Tests	Personnel Records Inspection	Voice Stress Analyzers	Fingerprinting/ Photographing	Arrest Records	Pregnancy/ Maternity Leave	Political Activities	Whistle-Blowing	AIDS Testing/ Confidentiality	Alcohol/ Drug Testing	Smoking Prohibitions
Alabama								✓						
Alaska				✓	✓						✓²			✓
Arizona		✓		✓	✓²		✓¹	✓		✓	✓²	✓		✓³
Arkansas		✓		✓	✓	✓								✓
California	✓	✓	✓	✓	✓	✓	✓	✓	✓	✓		✓		
Colorado								✓	✓	✓	✓⁴	✓⁵	✓	
Connecticut	✓	✓	✓	✓	✓			✓	✓⁴	✓	✓		✓	
Delaware		✓	✓	✓	✓			✓	✓	✓	✓⁴			
Florida		✓		✓	✓			✓		✓	✓		✓⁴	✓
Georgia								✓		✓			✓⁴	
Hawaii		✓	✓	✓				✓	✓		✓	✓		
Idaho		✓		✓	✓¹⁰				✓	✓				
Illinois		✓	✓	✓	✓			✓			✓			
Indiana		✓	✓	✓	✓			✓		✓	✓		✓	✓⁶
Iowa		✓		✓					✓		✓	✓	✓	✓
Kansas				✓					✓		✓⁴		✓	✓⁷
Kentucky		✓						✓	✓	✓	✓²	✓		

✓—denotes a state law related to the subject.

¹ Childcare employees only
² State and local employees only
³ State buildings
⁴ State employees only
⁵ Insurance businesses
⁶ State and local buildings
⁷ Public places
⁸ Childcare providers only
⁹ Private sector employees only
¹⁰ School employees

Source: Compiled by Benefit & Personnel Resources, Colorado Springs, Colorado, used with permission.

Summary of State Legislation (continued)

	Release of Medical Records	Military Service and Leave	Homework	Lie Detector Tests	Personnel Records Inspection	Voice Stress Analyzers	Fingerprinting/ Photographing	Arrest Records	Pregnancy/ Maternity Leave	Political Activities	Whistle-Blowing	AIDS Testing/ Confidentiality	Alcohol/ Drug Testing	Smoking Prohibitions
Louisiana		✓		✓	✓			✓	✓	✓	✓		✓	
Maine		✓		✓	✓				✓	✓	✓	✓	✓	✓
Maryland	✓	✓	✓	✓				✓	✓	✓⁴	✓²		✓	✓
Massachusetts		✓	✓	✓	✓			✓	✓	✓				✓
Michigan		✓	✓	✓	✓			✓	✓	✓	✓	✓		✓
Minnesota		✓	✓	✓	✓	✓			✓	✓	✓		✓	
Mississippi		✓								✓				
Missouri		✓						✓⁸	✓		✓	✓		
Montana		✓	✓	✓					✓	✓			✓	✓
Nebraska		✓		✓					✓	✓			✓	✓
Nevada				✓	✓			✓						
New Hampshire		✓		✓	✓				✓	✓	✓¹⁰		✓	✓
New Jersey		✓	✓	✓					✓					✓
New Mexico		✓	✓	✓					✓	✓		✓		✓⁶
New York		✓	✓	✓	✓		✓	✓	✓		✓			✓
North Carolina		✓		✓	✓⁴			✓	✓⁴	✓⁴	✓²	✓	✓	
North Dakota	✓	✓		✓				✓		✓²				

✓—denotes a state law related to the subject.

¹ Childcare employees only
² State and local employees
³ State buildings
⁴ State employees only
⁵ Insurance businesses
⁶ State and local buildings
⁷ Public places
⁸ Childcare providers only
⁹ Private sector employees only
¹⁰ School employees

Source: Compiled by Benefit & Personnel Resources, Colorado Springs, Colorado, used with permission.

Summary of State Legislation (continued)

	Release of Medical Records	Military Service and Leave	Homework	Lie Detector Tests	Personnel Records Inspection	Voice Stress Analyzers	Fingerprinting/ Photographing	Arrest Records	Pregnancy/ Maternity Leave	Political Activities	Whistle-Blowing	AIDS Testing/ Confidentiality	Alcohol/ Drug Testing	Smoking Prohibitions
Ohio	✓	✓	✓					✓	✓	✓	✓			
Oklahoma		✓		✓				✓	✓	✓				✓
Oregon				✓	✓			✓	✓		✓[4]			✓[4]
Pennsylvania			✓	✓	✓	✓		✓	✓	✓	✓			✓
Rhode Island	✓	✓	✓	✓	✓			✓	✓	✓	✓	✓		✓
South Carolina		✓		✓	✓				✓	✓	✓[4]		✓	
South Dakota		✓			✓[4]					✓				
Tennessee		✓	✓	✓	✓			✓	✓	✓	✓	✓	✓	✓
Texas	✓	✓	✓	✓	✓			✓		✓				
Utah				✓	✓[2]					✓	✓		✓	✓[7]
Vermont		✓	✓	✓	✓[2]					✓		✓	✓	✓
Virginia				✓			✓	✓					✓[2]	✓
Washington		✓		✓	✓			✓	✓		✓[4]	✓		✓
West Virginia		✓	✓	✓							✓[4]			
Wisconsin			✓	✓	✓			✓	✓	✓	✓[4]	✓	✓	✓
Wyoming							✓[4]			✓				

✓—denotes a state law related to the subject.

[1] Childcare employees only	[6] State and local buildings
[2] State and local employees only	[7] Public places
[3] State buildings	[8] Childcare providers only
[4] State employees only	[9] Private sector employees only
[5] Insurance businesses	[10] School employees

Source: Compiled by Benefit & Personnel Resources, Colorado Springs, Colorado, used with permission.

Pre-Employment Inquiries

MAJOR AREAS OF PREHIRE INQUIRY	IT IS NOT DISCRIMINATORY IF YOU ASK . . .	IT MAY BE DISCRIMINATORY IF YOU ASK . . .
ADDRESS	Applicant's current address.	1. Inquiry into foreign addresses which would indicate national origin. 2. Whether applicant owns or rents home. 3. Relationship of the persons with whom the applicant lives. 4. Previous address. 5. Length of time at present address.
AGE	1. IF HIRED, CAN YOU SUBMIT PROOF OF AGE? or statement that selection is subject to proof of age *if one is a legal requirement*. 2. If applicant is a minor, proof of age in form of work permit, certificate of age or birth certificate.	Requirements for birth or baptismal certificate as proof of age PRIOR to selection.
ANCESTRY OR NATIONAL ORIGIN	NONE	1. Any inquiry regarding ancestry or national origin of the applicant's parents, spouse or associates or any membership in associations which may indicate ancestry or national origin. 2. Language commonly used by an applicant or how an applicant acquired proficiency in a foreign language.
ARRESTS	NONE	Any inquiry related to arrests.
BIRTHPLACE	NONE	
CITIZENSHIP	1. ARE YOU A CITIZEN OF THE U.S.? 2. IF NOT, DO YOU HAVE THE LEGAL RIGHT TO REMAIN PERMANENTLY IN THE U.S.? 3. DO YOU INTEND TO REMAIN PERMANENTLY? 4. If hired, proof of citizenship or right to work may be required.	1. OF WHAT COUNTRY ARE YOU A CITIZEN? 2. Date of citizenship. 3. Whether the applicant or parents are naturalized or native born. 4. Requirement that birth certificate, baptismal or naturalization records be submitted as proof of citizenship PRIOR to selection.
CONVICTIONS OR COURT RECORDS	Actual convictions which are substantially related to applicant's ability to perform a specific job.	To inquire about any conviction or court record which is not substantially related to applicant's ability to perform job duties.
CREDIT RATING	NONE	1. Any questions about applicant's economic status or other source of income. 2. Whether applicant owns or rents home. 3. Method of transportation if not related to job requirements.
DEPENDENTS	NONE	1. If any children, number of, names and ages. 2. Childcare arrangements. 3. Marital status.
EDUCATION	1. Schools attended. 2. Academic, vocational or professional education. 3. Language, office or other skills if substantially related to the ability to perform job duties.	1. The nationality or religious affiliation of schools. 2. How language skills were acquired.
EMERGENCY CONTACT	Name of person to contact in an emergency.	Requiring the name of a relative to be contacted.
EXPERIENCE	Applicant's work experience.	
HANDICAPS	1. DO YOU HAVE ANY PHYSICAL, MENTAL OR SENSORY HANDICAP WHICH MIGHT AFFECT WORK PERFORMANCE OR WHICH SHOULD BE CONSIDERED IN JOB PLACEMENT? 2. Physical examination if required of all applicants.	1. DO YOU HAVE ANY HANDICAPS? 2. LIST ALL SERIOUS ILLNESSES FOR THE PAST 5 YEARS. 3. General inquiries concerning handicaps or physical conditions which do not relate to applicant's fitness to perform the job. 4. Inquiries concerning receipt of Worker's Compensation. 5. Physical examination if required only of some applicants PRIOR to or AFTER selection.
LANGUAGE SKILLS	If required to perform the job.	1. Requiring a level of language proficiency or the use of a particular language at ALL times if not substantially related to job duties. 2. "Mother tongue" or language commonly used by the applicant. 3. How applicant acquired proficiency in a foreign language.

Source: Colorado Civil Rights Division and Benefit & Personnel Resources, Colorado Springs, Colorado, used with permission.

The information in this table is to be used only as a guide to evaluate pre-employment inquiries for potentially discriminatory questions. This table concerns written and oral inquiries directed to an applicant PRIOR to selection or employment.

MAJOR AREAS OF PREHIRE INQUIRY	IT IS NOT DISCRIMINATORY IF YOU ASK . . .	IT MAY BE DISCRIMINATORY IF YOU ASK . . .
MARITAL STATUS	1. MRS., MISS, MS., when made in good faith and not for the purpose of discrimination. 2. Whether applicant can meet specific work schedules. 3. Any other commitments which might hinder attendance. 4. Anticipated duration on job or anticipated absences. IF ASKED OF BOTH MALES AND FEMALES.	1. SINGLE, MARRIED, DIVORCED, SEPARATED, WIDOWED . . . 2. Questions concerning pregnancy, birth control, children or future childbearing plans. 3. Spouse's name, age, place of employment or income.
MILITARY RECORD	Military experience and education in the armed forces of the United States which relates to specific job duties.	1. Type or date of discharge. 2. Applicant's general military service which is not substantially related to ability to perform specific job duties.
MISCELLANEOUS	Notice that misstatements, omissions and false information on the application may result in discharge.	Any non-job-related inquiry which is unnecessary to determine an applicant's eligibility for employment.
NAME	1. HAVE YOU EVER WORKED FOR THIS ORGANIZATION UNDER ANOTHER NAME? 2. IS ADDITIONAL INFORMATION CONCERNING CHANGE OF NAME NECESSARY TO CHECK WORK OR EDUCATION RECORDS? IF YES, EXPLAIN.	Inquiries about former names which have been changed by court order or otherwise if not required to check necessary records.
ORGANIZATIONS	Membership and offices held in organizations which relate to the applicant's ability to perform a particular job.	1. LIST ALL ORGANIZATIONS, CLUBS OR SOCIETIES TO WHICH YOU BELONG. 2. Inquiries about membership in organizations which would indicate race, color, national origin, ancestry, sex, physical handicap and creed or religion.
PHOTOGRAPH	May be required AFTER hiring.	Suggested or required PRIOR to hiring unless based on a Bona Fide Occupational Qualification (BFOQ).
PHYSICAL CHARACTERISTICS	Physical characteristics such as height and weight only if necessary to perform substantial job duties.	Characteristics such as height and weight if unrelated to abilities to perform substantial job duties.
RACE	NONE	1. Direct or indirect inquiries which would indicate an applicant's race or color. 2. Color of skin, eyes or hair. 3. Race or color is NEVER a BFOQ.
REFERENCES	1. WHO REFERRED YOU HERE? 2. Names of professional and character references.	Requesting or requiring a religious reference.
RELATIVES	1. Names and addresses of parents/guardians of MINOR. 2. Names of relatives already employed with the company if this affects company policy.	Name or address of a relative of an ADULT applicant.
RELIGION	NONE	Any inquiry to indicate or identify religious affiliation, denomination, customs, holidays observed or name of minister.
SEX	1. MR., MRS., MISS, MS., MALE OR FEMALE when made in good faith and not for the purpose of discrimination. A voluntary request only and stated as such. 2. Job advertisement or classification on the basis of sex and an inquiry concerning the sex of the applicant are permissible only if a Bona Fide Occupational Qualification (BFOQ) exists.	1. Sex of applicant or inquiries which would indicate sex if not a voluntary request and stated as such to the applicant. 2. BFOQ is interpreted very strictly by the courts. It is extremely difficult for the sex of the applicant to be considered a lawful pre-employment inquiry. Sex is NOT a BFOQ. • because a job requires physical labor, unusual work schedules or travel • because of the preferences of customers, employer, employees or others • because of stereotypes concerning attitudes or abilities on the basis of sex.
WORK SCHEDULES	Whether applicant can meet a specific work schedule.	1. REASONABLE ACCOMMODATION is required for an applicant on the basis of religion or creed. 2. Inquiry made prior to selection should be justified by BUSINESS NECESSITY.

Source: Colorado Civil Rights Division and Benefit & Personnel Resources, Colorado Springs, Colorado, used with permission.

The information in this table is to be used only as a guide to evaluate pre-employment inquiries for potentially discriminatory questions. This table concerns written and oral inquiries directed to an applicant PRIOR to selection or employment.

ABOUT THE AUTHOR

William R. Marvin, "The Restaurant Doctor™," is an advisor to restaurateurs across the country. He is the founder of Prototype Restaurants, a restaurant consulting, development, and management company based in Colorado Springs, Colorado.

Bill is a member of the Foodservice Consultants Society International (FCSI) and the Council of Hotel and Restaurant Trainers (CHART), and he was one of the first to become certified as a Foodservice Management Professional (FMP) by the National Restaurant Association. He has been a director of the Colorado Restaurant Association since 1986 and teaches a regular foodservice class for the city of Colorado Springs.

Having started in the industry at the age of 14, washing dishes in a small restaurant on Cape Cod, Bill went on to earn a degree in hotel administration from Cornell University. He moved to Colorado Springs in 1984 to design the foodservice system for the U.S. Olympic Training Centers. Before joining the Olympic Committee, Bill spent twelve years in San Francisco, where he was a supervisor in the management consulting department of a national hospitality consulting firm. He developed and operated two restaurants of his own in the San Francisco Bay area, and was an independent restaurant consultant specializing in marketing, new concept development, and Chapter 11 reorganizations.

Bill's hands-on operational experience includes hotels, clubs, restaurants, and institutions. He managed a condominium hotel in the Caribbean, was assistant manager of a prestigious New England country club, and worked as a consultant/designer for a national food facilities engineering firm. As an officer in the U.S. Navy, he operated several enlisted feeding facilities, the largest serving over 20,000 meals a day. His extensive experience has contributed to his broad perspective on the industry and has enabled him to be equally effective in all types and sizes of foodservice operations.

Bill's book, *Restaurant Basics: Why Guests Don't Come Back ... and What You Can Do About It*, is published by John Wiley & Sons, Inc. His next two books will be *From Turnover to Teamwork: How to Build and Retain a Service-Oriented Staff* and *How to Clean Your Restaurant and Most Everything in It*. Besides his private consulting practice, Bill is a frequent contributor to national industry trade magazines and conducts management training seminars across the country.

Contact Bill Marvin at:

Prototype Restaurants
332 West Bijou Street, Suite 107
Colorado Springs, CO 80905
Toll Free: (800) 767-1055